THE MAKING OF A CIVIL RIGHTS LAWYER

THE
MAKING
OF A
CIVIL RIGHTS
LAWYER

Michael Meltsner

UNIVERSITY OF VIRGINIA PRESS

Charlottesville and London

University of Virginia Press
© 2006 by Michael Meltsner
All rights reserved
Printed in the United States of America on acid-free paper

First published 2006

9 8 7 6 5 4 3 2 1

Library of Congress Cataloging-in-Publication Data
Meltsner, Michael, 1937–
    The making of a civil rights lawyer / Michael Meltsner.
        p.   cm.
    Includes bibliographical references and index.
    ISBN 0-8139-2501-0 (cloth : alk. paper)
    1. Meltsner, Michael, 1937–   2. Lawyers—United States—Biography.   3. Civil rights
workers—United States—Biography.   I. Title.
    KF373.M456A3   2006
    340′.092—dc22

                                                        2005024387

To Heli

History says, Don't hope
On this side of the grave.
But then, once in a lifetime
The longed-for tidal wave
Of justice can rise up,
And hope and history rhyme.

—Seamus Heaney, "The Cure at Troy"

Despite the Gregory Peck–Atticus Finch stereotype, most attorneys work alone in a room, eyes to print with their mouths shut, and aren't particularly handsome, but their clients go free or to prison—or forfeit their money, or get strapped to a table—because of what did or did not get perused in some fusty old casebook. Perused *and picked up on,* that is.

—James McManus, *Positively Fifth Street*

CONTENTS

Illustrations appear following page 98

A Note on Language

In civil rights history the words "integration" and "desegregation" are potentially loaded terms, to some observers taking on radically different meanings to which others appear to be oblivious. A common understanding holds that "desegregation" designates merely the obligation after a modest break from the past to desist from differential treatment on the basis of race. Integration, on the other hand, is said to imply an affirmative stance to take such action as will produce mixed race outcomes, an environment free of racism, or the adoption of means that will facilitate such results. Integration, therefore, is usually a far more extensive project than desegregation, or than simply ceasing discriminatory practices. I try generally to stick to this distinction, but because both terms have surfaced in a variety of contexts over the years, they may occasionally appear to be used interchangeably. Neither term, interestingly, was used by the Supreme Court in its seminal *Brown v. Board of Education* opinion, but soon a lower federal court mischievously glossed *Brown* as forbidding segregation but not requiring integration. I confront a similar problem in nomenclature with "Negro," "colored," "black," and "African American," terms that have been in fashion at different points in history and that also—along with "Black" and "people of color"—resonate in many ears with important political meanings. The historian Martha Biondi, for example, capitalizes "Black" because it is a proper noun that reflects "self-naming and self-identification of a people whose national or ethnic origins have been obscured by a history of capture and enslavement." "Colored" was fading away when I started civil rights work in 1961 but may someday surface again if we ever see a rainbow coalition of minority voters with any real electoral clout, as the Reverend Jesse Jackson once proposed. "Negro"—the racial term used in *Brown*—was the most common descriptor employed by the law in the early 1960s. "African American" and "black" have, of course, supplanted it. These shifts mark complex constructions of racial identity

A Note on Language

that while fascinating to analyze are not part of this memoir of civil rights history. In the pages that follow, when "Negro" is employed it signals the period in which it was in common use. I have employed "black" and "African American" interchangeably.

THE MAKING OF A CIVIL RIGHTS LAWYER

Introduction

I T was not until I arrived at the NAACP Legal Defense and Educational Fund (LDF) that I learned my profession, how to work with colleagues and clients, and how it might feel to grow up in the law. This book therefore tells two related stories. The first is a memoir of the civil rights movement, a critical period in American history whose unresolved issues still challenge us as a nation. The second story describes how a lawyer committed to social change discovered himself in his work. I hope that together they convey that practicing public interest law can yield enormous satisfaction. Because I have a particular interest in attracting young lawyers to the kind of work I know best, an appendix sets out the pitfalls and some suggestions for dealing with them.

While a range of political groups, right and left, now organize to use the legal process, strong forces in contemporary society reject the values proposed by lawyers doing civil rights and related work. Judges are far more result-oriented than most young lawyers expect. Representing outsiders instantly makes one vulnerable to bias and hostility. Embattled outsiders also tend to supply their own internecine warfare. Some of it is painfully, if unfairly, personal. Public interest lawyering is not for the thin-skinned.

I received no formal training in how to do or to enjoy my work. In a sense, it just happened. Not by osmosis, of course, but because of the context—the open setting that is one of the more benign legacies of the 1960s, the freedom to debate with like-minded colleagues, the egalitarian relationships, the relative absence of money-driven talk, and the laughter. The times made changing the world seem a thing we could do if only we joined together. To my surprise, I was overtaken by pleasure in the work and in the doings of the people around me. This reaction, I have learned, is common among veterans of the civil rights era. A mission to use the law for social change must have meshed with the person I was and wanted to be, in essence with my upbringing and hurly-burly New York City childhood. But these feelings took their energy, I am certain, from the core of the professional life at LDF, which arced toward service to others and support for the meaning in people's lives, with no pretense that we were nuns working for saints.

It may seem strange for a lawyer to say, but it was this fundamentally spiritual dimension of the workplace that made the difference. It would be a mistake to think that those good old days can never be replicated; the world is filled with horror, and the law is a toolbox to help fix it. One small example among many: no one talked of international human rights law when I was a full-time practitioner; there was no system, as there is now, of emerging remedies to bring the nations of the world up to minimum standards of decency.

For some fortunate few, concrete career choices are a given. In my case, the path favored by my family was hard to discern; my parents had long since made clear that they trusted me to make life choices that were right for me even if strange to them. If only I really knew then what those life choices were! Graduating from Oberlin College in Ohio during the Cold War, I first thought I'd join the U.S. Foreign Service, but the State Department's reputation for WASP exclusivity in those days put me off. Even before law school, I wanted to do what is now called public interest work—the term was born later, in the 1960s—but it was an unfocused ambition, more negative than positive and driven largely by a wish to defeat the enemies of liberty and culture as I understood them to be—Joe McCarthy, the censors of political satire and frank sexuality, southern bigots, anti-Semites, Richard Nixon.

I applied to law school because it postponed the need to decide anything, because it would keep me out of the armed services for at least a year, and because, broke and fatherless, I couldn't turn my back on the full-tuition scholarship Yale offered me. I knew so little about what lawyers actually did with their time that I cannot even claim my idea of the profession was distorted.

If put to it, I could have defined the world as I wanted it to be—Oberlin was good at stimulating such inquiries—but college also turned me into an observer, a would-be intellectual who thought he cared more about ideas than about actions, as if they were somehow exclusive. Unwittingly,

2

the Yale Law School redirected me toward the action of legal practice. I say unwittingly because the little bit of lawyering that was modeled consisted of a very elevated, smarter-than-smart gun-for-hire type, with the weapon held in a soft velvet glove and the bullets paid for by large-firm corporate clients instead of Mafia dons. Without examining the matter very closely, I knew I would not be very good at this work, but at the time the only difference I could see between me and the vast majority of my classmates was that I had to find an underdog to fight for, whereas they would forge remunerative careers in the service of high-paying clients. I didn't hold it against them. My choice may have expressed a set of ethical or political truths, but it represented for me then only the struggles of an insecure youth to integrate the strands of family, friends, education, and ethnicity with threatening contemporary events and personal opportunities.

The real power and dignity of the idea of equality, of battling stigmatization and "othering," was something I learned on the job.

Macon, Georgia

1992. Macon. The buckle of the Bible Belt, the band of dark, rich flat-land that runs south from Virginia, then west across Georgia to the Mississippi Delta. Long ago it was plantation country but today there isn't a cotton field anywhere to be seen; I'm mired in a common suburb, pushing a shopping cart full of diapers and groceries across a parking lot. Something I can't quite apprehend is wrong.

Well, it's bloody hot and humid, as it always seems to be in the self-styled "capital" of middle Georgia, eighty miles south of Atlanta. Some yards away is the brown line of the Ocmulgee River, behind me is the Kroger's supermarket where I've been shopping, and across the lot are an ice cream store, the Internal Revenue Service office, and an Army recruiter.

I can't see anything amiss in this ordinary Macon scene of converging Interstates, malls, and fast food. The only pedestrians in sight are a few grocery shoppers like myself. There is a pleasant path by the river but Macon is not for walking, except to and from the car. I see a Krispy Kreme baking in the sun off in the distance. This one has a visible doughnut machine that lures gawkers; to my right there's a Mexican restaurant where Brian, my son-in-law, says they have strolling mariachis during the dinner hour.

I still don't get it.

Brian is a college professor. His first job after earning a doctorate from the University of Chicago is at a local women's college, Georgia Wesleyan. He and my daughter Jessie will be moving on to greater things. I can't wait. In the decade I spent crisscrossing the South as a lawyer for the NAACP Legal Defense and Educational Fund (LDF), I never made it to Macon, a place with a reputation for an extraordinary number of attractive churches and a diehard resistance to ending racial segregation. Even though I handled plenty of Georgia cases, for me the action in the Peach State was to the south, near Albany or in Atlanta itself.

Macon was a backwater even for a race lawyer, but Jessie tells me it has its heroes: it's the home of Little Richard, the Allman Brothers, and Otis Redding; also the place where James Brown got his start. She teases me. "Even Cher lived here in Shirley Hills for a while. If you're interested in Macon lore, you have to visit the Rose Hill Cemetery, overlooking the Ocmulgee, where Duane Allman is buried. His devotees use the gravesite to party."

But I am here as a new grandparent and not interested in Macon history, especially Macon rock n' roll history. Nevertheless, I try to remember if Sherman burned the city on his way to the sea or left it alone as unworthy of his attention. That's when I see the sign rising above the parking lot entrance and it all comes together. A string of associations starts a relay through my brain. Sweating behind a loaded cart in front of a Kroger's searching for my rental car, I have discovered the place where my own history and Macon's intersect.

The sign says, "Baconsfield Shopping Center." The connection only leads to a few paragraphs in a Supreme Court legal brief but it is still overpowering. Baconsfield and its magnolias. Senator Augustus Bacon. Once his park. Is it the sign or the metaphor that gets me? I don't know.

The story is straightforward enough to be included in Aesop's *Fables*. In his will, an influential United States senator from Georgia, Augustus Octavius Bacon, born in 1839, died in 1914, left sixty-odd acres to his wife and children, then to be passed on to his home town of Macon in trust for use as a "park and pleasure ground" for "white women, white girls, white boys and white children" of the city. A veteran of the Confederate Army, Bacon was particularly chatty for a will writer, informing his descendants that while he had only the kindest of feelings for Negroes, he believed that "in their social relations the two races should be forever separate."[1]

Baconsfield was heavily wooded in 1920 when the city took the land over from Bacon's last surviving daughter, but it was soon landscaped by the municipal park department. Paths were cut through and flowering shrubs planted. The park was known for its lush magnolias. City-appointed trustees built a swimming pool, tennis courts, a petting zoo for children, and a clubhouse used for meetings by Macon women's groups — white women's groups, of course. Financial support came from the city government, the federal Works Projects Administration during the

Depression, and rents from a commercial area roughly contiguous to the park also donated by the senator.

In 1963, with court decisions ordering the end of segregated public parks finally becoming a reality throughout the South, park managers first closed the pool rather than see it used by black swimmers. Then the trustees concocted what they thought a clever strategy. They brought a lawsuit asking the Georgia courts to turn the park over to private trustees, removing the City of Macon from any role in running Baconsfield and thus defeating integration. While the case proceeded through the courts, the city kept the pool closed, settled the zoo's animals elsewhere, and made no effort to calm fears that if the park failed to remain in public hands, it would continue to be segregated. Angry Negro residents intervened in the case to assert their right to use the parkland, and the dispute finally made its way to the United States Supreme Court. In an appeal that I helped to research when I was an LDF lawyer in 1965, the Court decided that the racial restriction was unconstitutional, in effect holding that the park was still a public facility that had to be operated on a nonracial basis even if the City of Macon named new trustees and bowed out of any role in its management.[2]

But little rivals the persistence of claims of racial privilege. In a subsequent Baconsfield suit brought by the senator's heirs, the Georgia courts decided that his primary goal was a park that excluded blacks; if this result could not be accomplished legally, then there could be no public park at all. Using an ancient legal doctrine called cy pres, courts regularly allow property held in trust to be used in a way that differs from the trust's provisions when changed circumstances interfere with the original purpose of the trust settler. On the surface, cy pres plainly applied to the park. Bacon had planned it during the height of Jim Crow, a time when he couldn't be expected to anticipate an end to segregation or the many changes to come in the southern way of life. The attorney general of Georgia took the position that the courts should use cy pres to preserve the park for all Georgians, but the Supreme Court of Georgia decided the case in a way that would maintain segregation, holding that cy pres didn't apply because there was no alternative way to achieve Bacon's primary goal. In short, the Georgia judges ruled that Bacon wanted an all-white park or no park at all. The trust now failed under state law and Senator Bacon's heirs became the lawful owners.

With the support of several prominent legal experts, such as Professor Anthony Amsterdam and James (Jim) M. Nabrit III, an LDF senior lawyer and my first supervisor, local Negroes again appealed the case to the U.S. Supreme Court, arguing that Georgia could not divest itself of responsibility for a public park simply because of Senator Bacon's half-century-old racial views. Bacon wanted a park that whites could use, Nabrit insisted, and they still could have one; all Macon whites had to do was share it with others on a nonracial basis. He was seconded by Erwin Griswold, the United States solicitor general, who argued in a friend-of-the-court brief on behalf of the United States that Georgia could not hide behind supposedly obligatory state law: it had made an illegal choice to avoid integration.

But this time Nabrit and his local-resident clients were rebuffed.[3] Writing in 1970 for seven justices, Hugo Black thought that the state had acted neutrally, using its settled law of trusts to decide Bacon's "true intent." In other words, Georgia had authoritatively interpreted Bacon's state of mind as preference for no park for either race to one that blacks and whites could use jointly. According to Justice Black, once that mental state had been determined under the normal processes of Georgia law, it didn't matter that Bacon lived at a time when segregation was required in public facilities or that Baconsfield looked the way it did because of taxpayer money or that the park had been run by government for use of the white public for fifty years.

Black's opinion sealed Baconsfield's fate. The property now would revert to Bacon's two daughters and their children, even though his will had not provided, as wills often do, that the property would pass to heirs if the trust should for any reason fail and even though the heirs never could have expected to gain these assets. In short, the justices favored a windfall to the heirs over the black community's claim of equality in a public facility.

Suddenly furious and then—not unusual for me—just as suddenly sad, I stood in my tracks, for a few minutes stupidly staring at parkland converted to mall, market, and macadam. In a city where the population was divided between the races, the white powers that be had preferred a land sale to line the pockets of a few descendants of the senator rather than preservation of a public park. The eminent legal scholar Richard Posner argued a few years later that the Georgia court had no evidence to support its conclusion that "the dominant purpose of the gift was to foster racial segregation rather than to provide a recreational facility for the people of Macon," but other analysts disputed his argument, pointing out that Senator Bacon went to great lengths in his will to lay out views favoring segregation of the races.[4]

Still, who can really say what Bacon would have done if he knew what would happen to his country and state in the decades after his death? It's one of those unanswerable questions that the law feels it must pretend it can answer definitively. But no one can be confident of Bacon's actual preference under totally different circumstances. Courts can construct it, arguing that this or that is plausible, and as a result pass property from A to B because of the fiction, but in such cases they are never actually doing more than clothing surmise in the legal language of certainty. For all we know, Bacon would have preferred any kind of park to the sight of another bland urban mall with a McDonald's and a string of large For Rent signs.

The role of the judiciary in enforcing racial and ethnic restrictions in property transactions hasn't always been a subject of controversy. State courts long took for granted their role in implementing the prejudices of private persons who made explicit racial choices when they drew up contracts, conveyed land, and wrote wills and trusts, despite an 1866 federal law that prohibited racial discrimination in transactions involving real and personal property. While the courts always retained residual authority to void a legal instrument for reasons of what lawyers call "public policy," racial and ethnic conditions were for years deemed perfectly acceptable means of preserving the enjoyment and value of private property. In a 1944 report, the prestigious American Law Institute, an elite national (not southern) group of lawyers and judges, concluded that the resulting racial segregation played a "desirable" role in maintaining social peace.

Before 1948, virtually every court, state or federal, that considered the issue had approved the propriety of voiding deeds and leases in violation of covenants restricting black ownership or occupancy of residential housing. In blunt terms, courts could and did order blacks or whatever group was subject to the exclusion to vacate their homes in restricted areas forthwith. Ultimately covering vast amounts of American housing stock, racially restricted covenants had become popular after the Supreme Court decided in 1917 that municipal ordinances requiring residential segregation violated the Constitution. But the Court apparently saw no constitutional problem with restrictive agreements among private landowners until a dramatic about-face in 1948, reaffirmed in 1953, doomed restrictive agreements—which often excluded Jews, Asians, and other ethnic minorities as well as Negroes—as an effective means of perpetuating discrimination in housing.[5]

All six justices who heard the 1948 cases agreed that permitting courts to deny willing sellers the right to transfer property to willing buyers on racial grounds violated the Fourteenth Amendment's guarantee of equal protection of the laws. The Court ruled that property owners might agree to widespread racial restrictions but not call upon government to back them up. Taken together with the Court's 1954 decision in *Brown v. Board of Education,* the covenant case threw in doubt the validity of any judicial implementation of racial distinctions encumbering property. The 1965 Baconsfield appeal, which dealt with the withdrawal of the city and the naming of new trustees to run the public park, was just one of several cases that made it clear that courts must void racial restrictions and conditions when a state was significantly involved in enforcing property rights.

When courts found no governmental involvement, however, even if an intent to discriminate against a racial or ethnic group was obvious, they might continue to approve the restrictions. In the second Macon case, the High Court held that the fact that a state court honored a testator's last wishes did not amount to sufficient "state action" to invoke the Fourteenth Amendment of the Constitution. Consistent with the Supreme Court's reasoning, lower courts soon began to rule that no state law was violated simply by judicial implementation—the basis of the decisions voiding restrictive covenants—of wills and trusts or issuance of typical court orders governing the actions of trustees. A claim to the contrary, the Supreme Court implied, could convert every bequest into a potential constitutional affront, a result it was unwilling to accept.

One analyst, Florence Wagman Roisman of the Indiana University School of Law, lamented that in the vast majority of post-1970 cases involving racial and ethnic conditions the courts ignored the fact that the 1866 federal statute governing discrimination in property transactions had been interpreted to bar restrictions on transfers of private property along racial lines whether or not government was involved. But her view that use of this statute would have changed the result in many of these cases was opposed by other legal commentators, who argued that permitting transmission of wealth over the generations even for charitable purposes inherently discriminates against somebody: if any transfers of property are permitted, at least they should be carried out in a way that honors the autonomy and private choices of persons who were merely deciding what to do with their own money. Here was another instance of the overriding conflict in American legal policy—private autonomy versus communitarian consequences.[6]

None of these clashing ideas, of course, was on my mind in the parking lot of the Baconsfield Shopping Center in 1992. I knew something of legal developments as they affected notions of private property because since 1970 I had continued to practice and to teach constitutional law to students at Columbia and Northeastern law schools but I wasn't writing a brief in my head. I was stuck on irony, not legal doctrine. It amazed me that the people of Macon, white and black, were now the proud possessors of one more food market and several pedestrian low-rise office structures instead of a lovely public park by a river.

According to Frank C. Jones, the Georgia lawyer who argued both Macon cases in the Supreme Court against LDF, Senator Bacon's seven grandchildren felt that running the park as an integrated facility would contradict his last wishes. I wondered if the heirs had ever seriously considered giving the park back to Macon—to all of Macon, that is. "Several of them lived out of state," Jones remembered, "and had no particular loyalty to the City of Macon." After a moment of reflection, he added: "This was a time very different than now, when the white community was upset with school integration and other court decisions."[7]

If the politicians and judges of Georgia, with the apparent exception of Attorney General Arthur Bolton, were unwilling to defend a public park open to all, I thought, why should relatives who might live in Phoenix or Minneapolis turn down over a million dollars from a developer to do it? It wouldn't be the first or last time racial animus and greed, or maybe just indifference, had trumped community needs.

I also wondered about the peculiar all-or-nothing, either/or debate that surfaces every time a confrontation over affirmative action or resegregation of public schools captures the headlines. One side argues that racism and even its legacy are things of the past; to harp on them is to fail to recognize the massive changes that have taken place in public attitudes and behavior since the end of the civil rights era. Advocates of this position must travel around the country sealed in opaque plastic bags.

The other side tends to see belief in white supremacy and privilege as a persistent pathology of white Americans. The feeling—sometimes verbalized, sometimes not—is that racism will never go away. If opportunities to discriminate have been reduced and overt racial appeals are less tolerated, the explanation is that notions of racial inferiority have just gone underground. After all, housing and public schooling are still largely separated along racial lines; per capita income of blacks remains about half that of whites; longevity and infant mortality rates are still skewed. The underclass is still large; money accomplishes much the same exclusion from comfort, health, and security that race produced in the past. People in this camp are my natural allies, but I wonder about their reaction when (and if) something that looks like real change actually occurs. Are they setting the bar so high—the utopian goal of the complete disappearance of all racism—that permanent dissatisfaction is ensured? If this is the case, it is the kind of stuckness that only arrival of a new generation can fix.

Conservatives try to distinguish between irrational, old-fashioned, aversive discrimination, which is fast disappearing, they say, because it contradicts economic self-interest, and "rational" discrimination based on behavior they believe is not a product of group stereotyping.[8] They argue, for example, that a big-city cab driver who will not pick up young black males at certain times in certain places because of fear of robbery and murder isn't reflecting racial hostility but recognizing the facts of life.

I'll grant that in a nation that often takes historical accuracy lightly, it can be difficult to know how much of discrimination and prejudice is a holdover from the past and how much is the product of forces that are ever present if one will only look. But racial stereotyping or disparagement doesn't go away just because the laws change—though it is absolutely essential to change them—or because use of racial epithets becomes less frequent or even because people soften toward persons they once feared as outsiders and as threats to well-being. For many Americans a dark face immediately raises questions of who is on top. Moreover, a growing body of cognition studies document how seemingly neutral but powerful subliminal processes frame minorities as more dangerous and less intelligent than whites even in situations where the experimenters have made sure they're not. "Recall Amadou Diallo," observes the legal scholar Jerry Kang, "the 22-year-old West African immigrant . . . shot 41 times by New York police who 'saw' a gun that didn't exist. It should haunt us to read social science that suggests that if he were White, he [might] still be alive."[9]

On that day in 1992, I was standing on ground that bore witness to the proposition that racial ideas retreat into structure where they do their work invisibly. It's a lesson I learned every day of the ten years I worked as an LDF lawyer and one I still have to relearn far too often.

From the late nineteenth century until the early 1970s, for example, insurance companies sold life and burial policies to Americans and Canadians of modest means on a racially skewed schedule, charging blacks more and paying their families less on the basis of group estimates of risk. The companies targeted blacks for more expensive policies through the mechanism of requiring weekly payments and by limiting eligibility for benefits. Fee collectors regularly reported on the morals and habits of black customers. At least one company, Metropolitan Life, recently agreed to pay policyholders over $100 million in restitution, though it disclaimed fault.[10] Whatever your ultimate view of these industry practices, I think it is undeniable that their impact on the families concerned continued years into the future. Here the capital that racism kept from blacks was not only social capital, it was hard cash.

Another example: If you visit one of the arraignment parts of the New York Criminal Court you can wait hours before you see a non-Hispanic white person standing before a bail-setting judge. Some of this situation is probably due to overt racism of the sort that even conservatives dub irrational, but you don't have to be a social reformer to figure out that most of the offenses involve drugs, petty theft, or assault and are the products of lives that have conjoined the offenders' color, poverty, unemployment, and lousy education. Are all these people morally defective or have they suffered from the workings of arrangements rigged against them?

And another: In 1991, Professor Ian Ayres published empirical research that showed that white female car buyers were quoted car prices 40 percent higher than the prices offered to white males, black males were asked to pay more than twice what white males were quoted, and black females were given prices over three times more. Four years later, Ayres found the same patterns at work: car dealers were still offering lower prices to white males.[11] Mark Cohen's statistical "study of more than 300,000 car loans arranged through Nissan Motor Company shows that black customers in 33 states consistently paid more" in finance charges than white customers, "regardless of their credit histories." In Florida, the difference between the charges paid by black and white borrowers was $533 but in other states black purchasers paid as much as $800 more than whites. Data of this sort tell us more than we may want to know, that reservoirs of subliminally felt white superiority in the cultural heritage of Americans will continue to exert power over the way our market economy operates long after it may appear to some people that racial discrimination has been ended.[12]

And a last set of examples. According to the *British Medical Journal,* most of the 60,000 Americans forcibly sterilized between 1900 and the 1970s were considered "outcasts" by the white majority—"the mentally ill or retarded, 'sexual deviants,' the impoverished, African-Americans and immigrants."[13] In 1997, President Bill Clinton apologized for the government's role in denying treatment for syphilis to 399 poor black Alabama sharecroppers who were deceived as part of a medical experiment between 1932 and 1972 by physicians of the United States Public Health Service into thinking they were being treated for "bad blood." Forget that it took the federal government twenty-five years to make verbal amends. Apologies are important, but despite them, "if past disparities are morally illegitimate," as Glenn C. Loury puts it, "the propriety of the contemporary order must also be called into question."[14]

But how is the "contemporary order" called into question? There is certainly no shortage of books and scholarly articles imaginatively unearthing submerged structures with pronounced racial implications, deconstructing government rhetoric, and complaining that little change comes from litigation, once the primary tactic employed to increase racial equity. The books and articles are read and reviewed within the small world of academics and public interest activists, and the ideas that emerge are essential to a future renewal of social concern. (Sometimes their publication even creates a minor academic celebrity, such as Cornel West, late of Harvard, now of Princeton, or Columbia Law School's Patricia Williams.) But the vast majority of this commentary says very little specific about the next steps to be taken by those concerned with the costs of inequality. As if to match the bookish quality of the criticism of the "contemporary order," today civil rights leaders are almost invisible until some major, media-friendly event surfaces—an election, a misplaced racial reference, a questionable Supreme Court nomination, or crude oppression. The systematic pattern of action, the hallmark of the civil rights movement, now eludes us.

The pages that follow mark a personal journey to and through a place where that action took place. It is my hope that new energy will be liberated by an understanding of how civil rights work grew from small beginnings into a powerful means of change. The movement eventually subsided into a still valuable but too often marginal activity, and because it left many things undone, renewal is a necessity.

Too often the law stays permanently tilted; as studies such as those of Professor Ayres demonstrate, the free market can serve to reinforce racism rather than prove it inefficient. Like an old house that has settled, structures that arise from racial division take on unrecognizable shapes, resist improvement, and have consequences that reach far into the future. The events with deep structural implications I've cited go to measurable patterns of behavior. Less obvious but as important are the ways in which the existence of blacks as a group subjugated or covertly thought to be inferior organize and bond the other members of society by giving them something recognizable to fear and to feel superior to. Claude Steele and his colleagues at Stanford University have shown that when African Americans and whites are tested in a setting where it is obvious that blacks are supposed to do worse, they in fact do so. When test administrators make clear, however, that the tests do not measure traits such as intellectual ability that are stereotypically associated negatively with African Americans, blacks' test results are the same as whites'.[15] It is folly to shout about racism in considering such phenomena but just as silly to pretend, as the courts sometimes do, that our history of racial thinking ended two decades after *Brown v. Board of Education* was decided. The cables tying these events and their impact to the place of race in our society may be buried underground but they are still connected. Today, as the residents of Macon, now a city with a black mayor, search out a children's playground or do weekend shopping, few have any idea of the history of the Baconsfield and its descent from racial division. In part, the reason is that such history isn't taught in the schools, but there is also a more sinister explanation: when it comes to race, Americans are prone to *disassociation,* the separation of certain mental information from consciousness and its descent into the dark world of unawareness, where it is not subject to control.

In short, along with a shopping center instead of a park, white Maconites have a false sense of how things happen, a forgotten history of something that occurred because white people thought themselves better than black people. They may even say, "The bad old days are over. Things are different now." And to an extent they will be right. The America of my civil rights years is gone. One change is that the Macon shoppers who use the land that was once a farm that was made into a park that is now Baconsfield Shopping Center are usually treated with courtesy regardless of their race. But as the Baconsfield case shows, the law maintains a pecking order and stereotypes that usually change very slowly, if at all.

There is a postscript to the Macon story. A young lawyer who assisted in the litigation, Willis Sparks III, was one of Senator Bacon's heirs. "When the final court decision came down," as Joseph Claxton, an eminent legal historian who has taught at Mercer Law School since 1972, describes it, Sparks "was teaching a class at Mercer University Law School." His "wife came to the door of his classroom" and called him over to whisper that the family had won in the Supreme Court: Baconsfield was going to revert to the heirs.

Sparks stared at his wife, taking in the news. Then calmly he turned back to the class and, according to Claxton, without more ado announced, "Gentlemen, I quit." He gathered his papers and walked out.

While this episode occurred before Claxton arrived in Macon, he believes it happened as he has told it. "I have had the story confirmed for me over and over by alumni who were in the class. It is one of the most famous stories in the post–World War II era at Mercer." Sparks was not really a criminal lawyer, but later he took a job handling appeals for the district attorney's office in Bibb County. The DA himself was eventually killed while trying to stop a burglary, and Sparks, much against his real desires, was appointed to replace him. Years later, he sat down at his desk one morning, picked up a gun, and took his own life.[16]

It would be farfetched, of course, to connect this tragic event to guilt over seizing and selling Baconsfield. And to try to do so would be mean. Unworthy. Nevertheless, I must admit it pleases me to think there may be something in the idea.

How I Went to Work for
Thurgood Marshall

A FEW years ago I found a particularly battered old box in a corner of my damp basement. At the bottom was a yellowed sixty-year-old file of my father's. I had glanced at this inch-thick folder at the time of his death, decades earlier, but put it aside without serious inspection; not ready, perhaps, to learn its contents or more likely just not expecting to find much.

Now I inspected it more carefully, and as it became clear just what the file contained, I studied the contents as if I had discovered the Dead Sea scrolls. The file documented the employment struggles of Ira D. Meltsner—my father—in the Great Depression. I saw a drowning man begging for help.

Trying to learn your own history from your parents or from other relatives is difficult. Their information may seem reliable because they were there, but like a positive eyewitness identification offered in court, too often this testimony is virtually worthless, slanted in ways that are hard to pin down. The search can feel like driving at night without lights. You are moving but in what direction? Most of the time you look for a white line on the road, but even when you see one you fear it isn't really there—you may just be willing it into existence. Is this my history or simply a story that has been told?

I was aware of these risks while I studied—and later tried to corroborate—what I found in the file, but they deterred me not at all. The connection to my own life was just too powerful and seemingly incontrovertible. It was as if I knew the story, in the sense of living with its implications, although I had never heard it told. And equally startling was my recognition that this was hardly the first time my future had been shaped by messages from my parents that they hadn't seemed aware they had sent. At any rate, to understand what I was reading in the file, I had to travel backward.

While I was growing up, my father's work took him inside large corporations, where he persuaded top management to embark on sizable promotional campaigns using the calendars, ashtrays, desk paraphernalia, and what in the trade they called novelties—anything you could distribute with a company's name imprinted—manufactured by his employer. Because he was essentially selling the idea of an ad campaign—the products just gave it flesh—this kind of salesmanship required persistence, bravado, and a thick skin. For every successful penetration of the executive suite, dozens of times he was brushed aside, put down, strung along, or flatly rejected. The abrasive quality of the work was impressive. There were fierce gatekeepers to outwit; managers who pretended to have authority but didn't; buyers seeking kickbacks and a whole array of big-city chiselers. Tough negotiations about small differences in price often preceded factory delays that could kill a sale it had taken months to close. He disliked dealing with people who seemed perpetually irritated, but it was the necessary price to pay for taking home the best money he'd ever earned.

To compensate for the disrespect they suffered in the field, he and his co-workers constantly bragged about the size of their sales and commissions. The most adult I ever felt before the day of my father's funeral was the time I overheard some of this talk on a visit to his office and he took me aside to whisper, "They measure their pricks like this *all* the time."

At home, however, my father went out of his way to distance himself from this slick and assertive stereotype of the salesman. Ira tried to be self-effacing, lighthearted, and easily intimate and tried to emphasize his interest in serious culture. He had, for example, an extensive collection of classical records and somewhat ridiculously waved a white baton up and down while he listened to Toscanini conduct Beethoven. But even at work, he aimed to do things differently. He was the kind of gregarious, interested-in-their-problems boss that secretaries worshiped. Before product endorsements were common, he'd won the right to use the image of professional ballplayers, such as Jackie Robinson, on calendars that graced the walls of barbershops and package stores across the nation. He also had an interest in civil rights that seemed more suited to a clergyman or lawyer than to a man who made a good living thinking up better ways for his corporate customers to give away ballpoint pens. Whenever my father encountered anyone being judged by race or religion, he had a physical reaction that suggested powerful personal experience. Face turning red, body suddenly stiff, his round facial softness turned angular as he delivered a passionate condemnation of bigotry and injustice. He must have heard "Jew boy" or "kike" once too often, I figured, in his otherwise protected early childhood in Manhattan.

For most of his adult life, he was preoccupied with supporting a family, but his antidiscrimination advocacy wasn't just rhetoric. It was a major reason he once (unsuccessfully) ran for a minor office in New York State's Liberal Party—at a time when it *was* a liberal party—and devoted himself to B'nai Brith human rights projects, even though he had no other Jewish affiliation. He frequently distributed to neighbors the contents of a closet full of anti-Klan pamphlets, warnings of neo-Nazi conspiracies, and picture books touting the joys of brotherhood—black, brown, and white children holding hands; Christian and Jew in joint worship under "one God." But he would never acknowledge, much less discuss, any personal dimension of bigotry. The brawl that followed the first time I was called a Christ killer near St. Francis de Sales, the local parish church, was an occasion for a paternal lecture on the social dislocation caused by the Great Depression.

"The Depression?"

"Well, poverty does terrible things to people. It makes them fearful of their neighbors. The Irish kid who sucker-punched you probably had a father who had to explain why he was fired. Maybe he took it out on the Jews."

When it came to the Depression, he knew what he was talking about. He'd come from a comfortable Jewish family—his father moved a thriving Greenwich Village dry goods store uptown around the time he was born—and after college he planned to start an advertising agency with a classmate. But the family business collapsed with the economic downturn of the early 1930s, ending his hopes for financial support for the agency; by 1935, at age twenty-six, Ira was unemployed, married, and dead broke. But then he got a break. With the help of a veteran ad man who'd worked for both Macy's and Gimbel's department stores, he landed a job as the advertising manager of a retail store in Dayton, Ohio. To a New Yorker, Dayton was on another planet, but feeling confident about his knowledge of retailing, he expected to make his mark quickly and move up and, more to the point, away.

The Dayton Dry Goods Company, however, wasn't interested in the kind of advertising that passed for cleverness on New York's 34th Street. The store's approach was conventional—it used the word "thrift" in all its promotions—while my father's efforts ran to the tongue in cheek. One of his favorite ads featured a sketch of a mildly discontented husband who tries to think of tactful ways to tell his wife that their old furniture is "practically grounds for divorce." By the end of the copy, the guy will find "marital bliss" with a new bedroom set from Dayton Dry Goods.

Dad did his best to come to terms with what his New York mentor disparaged as "this small-town stuff," but his desire to get ahead was too strong. Quietly he started looking for a new job and heard of an opening for an advertising manager in Tulsa, Oklahoma. It was at this point, in debt because he had to support his parents (social security benefits had yet to begin), feeling trapped in a dead-end job, and eager for a fresh start, he began to recreate himself.

On the application form he sent the Brown-Dunkin Dry Goods Company of Tulsa Ira made himself six years older, covering some of the gap in employment by claiming he spent three years as a freelance copywriter. But the Oklahoma application probed more than age and experience. Incredibly to a contemporary eye, he was asked his political affiliation. My father, in most ways a typical New York liberal Democrat and great supporter of Franklin Delano Roosevelt, marked "Republican."

The store didn't stop there. It not only wanted to know what it called his "nationality" but insisted the answer be precise: "State specifically— viz: German-American, Scottish . . . Jewish, etc." In his firm hand my father wrote down "American." Staring at this entry, more than half a century later, I thought that it revealed more about what went on in the minds of American Jews in the 1930s than ten pounds of sociological text.

Of course, inquiring formally into the politics of potential employees may not have been routine even then, but the underlying message that hiring depended on more than job qualifications was. Employment discrimination on the basis of race, religion, ethnicity, and gender—but not politics—wasn't rendered illegal under federal law until President Johnson signed the Civil Rights Act of 1964; it must be some genetic code, I thought, reading my father's file, that explains how I would happen to be the lawyer who wrote the complaint in the first case—a suit against a North Carolina supermarket—brought under the fair employment protections of the new law.[1]

In the 1990s, after criticism from conservative co-workers, a southwest Virginia factory foreman was fired for wearing a small pin expressing his support for Bill Clinton, then being tried for high crimes and misdemeanors by the United States Senate; a South Carolina worker was fired for placing a representation of the Confederate battle flag on his toolbox. In 2004 a man who heckled George W. Bush at a political rally was fired from his job at a Charleston, West Virginia, advertising agency.[2] In most states, these actions by employers were perfectly legal; even in those few where a serious legal question would arise from such a firing, its answer would turn on whether it was "unjustifiable" under a particular state's laws rather than whether it violated some specific protection of political expression. The free speech guarantees of the First Amendment, it should be remembered, are addressed to government and fail to reach purely private action.

At first, Tulsa's Brown-Dunkin Company professed serious interest in my father's candidacy, but a few weeks later the store informed him laconically that the job was actually for an "entry-level assistant." How many times, I thought, had I encountered a similar dodge in a civil rights suit brought for a black plaintiff? Was I for that reason being overly suspicious when I considered the store's letter of rejection an obvious pretext? The file didn't tell me the answer, but it was clear that despite his newly discovered maturity and political conservatism, my father had been labeled "overqualified." Apparently it didn't help that because of his experience in Dayton he had demanded a minimum salary of $75 a week.

He gave similar answers to questions on employment applications sent to retailers and ad agencies in Little Rock, Detroit, and Columbus, Ohio, but failed to get even an interview. So my father made still another change. Instead of ducking the religious issue, he faced it head-on and lied. Ira represented himself as Christian—a Christian Scientist, a loyal follower of Mary Baker Eddy. It's unclear whether his new identity made the job search any easier, but when the Dayton store laid him off in 1936, he once again sent out the new résumé. This time it worked. He was hired to write ads, billboard copy, and press releases for the New Haven Railroad, then with headquarters in Boston. He took the job with hope that he had finally found an employer who would reward his creativity; my mother and he moved to New England, found a small but pleasant apartment on Dana Street in Cambridge, and settled in for a long stay. There were no Jews in his office, however, or, as far as he could tell, working for the railroad anywhere. When six months later he was laid off again, he wondered if his lie had been discovered.

For the rest of the 1930s, my father supported his wife, child, and aging parents with whatever short-term copywriting or advertising work he could find. He didn't drop his new age, political party, or religion until he finally made his way back to the safety of New York City, catching on with Brown & Bigelow, a large national corporation, where he would remain for more than fifteen years. The company had only a few Jewish employees and none in management, but it was more interested in profits than in ethnic and social distinctions. Its president, Charles Ward, who had met his future business partner in the federal prison at Leavenworth, Kansas, after conviction for a white-collar fraud offense, had a soft spot for outsiders.

Later my father became the company's first Jewish executive. With his new power, he hired an occasional African American and Latino to sell novelties in their own Brooklyn and Newark neighborhoods—not only as a one-man equal economic opportunity commission, I am sure, but for canny business reasons of the sort that had led the company to promote him. Nevertheless, even these small moves startled his bosses, and because at least one vice president seriously questioned them, Ira had to prepare a report that silenced corporate critics with the impressive sales figures turned in by his new employees. His argument was spiced with pure "How someone looks doesn't matter if they can pitch" logic of the sort then being used by Branch Rickey of the Brooklyn Dodgers and Bill Veeck of the Cleveland Indians as they introduced the first Negro players, Jackie Robinson and Larry Doby, into major-league baseball.

Papers in the old file mark many of these events but say nothing directly about the inner experience. Did he struggle with tangled feelings about pretending he wasn't Jewish during the Depression or not care a bit? Was his commitment to equality a well-earned identification with the plight of others or a way of legitimizing himself? How come he so fastidiously preserved the record of what happened but never spoke about the events?

My best guess is that he couldn't bring himself to admit that in remaking himself, he had turned away from his origins. Because he secretly believed that his actions reflected a character flaw, he'd do his utmost to eliminate from the wider society the social pressures to which in his weakness he had succumbed. This would certainly be consistent with a similar process that I observed over the years in many Jewish lawyers and activists. While a direct association of Jews and liberalism tends to overlook the diversity of opinion and increasingly conservative politics of an affluent community, Jews have long fought their own fears of persecution by trying to encourage tolerance and legal protections in the place where they lived.

Whatever the answers, it turns out that the best guide to my father's character isn't the documentary record contained in the file but the hours I spent studying him, allowing images to develop slowly over time until they became fixed only at his death. I saw a totally secular man who had no interest in a deity or anything smacking of formal observance or public

ethnic affiliation; he would have insisted that lying about religion or politics was merely the price of survival in a hostile world, and of course, just
a few years later in Europe successfully lying about being Jewish was literally a matter of life or death. I can imagine him shrugging it off and quip-
ping, "I owe honesty to my customers but not to a bunch of bigots."

When you consider that I was launched from law school in 1960 with
this pedigree, it isn't surprising that I became a civil rights lawyer. Nor is it
particularly remarkable. I have spent my professional life with advocates
who have some version of this tale to tell, some emphasizing how they
compensated for an early wound and others speaking the nonpsychologi-
cal language of radical social vision, but almost all if you really push them
connecting their work choices to family events or patterns.

Another aspect of those years plays a big part in the shape my professional life took. It was a simple warning that American Jewish children of
the times learned from the Holocaust even if they supposed it was not
meant for them, or if they, like me, had no interest in things officially Jewish: someone is out to get you, so take care!

This idea may not have gotten much air time on the West Side basketball courts or in the Greenwich Village cafés where I spent most of my adolescent days, but we all knew it nonetheless. It was there in the pictures of
the concentration camps that *Life* magazine eventually published,[3] which
seem to have been seen by virtually everyone alive; in the slowly emerging
story of the wartime behavior of the pope (no one I knew would have believed that Franklin D. Roosevelt had refused to bomb the approaches to
Auschwitz); in Ernest Hemingway's churlish treatment of the Robert Cohn
character in *The Sun Also Rises* and in movies such as the one made from
Laura Z. Hobson's *Gentleman's Agreement*.[4] It was there in the certainty
that New York was different from the rest of the country and disdained for
it as well as in the story of why my friends and I had been born in Manhattan and not, say, in rural Belorussia or a suburb of Dallas, Texas. It
seemed to be all over history itself.

No matter the escalating economy, parents coming up in the world, the
triumph of the Allies over the fascist forces of anti-Semitism, or the aggre-
gation of Jews in New York, someone (lots of someones) is after you simply because you are Jewish. My friend Judy Salzman was only three in 1945
but she remembers vividly learning to her horror what an evil force in the
world called Hitler meant for her when a buffoonish uncle spouting Ger-
man put a comb above his lips to mock the Führer, scaring her out of her
wits. You could hide, you could run, but the idea was there.

The linkage to black Americans was obvious. The amazing thing about the Nazis was not their anti-Semitism (join the club!) but their public reveling in a sense of racial superiority. The parallel to the way many Americans thought about the Negro was obvious to me even when I was in junior high school. I remember one well-publicized incident that drove home the point because it took place in New York City, not in Mississippi or Alabama. In 1951 Josephine Baker, a famous black entertainer, had been denied food service at a trendy, celebrity-studded New York night spot, the Stork Club, by its irascible owner, Sherman Billingsley—a buddy of the columnist Walter Winchell and the FBI director, J. Edgar Hoover.

Discrimination complaints were filed. The restaurant was picketed. Familiar Cold War charges of demonstrators playing into the hands of the Commie enemy were exchanged on the local airwaves.[5] I was only fourteen years old but I recognized a fight over who was high in society's ordering and who could be treated like dirt when I heard one. New York taught you that every day. To me, blacks and Jews (at least my kind of Jews) seemed very much in the same boat. From my first day in junior high school, when I was battered by random hallway violence, Manhattan was a polyglot place of colors and cultures, actual conflict and potential collision. I never would have made it to LDF, much less survived 1960s civil rights work, without New York City's basic training.

That was the public piece. The private side was my parents' relentless social liberalism—my father almost cried the day PM, New York's progressive daily newspaper, closed.[6] The pathology of the black ghetto was central to this way of thinking. Almost everything wrong with the United States could be traced to its continued existence, and the extent to which it was dismantled was the best measure of national progress. The message here was hard to translate into specifics but suggested that if everybody could be just given enough for basic satisfaction, if economic justice were afoot in the land, we'd all be a helluva lot safer. There would be less crime, disease, and dislocation. A humane society, moreover, was the best prophylactic against Nazis. My father was hardly unique. It is no accident that Philip Roth makes his alter ego, Alexander Portnoy, New York City's assistant commissioner for human opportunity. One strain of Judaism defined itself by good works rather than ritual or metaphysics: the obligation to feed the widow and care for the orphan, what I associate with the teachings of Isaiah: "Learn to do good; seek justice, rescue the oppressed, defend the orphan, plead for the widow" (Isa. 1:17).[7]

The funny thing was: How come I didn't feel Jewish? And, though I might look over my shoulder when I thought it, didn't give a damn? Oh, that Jews were supposed to care about the life of the mind, that was all right—by this time I'd discovered the joys of hours spent pulling books down from the shelves at the St. Agnes Branch of the New York Public Library—but this other stuff about God and obeying his rules for the clan, looking out for the well-being of other Jews—well, it just seemed un-American to be told who you were and whom you had to support, even what you could eat, and, implicitly, that you couldn't change anything.

But it must have been an absorbed Jew-as-victim history that led me to let that inept demagogue Senator Joseph McCarthy point me to a career. McCarthy helped make me and a lot of others of my generation into lawyers, and, more important, impressed on us a reason to be public citizens, long before we knew the difference between a contract and a tort. He stood for what Samuel Lubell, the sharpest political analyst of the time, called the politics of revenge—revenge against the necessity of the war with Germany, against the unexpected implications of the New Deal and a postwar psychology that was changing the country, moving it away from one set of assumptions bound to ethnicity, geography, and class to another set that I hoped was more open.[8] My first hero was Joseph Welch, the Boston lawyer who humbled McCarthy and his attack dog, Roy Cohn, when they went so far in their red baiting as to impugn the character of one of Welch's young assistants for having been a student member of a left-leaning bar group, the National Lawyers' Guild.

Watching Welch needle McCarthy into revealing himself to be a schoolyard bully in the riveting 1954 Army–McCarthy hearings, sprawled on the couch before the tiny black-and-white television set in our Manhattan apartment after the morning session at Stuyvesant High School (juniors and seniors, who started school around 8 A.M., were let out at 12:40), I discovered a spiritual self. It was based on democracy, equality, tolerance, the First Amendment, a fair fight, and the defining present more than on group affiliation, belief in God, a chosen people, the Torah, and the defining past. I simply ignored the fact that Welch was a Brahmin, an orderly Boston private practitioner for an elite firm who earned his living representing the wealthy. Or that he brought down McCarthy for going after the U.S. Army, our patriotic warrior self—not for destroying the lives of civil servants, diplomats, public school teachers (including one of mine), Hollywood scriptwriters, or Broadway actors.

It was enough for me that Welch was confronting the evil of McCarthy's zeal in attributing illegitimacy to a set of political views and doing it publicly. The congressional hearings engaged me in a political process for the first time at age seventeen, if only in my mind; they were Jimmy Stewart movies come to life, and Stewart stood for the ordinary guy, meaning you didn't have to imagine yourself a star to play the part. I certainly hadn't worked out what McCarthy meant to me or to American democracy, other than that by indiscriminate assault on Communists he was challenging the loyalty of my family's and friends' political and social leanings. In my family lexicon, Communists were understood more as innocent or distracted liberal idealists than as dangerous totalitarians. The real threat wasn't their allegiance to the Soviet Union but the targeting by anticommunists of anything that didn't conform to mainstream beliefs. As for the Russians, all I knew then was that they had fought the Nazis. The leftists McCarthy and Cohn fingered looked more like people with progressive ideas who might be seen browsing at the Eighth Street Bookstore than spies and traitors. No matter what he said, I decided, it was plain that McCarthy was really after liberals such as my dad.

I was hardly alone. Also in 1954, a Harvard senior named Arthur Liman attended a congressional committee hearing in downtown Boston where, to the cheers of the audience, McCarthy and Cohn browbeat a hapless Harvard physicist and a young psychology research assistant, threatening them with firing and prosecution. Their offense: failure to name persons they knew who had been members of the Communist Party. At the second day of hearings, McCarthy refused to let General Electric workers he claimed were Communists read a statement; when their lawyer tried to read the statement for his clients, he was carried from the room by U.S. marshals. Another lawyer tried to make a legal motion objecting to the proceedings. After consulting with Cohn, McCarthy refused. Later the lawyer objected to a question McCarthy had posed to a witness; the senator demanded the lawyer himself be sworn as a witness and interrogated about being a Communist. When the lawyer refused, he too was pulled from the room.

Liman was shaken and fearful. He wondered if McCarthy's jeering supporters knew he was a Harvard student, a Russian Jew, a New Yorker. Reflecting on the hearing years later, he thought that despite his childhood in a comfortable Long Island suburb and attendance at an elite university, he carried the insecurity of many Jews of the time. He lived in a period when Nazis would have killed him; when some of his neighbors taunted Jews as Christ-killers. Excluded often from housing, facing ethnic barriers to education and employment, Liman sensed the fragility of Jews' success. "Small wonder," he would write, "I grew up fearing the demagogue, the rabble rouser, the hater and the dogmatist and treasuring tolerance, fairness and respect for individual liberties." Watching McCarthy and Cohn abuse witnesses and the seeming powerlessness of their lawyers to protect them, Liman decided he would do something about it by going to law school. Years later, when he was a big-money New York superlawyer, he encountered Cohn in court. Impulsively he revealed to Cohn that it was what he saw as a young man watching him that had led him to become a lawyer. Thinking his ruthless form of practice had set an example, Cohn was "delighted." Liman said no more.[9]

My family and a postwar New York childhood may explain why I wanted to be a civil rights lawyer, but they don't explain how I got the job. That had to do with Babette Schiller Spiegel, a worried, intrusive mother-in-law.

After Babette counted the very few days I'd known her daughter Heli before we decided to get married and realized that her son-in-law-to-be had left the country for a whole year after law school, she viewed me with horror. Had her daughter been bewitched? Now that I had returned to the United States, she wondered what other radical stunts I was planning. Unable to get rid of me but not one to give up easily, she gathered her resources. If I had to join her family, plainly I must now clerk for a justice of the United States Supreme Court; or if for some strange reason a clerkship wasn't immediately available, I would go to work for the best firm in town. Nothing else would reassure her.

When faced with her employment suggestions, I ducked, evaded, forgot, stonewalled, would think about it, would definitely think about it, and so forth. In desperation, she insisted I seek advice from a sensible friend, a placid Boston banker named Philip Eiseman, in the hope that he would suggest something close enough to Cambridge to let her keep an eye on me. Unfortunately for her, Philip saw a son in every young man who asked for his help, and from the first he implied that he was on my side. To avoid Babette's wrath, however, he mumbled loyally that I should really try private practice with a conservative firm in Boston, but he wasn't convincing; he could read my body language. Deep down, I think, we shared a fear of Heli's mother, so after going through the motions, he passed me on to a New York lawyer friend named Ed Lukas.

I met Lukas at his Manhattan office. On crutches after a recent accident, he was grouchy and not at all sanguine about career opportunities for a recent graduate who wanted to find a job where he could work on constitutional law and civil liberties lawsuits. It was 1961 but the real 1960s hadn't hit the country with full force. Talk about rights was still heard through Cold War paranoia. To his generation, the petitions you signed or did not sign in 1936 were still important. Lukas made clear that progressive lawyers, especially civil rights lawyers, had to keep their distance from organizations believed to be under the influence of Communists.

After he thought I was properly cautioned, Lukas discoursed broadly about his legal specialty, the proper legal line separating church and state. Finally he let his eyes graze my résumé. He was pessimistic. "There are hardly any jobs—the ACLU has mostly volunteers—and the pay stinks."

But hobbling toward the door to see me out, not wanting to send me away empty-handed, he threw me a bone: "I hear Thurgood Marshall is looking for somebody. Call him."

But at first I didn't. Instead—trying to be a good son-in-law—I visited more of Babette's friends. One was a revered law teacher. He thought Ivy League law graduates should first work for established law firms, "for the training and discipline." This advice reminded me of a job interview I'd had during my third year at Yale Law School with Gerhard Gesell, then a partner at Washington's elite firm of Covington & Burling and later one of the great federal judges of the era. Gesell didn't suffer fools, especially naive young fools. Sitting behind a lacquered table in a small interview room off a courtyard at the law school's faux-Gothic building, he sized me up as a flake come to steal some of his very valuable time. Gruffly he urged a gradual apprenticeship starting with business clients: "You've got to know your specialties—antitrust, real estate, securities—before we can trust you with the *in forma pauperis* work." I was dismissed.

Hearing that I wanted to handle constitutional cases, a famous Boston federal judge offered to set me right. Over tea and cookies in his Cambridge study on a remarkably cool August day he told me I'd really do better making a pile of money; then I could write big checks to my favorite causes and become an influential supporter.

The odd thing about these advice givers was that none of them was an armchair liberal; all of them had given time as well as money to promote social justice. But when I appeared—a vicarious son figure—they had to do what they could to ensure that my future would include good suits, private school for the kids, and a summerhouse. Good works were fine; they just didn't see them as a life.

In a few short years, this sort of splitting the political from the economic self would fuel bitter charges of hypocrisy from the next generation, but in 1961 it wasn't surprising that I got similar readings from my classmates at Yale Law School. Leon Lipson, a member of the school's faculty, was said to have acidly labeled students of my years "young fogies," as opposed to the colleagues he put down as "old Turks." I was too close in age to my classmates to know if he was right, but it was clear that most of them would be making their way soon to large firms in big cities. With the exception of Stan Fisher and Harry Subin, my two closest friends, the Yalies of my year who heard I was considering going to work for Thurgood Marshall thought it a risky career choice. One wondered if working for a "Negro organization wouldn't be more social work than law." Because law school had taught us little about actual practice, some of my peers worried that I would never receive the right on-the-job training.

Such comments just encouraged me to believe that I was doing the right thing. With bravado, I told myself that at the very least I was doing something different. But deep down I was apprehensive about what I would find when I stepped into unknown space. Still the silent premise behind much of what I heard—that by my work I would make a personal sacrifice, a charitable contribution to the downtrodden—made absolutely no sense to me. I was much too egotistical, ambitious, and acquisitive to believe that my main motives were eleemosynary. No, I was doing this for myself as well as for others.

Nor was it that I disdained working for government—though a veteran Department of Justice lawyer had warned me in 1960 that the new Civil Rights Division (it had previously been only a lower-status "section") was a dead end—or couldn't use the superior salary offered by the firms or was at the time particularly clear about my ideals. It was more, I think, that the prospect of working for corporate clients terrified me and made me happy to go off in a new direction. Big-firm practice evoked memories of my father's love-hate relationship with his employer—the bittersweet of his dependency on the company and his dislike of persistent corporate infighting. In the end being a loyal corporate soldier hadn't protected him from losing battles in the quota wars, and he felt he had to leave the company to preserve his self-esteem. I didn't want to invite the kind of anxiety, suppressed as it was in him, I had grown up with.

Maneuvering in a government bureaucracy, as in a large law firm, struck me as asking for a self-containment that it was doubtful I possessed. And what would I do if some Joe McCarthy type started to demand obedience to the orthodoxy of the day? As self-suppression wasn't my strong suit, I ran the risk of going along and then feeling like a counterfeit. Even trying Washington for a short while might hold me back; and given a general driving impatience—my piece of the quintessential American impulse to transcend one's origins—I wanted engagement.

Most of all, I feared boredom. This was the slippery, hidden side of lawyering that was little discussed but omnipresent: the necessary long hours of gray paperwork that over time could kill the spirit if the task had no larger purpose to dignify it. At Yale I had heard horror stories of young associates buried for several years analyzing the dense and detailed testimony of economists who had been deposed before the trials of mammoth antitrust cases, trials that eventually became unnecessary when the cases were, as usual, settled.

Before speaking to Alex Bickel—my constitutional law teacher, a former clerk to Justice Felix Frankfurter, and soon to be the biggest name in his field—I was amazed that most of the lawyers I talked to thought civil rights law a backwater, at least for a white lawyer, and hardly any of them knew a black lawyer of any kind. When asked about Jack Greenberg, Marshall's first assistant, those few who had heard of him said he was the exception that proved the rule.

It was then that I went to the most unusual person I knew for advice. Alexander Mordecai Bickel had been brought to the United States from Romania in 1939 at fourteen years of age, when he spoke no English. In a few short years he would see combat in World War II, excel at City College in New York and Harvard Law School, advise Justice Frankfurter about constitutional history and racial segregation, work for the State Department, research his first book (about the unpublished judicial opinions of Justice Louis D. Brandeis), and the year before I arrived begin to teach at Yale.

I would spend as much time as I could in his classes, where he appeared, as the Yale Law School historian Laura Kalman described him, "in impeccably tailored three-piece suits, 'Phi Beta Kappa key displayed prominently,' hair slicked back."[10] Amazed that there was nothing about either his speech or his approach to the Constitution that suggested his European origins, I found that he both epitomized the constructed self and, because he radiated inner confidence, transcended it. At the very center of his thought was the challenge of deciding when and how the Supreme Court properly used its powers. Searching for interpretive guides to the Constitution intensely engaged his attention, but I felt him actually to be concerned less about text and history than about the tactics of justice. When was it compelling for judges to do the right thing and when did they have to pass, leaving the decision to others, in the service of more powerful values? A few years later—about the time I consulted him about my career—the legal world learned in detail with the publication of his book *The Least*

Dangerous Branch an elaborated version of what we had been hearing three days a week, and often disputing, in his classes.

Bickel, however, was always more than just a teacher we met in a classroom. His long-running feud with an iconoclastic colleague, Fred Rodell, was fodder for student gossip. After he showed up with his attractive wife at a party that Harry, Stan, and I gave at our Bishop Street apartment, we entertained each other with parodies of the teaching style of "our pal Alex." In fact, we were jealous: Bickel's eye often held twinkles that hinted at a more sophisticated life than we could know—and this was before his fame was widespread. It was rumored, for example, that he spent vacation time in such trendy, wicked resorts as Acapulco. We also sensed that he was a celebrity in the making, a member of a very elite group whose thoughts could energize government at the highest levels, and that by being his special charge for a time we shared in a meaningful public life. Bickel loved debate. He seemed to welcome our arguments even if he usually rejected them, but he could also get properly annoyed if he heard too much irreverence or student jibes that he was too wedded to Frankfurter's "Harvard-type" obsession with procedural nuances.

When I consulted him in 1961, I didn't even know if he would remember me, but he warmly endorsed working at LDF, dismissing others' concerns about a pace too frenetic to permit me to learn my trade. He never hesitated. How could one pass such a chance by? He'd write to Marshall. In the imperious but still friendly way he corrected student errors of legal analysis, Bickel settled the matter: "This is the job for you."

Why I became a civil rights lawyer in a day when there were very few such lawyers of any race and precious few who were white seemed merely a matter of serendipity to me at the time. Years later, looking carefully at how I'd been raised and what was going on in the world and remembering Bickel's words, I changed my mind, deciding I had been cut out for that work without even knowing it.

That's how, a year after graduating from law school, I accepted an offer from Thurgood Marshall, then director-counsel of the NAACP Legal Defense and Educational Fund, Inc.—variously called LDF, the Legal Defense Fund, the Fund, or the Inc. Fund in a usually hopeless effort to distinguish an organization of civil rights lawyers from its mother ship, the more conservative, membership-dominated National Association for the Advancement of Colored People. Across the desk in his cluttered, closet-sized office on the seventeenth floor of a Columbus Circle skyscraper, Marshall's deputy, Jack Greenberg, told me the pay was $6,000.

I was shocked. This was an unbelievably lordly sum. At the time, law school tuition was only $1,000 a year and downtown big-firm associates didn't make much more. I remembered my father's glow when he first made $10,000 a year. Most important, the salary was for doing work I wanted to do.

I gasped. "If that's too much, I could take less."

Taking in my confusion, Greenberg gently admonished me in words I would always remember with gratitude: "Never, never take less money for doing good."

Years later, I learned that in 1949 Marshall had originally hired him at a salary of $3,600 a year but hadn't cleared the figure with the NAACP board; in a humiliating move, the board forced Marshall to lower Greenberg's starting salary to $3,200. Marshall himself had been paid $200 a month a decade earlier when he had moved from Baltimore to New York to join his mentor, Charles Hamilton Houston, vice dean of Howard Law School and then the NAACP's "special" legal counsel.[11] The son of a Pullman porter, Marshall grew up with relative economic security, but the Baltimore of his youth was rigidly segregated, a social setting that was not so very different from the deep South. He studied at Howard only because the University of Maryland Law School did not accept Negroes. As many of his Supreme Court law clerks would emphasize in tributes upon his death, his background nurtured empathy with victims.[12]

After a year out of the country, I felt largely unprepared intellectually for the work ahead. I asked Greenberg what I could do to get ready. "Have you read the *Brown v. Board* opinions recently?" he asked.

Mercifully, he didn't wait for my answer—which would have been "Not since law school." Instead, he suggested I might get "an overview" by taking a look at his own 1959 book, *Race Relations and American Law*. So the next morning I took the Amsterdam Avenue bus to the Columbia University campus, walked over to the university bookstore on Broadway, and found a copy of Greenberg's book hiding under a pile of imposing United Nations pamphlets on race. In my eagerness to get prepared, I bought the whole pile.

Devouring Jack's book, I found that from law school classes I was familiar with many of the leading cases dealing with efforts to keep African Americans from voting booths and jury boxes. At Yale I had paid special attention to the way courts often used particularly egregious encounters between police and Negro men to announce new rules of criminal procedure somewhat protective of defendants' rights. But otherwise the book was an eye-opener. It was concise and readable but also a precise and authoritative survey of the case, constitutional, and statutory law governing race. When I finished it, three nights later, my head was swimming with the history of subjects I hadn't focused on before—failed efforts to stem lynching, abortive moves to ensure a level of nondiscrimination in housing beyond that facilitated by the Supreme Court's decision in the racial covenants cases, difficulties that were being faced in enforcing *Brown,* the fabulous story of legal evasions undertaken to keep Pennsylvania's Girard College exclusively white,[13] the founding of the NAACP and later the Legal Defense Fund.

Finally, here was my first encounter with the mythic figure of Houston—Thurgood Marshall's law teacher, predecessor at LDF, and guiding light. Greenberg did not go into the Houston-Marshall relationship in any detail, but it was clear from his treatment of the subject that the basic theory of challenging segregation in the courts had been laid down in the early 1930s by Nathan Margold, a white New York lawyer, a former United States attorney, and a Felix Frankfurter protégé, hired with a small amount of money from a private foundation as an NAACP consultant. Margold argued in a 218-page text dealing with both technical legal questions and high strategy that the NAACP should attack segregation, not unequal facilities, though his approach was cautious: "We are attacking segregation only because it is the only means now open to us of fighting the disgraceful discrimination that is being practiced against the Negro race." Also a man Frankfurter had mentored at Harvard, Houston had become the NAACP's "special" counsel in 1934 and had given Margold's ideas flesh. As Greenberg would write, Houston crafted a "grand strategic framework" to dismantle legal segregation, beginning with suits against white-only graduate schools. When he returned to private practice and teaching in Washington in 1938, Marshall took over from him.[14]

Today any lawyer even moderately interested in human rights or public law is aware of much of this history; in 1961 I felt I had been let in on a secret known by few.

Despite his triumph in *Brown v. Board of Education*[15] in 1954, when he persuaded the Supreme Court that legal segregation of the races was inherently unequal and hence unconstitutional, Thurgood Marshall was not yet a household name among whites, though he was the devil incarnate to enough southern segregationists to make him very careful about travel arrangements and particularly anxious if state police below the Mason-Dixon line were ordered to protect him.

Law teachers regularly obsess over the meaning of *Brown,* but then remarkably little attention had been paid to the decision in law school classes.

Nor was I much better informed than the rest of white America about Marshall or the NAACP or the history of Negroes in the twentieth-century United States, but at least I had been exposed to the basic principles of civil rights law in a course taught by Tom Emerson, who was both an influential scholar and a human rights activist. Aside from Emerson's offering, one of the few such courses in any law school, and Bickel's attention to such cases as *Cooper v. Aaron*,[16] the decision upholding the court order that led to federal military intervention in the schools of Little Rock, Arkansas, little was said at Yale about the doings of Marshall and the small group of LDF lawyers.

Among African Americans, of course, Marshall was already a legend, but there were hardly any African Americans at Yale Law School, fewer in fact than women, and there were only seven women in the class of 1960. The only black man I got close to at Yale was Clifford Alexander, later secretary of the Army, and that was only because I stood somewhere in his general vicinity when I was given the impossible task of guarding him in intramural basketball games. If you were guarding Cliff Alexander, you had either to foul him (and then you better back off quickly) or let him breeze by and hope he blew the layup. Getting very close was a decided risk to one's bone structure.

I would have to learn my Mr. Marshall on the job along with the history of the divorce of the LDF from the NAACP, how to navigate in our interracial office environment, and, not incidentally, how to practice law. Right away I could tell the soul of the place was in the secretaries. They were vivacious women who loved to laugh and gossip, to eat and drink, but would somehow find the stamina (as well as the child care) to type through the night when crisis struck. I learned from them that I could find enjoyment and hard work at the same place and the same time. And their memories were the main source of LDF history. They knew within a centimeter whom to rely on and whom to distrust in the national civil rights circuitry that flowed in and out of Thurgood Marshall's office and soon Greenberg's. They were experts at reading Marshall's mocking wit, cryptic allusions, and indirect leadership style. Was he serious when he told me to be ready to get on a plane to New Orleans in an hour or was he just telling me to have the papers he wanted on his desk forthwith? The two secretaries I worked with most often, Gloria Branker and Marcella Williams, were my mentors here. Urbane, wise women whose understanding of the male animal, at least the lawyer subspecies, was slightly intimidating; they could rip through Marshall's moods and the verbal traps he set for the unwary as nimbly as through a soul food recipe.

Much of his folksy macho talk was the thinnest cover for moving people indirectly. So was his glance; he could position his long dark body so that he looked you down or didn't look at you at all, all the time still speaking, probing, implying. He juggled these elements, choosing the mix that suited his purpose of the moment. There was something about being in his presence that was both comforting and unsettling. This must have been how he wanted you to feel. His manner left things unclear, where he stood and where you stood with him, but it also conveyed that he wanted results.

If he were a football coach, the message would have been "I expect to win." From us he was demanding the very best legal moves he could get. It was all right to joke casually, as we all did at LDF, about this or that strange way of some white person dealing with black folks or the equally strange way of some black person dealing with white folks, but Marshall took the anecdote to new heights. He used it as a didactic tool to express his numerous opinions on just how particular cases would turn on evidence, precedent, and cunning. It was an indirect means of expressing power and control. Most of all, I think Marshall had learned to be careful in expressing his opinions. His stories contained messages, all right, but the form in which he delivered them made it impossible to repeat them with total confidence of his meaning. If you were with him when he spoke, what he was driving at was generally clear, but the way he put things sometimes worked so that he could not be held fully accountable for a precise point of view unless he wanted to be.

I had never before encountered anything like these early lessons in Marshallese, but otherwise life at LDF was in many ways familiar. It felt very much like the mix, the shades, the talk on 79th Street and Amsterdam Avenue, on Manhattan's West Side, where I had lived as a teenager. It felt like the neighborhood, all right, just moved twenty blocks south to a high-rise office building.

I much needed, however, a serviceable explanation of what I was doing and why. As I slowly put the elements together, I concluded that I took the job with the Legal Defense Fund from a mixture of motives both high-minded and conventional. The primary reason to be a lawyer, I believed, was to fight injustice, but I also lusted after the action and esteem of defeating the bad guys and arguing before the federal courts. I tried to keep ambition and ideals in balance because I didn't want to feel (or to appear) either too greedy or too tender-minded, but even then I doubted (and I still doubt) that one serves society well without also pleasing one's private self.

When I went to work for the LDF, I didn't know much about it except that these were the folks who had won the *Brown* case and they were oiling a litigation machine to enforce it across the South. It came as a shock to learn that there were only six other lawyers on the staff (one of whom, another Stuyvesant High grad, the Harlemite Norman Amaker, soon left to spend most of the year in Berlin when John F. Kennedy called up the military reserves). I had to learn in fact as well as in theory that a civil rights case required just as much attention to investigating facts, hunting precedents, and acquiring technical proficiency as any other serious lawsuit. Moral truth didn't win them, but then neither did professionalism and craft. Both had to be present — not to mention luck and the right judges — in a seamless, persuasive whole.

My personal views about race, not that I gave them much thought at first, were linked like everything else to the atmospherics in my family and to growing up in the middle of Manhattan. I'd gone to integrated public schools; talked politics from age eleven, when Harry Truman surprised everyone by trouncing Thomas E. Dewey, Henry Wallace, and Strom Thurmond of the Dixiecrats to boot in the 1948 presidential election; played basketball on wide-open playground courts; skipped school to hang out in the unpredictable world of Greenwich Village; spent evenings hanging out on Broadway and persuading doormen and Irish bartenders at 52nd Street jazz joints such as Jimmy Ryan's that I was eighteen.

The New York world I confronted included plenty of nations, and there was very little that united them. In the city we were close but separate. It was no accident that my West Side neighborhood was often labeled "mixed" or "polyglot" by both politicians and sociologists or that Leroy Clark, a lanky Manhattan-bred colleague soon to join LDF, often sounded to me like a dark twin of my New York self. The melody of his youth was different but the urban rhythm was completely familiar. Or that many figures in the civil rights struggles to come emerged from the city — Bob Moses, the pied piper of the Mississippi movement, a math teacher at the Horace Mann School, had attended the same "elite" Manhattan public high school I had; Stokely Carmichael, the incendiary chairman of the Student Nonviolent Coordinating Committee (SNCC) during some of the tumultuous Black Power years, a student at Stuyvesant's rival, the equally well regarded Bronx High School of Science;[17] and red diaper babies too numerous to name.

If it occurred to me to ask, as later I would be asked numerous times in a range of linguistic styles, why a white man was going to work for blacks, at first I wished the thought into insignificance. Years later, when Greenberg, the only other white lawyer at LDF when I arrived, wrote his history of the Fund, *Crusaders in the Courts,* he brushed aside attention to his race; he had always thought it, he reported, the "least relevant" thing about of him. Greenberg would tell an interviewer that at the time *Brown v. Board of Education* was argued, LDF lawyers didn't think of themselves as white or black: awareness of race, he claimed, was not on the conscious level.[18] The comment must have referred to the inner world of civil rights relationships, because certainly it was noted that he was the only white lawyer among the LDF advocates. I felt Jack was saying something about his own thoughts and feelings but I also understood that many people would think he was expressing his aspirations for a color-blind society. In my case, friends and family and friends of family were mostly curious. Some thought the choice of work spoke of altruism; others supposed it reflected a quirk of personality. Blacks were less inquisitive but more likely to need some proof that I wasn't there to exploit the situation.

City life explained my own initial relative indifference to race, as it explained others' more concentrated attention. Still baffled by the need to be stable and specific in a nation that wouldn't and probably couldn't stop changing, I discovered that New York itself supplied both identity and difference. The distraught Puerto Rican classmate who out of the blue had stabbed me with the business end of a smoldering soldering iron in shop class at Joan of Arc Junior High School was Hispanic, all right, but only in the descriptive sense; to me, José was just another out-of-control hazard of city life, not an ethnic imperative.

But it was different for others. In 1963, Norman Podhoretz, then editor of *Commentary* magazine, dropped a bombshell on the New York literary world when he wrote about growing up in a poor Jewish, Italian, and black Brooklyn neighborhood in the late 1930s, when the animosity between white and black children often had brutal consequences. The conflict had "a special intensity and was conducted with a ferocity unmatched by intramural white battling." Much of the essay, which he called "My Negro Problem — and Ours," was a story of fights and beatings of what appear to be primary school children.[19]

How can blacks be the persecuted race, he thought, when where I lived and went to school they were doing the beating, robbing, and humiliating? Podhoretz attributed the raw and bloody encounters in his neighborhood to the mutual hatred of the antagonists, suggesting that whites devalued black children because they were far more persistently impudent and rebellious than white youths. The whites were poor but many of them, un-like the Negroes, were plainly bound for the middle class. The blacks were physically magnificent—"independent, reckless, brave, masculine, erotic" —and therefore, concluded Podhoretz, they became faceless, the objects of the envy and fear of whites, who had to deny or evade their own defiant impulses.

On the black side, Podhoretz argued, it was more than envy of the relative power and riches, the "possibilities open to me that were denied to him," that made a white kid faceless to a black one. "If I represented the jailer to him, it was not because I was oppressing him or keeping him down: It was because I symbolized for him the dangerous and probably pointless temptation toward greater repression just as he symbolized for me the equally perilous tug toward greater freedom."

If American whites were honest with themselves, Podhoretz wrote, they would have to admit that the result of these encounters has been hatred; whites are twisted, "sick in their feelings about Negroes," and—anticipating by years white flight and resegregation—even "middle-class liberals with no previous personal experience" will discover that "their abstract commitment to the cause of Negro rights will not stand the test of direct confrontation."

Is there any way for American society to solve its "Negro problem"? Podhoretz was pessimistic; the most he could offer was a prescription that showed how trapped he was (maybe we all are) in racial determinism. As a way out, he could think only of miscegenation. If blackness is a stigma, the "vision of the future is the hope of erasing the stigma by making color irrelevant, by making it disappear as a fact of consciousness." According to the Harvard legal scholar Randall Kennedy, Podhoretz was just the latest of "amalgamationists," entertaining the "idea of deploying intermarriage programmatically" as an "engine of positive social transformation." Thomas Jefferson and Patrick Henry believed "interracial intimacies"— the title of Kennedy's book—would whiten the Indians; and the noted twentieth-century anthropologist Franz Boas argued that if blacks became "octoroons . . . the color question would probably disappear."[20] Apparently the desire for our racial problem to simply go away is as old as our racial problem.

I long pondered the article. Some of it merited ridicule: Got a race problem? Why not take care of it by just abolishing race? After all, it's a cultural construct. But it's one thing, I decided, to point out the fragility in scientific terms of any conceptual clarity or definitional stability to "race" but quite another to argue that if millions of people have a troublesome idea, they could just plan to procreate its social significance into oblivion.

The article was published at a time when blacks were still denied service at lunch counters, when northern white liberal self-satisfaction and consequent patronizing of the South was at the high-water mark, and when interracial sexual contact was thought too inflammatory an issue to confront publicly. Miscegenation was still a crime in southern states; fearing political repercussions, Felix Frankfurter persuaded the Supreme Court to ignore prohibitions of interracial marriage in 1955. It wasn't until the *Loving* case in 1967 that such laws were abrogated.[21]

In my intellectual world, "My Negro Problem—and Ours" caused a furor. Much of the criticism centered on Podhoretz's suggestion of the wholesale merger of the races. The most telling comments pointed out that he saw the difficulty as a Negro problem, not a white problem—he was urging the obliteration of blackness to meet whites' need for social peace. Podhoretz got points for brutal honesty about his own feelings but he made no similar call for assimilation to heal the wounds inflicted on Jews by a legacy of anti-Semitism. Indeed, the end of the essay had him quaking at the thought of "a daughter of mine" marrying a black, but hoping he would have the "courage . . . to give her my blessing."

Podhoretz had not yet become a leading intellectual warrior against liberal American institutions and such liberal solutions to racial issues as affirmative action, but the drift of "My Negro Problem—and Ours" was unmistakably in that direction. In 1963, however, I was more taken by his careful description of neighborhood street violence between New York youths than his emerging neoconservatism. That had been part of my New York life too—not only among blacks and whites but with Hispanics and Greeks, members of gangs such as the Ramblers, the Scorpions, and the Lords, not to mention the unaffiliated but equally dangerous groups that hadn't yet acquired their own colorful, zip-front, script-lettered satin jackets.

I never went to school without keeping the possibility of attack in mind. I had developed New York radar. Healthy defensive paranoia could tell you the difference between a nut case and a head basher coming toward you on the cross streets near Broadway. And though I wore glasses, I was not small and did not look weak; I did not appear to be an easy mark, unless finding someone bigger was the very thing the basher was after, as was often the case. The fear left me mistrustful of adults also, especially those in authority. They seemed oblivious of what New York City school kids had to face. The police, moreover, were rarely where you wanted them to be. In 1950 I had been attacked from behind with an iron pipe after leaving a basketball game that my team had won by a large point margin; my nose was broken, but the officers on the case were best at documenting an event after it happened, seemingly more concerned about keeping proper records that trapping the mugger. We were a bunch of lost children in a crazy city run by big wheels who didn't much care what happened to us.

Unlike Podhoretz, while I too had plenty to fear, I never learned to attach my fears to a face of any particular color. Maybe Podhoretz's experiences with blacks, unlike mine, were all negative. Maybe he had a better sense of who he was and therefore knew what he had to defend. I'd had more tussles with whites than with blacks or Puerto Ricans. Perhaps the Manhattan of those years was an equal opportunity mugger. It helped that before going away to college I had lived in almost constant contact with blacks and Puerto Ricans and couldn't help but see them not as a homogeneous mass but as individuals. And it also helped that the only thing I had of real value that could be taken—the chance of realizing my vaguely defined ambitions—was at risk only from those above me in the social scale. Danger lurked in the New York of my youth, all right, but not in any one group. Nor was white supremacy in my bloodlines. My family tradition simply never included a role as subjugator; perhaps it contained some of the rebel and some of the victim but certainly not much at all of the master.

LDF society included a mostly black but integrated population of staff lawyers and an overwhelmingly black network of cooperating lawyers advised by a group of mostly but not exclusively white academics. In the background was a variety of Negro professionals and wealthy, socially concerned whites. I entered this new world alert to its novelty but with a comfort level that reflected a worldview forged on the streets of New York.

What They Didn't Teach Me at the Yale Law School

I CAME to LDF with very little knowledge of what lawyers actually did when they weren't behaving like Joseph Welch—saving the Republic from Cold War demagogues. Most American law teachers aim at being scholars, not trainers. It's a truth about legal education that most lawyers would like to forget and that the public is only dimly aware of. In law school, of course, I'd sometimes heard and read about lawyers' work with clients, but with one important exception, these were secondhand experiences. A typical war story was told by my trusts and estates teacher, Elias Clark, who vividly described to the class how as a young lawyer he had accompanied a senior partner to an elegantly furnished Park Avenue apartment to witness the signing of a will. We listened eagerly as he sketched the careful choreography of the event, down to the partner's weak joke that the elderly wealthy client would probably have to revise the document in a decade or so.

In those days, we were stuck with cameo narratives like this. No course was available where students could gain experience and earn academic credit while taking care of a client's needs under the guidance of a supervisor. At LDF, I would have to feel my way, and I came to resent that Yale hadn't better prepared me for practice.

The reason was that law schools—even Yale, which often claimed it was different from the rest—adhered to the view that students learned the law best by dissecting cases in the classroom. Indeed, if Yale differed in any way, it wasn't that the school much cared about educating practicing lawyers—we were so smart, the theory went, that we'd learn on the job— but rather because of the faculty's intense desire to see law school as a place where experts in many disciplines came together to craft public policy. The faculty had less interest in improving the classical model of professional training than in establishing law as a discipline as intellectually challenging and methodologically rigorous as any other taught in a university.

To be sure, as one faculty member would put it later, Yale Law had "a long tradition of attention to facts and problems of fact-finding" going back to a pioneering proponent of a school of thought known as legal realism, Professor (later Judge) Jerome Frank.[1] But in the late 1950s the little about practice that trickled down to students came not from what our professors said in class but from what they did outside of it: one leading light, Tom Emerson, founded a civil liberties organization and set out to legitimate family planning, playing a key role in privacy rights litigation that would eventually result in the Supreme Court's *Roe v. Wade* ruling protecting a woman's right to choose abortion.[2] Yale mythology had it that Fowler Harper, my torts professor, had sued the Hearst newspaper empire for calling him a Communist, won hefty damages, and with the proceeds bought an estate that he dubbed Hearst Acres. Louis Pollak and Charles L. Black advised LDF on litigation strategy, and Fleming James, who taught procedure, was the court-appointed boss of a major railroad then in receivership.

But to my classmates and me, parochial and career-focused as most of us were, the faculty's life outside of New Haven was really just background music. On the campus, the 1950s brought an oppressive calm; classes were the featured presentations and we rarely cut them. It never occurred to us to question the great liberal legalists on the faculty, who, Bickel more than most, did not believe democracy extended to law school governance. It was all a far cry from the decade or so to come, when Yale would suffer from a divisive student rebellion, intrafaculty turmoil, and a surprising refusal to promote or grant tenure to six bright young law professors for reasons that in some cases certainly included their challenges to liberal orthodoxies.

I remember one course especially. It was called experimental because the two teachers, Abraham Goldstein and Joseph Goldstein, tackled a subject rarely then taught in law school, criminal procedure—the steps to be followed in laying and resolving criminal charges. (Harvard didn't have such a course until Alan Dershowitz—who was also Joe Goldstein's student—joined the faculty five years later.) The novelty of the course's subject matter did not, however, extend to pedagogy. The Goldstein boys, related only in their love of things legal, left me a lifelong interest in how we treat people accused of crime, a subject I came later to practice and teach, but the class itself came alive only with their few stories of trial tactics and litigation strategy. They were brilliant, sophisticated analysts but largely unaware, or so it appeared, that just so much could be squeezed out from cases describing, say, the powers of the prosecution when one had never read a grand jury transcript, seen a trial, or watched even a slice of the kind of plea bargaining that almost always followed indictment.

Ironically, Abe Goldstein had come to teaching from practice, and Joe, even if he hadn't practiced criminal law, had served as clerk for Judge David Bazelon, the most active criminal law reformer on the federal bench. Somehow they conveyed a feeling that there was something illegitimate about teaching from experience—maybe they didn't have enough of it—in comparison with the supposedly hard-edged knowledge derived from the lifeless factual descriptions found in the opinions of the appeals court judges. Of course, questions of the sort laymen might ask—"What is it like to represent someone you think is guilty?"—were never discussed.

The Goldsteins' approach was hardly unusual. My partial disappointment with them was matched in almost all of my other classes. At the core, it wasn't so much that models of practice were absent but that too much class time was spent on dissection of the reasons—I experienced them as rationalizations—given by judges for their decisions and not enough on what would later be called "intense involvement with authentic dilemmas in a professional setting."[3]

Bickel could also dissect cases to the point of agony but he was dealing with the high art of analyzing constitutional principles; the man I saw and heard in class conveyed much of the time that the nation's future was at stake when such ideas were debated. He modeled for me, therefore, a way of integrating thought and practice that eventually would become my vision of a successful professional life. One memorable classroom event took place in September 1958. President Eisenhower had responded to widespread rioting against desegregation in Little Rock, Arkansas, by federalizing the state's national guard and authorizing the secretary of defense to send in troops to keep the peace. Bickel came into our constitutional law class that day carrying the text of the presidential proclamations and put us in the role of the president's lawyer. Disregarding the assignment for the day, he led us in a line-by-line deconstruction of the text and a search for the sources in the Constitution and federal law that authorized Eisenhower to act in such an extraordinary manner.[4]

Of course, that night I fantasized about arguing the case for the schoolchildren before the Supreme Court. Little did I know that in three years I'd be working with the lawyers who had done just that in the famous case of *Cooper v. Aaron*. For my taste, however, in most classes we were simply too far removed from the work I thought we should be trained to do and the settings where we would do it. And there were subtle pressures to resist complaining, even to oneself. I experienced my dissatisfaction with such brilliant teachers as Abe and Joe as churlishness. Something must be wrong with *me*. What we might call the elite law school syndrome was at work. Enormous intelligence was on display and available for the taking. A Yale Law School education was a gift to the mind and the career. Knock it and you were taking down the very thing that would lead others to attribute to you skills you weren't sure you actually had and opportunities beyond expectation. No wonder the alumni were so lavish in their attentions and financial contributions.

My dissatisfaction turned out to be more than a personal frustration. Much of it derived from the concept of law as a quasi-scientific enterprise, an assumption that had ruled the education of lawyers since Dean Christopher Columbus Langdell instituted the case method at Harvard in the 1880s. As law could be understood only by analysis of appellate court opinions, according to Langdell, the strategy and tactics of practice, the volatility of facts, and the patterns of institutional life were distractions, not sources of priceless learning from a master teacher. It was as if Michelangelo refused to explain to an apprentice how he held his chisel, much less to model its use with the apprentice at his elbow, though he was quite willing to debate endlessly the views of the art historian Giorgio Vasari; or as if a physician teaching would-be internists consistently substituted repetitive study of autopsies for hospital rounds.

True, some members of the Yale Law School faculty were in rebellion against the hermetic seal of appellate court opinions. These teachers thought the frontier of legal training was reached when economic and social science data were brought into the law classroom. In the abstract this made perfect sense. If the life of the law was, in Oliver Wendell Holmes's overused phrase, "not logic but experience," lawyers had to base their views of behavior more on solid empirical research than on subjective assumptions. But trying to shoehorn graduate-level social science into courses that could barely cover the legal basics produced the classic danger of a little learning. When they left the law for policy science of various sorts, too many of my law school professors, at least in comparison with my teachers at Oberlin College, seemed like amateurs, though undeniably talented ones.

Another variation from the case method took place in Joe Goldstein's class in criminal law, as opposed to criminal procedure. There we spent week after week examining a bizarre child abuse case—a physician or "therapist" given the name Dr. Martin set up an institute to "cure" homosexuals in part by encouraging sexual contact under "protective" conditions—from every conceivable legal and nonlegal perspective.[5] Goldstein's infusion of significant amounts of social science and factual readings was common at Yale but unusual for the times; unfortunately, despite the truly bizarre factual context, the case was presented in the same old bookish wrapper that was used in other classes.

Joe, who was to work closely with the psychiatrist Jay Katz and with Sigmund Freud's therapist daughter, Anna, was thought to be receiving training in psychoanalysis. There were days when he couldn't resist trying out this new learning on us. The questions of some fifty hyperactive and verbal first-year law students often elicited more looking at the floor or ceiling, nodding and shaking of the head, and grimacing than talking. He was expert at mimicking the famous psychoanalytic "Hmm." For some of us, the mustachioed Goldstein began to resemble Groucho Marx doing an impression of a Viennese shrink. But Joe was still one of the great legal innovators of the day—just not in the classroom. Most of my other teachers, brilliant as they were, also conveyed more of a need to distinguish their approach from Harvard's than any desire to examine the way lawyers were trained, much less change it.

Serious consequences for the way law was practiced and understood flowed from this state of affairs. Lawyers graduated with little experience of the critical relationships they would have with their clients. No wonder so many attorneys were thought to be arrogant and uncaring. They were unprepared, emotionally if not intellectually, for the intense personal conflicts, feelings, and doubts endemic to professional life. No wonder they drank too much and burned out early.

Trial work was slighted. It would be years before every law school made a trial practice course available so that at least graduates who were able to take it would have the important experience of actually questioning and cross-questioning witnesses. Such classroom sessions would be staged, but they provided only a first step toward mastering the art of direct and cross-examination.

Training in negotiation and mediation wasn't given even lip service. Indeed, I cannot recall even purely academic discussion of negotiation, although it was and still is by far the most frequent way legal disputes are resolved. It would be well over twenty years before dispute resolution gained enough acceptance to be a topic worthy of its own courses. It was thought somehow to be unscholarly for a law teacher to specialize in negotiation or mediation.

No attention was paid to the possibility that a moral or spiritual vision of legal work might alleviate the stress lawyers conventionally suffered or alter the perceptions of those who regularly trashed the ethics of the profession. Theories of justice were presented only ad hoc or in out-of-the-way corners of the curriculum. As I would learn three years later from the fifteen minutes devoted to it in my bar exam cram course, the study of legal ethics, when they were discussed at all, seemed a matter of self-protective, cover-your-ass maneuvers, not a guide to true professional responsibility. In any event, very few legal scholars of the time would devote a career to studying professional ethics.

In contrast to the atmosphere a decade later, institutions were understood more as repositories of rules than of social facts. In other words, we were being trained to work with business and government as they existed, not to transform them.

It cannot be denied, however, that the law school system I am criticizing was a great success. A success on its own terms, that is, because it functioned primarily to prepare young lawyers to do narrow tasks—write memos, take out-of-court depositions, prepare documents, and parse court opinions—in aid of well-heeled business clients while working for equally well-heeled corporate firms. The system produced exorbitantly paid worker bees in abundance, some of whom were so gifted that they eventually transcended the limits of their schooling. And it was a success in that some graduates of elite law schools—in those days virtually all of them white males—would become important national leaders. A naturally bright and unusually tenacious lot, they honed their skills so well that they would become the law partners who advised the most powerful government in the world and then move to Washington to serve in it, before (usually) returning to continue a remunerative corporate practice.

Even at Ivy League schools there were a few exceptions to the usual career path through the firms, in addition to then "odd" choices like mine to go to work for LDF: criminal lawyers; single small-town and suburban practitioners; career government attorneys drawn to a steady life of community service. These young lawyers got to try cases early in their careers, spend time with clients, and feel personally responsible for what happened to them, but they were (and still are) a decided minority of graduates from schools such as Yale. The law engages matters of such interest and importance in our society that even the stodgiest practice can involve strategic and tactical puzzles, fascinating personal dilemmas, and much human drama, but legal education at the elite schools wasn't organized with such possibilities foremost in mind. You might get there, but for most graduates it would take patience and probably partnership before intense client relationships were possible. Lawyers on the fringe, like me, who had to acquire the critical practical skills they needed quickly, had to do so any way they could because they weren't going to get them in a law school, no matter how glittering its reputation. The message was shockingly antieducational for a world-renowned educational institution: practice just can't be taught well in school.

Some of my frustration, however, came from the very substance of the law as it was revealed in statutes and court decisions. An example is a remarkable set of Supreme Court opinions in an unusual 1947 case involving Willie Francis, a black Louisianan who had been convicted of robbing and killing a white druggist when he was fifteen and sentenced to death.[6] In those days, Louisiana's executions took place in the local jail where the inmate was held instead of in a central facility; the electric chair, nicknamed "Gruesome Gerty," was hauled around the state on a truck to the parish in question. When the day arrived, Francis was hooded and electrodes were placed on his left leg. The sheriff of St. Martin Parish said, "Goodbye, Willie," and a police officer pulled the switch that would send 2,500 volts through his body. But though Francis groaned and his body strained against the straps that held him, he did not die.

The executioner tried again and Francis's body arched and his lips puffed out, but the electric current was insufficient to kill him. Pulled from the defective apparatus, a dazed Willie Francis was returned to his cell. Eventually a lawsuit was filed arguing that another attempt to electrocute Francis would constitute unconstitutional double jeopardy and cruel and unusual punishment. Efforts were also launched to ask the state board of pardons to commute the death sentence because Francis had suffered horrible pain due solely to the state's ineptitude.

The legal challenge eventually made its way to the United States Supreme Court, and it was the Court's resolution of the case, especially the way five of the justices treated the cruelty claim, that would fuel my youthful outrage. Four of the justices (Stanley Reed wrote the opinion; Hugo Black, Robert Jackson, and Chief Justice Fred Vinson joined him) basically decided that there was no constitutional violation because Louisiana didn't intend to act cruelly: "The fact that an unforeseeable accident prevented the prompt consummation of the sentence cannot, it seems to us, add an element of cruelty to a subsequent execution." There was "no purpose to inflict unnecessary pain nor any unnecessary pain in the proposed execution."[7] In short, it was just one of those things; get over it.

The four dissenters (Harold Burton, William O. Douglas, Frank Murphy, and Wiley Rutledge) took the position that a death sentence could not be implemented by causing unnecessary mental anguish and physical pain; there could be no death by installments: "Although the failure of the attempt" was unintended, Burton wrote, "the reapplication of the electric current will be intentional." How many attempts will be permitted, he asked, before attempting to execute Francis is seen as resembling burning at the stake?[8] For the dissenters, a second try was sufficiently barbarous to invoke the constitutional prohibition of cruel and unusual punishment.

What baffled me as a law student and then troubled me as a lawyer when I was trying desegregation cases, and still troubles me decades later when I consider the constitutional resolution of issues such as affirmative action, was the justices' easy disregard of the importance of results. I simply could not understand why the Court rejected Francis's cruelty claim because of the state's intentions. Did the Court think that just because you were a bigot or a discriminator you would be so stupid as to admit it or leave signs on the trail?

A state that inflicts unnecessary pain because its officials are thoughtless, indifferent to technical matters, or well meaning but insufficiently careful still inflicts extreme pain. It mattered not to Francis whether he was dealing with sadists or incompetents. It shouldn't, I thought, matter to the law, especially when the mental state of local officials was probably unknowable and the real culprit resided in the inadequately funded and monitored killing system the state legislature had authorized. When you are dealing with constitutional promises, it is results and not good intentions that should count. Why do we care if government officials are sincere when they are plainly wrong?

Questions of this sort have not, however, stopped the courts from continuing to require proof of bad faith before they honor certain constitutional claims. A particularly painful example is the case of Larry Youngblood, who served seventeen years in prison for child molestation after Arizona police improperly refrigerated semen-stained clothing that could have exonerated him. The Supreme Court of Arizona ruled that Youngblood's right to potentially exculpatory evidence had been violated by destruction of the semen stains, but the Supreme Court of the United States set that decision aside because he had not shown that the police acted in bad faith. Justice John Paul Stevens concurred in this decision because he didn't think it likely the missing evidence was important. In 2000, however, new evidence containing the attacker's semen was discovered; testing it led to Youngblood's complete exoneration.[9]

In 1983, decades after Francis was ultimately put to death, Louisiana still had problems with its manner of execution. Witnesses to the electrocution of Robert W. Williams reported burning flesh and "excessive burning"; according to the Fordham law professor Deborah Denno, four years later the electrocution of Alvin Moore was botched when he "was severely burned on the top of his head and his epidermis was found to be missing in a wide circular pattern."[10] In 1990, Louisiana substituted lethal injection for the electric chair.

I had strong feelings about the relative importance of intentions and results when courts were reviewing government decisions, but these were largely doubts of the sort that were subject to debate. Reasonable minds might certainly differ in respect to them. I felt no such tolerance, however, for the fifth vote against Francis, the opinion that sealed his fate. It was written by Felix Frankfurter and I regarded it as an act of cowardice. Frankfurter claimed to be a great humanitarian and opponent of capital punishment. He had certainly demonstrated his social commitment before joining the Court in attempting to win freedom for the questionably condemned anarchists Nicola Sacco and Benvenuto Vanzetti and by his record of advising President Roosevelt at critical times during the New Deal. As a justice, however, Frankfurter had too often for my lights offered precious procedural points as ways of avoiding significant constitutional claims. At times he was so worried about whether the courts might overstep their bounds that he let real injustice pass.

In the Willie Francis case, Frankfurter called the failure of the electric chair an "innocent misadventure" that did not offend a principle of justice rooted in the "traditions and conscience of our people." This sounded much like Justice Reed, but Frankfurter went further, and here I thought what he said was fatuous, self-inflated nonsense that would end up killing a human being. Frankfurter wrote that the Court "must abstain from interference with State action no matter how strong one's personal feeling of revulsion against a state's insistence on its pound of flesh. . . . One must be on guard against finding in personal disapproval a reflection of more or less prevailing condemnation. . . . I cannot," he added, "rid myself of the conviction that were I to hold that Louisiana would transgress the Due Process Clause if . . . allowed to . . . carry out the death sentence, I would be enforcing my private views" rather than the Constitution.[11]

Frankfurter may be a great man, I thought when I read the *Francis* case in Bickel's class, but here he is either deluding himself or being just another jerk. He wants us to conclude that he is mastering his smoldering passions in the service of democratic legitimacy, the idea that federal judges aren't elected and their job is to find law, not make it. But in fact Frankfurter's passion, his commitment to oppose cruel punishment, was just too weak. He wasn't compelled to the justification he offered but had discretion to do otherwise. Justice Burton's opinion for four of the nine justices showed him a respectable way it could be done, if he had the will to do it. Setting aside the death sentence would hardly have been beyond reason. The legal test Frankfurter proposed to his colleagues, as later revealed in Court conference notes, was nothing if not fuzzy: "Here, though it's hardly a defensible thing for a state to do, it is not so offensive as to make me puke—it does not shock my conscience."

In his concurrence, he also made empirical assumptions about "society's opinion" of whether Francis had been treated cruelly, but he had no evidence whatsoever to indicate what people thought or whether there was a national consensus about the meaning of cruelty. Nor did he vote to postpone the execution until proof could be assembled and offered to the courts. Such a delay might well have shown public opinion to be against a second try at execution. In short, Frankfurter was willing to rely on his personal opinion about public values but not on his personal opinion that the death penalty for Willie Francis was not defensible. His hallowed judicial restraint was just as selective as the supposed judicial activism of the judges he implicitly criticized.

Perhaps I had already been too exposed to a certain sort of cynicism about the reasons judges give for what they do, but in my judgment Frankfurter was simply playing to one crowd rather than another. To please his constituency of Ivy League academic lawyers and kindred judges, the people I would end up spending much of my professional life with, he was presenting himself as the good judge—the sort who avoids the unpardonable sin of writing his own views into law. In actuality he was just writing a different version of his views into law by placing the burden of establishing whether community standards of cruelty were violated on an indigent and his lawyers rather than on the state.

In my pre-law-school innocence, I had a vaguely positive sense of Frankfurter because of his effort to protect Sacco and Vanzetti from execution in what was then such a famous case that I had heard of it in high school. But in the *Francis* case I was stung by his judicial stinginess in applying constitutional rights. What I could not forgive was that the bill for all his opportunistic posing was paid in human life. Any hesitance I felt in reaching such a firm conclusion at such an early stage of my legal career was eased by the fact that Alex Bickel had made it clear to our class that when it came to Willie Francis, he parted company with his mentor.

Some years later the truth came out—or I should say a rumor of the truth came out. Frankfurter, according to the story, believed that Governor James Davis would commute Willie Francis's death sentence after the case was returned to Louisiana. At the very least it's clear he had tried to get the sentence commuted by "exhorting" Monte Lehman, a former Harvard Law classmate and roommate from Louisiana, to use his influence with the governor to save Francis's life.[12] It would be a nice out. Frankfurter would get to extol judicial restraint and no one would die.

Of course, it didn't happen; Willie Francis was successfully electrocuted in 1947. Frankfurter would continue his habit of going to great lengths to find reasons to keep the justices from making decisions he thought would bring criticism on the Court. In 1955 and 1956 he persuaded his brethren to pass on an appeal asserting that the states could not bar marriage between an Asian man and a white woman, consistent with the federal constitution's equal protection clause, even though the law was clear that the case fell within the Court's obligatory appellate jurisdiction.[13] (Later I would feel some satisfaction in writing a portion of LDF's friend-of-the-court brief in *Loving v. Virginia*, the 1967 case that declared antimiscegenation laws invalid.)[14]

When I was a law student, I didn't have a very farsighted view of how the *Francis* case or the way law was then taught related to my future professional development. Like my classmates, I mostly suffered from pure classroom fatigue. To breathe a little more life into my studies, to connect with what I hoped would be the law's human dimension, I decided to sign up with a student group, the extracurricular Jerome Frank Legal Aid and Public Defender Association, which offered me an internship with the New Haven public defender office. There a single lawyer tried to make a go of representing the catch of poor defendants netted daily by the city and state police. I don't remember the PD's name, but his worn and weary face is etched in memory. He was so overwhelmed by clients that he welcomed assistance from callow Yale law students and eagerly handed us case files to investigate. With scanty editing, he converted our research into motions to suppress evidence, trial briefs, and memos of law. We could go to court with him if we could find out when and where he was going, but he was simply too burdened and disorganized for us to count on anything he said about his schedule. He apologized for his inability to give us much explicit guidance about case planning and strategy; as he sadly explained, he was too busy to be a teacher. He would be happy to discuss the cases when there was time, he added, but this was almost never. As a supervisor, he was a well-meaning bust. As a mentor—someone who shows the path to professional enlightenment—he was downright destructive, because the working conditions he accepted made high-quality representation seem impossible. Unwittingly, this experience fostered the kind of disillusionment that turns many law students toward conventional corporate law.

I wanted to play a backup role in some of his misdemeanor trials but student practice, even under supervision, wasn't then permitted by the courts and wouldn't be authorized in most states until a decade later, when law schools began to set up in-house clinics.[15] Trials were few anyway. With a massive caseload and without any real assistance, the PD did a lot of plea bargaining.

Hanging around the courts and watching him interview clients in his office near the New Haven Green opened my eyes to this fact-bound plea-bargaining universe where legal rules and jury trials hardly ever entered. What mattered was what a cop would say privately to the DA, the kind of criminal record a defendant was carrying around, his race and social standing, how many more serious cases were waiting in the wings, how well the defense lawyer got on with the district attorney, and the mood of the man, and I mean man, on the bench.

This side of the criminal courts wasn't much discussed in the rule-dominated Yale criminal procedure class. Perhaps it wasn't intellectually rigorous enough or depended too much on anecdote, impression, and what happened out of sight. Only two other explanations could account for this educational gap in the course most relevant to the work of the public defender. One was true and the other was false. The true one was that it was statistically unlikely that any Yale Law graduate would practice this kind of law. The false one was that young lawyers needn't be trained in practice skills in law school because they could rely on receiving excellent and comprehensive job training from their future supervisors and more experienced peers. This tale was not true in the 1950s and 1960s—the time that some oldsters call the good old days—and today the claim that young lawyers get careful training by the firms wouldn't pass the laugh test.

Interning with the public defender was eye-opening in another way. No matter how well I knew that the criminal courts were places for poor people and black people, nothing prepared me for the experience of the defendants as they struggled with public assistance, ignorance, unemployment, drugs, self-hate and official disdain, dysfunctional families and lousy impulse control. Some of these clients had a dignity and stature that adversity couldn't touch; others lived with a violence or stupidity that made me cringe. They could be their own worst enemies. Harry Subin remembers a stubborn defendant whom the PD put on the stand in his own defense after he insisted he hadn't said a single word to the police at his arrest. He testified and was promptly impeached by the prosecutor with his own words in the statement to the police he had previously vociferously denied making. At the time we had no right to see such a statement before trial, and as Harry, who later had a distinguished career as a teacher of criminal law at New York University Law School, reminded me, there still is no constitutional right to do so, although most states have procedural rules that require disclosure.[16]

These clients all needed lawyers; they wanted any skilled assistance they could get to keep them from prison, though they often understandably treated us as second-rate representatives of the system that oppressed them. The law might be encouraged to yield some support; it might ride their backs more lightly. But I felt a truth long before I knew what to do with it: there was little a lawyer could do in any individual case that was going to change the logic of these lives. Part of the allure of LDF would be that it specialized in class actions, cases brought specifically to change laws and policies for large groups. Maybe that would work.

Though the Yale Law School would eventually hire talented lawyer-teachers to supervise students rendering legal aid to indigent clients, it long resisted granting them tenure because as academics clinicians were not deemed pureblooded enough. The Yale faculty couldn't get its collective mind around the idea that the people who taught students how to practice could provide enough conceptual sophistication and rigor to justify their equal treatment by the academy. Or that learning how to serve clients well was as important as case analysis.[17] Thus the faculty avoided making the clinics a regular part of the credited curriculum. Much of this attitude had to do with the pure self-interest of those with the power, but more of it derived, I think, from typical academic devaluation of learning through practice and direct contact with clients in contrast to the supposedly superior skill of doctrinal analysis and the conceptual refinements of economic and policy thinking about the law.

I would later have my own struggle with these attitudes, which were certainly not unique to Yale, when I set up a clinic for the legally indigent at Columbia Law School in the 1970s. While Dean Michael Sovern and such influential faculty members as the tax law expert George Cooper thought the school had an obligation both to help the poor in the Harlem community that surrounded it and to expose law students to actual practice, a few faculty members treated me and my colleague Philip Schrag as if we were tracking a virus into the house of the law. "So you're teaching them where the courthouse is" was a typical quip from skeptical colleagues. The mainstream faculty response, however, was ambivalence. Many were in sympathy with our approach, understanding that begrudging acceptance of clinics for poor people would reflect just another rationing of legal assets to people who needed them desperately. At the same time they had come to the academy to escape practice and weren't sure they could teach it wisely. Some feared losing control of institutions to which they had committed their professional lives. And clinics were expensive. How would they affect other worthy school programs? In the mid-1970s Schrag and I were voted tenure but were left with the confusing impression that the faculty vote was more a testament to our personal success than an endorsement of the value of student learning in the clinics.

Even more confusing were the crossed messages about what lawyers do and how they should do it. One signal told students of the importance of public service, but a look at the profession's allocation of legal services spoke eloquently of the necessity of keeping it rationed. Another emphasized loyalty to clients' ends, but gave little guidance how those ends should be balanced with the community's needs. Other messages made clear the centrality of money to what lawyers did but conveyed the strong impression that talk of money should be kept sotto voce. This had been the complex reality presented to a law graduate for some time; but with some shock and surprise at my certainty—at my having a belief at all—I decided it needn't be mine.

On-the-Job Training

ONE of the first things I was asked to do at LDF was to help prepare the main section of a document called a petition for a writ of certiorari, legalese for a request that the Supreme Court of the United States consider and then set aside a lower court's ruling. Since 1925, when Congress finally acceded to the wishes of the justices, the Supreme Court has had virtually total control over its docket and approves only a tiny percentage of the requests for review.[1] The case in question involved 187 South Carolina high school and college students who "peaceably assembled at the site of the state government," the capitol in Columbia, to protest segregation and were convicted of breach of the peace after they failed to disperse when the police ordered them to do so.[2] I reviewed the file sent from South Carolina to New York by two LDF cooperating attorneys, Matthew Perry and Lincoln Jenkins, with what I thought was great care and drafted a petition calling what the students had done the very essence of protected speech. I also emphasized the vagueness of the state breach-of-the-peace law employed by the police.

Later I would conclude that James Nabrit III, the lawyer assigned to break me in, was the most thorough lawyer I encountered in four decades of law practice and teaching. But even at this early stage of my LDF work, it was obvious that Jim, though no nitpicker, was extremely deliberate and cautious about his legal opinions. He was a key figure in plotting 1960s civil rights legal strategy even though he was not generally known to even an informed public.[3]

Born to the work, he was a civil rights diaper baby. When Jim was a first-grader his father won a landmark voting case in the Supreme Court broadening the opportunity of blacks to vote in Oklahoma. James Nabrit

Jr. worked closely with Thurgood Marshall and served first as a teacher and then as dean of the Howard Law School and later as president of the university. He was credited with teaching the first course in an American law school devoted exclusively to civil rights law. Many movement figures of the period were family friends; at college and law school Jim watched his father argue the District of Columbia case that was one of the *Brown v. Board* group in the Supreme Court. After graduating from the Yale Law School in 1955 he was hired by Frank Reeves, a former member of the NAACP's legal staff and one of the most politically influential black lawyers in the country. Jim even married civil rights—his wife, Jackie Harlan Nabrit, was the daughter of a Washington lawyer and later civil rights official in the federal bureaucracy. After a stint in the Army it was natural for him to find his way to LDF, where Thurgood Marshall declared to anyone who would listen that Jim's job was to be low man on the totem pole and he was to be called "boy."

This was 1959, and Jim became the fourth member of Marshall's legal staff. When I was hired two years later, the number had climbed to six. Although it was plain that Jim was far more than two years ahead of me in experience and civil rights savvy, he never made me feel like a rookie. But for the two days he looked over my argument and supporting papers, I was a mess: grouchy at home, unproductive at work, and full of doubt in both places. I was secretly glad that my wife, working hard that year as a teacher to a group of adolescent mental patients, had her own distractions to cope with. The longer Jim delayed in summoning me to his office, the more certain I was that I had chosen the wrong profession. Only a few months earlier I had been digging with archaeologists in the Negev Desert, carrying an Uzi on nighttime guard duty so as to warn the real soldiers if raiders crossed the border from Jordan. Was I too removed from current developments for this work? Did I remember enough constitutional law? Had I said enough, or maybe too much, to overcome the long odds of persuading the Supreme Court to take the case? In my three years in New Haven, what had I really learned of the law?

Maybe I should have stayed in Israel.

When Jim finally returned the draft, he came to *my* office, folded his six feet plus into a chair across from my desk, and appeared the very definition of casual. He told an anecdote about some trivial office incident and laughed the way a man who loves irony laughs. Then he lit up a King Sano, a cigarette with a filter he said was almost as thick and as dense as a slice of whole wheat bread.

I relaxed but, of course, should have been on my guard.

Jim's lungs strained to inhale and he spoke in a voice so low that I had to lean toward him across the desk to hear. Then he stubbed out the smoke in my ashtray and adopted a characteristic pose, holding his right hand against his chin, a pencil replacing the cigarette, pointing toward the ceiling. He had made, he said, only a couple of minor editorial changes. He thought I might develop a few points a bit more, but he praised my constitutional analysis. I'd done well.

Thank God, I silently rejoiced, for Alex Bickel.

"There is just one thing."

"Oh?"

A big thing, though he made clear there was no reason I should have known about it. The Supreme Court of the United States had a rule (it has been changed since): it wouldn't accept a petition for a writ of certiorari unless the clerk of the lower court certified the record of proceedings below. The clerk had to sign a statement saying, in effect, that he was sending on a true copy of the papers.

"You don't have one and better get it," Jim advised. He yawned before he continued, "And you'd better move fast. If it isn't done before the time for appeal runs out, the case is over and each of our clients may end up having to serve time in jail."

Then he asked me where I wanted to go to lunch.

I was soon introduced to less substantive but no less important aspects of legal brief writing. Today briefs can be typeset easily from disks and e-mail attachments or scanned along with documents that may be included in an appendix. With the right software and the click of a mouse, lawyers need never leave their offices to be able to provide high-quality text to the printer with proper fonts and correct margins. In the 1960s, however, Supreme Court briefs and those for many lower courts had to be done by a slower, labor-intensive, more expensive and time-honored technique, letterpress printing. In this method, based on principles that go back to the dawn of the printer's trade, the images to be printed are cast in metal, raised above the nonprinting areas, and rendered with just the right degree of pressure.

When I made last-minute changes to my arguments as a deadline approached—something that usually happened in the evening—I had to take the subway down to LDF's printer on Morton Street, in Greenwich Village. There I might sip burned coffee in a room off the main shop area while I waited for galleys so I could make my alterations and then take the finished product to the night window at the main post office on

34th Street. Walking the crowded streets to the train past packed Village bars and restaurants with Supreme Court briefs neatly stowed in my bag filled me with enormous pride.

With the continued help of Jim Nabrit, I learned how to translate an overpowering moral impulse into actual change through litigation. The task required habits of attention and order that I didn't know I possessed, finding in my chaotic city-boy makeup tolerance of frustration and a sense of technical proficiency. Fortunately, everyone at LDF was welded together in the early 1960s by a need for unity and support against common enemies. Rarely did anyone, lawyer or secretary, complain about the hours. Spouses or girlfriends of the then overwhelmingly male legal staff would arrive late in the day, after their own work, to bring in meals or help collate documents. We saw each other socially with a frequency I have never experienced in any other job.

Unlike most lawyers, we didn't have to develop rationalizations to justify advancing the prospects of clients whose interests were sometimes greedy, selfish, or even destructive. The civil rights movement had forced the country finally to pay some attention to hundreds of years of inequality. There was a growing consensus among Americans that something had to be done to eliminate legal segregation. As demands for LDF's assistance flooded in, we were too concerned about keeping up with the caseload to worry much about interference from the usual in-house power struggles, jealousy, or competition. It wasn't so much the burden of large numbers of cases. Compared to the caseload of a legal aid lawyer working in any major city, the number was manageable. But the cases themselves often were large, involved multiple parties, and were full of new issues and complicated institutional relationships. Rarely would the other side negotiate a settlement in good faith.

The cases also presented a difficult management problem: our clients never paid a fee, so we had no neutral principle, such as litigation costs, to tell us when to stop gathering facts and developing arguments. These cases had no built-in markers to tell a young lawyer he had done enough. When you were enmeshed in such a case, it could seem to embrace the whole universe of law. Yet each of us had several dozen such cases going at the same time. Outside advice about how to handle such problems wasn't always of much help, but it was important to staff morale that we could easily seek the help of great men of the law—Charles Black and Louis Pollak of Yale, Al Sacks and Benjamin Kaplan of Harvard, and Anthony Amsterdam of the University of Pennsylvania, later of Stanford and NYU, were frequent consultants—but in truth I felt I could pick up a phone and consult any one of a number of leading American legal scholars who knew something about a case-related problem I was trying to solve and get a response. Many nonlawyers freely donated their time during those years, such as the criminologist Marvin Wolfgang of the University of Pennsylvania, the nationally known pediatrician Allan Butler of Boston, and the New York surgeon Samuel Standard. In the civil rights era, volunteer experts who wanted to be part of our work were plentiful.

But mostly we had to rely on each other. And we had enough trust in the quality of the work and of our relationships to do just that. It was a peak experience that lasted no more than a few years, one that for me has never been repeated, at least on this scale.

At first my encounters with the federal government were not very promising. In the early 1960s, very few officials were willing to take a clear stand; most were extraordinarily cautious, as I discovered in the first major case that, in the trial court at least, was all my responsibility. This was a suit against two Greensboro, North Carolina, hospitals—one refused to admit black patients and the other segregated them, and both refused to permit local black doctors and dentists to work on the premises. Because a 1946 federal law, the Hill-Burton Act, funded the construction of these hospitals and explicitly permitted Jim Crow in medical facilities, one of our goals was to bring the United States Department of Justice into the case on our side.[4] Here was no regional preference for segregation but a racial distinction written into national law. The federal government's intervention in such a case would make a powerful statement about where the country was headed; it was almost as important to our long-term strategy as integrating every hospital in the country.

But the DOJ held back, afraid to alienate influential southern legislators; it was also unfamiliar with joining ongoing lawsuits in explicit support of black litigants. Until southern blacks began to put their bodies on the line, civil rights was low on President Kennedy's priority list. In an early North Carolina meeting about the Greensboro case one Justice Department lawyer baited me. He wasn't really hostile; more a hardheaded government lawyer trying to be professionally neutral about something I thought very one-sided. He pointed out correctly that federal law merely made money available to local communities for hospital construction; it permitted but didn't require race-based allocation of health-care dollars. Moreover, Greensboro had a hospital where blacks could be served. What was the big deal with separate but equal hospitals?

After some more of this, I lost it. "Do you propose," I raged at him, "that the Red Cross should give soldiers and accident victims different colored coffee cups depending on their race? The Red Cross 'just' takes government money too."

My local co-counsel was a gentle, balding, cocoa-colored lawyer from Durham named Conrad O. Pearson. He had been brought into the case because no Greensboro lawyer was ready to represent George Simkins, a maverick dentist who was president of the local NAACP chapter and a persistent critic of the medical establishment. Simkins, who had served time in jail for trespass in 1955 when he and three friends teed off at the municipal golf course, assembled a group of doctors, dentists, and patients to challenge the local hospitals. Conrad hadn't gone to a fancy law school (a classmate of Thurgood Marshall's, he had a Howard, not a Harvard, degree); though ever present at North Carolina rights battles, he paid the rent by doing deeds and divorces in a downtown walkup on Durham's Chapel Street. But in his quiet way Conrad was fearless; he also had an advanced degree in race talk. He knew an out-of-control kid when he saw one.

"Easy, now," he whispered. "He's just testing us."

He turned to the government man. One veteran lawyer to another, he drawled, "We bring hot bloods like Meltsner down here from New York just to keep you federals on your toes."

Affability was restored. Eventually the United States joined the case and provided critical support, but its hesitation even eight years after *Brown* left me with a general mistrust of reliance on federal lawyers that would take a long time to fade.

It is possible to take a very positive view of the Kennedy administration's civil rights record, and at the time liberal New York friends and former classmates found it difficult to accept my skepticism.[5] In contrast to Dwight Eisenhower, who declined to put the prestige of the presidency behind *Brown* even when he sent troops to enforce school desegregation in Little Rock and once urged Earl Warren to be more sympathetic to the concerns of white southerners, John F. Kennedy seemed to be ready to make the cause of ending segregation his own. His brother Robert and such Justice Department lawyers as Burke Marshall and John Doar tried to breathe life into existing civil rights laws; after a bomb killed four black children at a Sunday school in Birmingham, Alabama, President Kennedy eventually proposed the most sweeping rights legislation since Reconstruction. The Kennedy administration brought six times more cases to end refusal to register blacks to vote in the South than the Eisenhower administration, acted rapidly to ensure an end to segregation in public transportation, and ordered public contractors to cease discrimination. Most important, the Kennedys made it known to the civil rights community that the administration shared its goals.

But there were also major disappointments, especially in the first two years of the new president's term. The voting rights suits failed to register significant numbers of voters, as the head of the Civil Rights Division, Burke Marshall, was to concede only in 1964.[6] They required investigation of the circumstances under which applicants were rejected, a determination that black applicants were denied help offered to whites, and preparation of hundreds of witnesses to prove the government's case. Justice Department lawyers worked long hours in rural Mississippi and Alabama counties but ultimately, even when they obtained favorable court orders, local officials were able to block registration of more than a few new voters.

The new attorney general failed to protect the freedom riders who rode south to integrate interstate travel, and had even at first criticized them. His initial efforts to win over civil rights leaders had also failed, leaving a trail of misunderstanding. Despite his sympathy for the demonstrators, Burke Marshall again and again urged them to trust in court proceedings rather than take to the streets even after it should have been obvious that voting suits produced few results. The Justice Department allowed Mississippi to string it along when James Meredith won admission to the state university; as a result, opposition protests mushroomed into a full-scale riot. The White House civil rights adviser (later senator) Harris L. Wofford, denied the key Justice Department civil rights post given to Marshall because he was supposedly too emotionally committed to the black cause, was consistently marginalized and eventually stripped of any real influence over policy.

In the "stroke of a pen" controversy, Victor Navasky, a Yale Law friend turned writer and publisher, organized a campaign to mail ballpoints to the White House after President Kennedy declined to honor his campaign pledge to order an immediate end to federal support of segregation in housing. The president hesitated because he had been elected by a margin of only 119,000 votes, and more than a few observers thought even those few were produced by the finagling of the Chicago Democratic Party machine. Trying to avoid controversy and hold onto the support of key southern legislators, Kennedy waited until 1962 to sign an executive order on housing discrimination that in the 1960 campaign he had claimed he would issue upon taking office. The late-arriving order was a compromise that never really worked.

Later Navasky wrote what was generally regarded as the finest book on the Justice Department under Robert F. Kennedy. He focused on the struggle between Kennedy and J. Edgar Hoover over control of the implementation of policy on civil rights and organized crime. He concluded that Kennedy made "a Faustian bargain" with Hoover, permitting Hoover to enlarge the FBI's "formal jurisdiction, increase its budget," and authorize electronic surveillance of his personal nemesis, Martin Luther King Jr., if he "would agree to join Kennedy's crusade against organized crime and his maneuvers for equal rights." Later investigators uncovered evidence that Hoover knew of a series of the president's sexual escapades, but of at least equal concern to the Kennedys was the FBI's growing dossier of reports on two persons with ties to King who the bureau thought had associated with Communists.[7]

Bargain or not, changes in the FBI's civil rights practices proceeded at a glacial pace. FBI agents remained loyal to contacts on a local police force even when their commitment to segregation was unyielding. Despite hundreds of complaints that southern law enforcement officers had harassed, threatened, arrested, and beaten local blacks and civil rights workers trying to exercise their federally protected right to vote, it wasn't until 1964 that the FBI made any arrests. There were too many stories of FBI agents standing by taking notes at such encounters to doubt their authenticity. Robert Kennedy initially defended FBI inaction with the administration's common argument that interfering even when violence took place would, in effect, endorse creation of a "federal police force." Navasky repeats King's contemporary charge that despite formal complaints, "southern-based FBI agents didn't follow through on civil rights cases." Either way, he observes, "white agents seemed to black civil rights workers to fit into the white establishment like pieces of a jigsaw puzzle."[8]

Another part of the puzzle was the judiciary. Judges in the southern states, most of them elected, were unremittingly hostile to civil rights claimants. In contrast, a number of liberal Republicans appointed by President Eisenhower to the Court of Appeals for the Fifth Circuit consistently prodded lower federal courts to dismantle Jim Crow. To our amazement at LDF, the Kennedys at first nominated judges to sit on the federal bench in Georgia, Louisiana, and Mississippi who had been outspoken in their disdain for Negroes' civil rights claims. This was perhaps an excusable political necessity, even a laudable example of the famous Kennedy pragmatism, if you were reading about it in the *New York Times* over breakfast coffee in a northern city, but it was a personal affront if you had to deal, as we did, with the antics of the Mississippian Harold Cox (who called blacks "niggers" and "chimpanzees" from the bench) or the smoldering hostility of Robert Elliot of Georgia or E. Gordon West of Louisiana. JFK had reportedly traded Cox for the agreement of James Eastland (Cox's college roommate), chair of the Senate Judiciary Committee, not to block other appointments, including Thurgood Marshall's, to a federal court of appeals.

During the spring of 1963, when the hosing and beating of children in Birmingham, Alabama, by Bull Connor's police and fire departments provoked international condemnation, Robert Kennedy persuaded his brother to propose the massive legal changes that would ultimately become the Civil Rights Act of 1964. But even after the statutory initiative was announced and the administration loudly criticized Alabama authorities, civil rights activists and LDF lawyers felt they had to lobby Justice to act, or to act promptly, at every step of the way. Yet, ironically, many observers saw the Kennedy administration as far ahead of the country on civil rights. And it was. Once it was clear to the administration that protests would not cease and that the response to them was producing consternation in the rest of the nation, the Kennedys began to respond more actively. LDF was, of course, institutionally primed to demand speed just as the government was bound to move hesitantly. Still, I had to admire the legal skill—despite my frustration at the timid pace of their southern interventions—of the team of extraordinarily able and generally sympathetic lawyers who worked on the same civil rights issues I did. Marshall and John Doar were best known, but Harold Greene, later the judge who dismantled AT&T, and Howard Glickstein, later an official at the U.S. Civil Rights Commission and the dean of several law schools, were just two of an extraordinary group.

Perhaps the contradictions of those key early years of the 1960s at the Kennedy Justice Department are best summed up by something we soon would hear rumored but were not certain of at the time—that this was an administration and a Justice Department whose investigative arm freely bugged or wiretapped civil rights activists, including the LDF offices, while at the same time it also worked intimately with us and continually offered support. Though we were never able to substantiate our suspicions, LDF lawyers assumed the government was spying, and talk of "the taps" in phone conversations with colleagues in the South was a standing joke. Later, when I obtained my own FBI documents, the only evidence I uncovered was a wiretapped phone conversation with a lawyer in New Haven, Connecticut, who represented the Black Panther leader Bobby Seale at the same time I did. But widespread spying on SCLC activists was later substantiated and it became clear that there was little the Kennedy and Johnson administrations did not know about movement strategy and tactics. At LDF, at least, even if you thought your calls were being monitored, there was little you could do about it; it was impossible to conduct case-related business in code. If I heard any strange noise on a particularly sensitive call, I developed the nervous habit of referring humorously to the supposed listener. "Is the listener with us today?" I'd joke while brainstorming with a lawyer in North Carolina or Arkansas.

Still, I was shocked when Navasky told me at a lunch discussing his progress researching the DOJ book, one we had talked briefly about doing together, that he had come upon an incredible scandal. J. Edgar Hoover, he surmised, believed that New York lawyer Stanley Levinson, a King adviser, and an SCLC employee later identified as Hunter Pitts "Jack" O'Dell were closely tied to the Communist Party and were manipulating King. The whole thing had the odor of Cold War paranoia—what would the Kremlin get King to do?—masking Hoover's antipathy to civil rights and loathing of King. The FBI had a long record of covert actions against tiny radical civil rights organizations, based on its assumption that the groups were up to no good simply because some Communist Party members were involved. By holding compromising data on the Kennedys in his files and raising the specter of communism, Hoover managed to get the attorney general to approve electronic eavesdropping of Martin Luther King's office, home, and hotel rooms. Victor expressed surprise that the FBI had failed to tap Levinson's phone, as you would expect it to do if the bureau really believed he was subversive.[9]

Navasky quickly grasped Hoover's strategy of gathering information on the pretext of protecting King against charges that some of his advisers might have Communist affiliations while really putting together a dossier to embarrass the Kennedys for their public support of the civil rights leader. Tracking down the specifics took superior detective work, luck, and exquisite timing. Victor confided to me that his most successful technique was to imply to all the sources he interviewed that one of their DOJ colleagues had told him a great deal that he merely wanted to confirm. Thus he inched closer to the awful truth. Subsequently David Garrow and other historians would put together the authoritative and complete version of the events.

Rumors aside, the DOJ's attempt to serve different masters and our concrete knowledge of how much federal intervention was needed but not delivered left me and other LDF lawyers feeling alienated and embattled, convinced that even a friendly administration would end up viewing racial justice more as a narrowly pragmatic issue than as a moral one. They also taught movement activists a dreadful lesson: they would get little out of Washington unless they engaged in direct action, filled the jails, captured the media's attention, and shed blood. The Kennedy administration's temporizing may have been politically astute in the impact it had on national politics but it also helped bring on the divisive struggles fought later under the banner of Black Power which were to transform the public perception of the civil rights movement.

Like every LDF staff lawyer, I had my share of painful brushes with the department in the Kennedy years. One case stands out. In the early fall of 1963 I arrived in Americus, Georgia, after the state charged four young activists of the Student Nonviolent Coordinating Committee (SNCC) and Congress of Racial Equality (CORE), three white and one black, with the crimes of inciting and conspiring to incite insurrection, offenses subject to the death penalty in Georgia. Their insurrection consisted of trying to integrate the Martin Theatre, the town's only movie house, and later organizing and leading a protest march through the city's tiny downtown area that led to more than three hundred arrests. As I wrote of the confrontation that followed in a 1965 book called *Southern Justice,* edited by the constitutional lawyer Leon Friedman,

> The Chief of Police had warned a small group to stop picketing the Martin Theatre. When the pickets refused, he went to city hall, where a council meeting was in session; an ordinance banning picketing was quickly adopted, whereupon the Chief returned to arrest the pickets for violating it. Clubs and cattle prods, or "hot sticks" as they were called, were used freely by the police when making arrests. The police took special pleasure in using them on the backsides of young girls. Stitches were often required to close the wounds of demonstrators. One youth, James Williams, was set upon by police and clubbed until his leg was broken. Shirts taken from teen-agers shortly after arrest, and exhibited to the court, were hard-crusted with blood.[10]

The Department of Justice stayed as far as it could from these events, as it had done a year and a half earlier when Robert Kennedy had praised local officials in nearby Albany, Georgia, for avoiding violence. He didn't mention the thousands of arrests of persons demonstrating for the vote and for a desegregated city. Indeed, the only legal action the DOJ had taken in

Albany was to indict nine civil rights activists for perjury and interference with federal administration of justice after they urged a boycott of a grocery store owned by a man who had served as a juror.[11]

In the Americus situation, threats to the life of my local colleague C. B. King, the only black man practicing law in southwestern Georgia at the time, rolled in from surrounding counties. King was just one member of a family of activists—one brother, a history professor, had been committed to a state hospital as a lunatic in 1959 after he tried to attend the University of Mississippi; another, Slater King, was a leader of Albany anti-segregation forces; still another refused to comply with an order of his draft board to report for a physical examination for induction into the military, requesting that he be addressed as "Mr. King." He later fled the country, became a professor of politics in England, and was pardoned by President Clinton in 2000. C. B.'s wife, Carol King, was the director of the Albany Nursery School and would become the county director of Head Start. The nursery school was the first school in southern Georgia to have an integrated teaching staff and an integrated student body. Accompanied by two of her children, Slater's wife, Marion, tried to deliver food and supplies to imprisoned civil rights protestors. "She was told to leave, knocked to the ground, and kicked in the stomach by two policemen. Marion, who was six months pregnant at the time, lost consciousness—and later lost her child."[12]

Robert Kennedy announced that there would be no federal intervention in Americus; if an attempt to overthrow the government really was going on, the federal government would trust the Sumter County sheriff to handle it. But a Civil Rights Division lawyer, a man who later became a successful New York City politician, was sent to the Albany area with orders to keep his eyes open. Instead of looking for a way the department could intervene in the case, he spent his time reporting our doings to his superiors in Washington.

Serendipity put us in rooms next to each other in the same motel. One sultry October afternoon, he left the door to his room open while calling Washington. He loudly complained to John Doar, then second in command at the Civil Rights Division, that C. B. King and I were trying to manipulate him into recommending that the federal government intervene in Americus. Of course, we did indeed want to bring the DOJ into the case, but that was hardly a good reason for the DOJ to stay out. The government's authority to enter court proceedings in Americus was legally unclear because of Supreme Court decisions narrowly construing federal laws governing intervention, but that certainly did not excuse inaction. How could the courts clarify that authority, much less protect the demonstrators exercising their First Amendment rights, if the Justice Department didn't at least attempt to step in? Ironically, soon the administration would ignore arguments using federalism as a justification for staying aloof when events in Alabama and Mississippi forced Washington to act.

Even when the government was on solid legal grounds, however, as when southern blacks were denied the right to vote, the administration's policy was to act deliberately and hope for a settlement with recalcitrant local officials rather than to push the cases. This tactic would drive such LDF staffers as the Mississippi-based Marion Wright Edelman crazy. Listening to her reports of encounters between would-be voters and registrars could make me doubt that the state was really a member of the Union. Local registrars played federal authorities for fools, toying with Justice Department lawyers for months, promising cooperation while still requiring poorly educated sharecroppers to pass something called a citizenship test, asking prospective voters to interpret the Ninth Amendment, for example, or, as Thurgood Marshall had once acidly put it, "count bubbles in a bar of soap."

In Americus, an area of Georgia that a few years later was to send Jimmy Carter to the statehouse and presidency, we prevailed without the government on our side largely because the capital charges were so outlandish that they made local authorities look ridiculous. It didn't hurt that twenty-five years earlier one of the judges, Elbert Parr Tuttle, had represented Angelo Herndon, a black Communist Party organizer whose conviction for attempting to incite insurrection by distributing Party literature had been reversed by a sharply divided U.S. Supreme Court, or that King and I had been joined as counsel by Morris Abram, a respected and influential Atlanta lawyer.

The Americus case was a big part of my education, yielding legal success at thwarting elected officials' misuse of the law but also personal humiliation. Preparing for trial in a makeshift office off the viewing room of a mortuary owned by the Barnum family and eating lunch and dinner with the family brought me closer than I had ever been before to understanding the complex web of relationships between the races that governed daily life in the South. Family members knew their antagonists in the white community in a way that was infrequent in the North, where racism had a distant and physically aversive quality. The activists and locals who used the funeral home as a social center and a political clubhouse were more likely to give you the full pedigree of a sheriff or school administrator, where he came from, whom he'd first married, when he divorced her, and whom he married next as well as how he treated his secretary, than a dull stereotype of just another white man with power.

I wish my new friends at the funeral parlor had told me more about Ross Chambliss, the newly appointed local police chief. A few days later, when I had to cross-examine him before the three federal judges hearing the case, I was totally unprepared for his stonewall tactics. Impassive behind the girth poured into his starched uniform, the chief denied everything I thought obvious and turned my questions into mush. I was crushed and vowed never again to go into court unprepared. It dawned on me that, incredibly, I had never been schooled in cross-examination of truly hostile witnesses. In my two years of practice, I had learned a lot from my peers at LDF, but they were primarily constitutional litigators; trial tactics with uncooperative law enforcement witnesses bent on sowing confusion wasn't their strong point. I had crafted a winning legal strategy for the Americus trial but flunked out when it came to producing testimony from the chief that would have helped our case.

Fortunately, Morris Abram was there to pick up the pieces. Sounding a lot more like a good old Georgia boy than I did, he examined the considerably less hostile local solicitor, Stephen Pace, and easily got him to confirm that the demonstrators had been charged with a crime punishable by death merely in order to hold them in jail without bail. They were in custody, he admitted, awaiting action by a county grand jury on which a black person had never served, in plain violation of the Fourteenth Amendment to the Constitution and numerous Supreme Court decisions. The workers, therefore, could not have been constitutionally convicted of insurrection or attempt to incite insurrection, even if they had committed the crime. "Agree to leave the state," in effect they were being told, "or we will keep you in jail indefinitely." They were being held for ransom.

Judge Tuttle and another federal judge, Hobart Grooms, thought the state was using clearly unconstitutional means to prosecute the demonstrators.[13] A dissent in the case was filed by one of the southern segregationist judges, J. Robert Elliott, whom President Kennedy had nominated in 1962 to appease Senator James Eastland. Some years later it was estimated that 90 percent of Elliott's civil rights decisions during the 1960s were reversed by higher courts.

For a while I felt disoriented on my regular trips to places such as Americus and saw myself as an expert for hire—a sort of intrusive legal anthropologist—who flew off for a few days of action and brought a measure of civilization to a benighted southern society, then returned to real life in a Columbus Circle office tower and a Riverside Drive high-rise apartment. In the beginning it was easy to forget that it was my country, my constitution, and thus my struggle too, so heavy was the weight of history holding down the centuries of cultural accommodation we were trying to blow away.

Being an attorney made things more complicated to sort out. American lawyers are taught to see themselves as instruments, loyal servants of someone else's goals. The lawyer needn't share these goals, for his or her task is not, as the philosopher Richard Wasserstrom put it in a critical article, "to approve or disapprove" of a client's character or cause or even "the avenues provided by the law to achieve that which the client wants to accomplish." The lawyer needn't have a thought for the client's goal; his job is just "to provide that competence which the client lacks."[14]

Such an understanding of the lawyer's role sows moral ambiguity in a way that affects the way all lawyers think about their role. In a notorious Minnesota motor vehicle negligence case that law teachers love to use to shock students, defense lawyers failed to tell a young auto accident victim about the life-threatening aneurysm that an insurance company doctor discovered during a litigation-related medical exam because it wasn't in their clients' financial interest for the plaintiff to know.[15] Amazingly, Minnesota's highest court found the defense lawyers' behavior would have been totally consistent with prevailing legal ethics except for the fact that the plaintiff was a juvenile and thus was entitled to special protection by the courts.

In light of massive corporate frauds that company lawyers and accountants might have prevented if they had disclosed them to authorities, Congress enacted the Sarbanes-Oxley Act in 2002, requiring that lawyers make certain disclosures of confidential information to company directors and in some instances authorizing lawyers to report such information to the Securities and Exchange Commission.[16] It will, however, take more than a controversial statute applying only to securities specialists to bring about a general change in professional norms, because many lawyers still try to justify prohibitions on almost any form of disclosure. They will do everything they can to withhold information that they believe protects or advances a client's interest.

Protecting lawyers from having to approve of the ends of their clients has a range of consequences; for example, it permits them to claim their choice to represent the unpopular and embattled is professional, not political. Thus the client does not have to find an advocate who approves of his or her conduct. Access to legal assistance is more likely to turn on money or—where society provides an alternative, as in defense of criminal charges—on status rather than on the attorney's judgment that the client's case has merit. But the lawyer is protected from taint deriving from the client only at the price of a neutered moral sense. No matter the harm caused by the client's assertion of legal rights, the lawyer can just shrug and say: "It's him, not me. Just a job, folks." The resulting amoral universe, Wasserstrom argues, puts the "lawyer's words, thoughts and convictions" up for sale, explaining perhaps some of the hostility and charges of hypocrisy conventionally lodged against the profession by its many detractors.[17]

A typical lawyer's dilemma is the need to act when privately he or she has doubts or reservations about the social utility or ethical character of what the client demands. In all too many cases, the client's interests so shade the lawyer's perceptions that the lawyer isn't at all sure what he or she believes, or perhaps, even worse, almost completely dulls the lawyer's awareness that difficult ethical issues even exist. Sometimes law students learn their cynicism so early that they voice few objections to the conduct of the lawyers in the Minnesota case, where a life was put at risk for a few thousand dollars.

The LDF lawyer's problem was different, though it derived from the same perceived need for professional detachment. It was how and on what terms to take on legal work for clients with whom we identified closely. In my case, the civil rights movement's goals were my goals, but I had no desire to control my clients or do for them what they could do for themselves. I was not a political player—race, geography, and temperament made that impossible—but neither was I merely a technician with a license to practice who just happened to be available for hire.

I discovered that I loved doing for others—it gave me the sense of meaning that some people get from religion—but I wanted to do it only the way good lawyers did. That suggested a professional distance that might be acceptable on Wall Street or Main Street or in government but didn't fit the facts of work at LDF. In short, I didn't want to get so close to my clients that my judgment became clouded, but I certainly couldn't treat these cases as if they were like any others, either.

So I had to do the one thing that practicing lawyers are taught to avoid: figure out what I personally believed about my cases and clients and how those beliefs fit into my life. Mostly it was easy, as when I was dealing with physical brutality, plain injustice, or explicit racism; at times, when I was sorting out the best policy options among conflicting claims or determining where my work life ended and my personal life began, it made for doubt and anxiety about whether I had done the right thing, was the right person, or had crafted the best strategy for clients whose lives were often very different from mine. My black colleagues may have been just as middle-class liberal as I was but they had a different experience with these issues. When the community was divided or the client was ambivalent, their word might ring with an authenticity that few white lawyers could project. On the other hand, they might be stuck in a box that some people labeled "civil rights lawyers," as if that were a complete summary of all the interesting things about them and could be relied on to predict all their tastes and talents.

I remember one case that raised this issue, not because it was typical but because it helped me understand how hard it was to separate the personal from the professional in my work. In the mid-1960s I was in charge of developing a strategy to reform the money bail system, under which persons accused of crime were held in jail prior to trial not because they were dangerous or might flee but because they couldn't afford a bail bond—basically an insurance policy that would pay the state in case they failed to return for court appearances. Many cases could raise the constitutional issues that were involved in a challenge to this system, but finding a defendant who was willing to risk the hostility of a lower court judge that bringing such a case would engender and who would not be convicted or acquitted before we could appeal to a higher court was extremely difficult.

I had asked Harold Rothwax, then the legal director of New York City's leading advocacy group for the poor, Mobilization for Youth, and later the hard-bitten criminal court judge known as "the Prince of Darkness" for his heavy sentencing, to keep his eye out for an appropriate case. A few weeks later Hal found one that raised the money bail issue in a way that would allow us to get it before a higher court, but he warned me to be careful. The case involved an accused child molester who might be brutalized in jail but was otherwise unlikely to evoke sympathy.

Late one afternoon, I finished drafting the papers that would be necessary to bring an accelerated appeal challenging the pretrial incarceration of Rothwax's client solely because of his poverty. The draft did not shy from setting out the grisly allegations against the defendant, charging that he had tried to rape his girlfriend's young daughter, but it also alleged his insistence on innocence, that the events were based on a tragic misunderstanding. I gave a draft to the available LDF secretaries and returned to my office. When nothing had been done an hour later, I inquired and was told that they were refusing to type the papers. It was only after a frank discussion in which I learned of their dismay at helping this kind of client and they found out why the case was being brought on his behalf that we were able to produce the affidavits and briefs necessary to go forward.

Lawyering for a cause is now a fairly standard employment option for young attorneys—the woods are filled with defense funds and public interest groups advocating for protection of the environment, privacy, international human rights, and children's welfare, among many other causes—but in the early 1960s little had been written on this slate. There were no law school courses or guidebooks or law review articles on the subject. Those sage advisers who years later would have a lot to say about the dilemmas of public interest lawyers (who had to represent the public interest as well as particular clients) were still working out their own solutions. In the absence of such help, there was much I had to figure out through my own clumsy trials and errors.

Like the *New Yorker* magazine writer Calvin Trillin, then a *Time* correspondent who covered major integration stories, at first I often felt like "a visitor from a foreign land almost anywhere in the Deep South."[18] But it wasn't long before I lost forever any sense of being a tourist. Sitting up half the night in Albany, Georgia, with C. B. King or spending time in Little Rock to work with a determined Arkansan named John Walker or in Nashville to plan case strategy with Avon Williams Jr., Tennessee's first black state senator since Reconstruction, I learned the intricate history of black–white relations in dozens of southern cities. Between court appearances and witness interviews, I also got a short course on the divisions and alliances in the black community itself.

C. B. King, for example, had to deal with the typical tensions of a law practice and support a family quite aside from whatever modest income he derived from LDF's subsidy of his civil rights work. He sat at a desk under a framed saying ascribed to Abe Lincoln, distributed by a lawbook publisher, bluntly announcing to clients across the desk that "a lawyer's time is his stock in trade." It was just the sort of promotional graphic my father might have sold to his clients.

On the main street of Albany, C. B. might be cursed. His head had been bloodied by a local sheriff who had wielded a cane, called him "a black sonofabitch," and ordered him out of the county jail when C. B. tried to see a white civil rights worker whose jaw had been broken while in custody. In the Negro community, however, "Lawyer King" was treated with respect, his opinion sought on every major issue. The demands of being the only civil rights lawyer in town were extreme, and sometimes he would bend under the pressure. He was usually unflappable, but I had listened to him end an acrimonious consultation with a sharecropper, the bib front of his overalls barely covering a torn, mud-caked T-shirt, about a tractor accident with an angry command in his deep bass voice to "Just pay five dollars to the girl on your way out."

King mentored a small brigade of northern lawyers: a tough young attorney named Dennis Roberts (later a take-no-prisoners California litigator) was with him longest, but Drew S. Days III (later U.S. solicitor general and Yale professor), Elizabeth Holtzman (who later represented a Hew York district in Congress), and the future law teachers Kenny Hegland and Robert Cover were among the many who would learn their trade in his office. He served as house counsel to community groups, represented individuals, and exerted considerable educational efforts to demystify the law for the laity. According to Paul Harris, who worked for C. B. as a summer intern, he and another summer clerk saw in King's approach the model for the Community Law Collective they were to found in San Francisco in 1970. Another intern, Barbara Ratliff, became a leader of the black reparations movement. King would eventually run for Congress and governor of Georgia as a way of encouraging blacks to register to vote. He died of prostate cancer in 1988. In April 2003 I came across a news release on the Internet from the office of Georgia Senator Zell Miller announcing that the new federal courthouse in Albany would be called the C. B. King Courthouse. Some of the ironies born of the success of the civil rights movement are overwhelming; this one brought me close to tears.

Other LDF cooperating lawyers whom I first met when they were single or small-firm practitioners struggling to build a practice big enough to pay the rent became state representatives, mayors, and federal judges; Matthew Perry of South Carolina also eventually had a federal building named after him. Like Thurgood Marshall in Maryland, Perry had been blocked from attending law school in his home state's major university. He would overcome the hostility of local judges and black clients' fears that they would be punished for not having a white lawyer as well as the limitations of attending a school set up to train a handful of black students the state did not want to admit to the University of South Carolina. But not every southern black lawyer possessed Perry's tenacity, his physical stamina and good looks, and a winning personality that earned respect even from bitter courtroom adversaries; or John Walker's persistence or Avon Williams's courtly style and superb political instincts. Too many died before their time, some, such as C. B. King, exhausted from the effort required to bring vast changes to their local communities. Others paid the price of a fractured family life, chain-smoking to fuel a killing workload, or a liver destroyed by too much booze.

I had been given a short but intense introduction to their life when I was taken to juke joints, endless movement meetings, and lavish rib and chicken church suppers. Some of the drinking places had never seen sunlight. The buildings often squatted in the woods, surrounded by junked cars and mounds of empty whiskey bottles. Meetings were often held in whitewashed chapels, tiny places sitting proudly at country crossroads. Not a few of them were burned to the ground before the 1960s were out, but I have never heard of a successful arson prosecution for any of the blazes. At times I was presented like a mascot or an honored guest—"Lawyer Meltsner has come all the way from national headquarters in New York"— treated to soul food, soul music, and soulful people. I loved the music and the company, but when I was presented with the grease and gravy my outsider status was exposed. The befuddled Yankee lawyer would move the peas and fatback around his plate like a traveler presented with his first opportunity to sample a plate of haggis. Mostly, however, I was just given a corner of a stale-smelling central-city office and asked whom I wanted to see. Sooner or later everyone would stop by for a visit—local preachers, undertakers, schoolteachers who favored visits after dark, domestics, and young bloods. They were invariably friendly and some would do their best to make sure I didn't come to a bad end, warning me about reputed spies, bootleg whiskey, and particularly violent local police.

There was a whole culture of cars: where to park them to avoid vandalism; the best speed at which to drive through certain towns; most important, how to behave when the inevitable siren pulled us over.

Occasionally I had to deal with firebrands such as the student leader James Foreman, for whom lawyers, friends or foes, were a constant frustration. Once upon hearing that there was an LDF lawyer in the Atlanta SNCC office talking to Julian Bond, then SNCC's communications director, Foreman, whom I had never met but whose reputation for having a short fuse preceded him, burst in with his accumulated grievances about the law's delay in releasing demonstrators on bail. He kept shouting, "I'm sick of it. You can tell this to Jack Greenberg. I'm sick of it," until I calmed him down slightly by repeating, as if it were liturgy, "I promise I'll tell him. You can rely on me. I'll do my best. I promise I'll tell him. . . ."

There were whites—many of them exceptionally courteous—who claimed that the "local Negroes are perfectly content." Why were outside agitators like me upsetting them? Was I a Communist? they would ask in their lilting southern way; or with faux curiosity and no hint of disapproval, "Are you really just after black girls?"

Many white southerners had the startling habit of sincerely denying the reality of discrimination and racial thinking while at the same time upholding the wisdom of segregation and white supremacy. Defendant after defendant would claim both in open court and even in private negotiating sessions that despite the total absence of Negroes in a particular school, hospital, or public facility, there was no policy of racial exclusion. Administrators of huge all-white state universities, for example, men who had earned graduate degrees at elite institutions, would claim with all the disingenuousness that can be packed into a southern drawl, "Well, no qualified black has ever applied" or "No, we never talked about keeping Nigras out." These were the statements of men who were at the same time vigorously defending their right to segregate. The compartments of their minds apparently had been permanently sealed at birth.

Many in the black community, though they wanted change, were deeply and often wisely conservative. They wanted to know why we couldn't stop them from getting arrested, fired, and shot at. Why were we bringing down plagues upon them? I managed to win reinstatement for a number of Virginia and South Carolina nurses who had been fired after asking for integrated hospital facilities and the same pay as white nurses, but such cases, even when successful, imposed great costs on my clients and their families. The nurses had to wait years for the pay they'd lost and, of course, were never sure of the outcome until the case was over. The law's delay was always with us and our clients, though it was often forgotten when we won favorable rulings. A famous LDF story told of a New York clerical employee who got involved in a minor criminal court action and refused our offer of free legal assistance on the ground that he wanted the matter settled in the short run, "not some Supreme Court case."

Returning home after my trips to the South, I could be a burden to my family and friends. Something in me had changed that was hard to describe at the time it was happening; it was clear, however, that I was so intent on the demands of my cases that I had grown distant. I'd been lifted from the daily routine to a place where events were endowed with great significance. Like battles in a war, our victories and defeats were noted. The press sought our advice and opinions. Friends of friends called seeking help to get jobs in the South. A few short years out of school, I was suddenly being interviewed by academic researchers and asked to speak at symposia. I even had been on a panel at a meeting of the American Orthopsychological Association that had been canceled when rowdy demonstrators objected to one of the speaker's condemnatory views on movement violence. I never really understood freedom of speech until someone stole mine.

I started giving speeches about my cases at fund-raisers. At many a private New York dinner party, I could see the movement of eyes in my direction when I was asked about my work or latest trip. On these occasions, I was the most minor of celebrities, but still I wasn't ready for the attention. I tried to be humble, but because I thought LDF was doing God's work, I didn't always manage to restrain myself.

It took a while to find my lost sense of humor and perspective. At first I was sober to the point of piety about my clients' plight, and the feeling overflowed to the rest of my life and collected in occasional pools of self-righteousness. After all, I was connected by bonds of duty to people who desperately needed me. I could describe the black adolescents planning their first meal at the local Woolworth's lunch counter; the single-mother nurse trying to support her children by getting a job at the all-white hospital; the mortuary visiting room in Americus turned temporary law office where I often had to write pleadings to the sobs of a grieving family; the whiskered old white man in the Columbia, South Carolina, federal courthouse who misfired his spit so that it dripped down his own chin instead of on mine, where it had been aimed, and then, in utter frustration, called me a "fuckin' mixer" as he stalked away. Even the celebrations had a serious edge, as when I joined the often whimsical pear-shaped New Orleans lawyer A. P. Tureau for a gourmet dinner to mark our court-ordered integration of the expensive Moissant International Airport restaurant.[19] A. P. deadpanned that the meal didn't really count as integration because he was so light-skinned.

Oh, I had a varied collection of anecdotes to tell when I dined out in New York, but the real shift was inside, a teary, breathtaking, yearning, better-take-a-deep-breath feeling that comes from being there when people make the move of their lives and you identify with it, maybe even helped them make it.

My decisions were no longer purely career decisions, if they ever had been. But I still had to figure out just what that meant. I was certainly no revolutionary, and if any one thought impelled my politics, it was total rejection of the idea that great tomorrows justified violence today. I had never liked the violent images of my childhood—the Second World War, the gangs on the streets of New York. Avoidance of them was, I came to understand, the appeal of lawyering: it offered a promise, hard to see as it often was, of redistributing some of the world's goods, of bringing the outside closer to the center and the center closer to the outside, of stopping the victimization without taking prisoners. The rub was that much of the law was made in the image of the oppression that civil rights advocacy was supposed to cure and even at its best commonly responded to a need for order that could provide stability at the price of justice. Law could shape, protect, and mask the violence of rules, procedures, and policies that did not seem as unjust to the casual observer as segregation but were in every way as damaging. No matter how one felt about market capitalism, for example, or its traveling companions, bureaucracy and media, it was obvious that without some structural change in the way America did its business, the legatees of previous disability would do worse in the future than others. Civil rights law as traditionally practiced before the 1960s seemed to have no cure for this situation.

How, then, to use the stick that was beating my clients first to protect and then to enhance them? This was the right question for a civil rights lawyer to ask, but a personal one was increasingly on my mind: What did it mean that my work had become the most significant identifying feature of my life? With the memory of a father who felt his success at work came from a struggle against adversity, a sort of wrestling match with the devil, I might have had the same worry if I had been a baker, an actor, or a salesman like him. But even in my first year, I understood that being a lawyer at LDF wasn't just a job like any other.

The case that confirmed for me how engaged my sensibilities could become was a forgettable minor fracas, involving integration of several restaurant concessions on the Florida Turnpike owned by a national fast-food operation, the Hot Shoppes Corporation. Before the 1964 Civil Rights Act opened public accommodations to blacks once and for all, only eating facilities with a link to government or public property could be required to integrate. This company's restaurants blatantly turned black diners away but then amazingly denied doing so in court papers. Though Hot Shoppes restaurants in Virginia had opened their doors to blacks, when approached in 1961 to settle the Florida case quickly, the local lawyer hired by the company shrugged and said, "Heh, my client decides these things, not me."

In the weeks before the trial, our scheduled witnesses had received death threats. Several of their cars were vandalized in the Fort Pierce area. Local police were useless. Perhaps because of this attempt at intimidation, the witnesses faltered on the stand; they failed to convey a persuasive story of having actually sought and then been refused service, though that was exactly what they had told us had really occurred. During a recess, a prominent black clergyman and activist who had been seated in the courtroom approached my co-counsel, Derrick Bell, and me, offering to be a witness; afraid that the case would be lost, despite minimal preparation, we let him testify. He described vividly how he had been refused service and told explicitly by the manager that he would be arrested if he failed to leave the premises immediately.

His testimony was decisive, but because he had never mentioned the events before and because he gave me a conspiratorial wink as he left the witness stand, I was afraid that the minister had never been where he said he was. Had he simply made up his story at the last minute? I closed my eyes and called the next witness. A small matter, I told myself. The idea that this restaurant was open to all was the sheerest fantasy; its owners had fabricated a defense. That didn't give me license to use perjured testimony—indeed, I was supposed to unmask it—but the deed was done. Clients shouldn't be handicapped by my precious moral reservations; the policy of these hamburger joints might be a tiny twig on the branch of the tree of white supremacy, but it had to be cut if we were eventually going to get to the root. And by the way, I asked myself, was I really sure he had lied?

My justifications seemed eminently persuasive, but I still regretted the possibility of perjury. I told myself we probably would have won the case anyway and I should have made sure before letting the witness testify that he wouldn't let his zeal get the better of him.

A few years later, over an elegant Manhattan lunch, I told the Hot Shoppes story to an internationally famous writer, a woman who had lived in and courageously written about racism in one of the most viciously contested areas in the world. Familiar with political murder, she picked at her fettuccine Alfredo and sweetly ridiculed me to my face as displaying "typical American naiveté."

I half agreed with her but kept telling myself that, after all, I had chosen to bring this case and the courts had rules of professional responsibility that I had sworn to follow. The least I could do was be aware that I had violated them. While any ethical violation was my responsibility, however, I was not going to wring my hands over this one; my conscience would just have to adjust to the world as I found it. There was nothing to be done but be more careful next time.

I decided a lawyer's lot was not a happy one. It would be absurd to let a restaurant chain deny service to black people even one more day because a witness lied—racism was a system, not an isolated event or behavior—but sometimes, I concluded, we would just be stuck with muddy choices among lesser evils, truths forever partial and uncertain. One thing, at least, was clear: through their decisions lawyers make as much law as they find. Even though they often pretend it isn't so, the person of the attorney looms as large as the rules. Who I was—thought I was—would play as important a role as technical skill in what I did.

After a few years at LDF, I had come down to earth, landing in a world I could not have imagined. Big cases and argument of important points of law would lie ahead, but I was now linked to people who were in turn linked to me at the intersection of some fundamental beliefs and values. Those people would affect me—what I did, what I would become—and I would affect them. Sure, I'd have to know how to juggle the precise details that were the lifeblood of the law, but in civil rights work you brought all of yourself to the job. I would have to be a better lawyer *and* a better person. An attorney who did house closings or mergers and acquisitions might be able to nurture professional distance and reserve a moral calculus for his private life, but for me that sort of detachment was impossible. And a typical lawyer's fealty to rules had been displaced by absorption with the context and the concrete. Some might say with the novelist William Gaddis, "Justice?—You get justice in the next world, in this world you have the law," but in my work you had to live as if you believed the next world was nearby, maybe just an appellate court away.[20]

A Sense of the Work

I STARTED at the Legal Defense Fund in the late summer of 1961 and was given a desk in an already cramped office with Derrick Bell, a young black lawyer from Pittsburgh. He had been hired by Marshall the year before on the recommendation of William Hastie, a key actor in 1930s and '40s civil rights planning, later as a federal court of appeals judge in Philadelphia, the highest-ranking African American jurist in the United States. Even in my first weeks of sharing an office with Derrick it was clear that I was going to learn a lot more at LDF than how to practice law. He was later to become an imposing and controversial figure in the legal world—a prolific author of legal treatises and provocative fables about the enigmas of race in the modern world, a fierce critic of the LDF way of doing things, as well as the first black Harvard law professor and the first black dean of the University of Oregon Law School. Derrick would resign from both posts in protest of faculty hiring policies. We remain friends to this day, but it's a relationship built on loyalty to a shared past; we have opted to avoid conflict, to stay away from testing the boundaries with ideological debate, even though I suspect we agree far more than not.

What I saw in my officemate in 1961, however, was the man before he became an icon. With an extremely welcoming demeanor, he was carefully dressed in a manner that put my wan efforts to shame. He had an infectious laugh that could be heard an office or two away, and a sardonic wit about the foibles of the larger society. There was about Derrick a mixture of critical seriousness and good humor, though it was often difficult to know which feature dominated at any particular time. As Constance Baker Motley, who worked most closely with him, would write, Derrick "had never worn life as a loose garment."[1] If he got a trifle too preachy or garrulous, his delightfully outspoken wife, Jewel Bell, might be heard not so gently calling him back from the brink of excess. Two decades later, when Derrick would take up one of the most unusual protests in American academic history on behalf of female black law teachers, it was, I thought, as much homage to his remarkable wife as a provocative political intervention.

One of the first things I learned about Derrick was that he had decided to leave his job in the Civil Rights Division of the Department of Justice when his supervisors insisted he resign his $2 membership in the NAACP on the ground that it amounted to a conflict of interest with his responsibility to enforce federal rights laws. It took courage to leave DOJ when he was just starting out in professional life and was one of its few black lawyers, especially when those veteran civil rights figures from whom he sought advice suggested going along with the policy so as to help his career and ensure his ability to do good later on. Derrick never conveyed bitterness to me about having left DOJ; rather the experience, like most of his travails later in life, seemed to leave him in a better place, professionally and personally.

DOJ's insistence on Derrick's resignation from the NAACP illustrates the caution with which official Washington embraced integration even though it was now the law of the land. Nor was Derrick alone in facing a definition of impartiality required of government lawyers that treated advocacy of civil rights and opposition to it as equally unacceptable. In 1960 Howard Glickstein, a would-be Justice Department lawyer with whom I would later loosely collaborate on several cases before he became general counsel of the U.S. Commission on Civil Rights, had a job interview with the New York lawyer Harold "Ace" Tyler, nominated to head the Civil Rights Division in the last months of the Eisenhower administration. Tyler hired Glickstein but told him he must resign his membership in the American Civil Liberties Union. "After waiting briefly for the other shoe to drop," Glickstein asked his new boss, "What about my membership in the NAACP?"

Tyler said that would have to go also. Glickstein pointed out that he was a lifetime member of the NAACP and was not sure how he could give that up except by jumping out of a window.[2]

Derrick was well aware of the risks of launching protests on one's own, and would later write with insight and feeling of the turmoil caused by his refusal to teach his classes at Harvard Law School until a black woman was appointed to the faculty as well as his eventual departure from the Harvard faculty, one of the best-paid and highest-status academic jobs in the United

States.[3] Yet he always seemed to end up doing interesting work—he moved on from Harvard to a teaching job at NYU Law School, where at this writing he has been a visiting professor for fourteen years—and more important, had confirmed through his confrontations with authority his sense of himself as a black man who was committed to bear witness to the delusions of the white world. Though I would sometimes part company with his approach, it was clear that he was acting in the tradition of black truth tellers, such as Paul Robeson and W. E. B. Du Bois, both of whom had suffered harassment and ostracism for making white society uncomfortable about racial matters; perhaps later in life Derrick was even a little regretful at times that he had been spared more than frustration, extreme though it sometimes was.

Later in the year I began to work at LDF, I was shocked to learn that President Kennedy had nominated my boss, Thurgood Marshall, for an important federal judgeship. The attorney general, Robert Kennedy, had first refused to offer Marshall a seat on the influential court of appeals for the second circuit, which supervised federal courts in New York, Connecticut, and Vermont, insisting he become a trial judge. Kennedy relented only after hard lobbying by an influential black Democrat. Apparently RFK did not see Marshall's appointment as a way of grooming the first black Supreme Court justice, the way Lyndon Johnson would view his 1965 appointment of Marshall to replace Archibald Cox as U.S. solicitor general. Kennedy plainly expected little more than some marginal political gain from the appointment of the black lawyer, and even that gain, he was sure, would cost him political capital in the Senate; certainly he was not expecting Marshall to become an influential jurist.

So began a new phase in one of the greatest of all legal careers, beginning a course of government service for Marshall that would end only thirty years later, when failing health forced him to resign from the U.S. Supreme Court. LDF would always be associated with Marshall's leadership and the *Brown* case, but as 1962 began it would have to adjust to new leadership and novel forms of legal work that would dramatically change what lawyers asked of courts and the way courts might respond. The rights of minorities were about to be transformed; in many instances, for example, behavior that had been criminal under state law would suddenly become legally protected and privileged.

One of Marshall's biographers, Mark Tushnet, writes that in the years between the second *Brown* case (1955), which set the snail's pace of desegregation at "deliberate speed," allowing leeway to local federal judges and local conditions, and his nomination to the court of appeals, Marshall focused on fund-raising and organizational issues and left the actual litigation-related legal work to a staff he trusted.[4] That is certainly an accurate description of what I observed in the brief time I worked under Marshall, and it suggests one of the great joys of working for LDF—the opportunity early in one's career to make decisions of importance. LDF allowed me to argue a death-penalty appeal before the Supreme Court after I had been practicing law just two years, so early in my legal career that I needed to apply to the Court for special permission to appear before it. Most of my law school classmates were still begging to accompany senior partners to court and even to attend meetings with clients.

Though he wasn't present every day, Marshall was still a looming presence at LDF's offices at 10 Columbus Circle. He had the last word on any issue of consequence and made his views known, though often in his trademark enigmatic style. And he could materialize out of nowhere to read a brief or a set of pleadings. As almost everyone who has worked closely with him can attest, Marshall used jokes and stories as a way to connect with people as well as to convey a point of view. The jokes especially made him flesh and blood, an earthy figure to set against the pieties civil rights work pressed on the public utterances of its practitioners and an antidote to Marshall's deification in some circles after he became a justice. In one memorable story that I doubt he told in later life, he underscored his own notoriety and poked fun at the flamboyant Harlem politician Adam Clayton Powell. He recounted how the elderly African American elevator operator in a New York residential apartment building greeted him with familiarity and a knowing wink when he asked to be taken to a certain female resident's floor. An hour or so later, as the same car took him back to the lobby, Marshall, hoping to make a hasty exit, mumbled a quick goodnight. The operator replied in kind: "And good night to you, Congressman Powell."

Marshall was making the shift, as Tushnet says, from civil rights lawyer to civil rights leader and then to judge at a time when the movement and the reaction to it changed the shape of civil rights law. As has been described thousands of times, the demise of the "separate but equal" doctrine of *Plessy v. Ferguson* (1896)[5] emerged from LDF's management of an elaborately choreographed, lawyer-controlled, twenty-year series of cases. Once the Supreme Court settled the basic constitutional principle that segregation was inherently unequal, LDF lawyers turned their attention to enforcing and extending what they had won and to defending activists who were working to see that Court decisions were in fact honored. But after settling a matter of principle, the Court had turned political in *Brown II,* its 1955 decision on implementation. A critical point that had to be acknowledged but could not be publicly admitted at the time was that the Court's second *Brown* opinion was meant not to transform the public schools straightaway but to educate the public and calm southern white fears with a healthy dose of tokenism.

In their conference discussions, the justices emphasized moving cautiously, taking account of southern attitudes and giving lower federal judges the discretion to adjust their decrees to local conditions. Hugo Black, an Alabamian, bluntly told his brethren that "some counties won't have Negroes and whites in the same school this generation." He was concerned lest the Court issue orders that would not be followed. Felix Frankfurter warned that *Brown v. Board* implied novel group litigation challenging the courts with "a different kind of lawsuit," but he disagreed with polls that predicted overwhelming opposition and hoped that by "gradual infiltration . . . the process of desegregation can spread to the Deep South." He pressed Chief Justice Earl Warren to use the phrase "all deliberate speed," which would become the justification offered for delay in desegregation. The justices were aware that Court orders would be resisted, but few appeared to expect school segregation to last as long as it did.[6]

After the shock waves set off by *Brown,* the Court quickly and without discussion indicated that as a constitutional matter segregation was an improper principle to guide government action, not just in education but in all of its activities. But after stating an inclusive principle of equality, the Court rested. In the years to come exegeses of *Brown* would grow biblical in scope, but I found it hard to believe (wrongly, it turned out) that anyone could take seriously the lower federal court ruling, within weeks of the Supreme Court decision, that *Brown* had nothing to do with integration; it was just about ending formal barriers. While *Brown* may have been an ethical watershed, a coming to terms with a shameful past, *Brown II* made clear that it was also deeply calculated. That open-ended local conditions, as appraised by local federal judges, would guide the pace of change muddled the remedy for educational discrimination and ensured that implementation would depend on the political interplay of other institutions— national and local government and organized interest groups that had not yet acted to end segregation.

In our democracy, the Court seemed to be saying, law may be stated as a command, but whether it really is one, as they say, depends. It is understandable that politicians and police may treat law as elastic or inelastic as it suits their purposes, but only the naive can think that law as announced by courts is somehow different. Americans have a constitutional right to send their children to private schools if they wish, for example; they can vote down bond proposals for school construction, and they can move to another community to escape integration if they have the motive and the money. Ultimately all law, no matter its source, is regularly subject to major revision and reconstruction based on the level of its acceptance. Any set of legal principles that is not overwhelmingly popular, both easily comprehended and directory, will necessarily be shaped and formed by the act of implementation and the response to it.

Early in the 1960s, the first sit-ins at downtown lunch counters presented LDF lawyers with a new set of issues, requiring them to find legal theories to persuade the courts to draw the line between private property and state action in a place that would protect the demonstrators. The main thrust was to frame denial of service, arrest, and criminal prosecution of the protesters as the result of a series of decisions in which states and local law and law-supported custom played a critical role. As if designing a strategy to protect LDF's organizational integrity in the face of attacks by southern states and attempting to enforce *Brown* weren't enough, many of the demonstrations required LDF lawyers to become savvy First Amendment advocates also.

Charles Black of Yale Law School devised the essential legal approaches LDF used in the sit-in cases. I knew him as Charles Lund Black Jr., the constitutional law teacher whose courses I couldn't take because of my love for Alexander Bickel's classes on the same subject, and as Yale's expert on the law of the sea. Black was also a moonlighting poet for *Monocle,* a Yale political satire magazine co-founded by Victor Navasky and Larry Pearl. Navasky hoped eventually to take the magazine, devised to fight the 1950s blahs, to the national stage. When he graduated, a year ahead of me, and went to work as a speech writer for G. Mennon "Soapy" Williams, the long-time governor of Michigan, he needed a caretaker and asked me to run the business side of *Monocle* for a year. I was afraid the responsibility would ruin my studies, but I needn't have worried. Like so many other little magazines, *Monocle* had no business side.

For LDF's efforts to overturn almost three thousand trespass and related convictions of African Americans seeking food service at segregated facilities, Black devised a series of imaginative legal arguments that we freely incorporated into petitions seeking Supreme Court review of Maryland and South Carolina cases. We urged the Court to take a broad view of the many ways the states influenced business decisions to segregate, such as health regulation and licensing, and to recognize that because these were public facilities, an owner had little interest in a right to privacy worthy of protection by state trespass laws.

Later Black elaborated an argument first devised by Justice William Brennan in an earlier case, that state courts might abate, or set aside, convictions in nonviolent sit-in cases because of changes in the law. Ironically, Brennan applied a legal doctrine to the sit-in cases that went back to an 1801 Supreme Court case involving the law of the sea—Black's academic specialty. The Court ruled that the legality of seizing a French merchant schooner was to be determined by the state of the law at the time the courts considered the matter, not at the time of the vessel's capture. After Congress passed the Civil Rights Act in 1964, the modern version of the argument went, all pending state sit-in cases should be quashed on the basis that a new federal law had turned the crime into a right.

A minority of justices, however, thought they could not interfere with the sit-in convictions in the absence of greater government involvement in the segregation policy or at least explicit congressional intent to abate pending cases; another minority believed that government prosecutions that supported racial exclusion violated the Fourteenth Amendment's guarantee of equal protection of the laws. Finally, in a 1964 South Carolina case of two black men refused service at the lunch counter of a variety store owned by a national chain, Justice Tom Clark announced the compromise that carried the Court, holding that Congress should be understood as having abated the sit-in cases when it passed the Civil Rights Act, with its requirement of nondiscriminatory food service throughout the nation. Because Congress had not mentioned the act's effects on pending cases in the statute or in the extensive debates on it, it was obvious that the majority was acting—in words originating in a memo to Clark from Justice Brennan—"to obliterate the effect of a distressing chapter in our history."[7]

Before the final resolution of these cases in 1964, the key element for LDF lawyers in almost all early demonstration cases was that initiative lay elsewhere. Though we often consulted with protest groups when we were given the chance, the decision to march or sit in was made locally or by SCLC or SNCC leadership, with little if any consideration given to the readiness or advice of the attorneys. Of course, that's the way it had to be: if protesters had waited upon advice that what they were doing was probably legal, they might never have acted. Reflecting his NAACP heritage, Thurgood Marshall, for example, was early on very apprehensive, indeed at times oppositional, about protest demonstrations; so was NAACP leader Roy Wilkins. Fortunately, the freedom riders and sit-inners were more interested in taking action to hold up a mirror to the ugliness of Jim Crow than in these reservations.[8] One of the planners, James Farmer of CORE, announced that the goal of direct action was immediately to change actual practice on buses and in terminals. In this respect the demonstrators were true heirs of the 1930s labor union protesters who picketed despite injunctions and arrest on the theory that legislatures and courts would ultimately define their conduct as legal. They correctly predicted that the law would follow them rather than the other way round. But no one could be sure of that outcome until it happened. The strategy was a mixture of guess and hope.

By the time I joined LDF, six months after the first freedom rides, the LDF policy toward direct-action protesters had shifted dramatically. The talk was only about how to defend them. If I wanted to learn about Marshall's reaction to the sit-ins of a year earlier, I would have to go to a history book.

As with the rise of organized labor, the hoped-for impact of protest demonstrations was cumulative and systemic, making the lawyer's role one, though only one, of the elements necessary for success. Without it, activists would have had trouble putting demonstrators on the line day after day, raising bail money, neutralizing white control of local justice systems, and, most important, converting concessions into concrete negotiated or court-sanctioned results. It was widely acknowledged that one of the movement's greatest failures in the early days—Dr. King's 1962 campaign in Albany, Georgia—had been thwarted by an organized white community's willingness to arrest wave after wave of demonstrators. At the same time, the city abolished legal segregation but with police connivance privatized it. In part because the local federal judge was an avowed segregationist, the city was able briefly to enjoin demonstrators on the bizarre ground that the protests discriminated against whites. Because of Dr. King's initial belief that the federal government was sure to intervene, little effort was put into attempts to challenge the machinations of the Albany city fathers by pressuring them in court. It was a mistake that King and his southern allies would largely succeed in avoiding thereafter, and this solidified his future relationship with LDF.

Relations between movement activists and movement lawyers were subtle. There were places where direct action was the point of the wedge and places where it was litigation to desegregate a public facility that would in turn attract public protests until the matter was resolved. Planning with legal resources in mind was evident in some communities, totally absent in others. Dr. King counted lawyers, including but certainly not limited to Greenberg, among his most trusted advisers outside of the SCLC hierarchy, but many SNCC leaders tried to stay as far away from lawyers as they could, perhaps fearing they would end up hearing more moderate tactical suggestions than suited them. SNCC workers also wished to put distance between themselves and what they disdained as middle-class NAACP and Urban League tactics. SNCC's record of directly organizing the Deep South's forgotten black poor was one of the great movement success stories, one that was all too often forgotten after the mid-1960s, when the organization began its rapid decline into chaos and racial exclusion. Nevertheless, the harassment of SNCC workers was so frequent, relations with the police were so treacherous, and an effective federal presence was so rare in the early years of the decade that field workers could not at times avoid dealing with lawyers.

Many times, however, I first learned about cases that later became my responsibility not from the activists themselves but by reading about the events in question in the reports of journalists such as Claude Sitton of the *Times*. A southerner by birth, Sitton nevertheless was often in personal danger, though that fact never seemed to stop him from getting his story. He had a knack for being there when blacks seeking orderly food service were assaulted with fists, clubs, or coffee cups: "A dozen white youths and men in the small but angry crowd joined in pummeling the Negroes. They chased them around and over counters and tables in the waiting room of the terminal before kicking them out the door. The mob tossed one youth into the air again and again in the street outside, kicking and beating him as he struck the pavement."[9]

In their evocative book about efforts to register black voters in the 1960s, *Climbing Jacob's Ladder,* the journalists Pat Watters and Reese Cleghorn tell about a confrontation between Sitton and other reporters, including Watters himself and Bill Shipp of the *Atlanta Constitution,* and Sheriff Z. T. (Zeke) Mathews of "terrible" Terrell County, Georgia, and his armed deputies at a voter registration meeting. Entering the Mount Olive Church in rural Sasser, Georgia, on the night of July 25, 1962, along with a half-dozen white citizens, Mathews announced that "he was a little fed up with this registering business. Negras down here have been happy for a hundred years, and now this has started." Deputies demanded the names of those blacks in attendance at the meeting. Mathews then told a voting rights worker to leave the county for his own good.

While white deputies and citizens menacingly moved around the church, one of them observed that these "niggers down here . . . had just as soon vote for Khrushchev or Castro." As if the night weren't filled with enough theatrical elements, the Negroes in the church hummed "We Shall Overcome" as the deputies hassled them. When Mathews called Sitton a "Yankee newspaperman," the *Times* reporter replied, "I'm a Georgian, sir," and "an American like you." When the reporters finally left the church, they found a tire slashed and sand in their gas tank.[10]

Sitton's story of Mathews's invasion of the Mount Olive Baptist Church became, according to Taylor Branch, "the most remarkable news dispatch of the entire civil rights generation." It "made a mockery of the voting rights protections of the civil rights acts" that the Kennedys were then arguing should be used instead of protest marches. An outraged attorney general saw to it that a voting rights suit was filed against Terrell County within two weeks.[11]

After they were harassed, interrogated, and all too often beaten, the civil rights workers and local blacks trying to register or protest a lack of service were usually arrested and prosecuted for trespass or disorderly conduct. Police ignored the assailants even when they lingered in the vicinity or bragged about their conduct. The chaos produced by thousands of these prosecutions was usually left for us to sort out. It was no wonder that Marshall devoted his last years at LDF to raising money. Without a dramatic rise in the budget—less than $500,000 in 1960 but soon to rise into the millions—and an increase in staff, LDF would be unable to keep up with the escalating demand for its services.

While there was nothing new about civil rights protests, even college-level American history texts ignored them, and what they did contain even in the 1950s was shocking. At Oberlin College, liberal home of an important nineteenth-century underground railroad station, history majors such as Harry Subin and I were greeted with the following passage written by Samuel Eliot Morrison and Henry Steele Commager, the authors of the standard text:

> As for Sambo, whose wrongs moved the abolitionists to wrath and tears, there is some reason to believe that he suffered less than any other class in the South from its "peculiar institution." The majority of slaves were adequately fed, well cared for, and apparently happy. Competent observers reported that they performed less labor than the hired man of the Northern states. Their physical wants were better supplied than

those of thousands of Northern laborers, English operatives, and Irish peasants; their liberty was not much less than that enjoyed by the North of England "hinds" or the Finnish *torpare*. Although brought to America by force, the incurably optimistic Negro soon became attached to the country, and devoted to his "white folks." Slave insurrections were planned—usually by the free Negroes—but invariably betrayed by some faithful black; and trained obedience kept most slaves faithful throughout the Civil War.

Between a Virginian slave major domo, whose ancestors were likely to have been American for two centuries, and a Carolina rice hand, who might have been smuggled over from Africa within the year, there was an immense gap. Topsy and Tom Sawyer's devoted Jim were nearer to the average childlike, improvident, humorous, prevaricating, and superstitious Negro than the unctuous Uncle Tom.

One wonders whether what they were reading at the University of Mississippi could have been worse. After a few paragraphs about the down side of slavery, Morrison and Commager continue:

If we overlook the original sin of the slave trade, there was much to be said for slavery as a transition from a primitive to a more mature culture. The Negro learned his master's language, received his religion, and accepted his moral standards. In return he contributed much besides his labor—rhythm and humor, for instance—to American civilization.[12]

No wonder only a few people knew much about how and when protest demonstrations took place—that there had been freedom rides in 1947, for example, to test the actual practices toward Negro seating in interstate transportation. Negroes were obviously too busy singing and dancing to be protesting!

But now the worldview suggested by such trash would pass away. Linked through the law to a promise of permanent structural change and often prompting a brutal reaction by local segregationists and police, the protests struck a responsive chord in a larger population. During the early 1960s a lawsuit to establish or implement a right was often followed by a demonstration, protest, or some other form of advocacy, which in turn was followed by a lawsuit to establish or implement rights, which in turn was followed by a demonstration, protest, or some other form of advocacy, and so on. Which events you thought most critical or most responsible for change depended a lot on your perspective and when you thought things began. Perhaps the best example of this synergy is the successful lawsuit that followed the "Bloody Sunday" beatings of marchers in Selma, Alabama, on March 7, 1965. Physically blocked from protesting continued denial of the right to vote, Dr. King and his allies were faced with a brutal reaction by police and state troopers if they tried for a third time to cross the Edmund Pettis Bridge. King could not withdraw without facing ridicule, but the Alabama law enforcement posse was out for blood. Nonviolent northern movement supporters began to arrive in Selma. The stalemate was finally broken by Federal Judge Frank Johnson. After hearing LDF's First Amendment presentation and scrutinizing Jim Nabrit's plan for an orderly march, he enjoined the police from interfering and permitted it to go forward.

Even in a society given to litigation of all kinds, one Alexis de Toqueville described as historically dominated by lawyers, the critical interaction between social action and lawsuit was unprecedented. The Warren Court's decisions only occasionally had the dramatic impact claimed by both its supporters and its detractors, but they did represent a shift in willingness by the judiciary to honor constitutional claims evoking civil rights and liberties.

Previously, courts had been viewed as enemies of racial progress rather than engines of change; indeed, American reformers of all persuasions had reason to fear the judiciary. The liberalism of the Warren Court justices from the 1950s to the 1970s was an aberration, never seen before or since. The Supreme Court brought the Civil War closer with its 1857 Dred Scott decision, essentially ruling that Negroes were chattels, unprotected by the Constitution. After the war, the Court severely damaged congressionally enacted civil rights statutes and gutted the plain meaning of key constitutional protections such as the "privileges and immunities" clause of the Fourteenth Amendment. In the 1890s, lawyers had tried to invalidate post-Reconstruction segregation laws and been rebuffed; later the Supreme Court put together a dismal record by overturning basic social legislation of the Progressive era; during the Depression, the Court warred against Roosevelt's New Deal reforms until new appointees and electoral results led to a shift. Even the *Brown* case, a decision that heralded a change in both race relations and judicial openness to arguments expanding due process and equal protection rights, would have been impossible absent Cold War politics and the social forces unleashed by the Second World War.[13]

Jack Greenberg, who took over the Legal Defense Fund's reins from Marshall, dubbed this period the era of "trench warfare": the lawyers were engaged in an agonizingly slow battle to eliminate the vestiges of legal segregation, to enforce the rights won in court, and to protect their own position from attack. As in the trench warfare of World War I, it often seemed as if both sides would be forever immobilized in their dug-in positions.

As a leader Greenberg was totally different from Marshall, direct where Marshall was cryptic, orderly and unflappable where Marshall was unpredictable and mercurial. Marshall was a social animal, comfortable with janitors and Wall Streeters alike. He was the center of attention in every gathering and never at a loss for words. Greenberg didn't always seem at ease in unstructured situations, an aspect of his personality that at times complicated relations with a staff of aggressive, ideologically sensitive young lawyers. He would say, "I'm not very demonstrative, externally or internally," and when someone asked him if as a very young lawyer he had been nervous arguing one of the *Brown* cases, he sounded like a John Wayne character comparing his lack of emotion to his experience in a wartime firefight: "I just calmly did what I had to do." He certainly had a sense of humor, but if he ever told me a joke, I can't remember it. It was hard to believe that this boyish-looking fellow had commanded a landing craft at Iwo Jima, where 6,821 Americans and 21,000 Japanese had died fighting over thirty-six days for eight square miles in 1945, when I was only eight years old. He had such a youthful, open look that it was possible to imagine him as more of a peer than a boss.

But Greenberg was in fact full of iron and very much in charge. Both he and Marshall ran LDF in a fairly traditional way. Most policy decisions came down from the top, though staff lawyers had enormous control over their own cases. There was little organized talk about goals and objectives in the early 1960s; no one had any reason to doubt that integration was the end sought. Litigation strategy consisted of a refined version of the approach followed by the NAACP and LDF in the twenty years of planned class-action lawsuits marching toward *Brown*. The aim was to extend *Brown*'s view of equal protection of the laws to every corner of American life and to enforce it across the country, in many ways a more difficult and certainly more expensive challenge than obtaining a judicial statement of principle.

Emerging black nationalism, separate development of the sort promoted by the Black Muslim leader Malcolm X, and a movement in some quarters for local control of ghetto schools did not much figure in LDF's calculations during these years. Nor did a strategy aimed at rigorous pursuit of economic justice. LDF lawyers were fully aware of the limited value of integration without some redistribution of wealth and greater access to jobs with a future, but the civil rights movement had been forged in terms of racial equality, and there was plenty of work to do on that front. Americans were resistant to the very idea that there were social classes, much more so to the suggestion that their economic system needed to be altered. Moreover, there was little in the way of legal precedent for achieving redistribution aims through litigation. As a tax-exempt, state-chartered, court-approved legal aid organization, LDF was also severely limited during these years in its ability to lobby for new legislation. Efforts to create a national movement for a minimum income and greater public investment in support of children were in the offing, but the lawsuits they would generate would demonstrate how difficult it was to transform civil rights approaches into means of creating wealth. Despite the frustration caused by the knotty, indirect relationship between LDF's historic concerns and moderating the poverty of millions of vulnerable black Americans, LDF would remain primarily a litigator.

Consideration of tactics was another matter. Legal work at LDF was a daily colloquium on how to find the best plaintiffs to bring a case when there was a choice; on when, where, and with whom to litigate; on how to structure the most appealing legal argument; on how to manage the case in conjunction with other cases of the same sort, many of which were not brought by LDF; and on how to mobilize the support each case needed, which might include expert testimony, press attention, law review commentary, money from foundations, local counsel or favorable friend-of-the-court briefs from nongovernmental organizations or the U.S. solicitor general.

In the years leading to *Brown*, LDF had worked with a small group of local lawyers on a clearly defined basic issue. The leadership of Marshall, Robert Carter, and NAACP executives such as Walter White, Roy Wilkins, and Clarence Mitchell was generally accepted. The organizations were not rich, but they occupied the field and had no real competitors; the NAACP received most of such financial resources as were available for civil rights work. The leadership was familiar with key Washington players in Congress and the judiciary and could exercise a measure of centralized control over members and associates in the South. Unfortunately, a legacy of the *Brown* history was an exaggerated belief in the LDF's capacity to map and manipulate streams of lawsuits. No matter the messy reality, we would learn that many judges, even a few Supreme Court justices, could not be shaken in their belief that LDF was in total control of the content and timing of all major civil rights cases. Where some judges just saw legal arguments, others perceived ploys and stratagems.[14] Of course, the organization at times colluded in maintaining the misimpression of control, doing its part to keep the more legendary portions of the story believable by issuing press releases and publicizing victories in a manner that would help it raise the money it needed.

Many observers believed, in the continued viability of the *Brown* story, that an all-powerful NAACP was responsible for setting before the courts tailored lawsuits with scripted clients, and in cases involving public school segregation, this perception was largely accurate. Most approved and very few in the black community objected to class-action lawsuits whose objective was to end rigid, law-backed racial segregation. So far as pulling down the barriers was concerned, support for the cases was nearly total, the main exceptions being some teachers and administrators who rightly feared losing their jobs to whites in a newly desegregated system. But after 1971, when the Supreme Court explicitly approved busing and rezoning in aid of further integration of systems that had experienced some desegregation, such as Charlotte, North Carolina, and as more cases were brought against segregation in the North, black communities began to display diverse class and geographic reactions to integration proposals. A painful moment came in Atlanta in 1972 when black and white members of the city's elite engineered a revolt against "outsiders" such as LDF, won the support of plaintiffs for a new legal team (ousting LDF from its own case), and ultimately gained approval of the courts for a desegregation plan that traded away further transfers of black students to white-majority schools for promises of hiring more black administrators and teachers. Low-income blacks who favored an integration plan were represented by the ACLU, not LDF. A detailed study of the Atlanta experience found that LDF's hands were tied by "disengagement from the client community it represented."[15]

As the number of divisive intraracial issues in school cases grew, the result was rising fear among judges that the strategy and tactics of cunning case planners had been crafted to box them in. They asked, for example, if they could trust that testimony and documentation had not been manufactured by lawyers rather than simply arising spontaneously from the swirl of social life. This was plainly a set of perceptions that could cost LDF votes in close cases, and there was more truth to the charge than we wanted to admit. School cases had always emerged from an interchange between local communities wanting to bring a suit and national civil rights policy that encouraged finding such plaintiffs because it wanted such suits brought. The case would be filed by LDF and local lawyers, but as it continued, LDF, with its national perspective, planning expertise, and checkbook, would play more and more of a policy-setting role. But the cases went on and on as plan after plan was proposed, challenged, adopted, and then revised in light of new court rulings and changes in local demographics and funding. The suit against the New Orleans schools went on so long that one of the key plaintiffs was teaching in the same school system he had sued as a child. Communication between LDF in New York with local client groups was only as good as the on-site counsel could make it. But not all attorneys were skilled at such communication, and they were typically overtaxed with large caseloads and public service responsibility; LDF had its own problems with over a hundred often detail-oriented cases to keep track of. The path of least resistance was to assume that plaintiffs still wanted what they had wanted when the suit was filed.

Whatever LDF's capacity to control litigation in the run-up to *Brown*, the number of cases, issues, and lawyers involved in 1960s civil rights work changed the equation. Most LDF cases still came from the several hundred cooperating attorneys in the South and border states, most of whom had been sending civil rights cases to LDF for years. It is also true that when LDF pushed ahead in its efforts to get the courts to rule in ways that recognized a constitutional violation in discrimination against the poor, its docket came to include cases in a range of areas that had been identified by lawyers in New York, who then contacted local lawyers in search of clients willing to sue. But soon LDF would be just one player among many. Too many litigants across the country had interests they wished to press; with a national belief in a "rights explosion" and the emergence of poverty law as a recognized legal specialty, both LDF and its cooperating lawyers had to move on the issues they felt were important, or someone else would. Of course, even the best-planned cases could settle, veer off into unpredictable areas of law, or be abandoned by a client. And especially in the early years of the movement, many cases were defensive—control was in the hands of segregationists who initiated legal action or government agencies or a prosecuting authority.

In the LDF office, there was a remarkable informality about taking on cases. I don't want to suggest that the process of identifying potential lawsuits was taken lightly, because it wasn't, but the decision was usually based on a brief conversation with Jack Greenberg or even a short note. We had no formal case intake process or committee structure to deal with such matters. Moreover, when disputes about tactics surfaced, staff lawyers had remarkable access to the leadership to argue for what they wanted. I always found Greenberg open to this sort of dialogue on a one-on-one basis; my colleagues Leroy Clark and Norman Amaker were particularly adept at getting his attention and turning their views into policy. These initiatives could lead to altered and important moves in cases or clusters of cases, but they rarely resulted in a significant change in overall strategy. Even a major effort such as Clark's idea for a national program of test cases raising poverty law issues, which was ultimately funded by the Ford Foundation, was less a shift in policy than a timely way of raising money for what LDF had been doing or would do anyway.

Occasionally the LDF staff and brain trust of advisers would meet in conference at New York's austere City Bar Association building or retreat-like rural settings such as Airlie House in Warrenton, Virginia, to discuss where the organization was going, but I rarely felt these meetings made any real progress in examining basic assumptions. Perhaps we were too busy and overcommitted, or perhaps integration through major litigation in the federal courts was simply too firmly built into the organization's identity to tamper with. Periodic staff meetings in the office were no better. They often consisted of show-and-tell renditions of the caseload by the attorneys responsible for the various cases, all of whom wanted to get back to work in their offices. At the meetings I usually had the draft of a brief hidden under my docket report, and I would proceed to edit it, occasionally looking up in an attempt to appear attentive.

In sum, our approach to policy and litigation suggested a professional ideal of competence related primarily to cases and groups of cases rather than one aimed at developing a strategic plan crafted to gain clear resolution of explicit and detailed social goals and objectives. This may seem like seat-of-the-pants management, but it was fairly representative of the way law firms of all sorts operated in those days, before the big firms hired communication consultants and managers with MBAs or commercial backgrounds to propose business plans, mission statements, and glossy promotional material.

Even though LDF was a nonprofit with an active board of directors, a public law agenda, and hundreds of friends and as many adversaries in the ranks of government and academia, the feel of the place was more law firm than policy think tank. Like most law firms, LDF was better suited to finding lawyers to further develop areas in which it had already been working or handling cases that arrived at its door and interested a staff member. This law firm model was both good news and not so good news. It made pressured litigation bearable because LDF was populated by people who understood that litigators had to be decisive. They could talk but also had to act. But it also left us with a social agenda that often consisted of a string of cases that, valuable as they were, only indirectly and inconsistently related to changing the basic structural obstacles to equality in legal arrangements governing housing, education, and employment.

Recently, after studying NAACP/LDF files from the 1940s, the Virginia legal historian Risa Goluboff found a pattern of rejecting or evading claims for assistance from southern black tenant farmers and sharecroppers who had encountered racial and economic domination.[16] There were many potential reasons for not coming vigorously to the aid of these poor and vulnerable workers, from a shortage of personnel to a preference for assisting organized groups such as unions to the overriding needs of the campaign to override *Plessy v. Ferguson,* but as I read Goluboff's findings, I was most impressed by the sense she conveyed that the NAACP had nothing like a considered strategy directed to economic matters.

Twenty years after these events, similar dynamics still dominated the thinking of civil rights activists. There were exceptions, such as the 1966 effort by A. Philip Randolph, the influential founder of the Brotherhood of Sleeping Car Porters, and Bayard Rustin to build a head of steam behind a "freedom budget" based on the principles of job and income security. In the 1960s, fair employment litigation at LDF reflected more than usual long-term planning, but its impact on economic system fundamentals was uncertain. Dr. King became increasingly aware that the movement had not addressed economic justice or general living conditions in the North. Frustrated by urban riots, a distracting and costly war, and the growing appeal of Black Power rhetoric, he decided on a dramatic shift in strategy: he would open a "second phase" of the movement devoted to economic discrimination.

Organizing efforts and demonstrations in Chicago in 1966 were aimed at better housing and jobs for ghetto residents. In 1967, SCLC planned a Poor People's Campaign that after Dr. King's death would bring a tent city to Washington, D.C., with the goal of lobbying the national government for a guaranteed annual wage, full employment, and low-cost housing. In 1968 King supported decent wages and working conditions for sanitation workers in Memphis, where he was fatally shot. None of these efforts, however, achieved anything approaching concrete economic goals. In Chicago, a face-saving compromise with powerful Mayor Richard J. Daley was engineered; the Washington campaign was treated with derision; violence in Memphis culminated in the assassination. Today many of the Chicago and Washington events are viewed through the distorting lens of a great leader's final days; at the time they seemed earnest, amateurish, and ultimately embarrassing, largely because of the shortsighted planning that went into them. Local and LDF lawyers, most prominently Leroy Clark, tried to channel the efforts of the ministers who constituted the main body of leadership toward practical, specific results, but negotiations with politicians and bureaucrats produced little in the way of aid to the poor. There were no legal victories of the sort LDF counted as measures of success. Neither Dr. King nor LDF had evolved a broad theory of change where poverty was the issue.

We were, in short, experienced litigators but didn't always consider why we were litigating some cases and not others or to what long-term end. When we did, the reasons given were more operational and tactical than responsive to measurable results on structures and policies that affected the black community. We were lawyers first, and our training did not prepare us to plot a course for black economic growth or to measure rigorously the impact of what we did do in particular cases. In fact, the case—our bread and butter, our glory—was also a kind of tyranny. You could easily be seduced to measure progress by winning the case and the judicial opinion, no matter how remote their impact on the real world of work and family life. At LDF, decisions were often ad hoc, position memos were the exception, and Jack Greenberg was mercifully quick with approval or rejection of case plans. The message was: Do your work as well as any other law firm would, even better given the forces arrayed against us; do it as good lawyers would do it and all will be well, at least as well as can be expected.

The white-only Baconsfield Park. (Courtesy of Hargrett Rare Book and Manuscript Library/University of Georgia Libraries)

The developed Baconsfield site after it had been sold to avoid integration. (Courtesy of Annette Anderson)

Five LDF lawyers behind Thurgood Marshall's desk in 1962 (*from left, clockwise*): Derrick Bell, Frank Heffron, Norman Amaker, Leroy Clark, and Constance Baker Motley. (Courtesy of the NAACP Legal Defense and Educational Fund, Inc.)

Four LDF lawyers in 1964 (*from left, clockwise*): Jack Greenberg, Norman Amaker, James M. Nabrit III, and Michael Meltsner. (Courtesy of the NAACP Legal Defense and Educational Fund, Inc.)

"Sorry, But You Have An Incurable Skin Condition"

NO ADMITTANCE

Lilywhite MEDICAL SOCIETY

Lilywhite HOSPITAL

M.D.

©1963 HERBLOCK
THE WASHINGTON POST

---from Herblock: A Cartoonist's Life (Times Books, 1998)

My first big case ended a several-hundred-million-dollar federal subsidy to segregated hospitals and inspired this Herblock cartoon. (Courtesy of the Herb Block Foundation)

Derrick and Jewel Bell in 1964, holding Douglas Du Bois Bell and Derrick Bell III.
(Courtesy of Derrick Bell)

Philip Schrag,
LDF's consumer
lawyer. (Photo by
Tom Holzel)

The Americus Four about to be freed from capital charges for
marching against segregation in 1963. (AP/Wide World Photos)

The author and Robert Lypsyte of the *New York Times* present Muhammad Ali with
the 1994 Sportsman of the Year award. (Northeastern University Libraries, Archives
and Special Collections Department)

The legendary Georgia civil rights lawyer C. B. King (*right*) and Congressman Ron Dellums (D-Calif.). (Photo by Syd Harris, courtesy of Paul Harris)

Framed by the
scales of justice,
Anthony Amster-
dam testifies
against the death
penalty in 1972.
(Corbis)

Margaret Burnham and her client Angela Davis, released on bail after sixteen months in custody. (Archives of the National Committee to Free Angela Davis)

The LDF prison lawyer Bill Turner in 1968. (Courtesy of William Bennett Turner)

In 1964, the Supreme Court found a formula that led to the dismissal of thousands of sit-in convictions. *Bottom row:* Justices Tom C. Clark, Hugo Black, Earl Warren, William O. Douglas, John Marshall Harlan; *standing:* Justices Byron White, William J. Brennan Jr., Potter Stewart, Abe Fortas. (1965 photo, reproduced from the Collection of the Supreme Court of the United States, Office of the Curator)

By 1972, the Court that decided LDF's leading capital punishment case, *Furman v. Georgia,* had five new members. *Bottom row:* Justices Potter Stewart, William O. Douglas, Warren E. Burger, William J. Brennan Jr., Byron White; *standing:* Justices Lewis F. Powell Jr., Thurgood Marshall, Harry Blackmun, William H. Rehnquist. (Reproduced from the Collection of the Supreme Court of the United States, Office of the Curator)

A White Civil Rights Lawyer

I N 1961 few paid attention to the significance of selecting a white leader at LDF. Jim Hicks, a columnist for New York's leading black paper, the *Amsterdam News,* mildly questioned Greenberg's appointment, and the following year the journalist Louis Lomax speculated that the black man in the street would resent anyone who wasn't black in power at LDF: "The Jews would die before they would let a Negro rise to the leadership of one of their organizations; so why should we let Jews, or any white man . . . head our organization?" But in truth there was remarkably little negative comment from the African American press and a great deal of support for Marshall's choice. Some gripes from NAACP board members had more to do with their desire to reassert control over LDF, now a totally separate organization, than real opposition to Greenberg.[1]

Jack's assumption that his race was unimportant to most of the people who dealt with him fascinated me because it mirrored my own wishes about life inside LDF. It also seemed plausible at a time when we were arguing to the world that invidious racial distinctions should be banished from public life. In those early days, I saw myself as a civil rights lawyer, not as a white civil rights lawyer, as if I could pack my color away in an attic trunk for the duration. Indeed, for a short time at the beginning of my tenure I had to figure out if there was something in being Jewish that had led me to LDF. It was soon apparent that while there were many Jews in the civil rights movement, both as participants and as donors, there were also many who evidenced none of the vicarious identification with blacks that oppressed Jews were supposed to feel and who could be every bit as disparaging of Negroes as white Gentiles. Jews in the latter category, however, seemed far less willing to express their views in public than other Americans.

There was something appealing to Jewish lawyers, however, in the logic behind my father's basic teaching that social and legal action to end mistreatment of any minority helped all minorities; at least it helped the Jews. Indeed, the survival of the Jewish people despite centuries of adversity was attributed to Jewish law emanating from sacred texts. It was not a great step from here to liberal American constitutionalism. In the end, I decided that if there was any Jewish legacy that played itself out for me at LDF, it was that Jews had lived for centuries in nations where they were regarded as outsiders. I had somehow learned from my parents' experience, though they were the children of native-born parents themselves, the ability to feel part of a society while at the same time devoting my career to challenging some of its cherished beliefs.

But it was the color-blind issue that fascinated me. All I had to do was carry a suitcase downstairs for my colleague Constance Baker Motley and note how much more easily I hailed a cab to the airport than this handsome and obviously respectable woman to be reminded that American society had other ideas about race. Once when I saw a taxi driver apparently speeding away to avoid taking Mrs. Motley to La Guardia Airport, I wanted to attack him physically. I jumped in front of the cab and came to my senses—don't ever mess with a moving New York taxi—only when contact with a hard yellow bumper thrust me to the curb. Aside from a slight pain in the thigh, I suffered from a profound feeling of racial shame. No, I couldn't fully share Jack's assumption that his race was unimportant.

How much race matters, however, is rarely so easy to decide in this country as it was with regard to that taxi driver. In 1998 Mrs. Motley, now a federal judge who in the 1970s had appointed me as counsel to represent several indigent prisoners in challenging criminal cases, published her evocative autobiography, *Equal Justice under Law,* observing that "during my years at LDF" Jack Greenberg "was the only white lawyer" other than a woman who had left in 1948, "who worked as a staff member."[2] The error was palpable; an obvious oversight, as I worked with her directly on only a few cases, or just a matter of forgetfulness: Judge Motley left the Fund to serve as a New York State senator and Manhattan borough president four years after I arrived. But my feelings were hurt. Actually, this once I *was* an invisible man, given a taste of what then was for too many just the ordinary pain of blackness.

As I saw it at the time, Jack Greenberg had prevailed in what was an elemental struggle with a black rival for the boss's job. And Marshall himself had given it to him. It was clear to me that Greenberg had the inside track because he had been increasingly running the LDF legal program in the post-*Brown* era after Robert L. Carter, once Marshall's second in command, left LDF in the late 1950s to become the NAACP's general counsel. As lawyers, there was little to choose between them. Carter, later a New York federal judge, and Greenberg, later the dean of Columbia College, were both superb tacticians who also saw the larger picture of how litigation, demonstrations, and politics intersected. They both could be tough; both had cut their teeth on pre-*Brown* civil rights law and played important parts in several of the five cases considered by the Supreme Court, though Carter was senior and had more of a leadership role. Both knew well the players in the small world of civil rights activists. Neither was thought to be warm and cuddly but both were honest and fair-minded.

My intuitive understanding of Marshall's decision to choose Greenberg instead of Carter as his successor had nothing to do with brains, legal ability, or leadership skills. I sensed from the way he talked about him that Thurgood Marshall thought of Bob Carter more as a force to be reckoned with, a rival or potential rival, than as a loyal lieutenant. Jack Greenberg was just as able but he had clearly been less of a threat to Marshall's leadership, and the same would be true for his legacy. While it was impossible for me to divorce either man from his race, at the time I saw Marshall's decision as turning primarily on competition, which of course could have a racial dimension. The only evidence I had at the time to support this conclusion was the fact that I reached it after listening, like a fly on the wall, to late-afternoon conversations between staff members and their boss in Marshall's office. That the future justice would sometimes pull a bottle from the bottom drawer of his desk added to the authenticity of these let-your-hair-down sessions. There was something in Marshall's relationship with Carter that was absent from his dealings with Greenberg; it reminded me of a men's locker room.

Later I learned my intuition was probably correct. Marshall wanted to control the civil rights legal program. After seeing to it that Carter was made the NAACP counsel, a move that left him with a title but, as Greenberg would put it, "no budget and no staff, and he didn't even have a law library," Marshall set out to make LDF independent of the NAACP hierarchy.[3] At the behest of southern senators, the Treasury Department forced the two organizations apart in 1957, ordering separate boards because the NAACP was a political and lobbying organization and LDF was considered a charitable entity doing legal aid work, unable to do substantial lobbying until federal law was amended twenty years later. These changes left

Marshall in charge. Adrian DeWind, the prominent New York tax lawyer on the LDF board, warned that it could not subsidize NAACP legal cases if they dealt with issues specific to the NAACP without losing its right to offer contributors a tax deduction.[4] On the other hand, it wasn't perfectly clear whether LDF would be barred from providing major financial support in some cases and legal programs for which the NAACP had just provided counsel to others. This was a perfect framework for Marshall and his successors to avoid NAACP issues they wanted to avoid but get involved when they thought it wise.

In his *Thurgood Marshall: American Revolutionary,* written without benefit of access to LDF files, Juan Williams summarized the Marshall–Carter ego battle that emerged from his researches: "Marshall saw Carter as a first-rate legal mind who handled the office's affairs expertly. But Marshall also saw Carter had come to resent him. Carter complained to board members that Marshall often behaved like a prima donna. He wanted all the public attention, he made all the speeches, and he got all the credit, while day-to-day issues and concerns fell on Carter's desk." Gloria Branker, the astute secretary I shared with Derrick Bell for several years, told Williams that Carter would report to "board members his boss's personal and professional problems." As Marshall was a serious drinker with an active social life, there would have been plenty of gossip to fuel mistrust between the two men.[5]

Carter felt Marshall had long taken credit for creative legal work that had been Carter's. At first, he had accepted this subordinate role as the price of learning how to be a better lawyer but tension between the two men increased. When Marshall saw to it that he was shunted off to the NAACP general counsel job, Carter was hurt and angry at what he regarded as a demotion. In a memoir written in his mid-eighties, he remembered that Marshall had in effect "kicked me in the head." Over the years, Carter wrote, he had come to understand that by selecting Greenberg as his successor his boss was showing the politicians who would have the final say over his judgeship that he harbored no resentment toward whites. Carter also believes his relationship with Marshall "soured so rapidly" because of Greenberg's Iago-like machinations. According to Carter, Greenberg and he were friends but then Greenberg betrayed him by "coming to me regularly to pass on some crude uncomplimentary remark he said Thurgood had made about me; I would in turn make an equally foul, denigrating remark about Thurgood." Thus, says Carter, "he stoked my anger." Carter believes he was too naive and did not spot Greenberg's "hidden agenda." (Greenberg, in contrast, has said that he was "astonished" by his selection to head LDF.) Carter unburdens himself of what must be a lifetime of bitterness by describing a call made to him years later when he was practicing law from Greenberg's first wife, Sema, then engaged in a vicious divorce action. Sema Greenberg sought his testimony against her husband by telling him, "We know what he did to you."[6]

The succession struggle has a certain interest to historians and still fascinates those of us who watched it close up. The enduring lesson it taught me was not to assume that persons who did good deeds were necessarily kinder, gentler, or more sensitive than others. Power politics is not alien to the world of high ideals.

The struggle had another dimension also. Carter had different organizational interests to pursue now that he was an official at the NAACP. There was a built-in rivalry between LDF and the NAACP over influence and money that one day would fester and the next turn into an ugly lawsuit when the association claimed the exclusive right to use the NAACP name.

In 1962, however, shortly after Greenberg took over for Marshall, the NAACP and LDF set up a high-level committee of lawyer members of both boards of directors to monitor tensions and "minimize misunderstandings." But conflict continued over who should get the lion's share of the limited number of dollar contributions available for civil rights work, and be able to claim full credit for the victory in *Brown*. The files of both organizations have their share of letters transmitting to LDF checks that had initially been sent to the association so that the donors could receive their tax deductions. In July 1964, for example, Roy Wilkins, the NAACP executive director, had to send a $10,000 gift from a benefactor named Lenore Marshall to LDF, even though the NAACP was in a perilous financial situation. A frustrated Wilkins expressed gratitude for the gift, "even though the NAACP itself will not benefit directly." Facing a $250,000 deficit, he announced the creation of a tax-deductible fund—an alternate to LDF—and expressed the hope that Ms. Marshall would mention it to "interested friends."[7]

The same day Carter wrote Greenberg begging LDF to pay almost $14,000 in fees to seven South Carolina lawyers who had represented more than 700 civil rights demonstrators in Charleston. The request was the latest in a series. Greenberg responded that he knew nothing of the cases and found it difficult to pay for them as LDF hadn't been given an "opportunity to conduct" the litigation. He told Carter that the LDF board had taken this position when the NAACP had sought reimbursement in a similar situation in Jackson, Mississippi. LDF would pay fees, he reiterated, when it was handling the cases.

Carter and Greenberg were at odds, though they struggled to keep such tensions from becoming public knowledge. Still Carter made efforts to order NAACP-affiliated lawyers not to deal with the LDF; he believed, however, that Greenberg wanted all NAACP cases turned over to LDF. LDF depended on the same lawyers, most longtime members of and counsel to local NAACP branches, who Carter had used in the demonstration and other cases. Despite criticizing Carter's request, Greenberg indicated that LDF would "make an effort" to work things out with the South Carolina lawyers. But he was hardly indirect about his larger goal: "In the future, however, it would be less difficult to come to such a decision if the cases were presented to us at the outset." Carter now regarded Greenberg as an "enemy" and redoubled efforts to expand his legal staff.[8]

This sort of organizational infighting over money and turf was not to diminish during Carter's tenure as NAACP general counsel, but blame could hardly be ascribed to him personally; the conflict would periodically recur long after he had left civil rights work for the private practice of law. LDF's pockets were just too deep and it took in funds that the NAACP believed contributors really had meant for it. As the years passed and the two organizations grew farther apart, frustration increased until eventually, in 1982, it provoked the embarrassing litigation over the use of the name, which resulted in a decision that too much time had passed for the courts to now order LDF to cease using the initials of the NAACP in its name.[9]

The exclusivity of the legal profession also played a role in Marshall's decision to choose his LDF second in command over the NAACP general counsel. Marshall was a lawyer first and foremost in much of his thinking; he liked the way lawyers did things and he had a mistrust of the NAACP organizational life that was based, justifiably or not, on incomparable experience with both national leadership and local branches. Subsequent scandals over NAACP finances and personnel and conflict of interest among board members would only confirm Marshall's assessment of the NAACP as a leaky ship.

In 1961 he may have viewed Carter as having become more a creature of the NAACP than he in fact was. Ironically, Carter would have his own problems with the very attitudes Marshall mistrusted, courageously resigning in protest in 1968 along with several members of the legal staff after the NAACP board without consulting him disciplined Lewis M.

Steel, one of his lawyers, for publishing an unflattering article about the Supreme Court of the United States in the Sunday *New York Times Magazine.*[10]

Significantly, Carter's key policy views put him at odds with LDF. An ambitious and experienced lawyer, as NAACP counsel he wanted to grow a docket that included more aggressive civil rights cases than was possible if he was just defending the narrow interests of the association. When foundation grants and the tax-exempt fund Wilkins had set up generated enough cash, he expanded the legal staff and moved into an area that LDF left largely unattended while it litigated literally hundreds of cases in the southern states. Carter mounted suits against northern school systems that had never been segregated by force of law but nonetheless were virtually racially exclusive. His approach, generally known as attacking de facto rather than legally imposed de jure segregation, could be described in various ways, but at the heart of it was the idea that state and local authorities had structured the educational system by facilitating or at least knowingly accepting segregated residential housing and zoning patterns in full awareness that they would result in segregated schools. *Brown* had been unclear as to whether blacks were denied equal educational opportunity when segregation of students by race was a fact but not a product of intentional conduct by school officials to keep the races separate. Put otherwise, was constitutionally recognized harm to students caused by segregation itself or by segregation only when it was imposed willfully by particular agencies of government? Carter began his efforts to reenergize the NAACP's legal program by moving ahead with cases brought in Massachusetts, Ohio, Indiana, and Kansas, arguing that to justify court-supervised reorganization of the public schools, it was enough just to show a serious racial imbalance.[11]

Neither Greenberg nor Constance Baker Motley nor Jim Nabrit—the LDF leadership during the first half of the 1960s—would give house room to this approach. They did not deny the facts of segregation or the hypocrisy of condemning school patterns in one region and leaving them untouched in another or the need to attack northern racial patterns; rather they thought the legal theory by which Carter sought to advance his approach was unlikely to succeed in the federal courts and that raising it was premature at best. It was just plain bad tactics, they believed, to ask the courts to shift attention from ending segregation that a few years earlier had been required by law to achieving in the public schools what opponents would label a "racial balance" quota system. Thus they saw

Carter's campaign as merely a way to make points by losing cases, an approach they disdained. Federal courts, they accurately if somewhat dismally predicted, would force school authorities in the North to move toward integration only if they could point to construction, pupil assignment, transportation, and other policies in at least some schools in a district that could be proved to be based on racial considerations. Others at LDF wondered whether the cases were simply Carter's way of trying to restore prestige to the NAACP after SCLC and direct action approaches the NAACP initially spurned had captured the national civil rights spotlight.

Focused on winning the hundreds of cases to integrate schools it had brought mostly in the South, LDF may have missed the importance of putting its entire weight behind the challenge that Carter mounted in the de facto northern segregation cases. At any rate, soon courts would begin regularly to reject constitutional claims of discrimination because disparate treatment could not be proved intentional. Even if blacks were a fraction of the whites in a particular group—students in a certain school, say, or police and firefighters who had passed a test—in many situations courts would insist on a finding of animus, some evil motive by a particular decision maker, to rule for the minority unless Congress had specifically indicated in a statute that a purpose to discriminate was unnecessary.

The point was critical—did the *Brown v. Board* view of the world require fault, that is, a close correspondence between the behavior of the rights violator and an egalitarian result? Was the constitutional promise that of a nation where law acted to provide equality, whether or not some wrongful set of particular decisions could be identified that closely connected causally with a racially divisive result?[12] What had to be done to make a significant break from the past when it was obvious that taking a "We can't do anything about it" attitude left in place an unequal distribution of jobs, privileges, and benefits? How far could a plan to end discrimination go beyond addressing the precise situation of the litigants who'd brought the successful case without itself promoting discrimination against innocent bystanders? Dwarfing these questions was the political reality that white voters could be mobilized, and not only by the racist appeals from figures of the stripe of Alabama governor George Wallace, around fear that what was given to blacks would be taken from them.

Such questions had lurked in the shadows as long as the main issue for the civil rights movement was toppling formal barriers. The first time I appeared in a courtroom as a lawyer in a school desegregation case, the federal judge, Thomas Michie, called a meeting between the LDF team and the school board attorneys in his chambers in Lynchburg, Virginia.[13] A small group of Negro parents and their children had sued the school board seeking to represent all persons subject to the board's segregation policy. The judge told the board lawyers in no uncertain terms that their client had failed to make a voluntary start toward desegregation and had made things worse by illegally refusing to grant the application of at least two of the named plaintiffs who wanted to transfer to previously white schools. Then he turned to Jim Nabrit and me and just as forcefully announced that the only present remedy he would require would be limited to assigning those children who had affirmatively requested transfer to the white schools. Basically, the judge was saying it was appropriate to leave the racial system in place for at least a dozen years until the schools were desegregated at a rate of a grade a year. Such reactions, limiting *Brown* to individual relief, were common until the mid- to late 1960s in southern districts. The de facto segregation cases ultimately brought such questions to the fore in an even more explicit manner because they asked the courts to change one system for another, not assess individual fault or attempt to fashion remedies that tightly fit the mold of a specified intentional violation.

The Supreme Court would vacillate between upholding claims seeking equal treatment by looking at results and in other cases requiring proof of fault, between rulings that displaced whites had to be treated the same as members of traditionally rejected minority groups and others recognizing that the impact of a history of invidious social arrangements couldn't be wished away in the name of a superficial equal opportunity. Looking to consequences alone posed dangers when it enmeshed the courts in "seemingly neutral governmental choices about the allocation of public funds, the zoning of land in residential areas, the elimination of traffic problems and the very structure of local government." Virtually every action of government could be challenged for inequity, engaging the courts in trying to find remedies beyond their competence or in writing orders they could not enforce. But after canvassing the risks, Harvard's Lawrence Tribe, partially relying on the pioneering work of Charles Lawrence, concluded that rather than trying to restrict government support of equality by a "pseudo" intent principle, the Supreme Court could impede "government acts that given their history, context, source, and effect seem most likely to perpetuate subordination" and to reflect hostility to the interests or indifference to the needs of historically subjected groups. In short, zoning a "white neighborhood for large lots that exclude the possibility of low-income housing is more likely to be the product of racial animus or indifference than is a decision to subsidize a shopping mall project." Eliminating an employment test with a racial impact that was not correlated with job performance was different from restricting additional government payments to the handicapped. The proper test, then, was to examine the roots of a policy, how it worked and how in context it affected racial minorities, not robotically search for culpability and bad intent.[14]

A related uncertainty could be found in Court pronouncements governing race-conscious affirmative action plans, emanating from Justice Lewis Powell's single but controlling (until limited affirmative action was approved in 2003) 1978 opinion in the famous *Bakke* case, where he spoke approvingly of using race as a factor in admission to higher education, there medical school, solely to facilitate a diverse student body.[15] On his way to this conclusion, Powell rejected affirmative action as a means of remedying either the results of historic patterns of exclusion from the medical profession or the legacy of general societal discrimination because in part doing so would burden innocent third parties.

When it could be said, however, that Congress had decided it was effects rather than fault that counted, the Court did not require intentionality. In *Griggs v. Duke Power Co.*[16] it ruled that businesses had to justify the necessity of occupational tests that led to differential racial results in hiring and promotion without regard to fault. But when Congress's intentions were uncertain or when the Constitution rather than an act of Congress was the guiding principle or when changes in the Court's composition had shifted the controlling majority, significant racial imbalance wasn't enough to win a lawsuit. As the years passed, the Court increasingly abandoned efforts to reconfigure the country's economic and political landscape along nonracial lines.

Perhaps the best example of the tension between the polar views was not a lawsuit but a federal statute. Like every other major civil rights legislation of the 1960s, the Voting Rights Act of 1965 came about as a result of a reaction to violence. Confrontations in Selma, Alabama, riveted the attention of the world after years of failure to bring large numbers of blacks to the voting booth by registering them via court challenges of electoral moves by the states deemed to have adverse effects on minority voting patterns. Tired of local officials' efforts to thwart the most basic democratic right, informed of the limited impact of a case-by-case approach, and pressed by militant demonstrations and an increasingly brutal police response, Congress finally legislated a scheme that produced changes in practice without any inquiry into fault.

The official government description of the way the Voting Rights Act operates makes its system-wide reach clear:

> Section 4 ended the use of literacy requirements for voting in six Southern states (Alabama, Georgia, Louisiana, Mississippi, South Carolina, and Virginia) and in many counties of North Carolina, where voter registration or turnout in the 1964 presidential election was less than 50 percent of the voting-age population. Under the terms of Section 5 of the Act, no voting changes were legally enforceable in these "covered" jurisdictions until approved either by a three-judge court in the District of Columbia or by the Attorney General of the United States. Other sections authorized the Attorney General to appoint federal voting examiners who could be sent into covered jurisdictions to ensure that legally qualified persons were free to register for federal, state, and local elections, or to assign federal observers to oversee the conduct of elections.[17]

In its 1966 decision upholding the constitutionality of the act the Supreme Court put it this way: "After enduring nearly a century of systematic resistance to the Fifteenth Amendment, Congress might well decide to shift the advantage of time and inertia from the perpetrators of the evil to its victims."[18]

The Court acted in similar fashion when in 1968 and 1969 LDF school cases it placed the burden for integration on local school boards, insisting that no longer were the *Brown II* administrative factors grounds for delay. Along the same lines, in 1971 the Court approved busing schoolchildren as a means of overcoming segregated neighborhood housing patterns and again in 1973 it was willing to hold Denver's school system to strict desegregation standards even though only certain schools had been intentionally segregated.[19]

But different results obtained in the North and, reflecting the decreasing political value of civil rights currency, would soon be evident everywhere. Before the century was out, desegregation would be replaced by resegregation in many districts. But long before these events, federal courts of appeal consistently rejected Robert Carter's approach, ruling between 1963 and 1966 that school boards had no duty to transfer students to achieve racial balance unless it had been caused by intentional discrimination. The courts in question assumed that under *Brown* the Constitution did not require the intermingling of the races, only *prevention* of intermingling on the basis of race. The holding that LDF lawyers had expected had come to pass: racial isolation was perfectly acceptable legally, notwithstanding its negative consequences for the educational opportunity or achievement of the persons who were isolated.

It might be argued that the de facto cases significantly closed the door on meaningful desegregation in key northern cities, though it is highly unlikely to have occurred under any circumstances. The Court rejected a plan to require the Detroit schools to desegregate by incorporating suburban districts in its desegregation plan, the trial court having found persuasively that there was no other way to integrate public schools in which so many students were black. Stephan Roth, the anything but radical judge in the case known to lawyers as *Bradley v. Milliken*, also found that governmental actions had created a segregated school system and that Michigan officials at all levels had combined to establish and maintain an explicit pattern of residential segregation throughout the city and its environs. Ironically, it was not the NAACP lawyers who demanded a broad multidistrict remedy but the Detroit school board itself that made the factual showing that persuaded Judge Roth, who initially had been hostile to arguments that desegregation should transcend city limits.[20]

Though the original impulse behind *Bradley v. Milliken* derived from the NAACP's northern school segregation approach, the most devastating aspect of the case affected school systems segregated both de jure and de facto. Both NAACP and LDF lawyers ultimately appeared in the case, perhaps because Carter had been replaced by Nathaniel Jones, who was friendly to LDF, as the NAACP's general counsel. The Supreme Court's decision would turn on remedy—no matter the racial policies of the local board, it ruled, the federal courts could not require compliance from unintentionally discriminating suburban districts. Michigan school districts outside of Detroit, according to the Court, had not themselves contributed to the segregation of Detroit schools, so an overwhelmingly black school system (soon to become more so as whites fled the scene) surrounded by practically all-white suburban school systems could remain. That the result would clearly leave the entire Detroit public school system "racially identifiable" with "many of its schools 75 to 90 per cent Black" was insufficient to justify looking "beyond the limits of the Detroit school district" for a solution to segregation in the Detroit public schools.[21] It didn't seem important that the Fourteenth Amendment required states, not cities or school districts, to provide equal treatment; for the purposes of *Brown v. Board*, in most instances large northern cities were on their own.

The Supreme Court's unwillingness in 1974 to focus on results even when it assumed there had been some fault—for example, segregated housing patterns fostered by city, state, and federal governments—and its refusal to see discrimination in many situations where racial outcomes were extreme would be a harbinger of things to come. In 1978 the Eagleton-Biden Amendment tightened restrictions on the Department of Education's authority to force school districts to comply with the 1964 Civil Rights Act by prohibiting busing to carry out desegregation plans.[22] In a powerful essay often cited by civil rights lawyers, the late Alan Freeman charted how the Supreme Court acted when it wanted to abandon use of statistical disparities and requirements for numerical results and employ instead a perspective concerned with "rooting out the behaviors of the individual bad actors who have engaged" in discriminatory conduct.[23] Instead of the result-oriented approach of the Voting Rights Act, which treated race as an exceptional concern, the Court would more often consider it as simply one more socioeconomic factor among many to be weighed. So under the *Bakke* formulation, universities could consider race in making admissions decisions not because of the powerful impact of racial history on academic admission policies but because educational institutions had an interest in diverse student bodies. This ruling equated the social import of race, as Freeman put it, with being a "farm boy from Idaho."

By the late 1980s, logic of this sort was commonplace. The efforts of the Richmond, Virginia, City Council to set aside 30 percent of the dollar value of its contracts for minority contractors, who previously had garnered only 1 percent of the city's business, were not sufficiently based on a history of discrimination to survive challenge as a proper remedy.[24] In the famous *Mc-Cleskey* case, the Court required a showing of animus for relief against systemic policies that produced racially disparate sentencing in capital cases.[25] An Alaska cannery did not have to justify two separate job classifications, one for unskilled, lower-paid minority workers and the other for white, skilled, higher-paid workers.[26] If employers are successfully sued when they are not at "fault," the Court warned, they might hire on the basis of race, unlawfully discriminating, to protect themselves. In such cases, discrimination against racial minorities was stripped of its exceptional character as a grievous harm, the continuation of which affected the essential character of American life, and clearly weighed less than business efficiency. There was a sense of quick switch about this approach. Yesterday we took account of the fact that we had treated you badly, cheated you of resources, and favored others; but this is today, and we're not going to give you a break anymore. Get over it.

But in 1961, when Marshall chose Greenberg to replace him, these developments could not have been predicted. Civil rights forces were still trying to upset explicit segregation laws and visible racial policies; breaking the color line in restaurants, swimming pools, and even golf courses was a worthy way to spend time. Less than 2 percent of previously de jure segregated black schoolchildren were in integrated classrooms. Beatings and firings of Negroes who sought to vote in the South were commonplace. Federal money had built separate emergency rooms, maternity wards, and intensive care units and financed segregated housing projects. In the North, attention was slow to focus on the implications of the civil rights movement for the inner-city ghetto and the suburban enclave. Efforts to attack disparate impact and refashion government programs and corporate employment norms were still in the future. In sum, the claims of a litigant who expressed worry about race discrimination against whites wouldn't have passed the laugh test.

Whatever Marshall's motive for choosing Greenberg, his decision added a personal dimension to a growing institutional animosity between LDF and the NAACP. It had long been assumed by the civil rights bar that Carter was Marshall's heir. When Marshall chose Greenberg to succeed him, there was undeniable surprise, complicated by several facts: the Fund's star was in the ascendant and the association's was in decline. By the mid-1960s, LDF had a New York–based staff of more than twenty lawyers and the number was growing. LDF had become known as the legal arm of the civil rights movement after it started to represent Dr. King and a whole cohort of activists regardless of affiliation. While LDF's budget grew steadily, the NAACP was still hurting—losing members and spending more than was prudent. Most demoralizing to the NAACP was that its old guard was being upstaged by a new generation of leaders from other organizations. To the outside world, even to many journalists, the NAACP and the LDF were indistinguishable, but more important, LDF had the money.

In these years the two organizations were bound to present a united front in civil rights matters, but the personal tension between Carter and Greenberg remained just below the surface. Conflict between the NAACP and LDF would soon seem trivial. More strident voices in the black community came to the fore in the mid-1960s as the depth of white resistance was exposed, the pace of integration slowed, and riots, assassination, and war made this one of the most turbulent periods in American history. They demanded a more aggressive stance toward poverty and structural discrimination. Derrick Bell, a close friend of Carter's, also wanted to move the emphasis of LDF activity away from southern integration suits. Bell's approach, which he spelled out in greater detail in a series of oft-cited books and articles beginning in the 1970s, after he became a Harvard law professor, was to seek greater resources and instructional quality for black students, even if that goal required acceptance of their attendance at all-black schools. In a 1976 article that did much to establish his reputation in the academic community he directly challenged the LDF's way of doing things:

> But neither NAACP nor the court-fashioned remedies are sufficiently directed at the real evil of pre-*Brown* schools: the state-supported subordination of blacks in every aspect of the educational process. Racial separation is only the most obvious manifestation of this subordination. Providing unequal and inadequate school resources and excluding black parents from meaningful participation in school policymaking are at least as damaging to black children as enforced segregation.[27]

Derrick not only accused civil rights groups of opposing school plans that would "upgrade educational quality" because they might sacrifice integration; he widened the gap between him and former colleagues by supporting claims that lawyers at LDF and the NAACP followed a "We know what's best" attitude in choosing what remedies to pursue, disregarding the desires of the black community they were representing in class-action lawsuits and taking advantage of clients' passivity in the face of lawyers' assurances. This picture of an LDF that didn't listen to its clients was followed by a broad claim that contributors influenced LDF's selection of cases.

Twenty-five years later, flagging black interest in school integration as a workable solution, judicial hostility to continued court administration of local schools, and more evidence that there were two Americas when it came to public education seemingly confirmed Derrick's prophetic and deeply pessimistic judgment that racial subordination was inevitable and intractable. According to him, integration would remain marginal in many school districts, including those that needed it most, as he explained in his contribution to an imaginative 2001 book in which Jack Balkin of Yale was joined by eight other scholars in writing versions of the *Brown* opinion as they would have written them in 1954, although of course they could be guided by insights acquired since. Of the nine opinions, Derrick's was the only dissent.[28] He held, as he had long done, that integration didn't work, and called for strict enforcement of the "equal" in "separate but equal"— as strict as the "separate" had been treated. While he denied that he intended his opinion to be merely provocative, his emphasis on giving the black community the opportunity to control and improve its own schools made most sense when one thought whites would always find a way to defeat integration unless their clear interest, as he put it, "converged" with that of blacks. Of course, the question then arose why a white community that was as hostile to black educational gains as this argument implied would devote the substantial resources required to change the black schools dramatically.

Derrick kept searching for models of communities that had achieved significant change by setting up alternative schools or financing arrangements, but even as late as 2004, when he wrote on *Brown's* fiftieth anniversary, he had yet to find more than promising experiments in certain charter schools, independent inner-city schools, and voucher programs. Without broadly applicable hard evidence verifying superior educational quality, the available alternatives looked more like refuges from failing public school systems than responses to levels of integration or segregation. A case still could be made, moreover, that integration, even if it was just a surrogate for better schooling, was the most efficient means available to promote a higher level of educational performance.

By the new century there would be fresh evidence that without the national government's intervention—which was not forthcoming—previously integrated schools would be resegregated at a rapid pace. A Harvard study found 70 percent of the nation's black students attending predominantly minority schools, while 37 percent of Latino students went to schools where 90 to 100 percent of the students were also minorities. Thirty-five percent of black students attended schools that were 90 to 100 percent black. Where black students and white students attended the same schools, they were often separated into segregated classrooms. Ironically, when resegregation came, it was less pronounced in districts previously segregated by law than in the North and West.[29]

But these developments could hardly have been predicted in the 1960s. We were more concerned with the fact that *Brown* had declared segregation a constitutional wrong and we believed that ending it was the best remedy for inadequate schooling. With his de facto cases, Carter had tried creatively to expand and to amplify *Brown's* promise of equal educational opportunity, but white America's image of acceptable integration was a minority of black students attending a school with a majority of whites. The converse was unacceptable. Derrick Bell's views, on the other hand, ultimately challenged *Brown's* very premises: though he failed to present a politically practical means of achieving it, his goal was clear—it was equal education, not moving bodies. Not only was his approach rejected at LDF but he felt that he had been treated more like a heretic than as a dissenter. He left LDF in 1966 for a job in Washington where his charge was to enforce federal civil rights laws requiring school desegregation. Two years later, feeling trapped by Washington bureaucratic inertia, he made his way to the academy.

The departures of Derrick and Constance Baker Motley were just two of the many events that led to a change in the atmosphere at LDF in the second half of the 1960s. The legal staff doubled and later would double again. No longer could you stand in the middle of the office and like some town crier of old expect everyone to hear your news. The interoffice memo replaced word of mouth. The powerful interracial consensus of liberals that had backed national civil rights legislation began to fray and Black Power rhetoric had seized public attention. But these developments never came anywhere close to putting Greenberg's leadership in doubt, in part because a wide range of movement activists viewed LDF as a common resource.

By this time white lawyers had been in court on behalf of movement clients for years. William Kuntsler, who previously had a small practice with his brother focusing on typical civil law matters, had been one of the first and was certainly the most visible and noisy. I first meet him before he had been overtaken by fame. In late 1961 he had been brought to the LDF's Columbus Circle offices by Carl Rachlin, then the general counsel of CORE, to attend a meeting about providing legal assistance to the civil rights workers then beginning to organize in Mississippi.

Before the meeting began, a call came in from Mississippi about an incident that had led to arrests in Poplarville, a notorious Delta town where William Mack Parker, a black man charged with raping a white woman, had been taken from jail and lynched two years earlier. Not finding any staff lawyers at their desks, the switchboard operator, who in those days distributed incoming calls, simply announced the basic details of the call to the group of attorneys standing near Greenberg's office waiting for the meeting to start.

Immediately Kuntsler became agitated. He announced loudly, his voice going up a register, "We have to get there now. This is Poplarville. I mean *Poplarville!*"

Rachlin had to restrain him. "Later, Bill. Later." Plainly Kuntsler wanted to leave the meeting immediately, go directly to La Guardia, jump on a plane, and materialize magically in some southern courtroom.

Even though I was greener than green, his reaction struck me as too much larger than life, displaying the kind of excessive earnestness that usually meets with trouble in the law courts, but while Kuntsler would have more than his share of problems with judges—one notoriously (and abusively) sentenced him to over four years for contempt—he turned out to be as brave as he was daring. In movement legal work he found an outlet for whatever demons had been driving him and he proceeded with a flamboyance that was very different from the more cautious and measured approach of most LDF lawyers. Unfortunately, as time went by, he developed a habit of crisscrossing the South and filing a wild array of cases—an itinerant, a sort of legal Johnny Appleseed—that other lawyers would have to take over after he moved on.

Kuntsler had an undeniable talent for choosing skilled collaborators, such as Arthur Kinoy and Morton Stavis, whose research and writing masked his limitations. With his love of the spotlight, he earned a "There he goes again" reputation at LDF, but of course to him LDF lawyers were much too conservative in personal style and conventional in legal approach and, even worse, given to protecting the turf of the nation's leading civil rights legal organization. Kuntsler and his clients, such as SNCC's James Foreman, thought of LDF as too closely linked to the DOJ, a notion I thought spoke more of their frustration than of the reality. But Kuntsler was certainly right about style. No one at LDF stood within a mile of him when it came to celebrity or capacity to engage the media. The distance grew as he came to work on cases arising out of the 1968 demonstrations at the Democratic Party convention in Chicago; the Attica prison riot; the FBI's pursuit of Native American activists; the murder of the Jewish Defense Fund's founder, Rabbi Meir Kahane; and the 1993 bombing of the World Trade Center. While Kuntsler was a media darling, during these years frustrated LDF lawyers were still trying to explain the basics to reporters: they worked for LDF, *not* the NAACP—the two were separate organizations.

I have little idea of the man's private life but I always thought there was something of the dance-away lover in the way Kuntsler approached a lawsuit—promising much, delivering a dollop of charisma, and then moving on. He might popularize an interesting tactic—say trying to remove prosecutions of rights workers from state to federal court under a Reconstruction-era statute—but he wasn't always around for the heavy lifting or the

A White Civil Rights Lawyer

dénouement. Actually, sex was often the "cement" that bonded movement workers, as the activist Robb Burlage once put it in reference to the leaders of the Students for a Democratic Society (SDS).[30] This idea probably was much less applicable to the bands of civil rights lawyers working in the South than to youthful activists, but in Kuntsler's case, at least, one wondered; where the press and public were concerned, he was as eager for attention as a would-be seducer.

Kuntsler would go on to become *the* celebrity left lawyer of the period; to the irritation of judges everywhere, he was always willing to put the state or the court on trial by injecting claims of government oppression into the defense of his clients, increasingly men charged with murder, and winning his share of difficult cases. In 1974 Steven Phillips, a former student of mine at Columbia Law School, prosecuted a bizarre murder case against a hospital worker named James Richardson, charged with killing John Skagen, an off-duty police officer who had been shot while trying to search him at a subway station in the Bronx. After firing his revolver at Richardson, Skagen himself was shot by another policeman, who didn't realize he was a cop. Kuntsler took the case pro bono, though he later petitioned the court for payment. In his 1977 book about the case, *No Heroes, No Villains,* Phillips describes his adversary as the epitome of a "society is to blame" defender, "obnoxious" but also "endearing."[31] By the end of the hard-fought trial, which resulted in Richardson's conviction for manslaughter (later reversed by an appellate court because of insufficient evidence that his shot had actually caused Skagen's death), the two lawyers were continuously snarling at each other. Kuntsler constantly baited Phillips, trying to get the young prosecutor to lose his cool and commit an error that could lead to reversal of a conviction. Phillips struggled to maintain his composure by telling himself he'd truly arrived as a lawyer when Kuntsler attacked him before the jury as a "puppet of the establishment."

Kuntsler died of a heart attack in 1995 at age seventy-six. After his death the Harvard law professor Alan Dershowitz memorably said: "I have great compassion for God now, because I think Bill is going to start filing lawsuits as soon as he gets to heaven."[32]

The civil rights turf grew crowded in the mid-1960s as Greenberg brought on new lawyers, hiring both blacks and whites to maintain an integrated staff, to engage in widespread litigation over employment discrimination and the rights of the poor—issues that would have seemed fanciful early in the decade. No longer was there a feeling of an LDF monopoly; more lawyers for government and other organizations found themselves doing work under the umbrella label "public interest law," which included civil rights law but also encompassed a vast range of other issues and activities.

Civil rights law itself had been viewed skeptically just a few years earlier when I had finished law school. Now it was the professional place to be for many talented recent graduates and young practitioners. Some volunteered to go south for a season, consulted on complex lawsuits, and then returned to private practice. Others changed the path of their lives by affiliating with interracial firms in such places as Charlotte, New Orleans, and Memphis, joining the Lawyers' Committee for Civil Rights under Law (launched at the urging of President Kennedy in 1963) or working hard to raise enough money to pay for its regional offices. Still others flocked to the new Legal Services Program funded by the Office of Economic Opportunity under Lyndon Johnson's War on Poverty or set up advocacy programs of their own to assert the rights of women, ethnic minorities, or discrete interest groups like the disabled. Some stayed at private law firms but brought major cases on a pro bono basis in their own communities. In one of his books, Kuntsler actually tried to list all the lawyers, black and white, doing the kind of "people's law" he like to call his work, but though the list was long, it was hopelessly incomplete. In LDF, Charles Houston, Thurgood Marshall, and Jack Greenberg had created the model for a new professional role.

Greenberg and Bell

PROLIFIC as well as visionary, Derrick Bell has often referred to the personal dimensions of his role in civil rights history. In his *Confronting Authority* Bell describes the mixed blessings of a go-it-alone maverick's life; how his protests have often led to as much consternation in his friends as in his enemies, as when his challenge to Harvard's failure to appoint Professor Regina Austin upset her and may actually have cost her the job; or when his wife of thirty years would admonish him gently: "There you go again. After all these years, still trying to teach the white folks."

Bell tells of reminiscing about his time at LDF with Leroy Clark several years after leaving the Fund only to learn that Clark was still angry that Bell would "invariably go off on my own in protesting to Greenberg about one or another policy that we all felt was wrong." Bell is amazed by the intensity and longevity of Clark's feelings: "For the life of me, I can't remember preventing others from challenging Greenberg or any of them complaining to me about my tactics. Given Clark's outburst, I wondered whether the staff might have been angrier with me for protesting than with Greenberg for the actions that made the protests necessary."[1]

From a historical perspective, this is a fascinating passage because it implies without specifying any particulars that Bell saw LDF as seething with dissent; staff lawyers, he suggests, felt so intimidated that they couldn't express their frustration. That's not the way I remember it. Did an interracial staff of ultimately twenty-five-plus lawyers dispute, compete, bitch, and moan, often aiming their barbs at the boss? You bet. Did black and white lawyers sometimes take different positions on grounds that seemed to reflect race or political views born of race? Sure. Did they care that even the minutest decision might have adverse effects on a fragile civil rights movement? Absolutely.

But was LDF in the 1960s more a group cohering around a commitment to end white supremacy or a metaphor for the diminishing possibilities of honest talk across the racial divide? Certainly, I think, the former. Despite a few exceptions, respect and collegiality were the hallmarks of staff relations during my years at LDF.

In 1995 Leroy Clark pushed back at Bell. He was "ambivalent" about criticizing a former colleague but it was "urgent" to do so because Bell's work "propagates a damaging and dampening message which must be confronted and rejected." In *Confronting Authority* and *Faces at the Bottom of the Well,* two of Derrick's better-known books,

> nowhere . . . is there a recognition of the long history of effective white cooperation with blacks in ending segregation, such as the fact that two major civil rights organizations, the NAACP and the Urban League, originated with whites and blacks acting cooperatively. Nowhere in either book is there a recognition of white financing of the civil rights movement. Black lawyers, like Charlie Houston and Thurgood Marshall, theorized the legal battle to end state-enforced racial segregation, but when Professor Bell and I were lawyers for the NAACP Legal Defense Fund, at least one third of the lawyers were white. . . . Indeed, from the very beginning, some talented and dedicated whites have been critical actors producing positive results in the black freedom struggle. That they may only have been the "few" whites that Professor Bell claims would "actively support civil rights for blacks" does not defeat the point. Most movements began with a "few." The larger public, white and black, becomes educated and drawn toward their direction.

Clark went on to dispute Bell's views about the intractability of racism, rejected his use of allegory instead of coming forth with "objective proof" of certain assertions, and took on a central thesis:

> Nor do I agree with his implication . . . that racism is the paramount factor in the absence of class awareness. Undoubtedly other factors like Americans' steady belief—at least until recently—in the myth of unlimited mobility, the absence of a history of a hereditary aristocracy, and America's high standard of living after World War II, explain much of

the belief that one's future is not unfairly controlled by one's class level. However, the absence of class consciousness is not a phenomenon "owned" exclusively by whites. Despite strong forces compelling racial solidarity amongst blacks, such as racial segregation, E. Franklin Frazier, in his celebrated book, *Black Bourgeoisie,* showed the multifarious and strenuous ways in which a black elite separated itself from poor and working class blacks.[2]

Derrick's best-known fable, "The Space Traders," also comes in for Clark's acid pen. There, visitors from outer space arrive at a time when the United States is deep in debt, plagued by pollution and lack of nuclear safety. In return for taking all African Americans back to their home star, the traders will present the administration of the day with gold, magical antipollution chemicals, and the key to safe use of nuclear energy. After a period of shock and initial rejection, Americans first debate and then finally accept the offer.[3]

Clark relates the story "to the American past . . . lurking in the wings for blacks, there is an American version of the Nazi 'final solution.' From one perspective, the secession of the Southern States from the Union, which precipitated our Civil War, is as close as America has come to the ominous threat to expel blacks that Professor Bell creates fictionally in 'The Space Traders.' Rebellious white southerners proposed taking black slaves into a separate land—the plantation. The pay-off to the North was the end of strife and conflict over the importation of slaves, and the end of a nation divided into territories where slaves could or could not be owned."

But, Clark continues, the "actual history of this near holocaust for blacks contradicts Professor Bell's predictions. White abolitionists saw the Confederates as the 'Space Traders' of their day, and fought a bloody and costly Civil War to successfully prevent blacks from being carried off into the continued hell of slavery. None of this history of positive white involvement in ending slavery is recognized."[4]

I think Clark gets much the better of this debate, certainly to the extent that his critique implicates the LDF staff and its integrationist stance. Though the world of civil rights lawyers has changed significantly in years that have seen the steady closing of the reformist vision of the 1960s, LDF was then and remains today a model of racial partnership. William Robinson, for years the dean of the University of the District of Columbia School of Law, worked at LDF from 1967 to 1973. I remember him as a fiery African American lawyer with definite views that LDF had to aggressively relate better to the black community; Robinson believes LDF is still doing the right kind of work and doing it well.[5] Norman Chachkin, at this writing LDF's director of litigation, who is white, has been with the organization on and off more than thirty-five years, initially as an NYU law student moonlighting as a part-time secretary. "There's plenty of tension in this kind of pressured legal work," Chachkin has commented, "but racial tension rarely appears at LDF."[6]

This remark may be hard to swallow in a country with few examples of true racial integration among people doing highly visible, stressful work. But in a real sense the few exceptions prove the accuracy of Chachkin's observation. And there were exceptions in the late 1960s and early 1970s. No matter how irrelevant Jack Greenberg thought his race or how much I wished I could agree with him, it was just a matter of time until a challenge to a white head of LDF arose. In October 1970, shortly after I left the organization to teach at Columbia Law School, a recently hired staff lawyer, Margaret Burnham (later a colleague of mine at Northeastern Law School), urged LDF to represent Angela Davis, the controversial black academic, American Communist, and militant who had been arrested in New York on charges of murder, kidnapping, and conspiracy stemming from a notorious shootout in a California courthouse. The violent encounter left four dead, including a state judge and Jonathan Jackson, thought to have instigated the violence in an attempt to rescue his brother George, an inmate at Soledad Prison, whose letters from prison, published in October 1970, had attracted international attention. Guns carried by Jonathan Jackson were registered in Davis's name and she had been active in the defense of George Jackson and others charged with the death of a Soledad guard. She was taken into custody on the theory that she had planned or facilitated the courthouse invasion, even though she hadn't been present. After her arrest, Davis was held in solitary confinement in the Women's House of Detention in Greenwich Village.

Burnham had grown up with Davis in Birmingham, Alabama, where her father, Louis Burnham, was running a Communist Party–supported group called the Southern Negro Youth Congress (SNYC). Working class in spirit, revolutionary in tactics, the SNYC tried to register voters, interest local blacks in progressive causes, and raise awareness of ways to fight segregation in Birmingham. In 1948, when Burnham brought Senator Glen Taylor (D-Idaho), the running mate of Henry Wallace in his bid for the presidency on the Progressive Party ticket, to town for a speaking engagement, he came in conflict with City Commissioner Eugene "Bull" Connor. Even then Birmingham's chief power, Connor made sure there were enough threats of violence, Klan bombings, and arrests to ensure that few people would show up for the speech. He also put Burnham in fear for his life. As Diane McWhorter tells it, one night Burnham and his wife vacated their apartment "after receiving threats from the Klan. Crouched on the floor of a friend's car, they arrived with their baby daughter [Margaret] at the house of the youth congress's most active lay member, a schoolteacher named Sallye Bell Davis, whose four-year-old daughter [Angela] was overjoyed at the unexpected company." The two renewed their friendship as teenagers when both were attending high schools in New York City.[7]

Though she hadn't seen Angela Davis in several years, as soon as she heard of the arrest, Margaret Burnham sought access to her. Entering the jail, she encountered the Communist Party counsel John Abt, an old friend of her father's, who was also trying to get in to see Davis. Later both lawyers would try to head off the return of Davis to California after it became obvious that New York officials couldn't wait to get rid of her.

Greenberg believed that any defense Davis could offer to a request for extradition would be frivolous (though he probably didn't know at this point that California had arguably failed to supply New York authorities with the proof required to detain her even under the loose requirements of extradition law), but, more important, that LDF had no business, absent a claim of discrimination, representing a client "associated with violent resistance to the justice system." He refused to get involved in the case, even though the entire legal staff, with the exception of Jim Nabrit, adamantly opposed his decision. When, as a representative of the staff, Conrad Harper—later the first black president of the Association of the Bar of the City of New York—urged him to reconsider, Greenberg was steadfast. Later the LDF board backed him unanimously. Press reports tried to paint the controversy as turning on Jack's race, and certainly some staff lawyers saw it that way, but I can find none who were willing to be quoted at the time.[8]

The conflict also had a strong (and quintessentially 1960s) generational cast, stemming from the experience of feisty young lawyers, most of whom hailed from the urban North, representing a client population that was growing disillusioned with the promise of a nonracial society and a leadership that the staff thought was wedded to an emphasis on integration simply because it had been responsible in the past for dramatic changes in race relations. Revolutionary talk was in the air. First inner-city riots and then acts of domestic terrorism linked to frustration with the war in Vietnam had become common. Even peaceful protests over war or race had a way of turning ugly and leading to injury and death, as in shootings by law enforcers in Orangeburg, South Carolina, Kent State College in Ohio, and Jackson State College in Mississippi. Everyone at LDF believed that in a nighttime raid Chicago police had simply murdered Fred Hampton of the Black Panthers. What someone stood for became more important than the particulars of his or her legal situation. In this increasingly polarized environment, the staff viewed Angela Davis as a black leader who needed legal protection; Jack Greenberg saw her as the object of a romantic, even violent, militancy, and the LDF board considered her a threat to the organization's working consensus—change through peaceful integration and legal processes.

Greenberg agreed to let Margaret Burnham go on half-time status to represent Davis but refused to commit LDF resources to assist her. He had come to believe that Burnham had attempted to defy his refusal to represent Davis by filing a case dealing with the conditions of her prison confinement in Manhattan without his approval. Apparently discovering legal papers Burnham had prepared that indicated affiliation with LDF, Greenberg concluded that she was engaged in a surreptitious "effort to associate LDF publicly with the Angela Davis case." But in the prison case Burnham assisted a group of lawyers that included one former LDF staffer and a current staff member in whose involvement Greenberg eventually acquiesced because the suit involved constitutional terms of confinement instead of a defense of Davis's alleged crimes. And Burnham was vindicated, as the suit resulted in a difficult-to-get federal court order for Ms. Davis's transfer to the general prison population on the grounds that her solitary confinement was unconstitutional.[9]

Margaret Burnham continued for several months to work half-time at LDF while spending the rest of her day helping Davis, who was held in custody for sixteen months when California refused to admit her to bail; eventually Burnham joined the defense team that in 1973 won Davis's acquittal—by an all-white jury—of all charges stemming from the courthouse shootout.[10] Although the state had almost no direct evidence against Davis, the outcome plainly surprised Greenberg, but he wasn't alone—pretrial press reports had virtually convicted her. At the time of her arrest, President Nixon had lauded the FBI for apprehending a dangerous "terrorist." But long before her vindication, Greenberg had been badly stung by the staff dissension.

In his history of LDF Greenberg said that objections to his decision not to represent Davis reflected the desire of staff attorneys to "be seen as allies of the Black Panthers, students who tore campuses apart and paraded with rifles, draft resisters, and prisoners who fought jailers." He thought these activities "led to self-destruction" and reminded the lawyers that "those who live by the sword shall die by the sword." This characterization of the staff was unfair. Greenberg had weathered criticism of his decision to keep LDF away from certain left lawyers without losing his cool, but facing near unanimous in-house dissent over representing Davis must have been humiliating. In light of Davis's notoriety and the difficulty of a black Communist's being treated fairly by the judicial process without agile representation, Greenberg's stated reason for rejection of the case—lack of a constitutional claim that "LDF historically had addressed"—is not persuasive. LDF represented all manner of black public figures. In years when Muhammad Ali was reviled, Jonathan Shapiro (his draft evasion criminal case) and I (his right to box case) were Ali's lawyers. At the time, LDF was representing hundreds of convicted murderers. While Jack criticized the staff's attraction to the Panthers, whose image had a lot to do with armed resistance, he had authorized participation in the defense of party chairman Bobby Seale for his role in demonstrations at the 1968 Democratic Party convention. Five of us, including Jack himself, would be named in a letter signed by Seale and Huey P. Newton stating, "Words cannot express our thanks and gratitude for the fervor and political and legal acumen that you devoted."[11]

Why an accused Angela Davis was so very different was hard to grasp, if it wasn't the Communist label attached to her.

Months later, an LDF board committee announced a policy covering cases the staff could appropriately take on. In a thinly masked reference to the charges against Davis, the LDF statement rejected views of "racial separatism," even if held sincerely, as well as violence that would "undermine the law courts and the legal system." But the specific policy would actually have permitted representation of Davis if her case affected the legal rights of blacks or if she had substantial claims and no lawyers to raise them. Burnham had met with William T. Coleman, LDF's president, leading Philadelphia lawyer, and secretary of transportation during the Gerald Ford administration, to explain her position and thought she might have convinced him that Davis was an appropriate LDF client. At the board meeting adopting the anti-Davis policy statement, however, Coleman "observed that Angela Davis had five lawyers and eleven black law professors on her defense team. Tony Amsterdam"—who had tried to obtain her release on bail—"also assisted in her defense."[12]

Soon after helping defend Davis, Burnham moved to Boston, where she had a successful career as a practitioner before Governor Michael

Dukakis of Massachusetts appointed her to a judgeship in 1978. Later she was named director of the National Conference of Black Lawyers, a new African American bar association, and subsequently became a full-time law teacher. Derrick Bell would write in 1976 that staff lawyers regarded the unwillingness to represent Davis as "an unconscionable surrender to conservative contributors," but he failed to explain why LDF had so often been able to disregard these unnamed "conservative contributors." He also claimed that because of the controversy "a few lawyers resigned"—a statement that appears to be in error.[13] Burnham formally left the fund when she returned east, feeling that Greenberg didn't want her to stay, but I could find no other LDF attorney who resigned because of the Davis affair.

It was not difficult for me to decide which position I would have supported had I still been an LDF staff member, but I certainly felt fortunate in being almost totally disengaged from the controversy by my new teaching duties at Columbia Law School. I respected Greenberg's leadership but I also felt that, like many of his generation, he had a blind spot when it came to a civil rights figure allied with the Communist Party. To me it was the Communist factor, not the views of contributors, that explained his actions. He probably believed my generation had its own blind spot about the risks of associating civil rights activism with membership in the Communist Party, but any doubts I might have had were smothered by having seen the harm done to Martin Luther King Jr., the credibility of the Kennedy administration, and indeed the civil rights movement as a whole by the FBI's fraudulent hunt for Communists in the SCLC.

Jack had come into civil rights work when the NAACP and LDF were at great pains to deny the charges of Communist conspiracy trumped up by segregationists to taint the movement. Civil rights workers were extremely vulnerable to such attacks in the 1950s, and the NAACP had to walk a fine line to deal with them, maintaining its liberal stance toward civil liberties while distancing itself from the Party. (There had been disturbing rumors, for example, that Thurgood Marshall had agreed to furnish J. Edgar Hoover with information about movement figures he thought were Communists.) In 1963 Martin King had asked for the resignation of an employee that the FBI had identified as having Communist ties because "in these critical times we cannot afford to risk any such impressions." With the LDF board's support, Greenberg refused to collaborate in the representation of 1964 Mississippi Freedom Summer rights workers if the National Lawyers' Guild—from which Thurgood Marshall had resigned—became involved.[14]

Not only had Davis used her Party affiliation for full media shock value, but the involvement of John Abt, at one time the Party's general counsel, was a reminder of how fears of Communist affiliation and subsequent use of it to smear civil rights organizations could become a major distraction. To Burnham, Greenberg's claim that Davis had little support in the black community proved him to be "totally out of touch." Davis support committees around the country (and the world) had raised significant amounts to pay for her defense and generated an outpouring of petitions and letters demanding her release. Greenberg found evidence of a lack of black support when the Davis defense refused to permit the trial to be transferred to Oakland or San Francisco, where there was a substantial chance of a jury with black members, and opted instead for a trial in San Jose, in Santa Clara County, "an upper-class suburban area where the residents were people like our staff lawyers."[15] He was arguing in effect that Davis was not a legitimate black leader because she thought she faced hostility in a black working-class community. But it was obvious that the state's lawyers would have successfully objected to a trial in Oakland, the home base of the Panthers, and, in fact, court papers establish that the Davis defense team had vigorously sought a change of venue to San Francisco County, whose population was about 15 percent black. The trial court ultimately ordered the trial held in Santa Clara County, where the population was less than 2 percent black and contained many more poor Latinos.

For Burnham, Davis was not only a longtime friend but an eloquent fighter against racism who proclaimed her innocence; her political affiliation was secondary. When Davis insisted that the weapons used in the shootout had been stolen from her house, Burnham believed her. Obviously Greenberg did not.

I could appreciate the pressures faced by both Greenberg and Burnham. Ever since 1966, I'd found myself increasingly muddled by the way the civil rights movement had developed and was perceived. Just when it was time for the movement to broaden to the North and deepen to firmly connect race and class, traditional civil rights forces suffered their own outbreak of racism. SNCC acted to purge whites from the ranks of people working in the South for integration—a devastating symbolic blow to what had been a biracial compact—and joined what would become a decades-long war fought by both right and left against liberalism. SNCC chose as leader Stokely Carmichael, whose calls for Black Power were widely understood to refer as much to hostility to whites as to black pride. Malcolm X, assassinated in 1965 by followers of Elijah Muhammad, his former Muslim mentor, was a complicated figure whose racist reputation among whites stopped far short of revealing a full picture of the man; but it is undeniable that his appeal to northern blacks, based largely on his utter mistrust of whites' intentions, rivaled Martin Luther King's.

Beginning in the Watts neighborhood of Los Angeles and continuing in city after city, urban riots displayed the vicious consequences of disparities between whites and blacks in money, opportunity, and power. In the most common scenario, police officers killed a black man after some typical inner-city confrontation—apprehension of a criminal, stopping a driver for a traffic violation, or just a lethal misunderstanding. Then the neighborhood responded by burning and looting businesses and savagely beating and sometimes killing any whites in the vicinity. Soldiers or police moved in and shot the rioters, bringing a measure of order to burned-out city neighborhoods. Officials then lamented the violence, demanded that it cease, but also called attention to legitimate community demands for more government financial assistance and private investment. Some people said we had to understand about ghetto poverty and despair; more insisted on punishment. It took years for the scenario, like some viral epidemic, to run its course.

Although violation of civil rights or longstanding perception of grievances often lit the fuse, no one could confuse the rioters with the largely peaceful southern demonstrators.

These developments, played out in a nation that was at war in Asia against a nonwhite country and at times seemed to be at war against colored people in its own cities, were bound to change life at LDF. I found the impact marginal but still painful. One of my colleagues was put down by another in a way that persuaded her that she had basically been disrespected because she was white. Recently hired white and black lawyers seemed to hang out more often with colleagues of their own race than staff members had done in the past. A black lawyer I'd worked with for years made what I thought was a pejorative reference to me in a fund-raising talk that I hoped he intended as a joke but I was not really sure. Notice my use of "persuaded," "seemed," "not really sure." I hope I am not usually given to so much equivocation, but here it is necessary because for me the essential quality of the experience was ambiguity, if not denial.

My wife got it immediately. "You are upset that things are different," she informed me authoritatively, and added, "I don't think you even know you are suffering that the feeling at the office is no longer 'all for one and one for all,' that there is less putting aside individual predilections for social consensus. I wonder if deep down you feel you are being held accountable for what white America does."

If it was true, I found it hard to admit to her or anyone else. Alienation was acceptable for the average disillusioned white liberal who naively expected the road to brotherhood to be paved with good intentions but not for *me*—after all, I was a *professional*. Hence the qualifiers. To be sure, exhausted from day-in-day-out stressful litigation, I had a growing sense that there was a limit to the number of years I should spend in a job that often had to be performed in a fishbowl atmosphere, one in which the throttle was always out full bore. I had also come increasingly to deal with literal life-and-death issues.

But while I could leave LDF, I couldn't leave the work. That's why in 1970 I finally accepted an offer to join the faculty at Columbia Law School and left the job I once thought I would have for the duration to start a legal clinic for the poor.

Larger issues than Jack Greenberg's leadership and my career plans were lurking in the Davis controversy—issues of LDF strategy that were never fully aired, perhaps because the case combined a notorious public figure, the almost always wild card of communism, and political violence.

How far should LDF go in risking its legal firepower and credibility with persons in positions of power by representing black separatists, some of whom were plainly understood on the streets of black America as standing for "Get Whitey"? One could honor the LDF board for tackling the question without finding that the policy it adopted provided much guidance.

Why shouldn't LDF, as Derrick Bell kept urging, rely less on integration and begin to develop alternatives to promote equality in education? When I read the 1976 article in which he claimed that civil rights lawyers were captured by the need to keep their (mostly white) contributors happy and too often refused to listen to clients who cared little about integration, and especially busing of blacks for integration, I thought it overstated both problems.[16] But, as always, Derrick had a point. LDF did seem to hold itself remote from the problems plaguing the black poor when it automatically gave priority to integration as a remedy for the ills of poor and working-class black neighborhoods.

In the Davis affair, the LDF board's answer unmistakably rejected separatism and violence, but the specifics were few and limited understandably to the controversy before it: Jack's authority to decide litigation priorities was confirmed. LDF could represent Black Power advocates under certain circumstances but it was committed to integration; Greenberg symbolized this stance in his person, record, skill, and links to Thurgood Marshall and *Brown v. Board.* Some observers noted that under his leadership LDF had in fact done a great deal to support a wide range of black political opinion, from Black Muslims to Panthers to members of SNCC as well as the NAACP, and an equally wide range of clients, from criminals to schoolchildren, blue-collar workers, and ministers, when it had positively evaluated their legal claims. But this record just made it all the more difficult to understand Greenberg's adamancy in refusing to represent Angela Davis. Still I wasn't surprised when the staff accepted the board's decision and the organization continued to play its role in hundreds of pending lawsuits without disruption. School desegregation, employment discrimination, and appeals of the death penalty dominated the docket. LDF held a unique place in presiding over efforts to reform American society through legal action, and no one knew this better than staff lawyers. The Davis case had chipped but hardly broken my faith in the quality of LDF organizational life.

When the white leadership issue came to the fore again, I was a decade away from LDF and to me the controversy bordered on the surreal. During the 1970s I had been earning my living running the poverty law clinic at Columbia with Philip Schrag and teaching criminal procedure at the law school as well as a course that had been bequeathed to me by Telford Taylor, a retiring faculty member, in which law students autopsied important constitutional law cases to learn the tactics and strategies used by the actual lawyers. But my most important duty was developing a program to train clinic students, who Philip and I hoped would ultimately go on to work for legal services offices or advocacy groups such as LDF, the ACLU, and the host of new organizations cropping up everywhere but especially in Washington. I was but a few subway stops from LDF's Columbus Circle office, but the intensity of my new work forced me to keep my distance, except when (as in 1972) I argued one of my old LDF cases before the Supreme Court or consulted on pending litigation. Like Amaker, Bell, and Clark—all of whom also became law teachers—I found that time away from day-to-day LDF practice soon made me just another (very) interested alumnus. A new generation of LDF lawyers seemed to be remarkably well trained in civil rights law in comparison with the little available when I was in school, a testament to the fact that now hundreds of such courses were being taught by teachers who had been on the firing line themselves, and to the wealth of work-study opportunities made available by the new clinical programs.

In 1979 the president of Northeastern University gave me the opportunity to run a whole law school devoted to making work-study training the heart of its curriculum, not just an elective course for a few, as it had been at Columbia. A lifelong New Yorker, I was still getting used to more sedate Boston and Cambridge ways when the drama began to be played out at the Harvard Law School. It is no accident that when screenwriters or novelists want to put a character in law school, they almost always choose Harvard. Other schools also have fine faculties and lavish benefactors, but Harvard is where modern legal education began, the school that sends more graduates to the high courts and sought-after teaching jobs than any other. Regardless of the ebb and flow of magazine ratings, which usually place it behind Yale and Stanford, it has the elite franchise sewn up. When Americans think law or law school, they usually think Harvard.

It didn't matter all that much, therefore, that the controversy took shape as a mostly symbolic matter, cut off from any real consequence to the lives of black Americans. Even if there hadn't been signs of typical academic intrigue, it would have captured attention. This was Harvard.

In 1983, with Derrick Bell gone to become the dean of the Oregon Law School, Harvard Law School's dean, James Vorenberg, invited Greenberg and J. LeVonne (Julius) Chambers, an experienced and effective North Carolina black lawyer who had shared an office with me for a year at LDF, to teach a course on civil rights law during the school's three-week intensive winter term. At the time Harvard Law's faculty had one black man and one white woman, and the school's failure to hire more minority and female faculty was an open sore to many students and to some members of a faculty that was increasingly divided along political lines. Still, Jim Vorenberg, a great public lawyer himself, couldn't have predicted the hornet's nest he had disturbed by simply hiring two extraordinarily qualified lawyers to share a teaching platform.

With the announcement of the course, the Black Law Students' Association and the Third World Coalition quickly organized a boycott on the grounds that only a black teacher could bring a full understanding of American racism to the classroom. Greenberg, student leaders complained in widely disseminated statements, could not serve as a role model for black students. They claimed, without elaborating, that Greenberg and Chambers were committed to "civil rights goals of the 1950s" and were unable to question LDF "litigation priorities."[17]

Derrick Bell, by far the most influential black law professor in the country, lent his support to the students. A single black but about thirty whites eventually took the course, although, according to Greenberg, students of both races came to him to indicate that only fear kept them from enrolling. Bell, who later returned to Harvard to teach, opened another front when he argued that Greenberg "should long since have recognized the symbolic value of his position to the black community and turned over the leadership post [at LDF] to a black lawyer."

For me, as I watched these events from across the river in the dean's office of Northeastern—which, like every other law school, had its own struggles over how to diversify the faculty—the boycott and the raw conflict between my former colleagues indicated how much poison had leeched into the system. In a conflict remote from concerns of most Americans, here were two of the nation's premier civil rights figures locked in a nasty public dispute that turned on whether race would decide who would play a leadership role. There were meaningful ways to debate LDF's priorities and the leadership needs of civil rights activists, but this hardly seemed a promising occasion to do so.

Worse, the spat took place at a time when the Reagan Justice Department's civil rights division under William Bradford Reynolds was urging the courts to take the narrowest view possible of federal rights laws. The department argued that the Internal Revenue Service lacked the authority to deny tax exemption to racially discriminatory schools, tried to reopen fifty-one court decrees in affirmative action cases, and supported increasing the proof required of black plaintiffs while making it easier for states that had previously discriminated to avoid submitting electoral schemes for the Justice Department's approval, as required by the Voting Rights Act. The Reagan administration was putting in place the strategy that would end in the resegregation of many public schools. It even opposed voluntary affirmative action agreements that had been freely negotiated by school boards and employers.[18] In his one term as president, Jimmy Carter had named thirty-seven blacks to the federal bench; in two terms Reagan's total would be fewer than ten.

Hostility radiated out of Washington, yet we were devouring our own. Derrick was a gentle and considerate man with many white friends. He and I had never lost touch, and when we got together we found there was no need to list our policy differences. Even when I thought he had taken a wrong path, I admired him for acting on his beliefs and for doing so as a teacher— acting with a view to educating those who were watching. In a relentless yet heroic way he had taken up the responsibilities of the "talented tenth," the "exceptional men" who long ago W. E. B. Du Bois believed might guide the race away from the impact of slavery and segregation; certainly by personal courage and resolve he had earned the right to have his protests taken seriously. His scholarship, including the first rigorous text dealing with American race law, had been a source of inspiration to thousands of students and he had served as the model for many a successful academic career.

He had long been critical of Greenberg's leadership, but in this fight he seemed to be permitting himself to be misunderstood as arguing that only an African American could properly teach civil rights law and only an African American could direct a civil rights organization. Not only did I think both notions nonsense, I found them personally insulting. To be sure, Derrick argued that the student action was a protest against a faculty hiring policy, not really a comment on Greenberg's ability to impart the law, and it was merely the right time for Jack to step down. Christopher Edley Jr., another Harvard law professor, tried to accommodate both sides with a more moderate line by arguing in the *Washington Post* that the issue wasn't whether Greenberg could teach an excellent course—anyone who disagreed with that was "stupid"—but whether in a still bifurcated society race could be considered at all in making teaching appointments.[19] Unfortunately, the parties to the dispute communicated through the media, no longer directly with each other, and the message, if this was the message, got garbled. To the world outside Cambridge, these events were all about racial exclusion.

With all the press coverage, it was easy at first to put the boycott down to personal animosity between Bell and Greenberg derived from twenty years of policy differences, and perhaps was a legacy of disputes between Greenberg and Derrick's longtime friend Bob Carter. Or to see the Harvard students as a bunch of spoiled brats who, totally secure about their own job prospects with a Harvard Law degree, could afford to promote a media frenzy to show up their own dean and faculty. When they treated Greenberg as an object or a symbol and not as an individual, however, their actions were similar to those of the racists they detested.

Along the same lines, they acted as if a lawyer as knowledgeable as Julius Chambers, who was sharing the platform with Greenberg and was then the corporate president of LDF, simply did not count. In a way, Julius had more front-line civil rights credentials than anyone else involved. Founder of a successful integrated law firm in Charlotte, he was Mr. Civil Rights to the whole state of North Carolina and the main force behind the desegregation of the Charlotte schools. His life had been threatened and his house and car bombed as a consequence of his activism. In a letter to the *Civil*

Liberties Review Derrick had called Greenberg a "self-appointed, contemporary abolitionist" operating out of a New York City "plantation penthouse"; even the unflappable Chambers—a man whose career rested on a capacity for firm but quiet resolve—had had enough. He deplored the "personal attack." LDF believed in school integration even if Bell did not. There was no evidence that contributors had dictated LDF's decision in the Davis case or in an earlier unwillingness (another charge) to file a brief in a case involving efforts in the Georgia legislature to unseat Julian Bond because of his statements against the Vietnam War. LDF had represented plenty of political dissidents, including Black Panthers and even Ms. Davis in a suit over prison conditions. According to Chambers, Bell had even misstated a Bible reference: James 2:17. He reminded Derrick that the passage dealt with the need to join faith with works and that LDF was black America's "finest embodiment" of the principle.[20]

Criticism of the students was powerful, but I couldn't quite rest with it. While the students were totally off the mark in going after Greenberg and treating Chambers as a nonperson, they were trying to achieve something in which they had a legitimate interest. There was an obvious connection between "race-conscious measures . . . to increase minorities' political and economic power" and remedy past discrimination, as the New York lawyer Jonathan Feldman later put it, and "strengthening minority leadership," as in the presence of minority faculty on the Harvard Law School faculty.

There is a long tradition of Harvard law teachers, both white and black, who are both brilliant lawyers and brilliant publicists, among them Charles Ogletree, Arthur Miller, Alan Dershowitz, Randall Kennedy, and Laurence Tribe. With Derrick's support, the students were apparently taking a page out of the faculty's book in using the boycott as a way to get their message across. And because events that occur at Harvard will be noticed when similar occurrences elsewhere are ignored, the press went for the bait big time.

Effective marketing maybe, but what meanness, and misdirection. It wasn't a question of being respectful of Jack Greenberg's contributions to civil rights law—though that would have been appropriate—but the scenario was played out without any serious evaluation of LDF or of Jack's leadership aside from the fact that he was white. It had been composed largely of slogans. I realized that I had been looking forward to a debate about LDF's priorities ever since the Davis affair, even though my own tentative conclusion was that there was little more a centralized organization of lawyers could do to facilitate social change but file suit when it had a viable case.

Two years later Greenberg moved on to a teaching job at his alma mater, Columbia Law School. Later he served as dean of Columbia College. He was not forced out. After thirty-five years at LDF, twenty-four of them as director-counsel, he simply thought it was time to leave. His successors, first Julius Chambers and later Elaine Jones, LDF's effective Washington lobbyist, and then Ted Shaw, Jones's deputy, were all black, all formidable legal figures. They had a lifetime involvement with the organization but none of them would have been selected as director-counsel had they been white. No matter the situation in 1961, it would have been a mistake to choose a white person to run LDF in 1985, when numerous qualified blacks were available, when the overriding civil rights issue was (as it still is) mobilizing the African American community. But it was just plain bigotry to hassle Jack Greenberg because of his race when he was clearly a brilliant choice as a civil rights law teacher—that I knew from personal experience.

The boycott, then, was an artifact of stereotypical racist thinking. Only members of your own group can understand, empathize, point the way, and be trusted. The most knowledgeable civil rights lawyer in the country was being told to keep out of a classroom because of Harvard Law School's agonizingly slow movement toward increasing minority faculty. I was not much concerned about the offense to Greenberg—his place in history was secure. While every lawyer who was ever in the same room with Martin Luther King has claimed to have represented him, it was Greenberg—and LDF—that King asked time and time again to do his most important legal work. But when law students and law professors refuse to make distinctions between people on the basis of who they are, we are back to the same process of othering that created segregation in the first place and then hardened it into law. It was more than accidental, I thought, that some faculty members at my school, Northeastern, actually opposed certain African American teaching candidates not because of their race but because of their politics. Was I looking at the future?

As long as housing, schooling, and political power were racially bifurcated, blacks weren't always going to cherish whites' assistance, no matter how well it was meant. But it was just too easy to turn frustration with lack of change on the streets of the black community against white liberals. Dim recognition of this fact must have figured in my own decision to leave the LDF for Columbia Law School a decade earlier, in fear that I wouldn't be listened to for reasons other than what I had to say. Apparently history was no protection. No matter whether you, like Greenberg, had been one of the lawyers in *Brown v. Board of Education* and had over three decades on the firing line, young people were going to ask, "What have you done for me lately?" The tragedy, of course, is that the nation's racial problems are certainly not black problems or even white problems but our problems, and as long as we fail to claim them, we're going to stay stuck with them.

Unfortunately, the leadership conflicts that began with Angela Davis's notoriety and a tangential extradition case and a decade later focused on the teaching of a civil rights course at Harvard had been too crude to permit anyone to learn much from them. There had been an opportunity on both occasions to talk more explicitly about LDF's future growth and development, whether the organization should or could change its approach, but nobody had done so. The result of the flap over the civil rights course differed not at all from what happened in 1970.

Apparently, aside from Derrick Bell and a number of his academic followers in what would be called the critical race theory movement, LDF had few critics who offered specific correctives—which meant that either it was doing a splendid job or what it was doing was no longer all that important. Certainly civil rights issues themselves had a shorter shelf life, except for such hot-button matters as affirmative action. Theodore (Ted) M. Shaw, who succeeded Elaine Jones as LDF director-counsel in 2004, had said some years earlier that 1980 marked "the end of a period in which civil rights litigation was viewed expansively and offensively and [the beginning of] another in which by necessity it was viewed less expansively and defensively."[21] Increasingly, system-challenging racial litigation was harder to bring and harder still to win; fewer people with the power to do something about it really cared about finding a way to change the ghetto or to make eradicating the consequences of poverty a primary domestic policy issue.

But Harvard Law School apparently had been affected by the student protest. A few years later it invited Bell back on the faculty and soon thereafter began to hire black law teachers in greater numbers. For some years the new professors were all male, however, so the change failed to satisfy my old officemate. In 1992, when the university insisted that Bell return to full-time teaching after two years of protest against failure to hire a black woman teacher, Derrick would depart Harvard for good.

Me and Muhammad

IN troubled years of war and riot, I had one case that lightened the heart, eased my burden, and gave me hope of at least a symbolic victory over the increasingly bad news.

My involvement actually had roots deep in childhood. My father had early on conveyed a cynical notion about his boxing bets, which, unlike his other gambles, were almost always profitable. Making money from gambling was notable in itself for a man whose loyalty to games of chance was so great that his bookmaker gave him Christmas presents.

"Look at the fighter's record," he instructed me, "and ask yourself whether, if the guy you like wins, will there be a lucrative rematch. If the answer is yes, then bet him. If not, pass up the fight or bet his opponent."

Boxing didn't much interest me so I never "liked" any fighter, but for a time in the 1950s I followed any sport my father had taken up. When he started betting on boxing, I had to learn something about it. One way to learn was to read copies of *Ring* magazine at the local barbershop and then listen with him to the frenetic Friday-night radio broadcasts of boxing matches from Madison Square Garden. This way I collected gym lore about the leading champions of the time—Willie Pep, Sugar Ray Robinson, Joe Walcott—as well as about dozens of leading contenders. Someday, I supposed, I might have to support myself by figuring out which boxer's victory would lead to the big rematch. Little did I know how my store of boxing trivia would come in handy.

By the time I first heard of Cassius Clay, as Muhammad Ali was then called, my father was dead and his gambling lectures were long forgotten. Ever since Ali turned professional, shortly after winning the 1960 Olympic light heavyweight title in Rome, his life has been chronicled like that of a head of state. He was news then and as the press-declared best-known face on the planet he is news now—though even with the publication of adoring biographies by Thomas Hauser and David Remnick and Mark Kram's Ali-battering *Ghosts of Manila,* curiously little has been said about his epic courtroom struggle to return to the ring after being banned during the Vietnam War.[1]

From the beginning Ali stood out, even in the hype-driven promotional world of boxing. He made outrageous victory predictions, called himself "the greatest," and delivered his doggerel verses to an eager audience. By 1964, when Ali knocked out the heavyweight champion and overwhelming favorite, Sonny Liston, in the seventh round of his first championship fight, I had been at LDF for three years and thought of him less as a fighter than as a racial icon. If Joe Louis, the heavyweight champion of my father's generation, presented to the white world a vision of patience and restraint mixed with the superhuman strength of the good, loyal black man beloved of white mythology, Ali was at turns the irreverent voice of a court jester and the symbol of a liberated race that would be defined only on its own terms. Louis gracefully occupied the place he had been given; Ali was out to seize his. Naturally, whites couldn't figure him out. Was he serious or just putting his audience on?

At first the underdog Olympian's brashness seemed just the freshness of youth, but soon enough the man and his image, like the 1960s themselves, turned problematic and contradictory for most Americans. When Cassius Clay became Muhammad Ali, an outspoken proponent of Elijah Muhammad's separatist Lost Found Nation of Islam, his popularity among whites plummeted. The Nation of Islam was feared by those who understood its message as condemnation of the entire white race—Satan, murderers, thieves—but while Ali often praised Elijah Muhammad, he rarely if ever repeated a message of hate.

Like every other well-known racial figure of the time, Ali soon came to our professional attention at the Legal Defense Fund. His local draft board in Louisville, Kentucky, had earlier classified him as unacceptable for military service because of a low score on a mental acuity test. Two years later the selective service system was told to increase the number of young men available for Vietnam War service and it lowered the passing grade on the intelligence test. Along with thousands of others, Ali was reclassified 1A, or fit for service. He complained that he hadn't been given any warning of the shift and appeared before his draft board to claim for the first time that he was a conscientious objector who had "no personal quarrel with those

VietCongs."[2] He also sought exemption from a 1A classification because he was the sole support of his mother, had to pay alimony to his former wife, and because military service would cause him serious financial loss—"I may never be able to overcome this time of loss of boxing sharpness and come back from the service and earn the kind of money required to pay off these financial obligations."[3]

Along with these grounds, the core of Ali's claim—that his religion taught him "not to take part in any war with infidels or any nonreligious group"—was rejected by the local board as well as an appeal board. The matter was forwarded to the Department of Justice and referred to an independent investigator—Lawrence Grauman, a retired Kentucky judge—for evaluation. Grauman reviewed the evidence and concluded that Ali was of good character, sincere in his claim of eligibility for exemption on religious grounds, and legally entitled to it.[4]

Despite the strength of Judge Grauman's recommendation, no one was surprised when lawyers at the Justice Department ignored it, concluding that Ali's beliefs were based on political and racial doctrines, not religious or ethical precepts. According to the DOJ, Ali opposed only certain wars, not war in all its forms, because he excepted a holy war to defend Islam from his general condemnation.

Ali's lawyer at the time was a legendary figure in legal circles named Hayden Covington. As the counsel to the Watchtower Bible and Tract Society (the Jehovah's Witnesses), Covington was as familiar as any lawyer in the United States with the labyrinthine regulations governing religious exemptions from selective service. Between 1939 and 1963 he had appeared as the Witnesses' attorney in 111 Supreme Court cases.[5] In fact, largely through Covington's efforts the Witnesses held a unique place in American constitutional law. Their practice of door-to-door proselytizing and refusal to serve in the armed forces had spawned hundreds of selective service appeals and successful challenges to local regulation of speech and religion.

Covington had increasingly prevailed in these cases. At first the Supreme Court turned away many of the Witnesses' claims, but as new justices appointed by Franklin Roosevelt developed confidence in their more expansive view of the First Amendment, judicial attitudes changed. The key case was one in which the Court reversed—despite wartime passions—a three-year-old precedent that permitted public schools to require children to salute the American flag, viewed by the Witnesses as a blasphemous bowing to a graven image.[6] Despite involvement in such epochal cases, Covington was hardly a sophisticated constitutional advocate. But he did have custody of important cases in which the conflict in values between the Constitution and local political and police officials was manifest, and he knew how to frame constitutional questions that would attract the Court's interest. In the United States, in contrast to some other countries, a lawyer needs no special expertise or credentials beyond admission to the bar to seek review of a case before the highest court in the land.

Covington's influence on Ali's increasingly complicated legal situation could be seen in August 1966, when he added a claim of the sort that the Witnesses often employed, asking the selective service system to consider Ali exempt from military service because he was a "minister" of the Lost Found Nation of Islam.[7] Despite Judge Grauman's finding that Ali's beliefs were sincere, this sort of claim — that the heavyweight champion was also a full-time man of God — brought out the knives of even more editorial writers.[8]

The press had paid enough attention to Ali's efforts to avoid induction to call forth mountains of hate mail and adverse editorial comment across the nation: he was both affiliated with the reviled and feared Muslims and a draft dodger — by definition an unpatriotic American — not to mention a provocative and assumably rich black public figure. He was called a coward and a traitor. The storm of criticism receded somewhat while Covington bought delay with administrative appeals but it broke out anew on April 28, 1967, when Ali declined to take the traditional step forward to signify his acceptance of induction into the armed services.

Edwin Dooley, the chairman of the New York State Athletic Commission, was a defeated Republican officeholder who had wangled his job regulating boxing from Governor Nelson Rockefeller by threatening to run as a spoiler, splitting the GOP vote in a New York congressional election. Within hours of Ali's refusal of induction Dooley announced that the commission had lifted the champ's license. Preening before reporters, he declared that Ali could no longer box in the state and that New York no longer regarded him as heavyweight champion. There was no notice, no hearing, no waiting for the formalities of trial and conviction; just the commission's conclusion that licensing a man who refused induction was "detrimental to the best interests of boxing."[9] You can get a measure of Ali's unpopularity and the level of racial tension in 1967 from the fact that within days, even before he was actually convicted, almost every important state boxing commission in the nation had followed Dooley's lead. Ali was barred from fighting throughout the United States.

Indictment and trial followed with lightning speed. By June, Ali had been convicted and given the maximum sentence of five years in prison and a $10,000 fine by a Texas federal judge, Joe Ingraham.[10] He had moved to Houston and transferred his selective service file to a local draft board, in part because of the supposed liberal orientation of the Fifth Circuit Court of Appeals, which would have ultimate jurisdiction over any criminal case. Covington's defense strategy was to preserve the conscientious objector claim but also to urge federal courts to stop the classification and induction of blacks until they were represented on local selective service boards in proportion to their percentage of the population (0.2 percent of local Kentucky draft board members were black, even though blacks accounted for 7 percent of the population; the situation was just as bad in Texas, where 12.4 percent of the population but only 1.1 percent of the members of selective service boards were black). Hoping the boards would be treated like trial juries, Covington aimed at getting Ali's induction postponed while the issue of Negro board members was litigated. It was a serious miscalculation: no federal judge was going to block conscription of a sizable proportion of the eligible population on any theory, much less this one.

Another tactic was to seek extensive disclosure of selective service documents and records in Ali's case to search for evidence of prejudice. A subpoena sought statements by General Lewis B. Hershey, the director of selective service, and Representative Mendel Rivers, chair of the House Armed Services Committee.[11] Rivers had threatened congressional action if Ali was deferred; Hershey had made an unusual public statement predicting that the conscientious objector petition would not be granted.[12] If the subpoena was upheld, the defense would have factual ammunition for its arguments; if it was quashed, the defense would at least have an issue to appeal.

But the Fifth Circuit rejected these and all other claims raised by a new team of lawyers, including such high-profile movement attorneys as Charles Morgan and Howard Moore of Atlanta. The judges pointed out that under established law the court could reverse the conviction only if Ali's classification was without basis in fact. In other words, even if the evidence favored Ali on his conscientious objector claim, he could lose because Congress had given the courts very limited room to review what draft boards did when they classified registrants. Regular or duly ordained ministers were exempt from service but the law was meant to protect leaders of religions, not members. Ali's claim that he spent 90 percent of his time as a minister had been supported by 43 affidavits and the signatures of 3,612 persons who had participated in his ministry, but the court ruled against him largely because he had listed his vocation as a professional boxer, never claiming he was a minister, until after he had been reclassified. The court also ruled that there was sufficient evidence for a draft board to conclude that he didn't fall within the legal definition of a conscientious objector.[13]

That would ordinarily have ended Ali's hopes of avoiding prison, but while his final appeal was pending before the United States Supreme Court, one of those unpredictable events took place that have marked the boxer's public life. Erwin Griswold, former dean of Harvard Law School, who as solicitor general represented the United States before the Court, informed the justices that defendants in a number of pending cases, including Ali's, had been the subjects of potentially illegal wire tapping by the FBI. Because Ali had been a party to five calls that had been intercepted by taps on phones used by Elijah Muhammad and Martin Luther King, the Court sent his case back to the lower courts to decide whether the taps had gathered illegally obtained evidence that affected the draft-dodging conviction.[14] If it were not for this reprieve, Ali's conviction would undoubtedly have been affirmed and he would have been sent to federal prison to serve his sentence.

During the months that followed, Ali's Chicago business lawyer, Chauncey Eskridge, began for the first time to consider seriously LDF's offer to challenge the boxing ban. He'd held off, he told me, fearing that if Ali did start fighting, pressures from organized veterans' groups would make it more likely that a judge would send him to prison. Four months after the Supreme Court sent the case back to him, Judge Ingraham decided the conversations tapped by the FBI contained innocuous materials that had nothing to do with Ali's conviction for draft evasion and thus upheld it.[15] Feeling he had nothing to lose, Ali decided to follow Eskridge's advice and agreed to a court challenge to restore his license. Attitudes toward the war were shifting, he thought; more to the point, perhaps, after almost three years of inactivity he was running out of money.

In November 1969 we went to federal court in New York against Commissioner Dooley while other lawyers once again appealed the criminal case to the fifth circuit.

By this time I had been at LDF for eight years and my responsibilities were equivalent to those of a partner in a private firm. Only three members of the legal staff had been there longer. (I even had a new title—first assistant counsel—which meant almost nothing in the egalitarian world of LDF.) It was therefore no surprise that the licensing case was totally in my hands or that I could arrange to be assisted by one of LDF's most tenacious young lawyers, Ann Wagner, a recent graduate of NYU Law School.

Ann had done research for LDF as a student and was willing to take whatever piecework she could find until a regular staff slot opened. She was intelligent and aggressive, but her most important qualification for this case was that she had helped put herself through law school by working in the New York courts sifting through records to determine whether alleged criminals showed sufficient community ties to warrant release on low bail. Ann was one of the few people who knew their way around New York's often arcane record-keeping system.

We decided that Ali's case would go nowhere in the state courts. They were clogged with cases and populated by too many judges chosen by political insiders for a controversial case like this, and so we filed in federal court. To win we would have to persuade a judge that Ali's constitutional rights had been denied by the New York State Athletic Commission. We could pick among a cluster of claims to raise but all were novel and there was very little in the way of precedent to back them up. The main ones—first, that refusing induction in the armed services on the grounds of conscience had no rational connection to the evils the commission was supposed to cure by licensing boxers; and second, that because the federal courts had permitted Ali to remain free while appealing his criminal conviction, the State of New York had no justifiable interest in keeping him from working while his appeal was pending—evolved from a criticism of the criminal justice system popular at the time. Restrictions on the ability of convicted criminals and former convicts increased the difficulty of rehabilitation; a national crime commission had recommended that such "civil disabilities" be limited to those that related closely to the crime committed by the offender—say, not letting a convicted embezzler be employed as a bank teller.[16]

Today many people doubt the effectiveness of efforts at rehabilitation, and that skepticism is used to justify an undifferentiated and often self-defeating punitiveness directed at persons convicted of crime. Federal law, for example, makes anyone who has been convicted of possessing or transferring drugs ineligible to receive a student loan, grant, or work assistance —a policy choice that, of course, makes it harder for ex-offenders to find remunerative work. Public-interest organizations struggling against the tide of this attitude, such as the New York–based Legal Action Center, point out that the vast majority of prisoners will return to their communities, and keeping them unemployed because employers hesitate to expand work opportunities for people with criminal records has drastic consequences.[17]

In 1969, however, I was less concerned with systemic reform that with Muhammad Ali's personal situation. Ann and I concluded that the lack of relationship between any valid regulatory purpose of the Athletic Commission and Ali's particular conduct exposed how clearly the government officials in question were out to get him. Commissioner Dooley was basking in a media spotlight turned on by Ali's fame, fear of anyone connected to the Black Muslims, and the brand of patriotism stirred up whenever anyone is accused of draft dodging.

Our other major argument was a long shot with very different origins. Reading the sports pages to learn how to follow my father's gambling strategies had taught me that many professional boxers not only had been brushed by the law, they had been squeezed hard by it. I couldn't at first remember the names and dates, but I was certain that felons and others involved with the criminal law had been commonly licensed to box in New York State. So why, I asked myself, not Ali?

Of course, making this unequal-treatment argument into a successful legal claim would take time: it depended on digging up facts showing exactly what the commission's licensing practices had been in the past, as well as on persuading a federal judge that any unequal treatment of the champ was serious enough to violate the Constitution. Because of Ali's financial crunch, Chauncey Eskridge pressed us to get Ali a license to fight before he was jailed. If we did that, we couldn't wait to develop the necessary facts for this claim but had to go ahead with our other arguments in the hope of getting a judge to order Ali's suspension illegal as a matter of law without the necessity of a full factual investigation.

When the case was filed, Marvin Frankel, a former Columbia Law teacher and LDF consultant and a close friend of Jack Greenberg's, was the judge randomly assigned to hear motions in the federal district court. We didn't think we could get a judge more well disposed to us than Frankel, so I quickly filed a motion for a preliminary injunction that if granted would get Ali a boxing license immediately. Judge Frankel had other ideas, however, and he quickly threw our claims out of court. The Supreme Court, he concluded, had often approved of denying state licenses to felons, and in a business so much given to corruption, state boxing commissions had broad discretion to decide what did and did not relate to the good character of its licensees.

But Frankel also saved us from defeat. In one of those technical moves that only a litigator can fully appreciate, before dismissing the case for good he gave us a chance to make a factual showing that the commission had been unlawfully selective and had taken criminal conviction into account only in respect to Muhammad Ali.

Ann took up residence for a time in the commission's dreary Manhattan offices, and what she discovered was so astonishing that Judge Walter

Mansfield, Frankel's successor on the case, condemned the state officials and enjoined them from denying Ali a license. It turned out that over the years state regulators had licensed at least 244 men who had criminal records, including murderers, rapists, burglars, robbers, and army deserters. Though the names of the men were not disclosed to protect their privacy, it was obvious that among them were both champions and highly rated contenders. Some had been licensed after indictment and before conviction; others after conviction but on appeal—Ali's current status—as well as while on parole or probation.

It didn't seem to matter. In fact, looking at these files led inevitably to the conclusion that the commission had never taken a negative view of involvement with the criminal law. No case could be found of anyone the commission had treated as it had treated Ali. It was all too plain that the commission had maliciously attempted to punish him for what he represented: the Muslim; the draft dodger; the self-defined, outrageously provocative black champion.

Judge Mansfield (a former Marine Corps major with an outstanding war record) did not, however, try to plumb motives. He found the commission's conduct unconstitutionally arbitrary and ordered it stopped.[18] A few weeks later, at my urging, Jack Greenberg called Louis Lefkowitz, the state attorney general, and persuaded him that New York State had no legal grounds to appeal, and no political interest in doing so, for that matter. Lefkowitz must have been moved by the overwhelming statistics Ann had gathered and by the intervention of Arthur Logan, a prominent black physician. Moreover, by 1970 the Vietnam War had another face. Politicians of all stripes were now coming out against it—they differed only in whom they blamed and how fast they wanted to get U.S. troops back to this country. To many Americans, Ali looked very different from the man vilified as unpatriotic in 1967.

Promoters quickly scheduled a Madison Square Garden warm-up with the journeyman heavyweight Oscar Bonavena, but Ali's real goal was the great payday that would follow an attempt to regain his crown from the current heavyweight champion, Joe Frazier. Still standing in his way was the five-year sentence handed down by Judge Ingraham in the criminal case.

Chauncey Eskridge had a habit of trying to deploy lawyers like a football coach shuttling substitutions in a search for the winning combination. As he focused on Ali's last chance to upset the criminal conviction in the Supreme Court, he changed lawyers again, bringing in an LDF staffer, Jonathan Shapiro, a Harvard graduate who had done civil rights work in

Mississippi before joining LDF. Shapiro pressed hard the notion that Ali's beliefs were of a more religious nature than others the Court had accepted as grounds for exemption and argued that his willingness to defend Islam was more a theological than practical reservation about war. But before the Court could consider Shapiro's theory once again, a concession from the United States came to Ali's aid. The solicitor general admitted that Ali's beliefs were founded on the basic tenets of the Muslim religion rather than on politics or race, as had been argued earlier, and that he was sincere in his beliefs. Since the local draft board had given no reason for denial of Ali's claim, there was no way of knowing which of the potential grounds it had actually relied upon. As two of the three justifications were now admitted to be invalid, the source of Ali's conviction might have been—no one could know—one of the illegal two. On this reasoning, the conviction was set aside.[19]

The theory applied by the Supreme Court had a respectable history but it hadn't always been used when it could have been. If Bob Woodward and Scott Armstrong's 1979 book, *The Brethren,* is correct, the original vote of the Court had come out 5 to 3 against Ali. But heeding the pleas of a law clerk, Justice John Harlan, a member of the majority, sequestered himself with background materials about the Black Muslims and after a period of study changed his vote. He now thought the government had misled draft boards as well as the courts by insisting that Ali's religious beliefs weren't authentically pacifist. According to Woodward and Armstrong, after he read an earlier draft of Harlan's opinion, Chief Justice Warren Burger told a clerk that Harlan had become "an apologist for the Black Muslims."[20]

It was a moderate justice, Potter Stewart, who pushed the "might have been illegal" solution as a way to persuade all the justices to reverse the conviction but not to expose the Court to criticism that its decision was a broad endorsement of Black Muslim racial and religious views as peace-loving.[21] Burger was relieved. Harlan went along. Ali won, and the country was spared the prospect of a deeply divisive imprisonment.

As for Ali–Frazier, the actual fight succeeded both as boxing match and as symbol of vindication. It was hugely profitable for the fighters and promoters. The fighters were paid $2.5 million each; ringside seats were $150; the gross was apparently close to $30 million—all records for the time, though today the numbers look puny.[22]

The two men soon seemed genuinely out to damage each other physically. Ali had viciously bad-mouthed Frazier before the fight, as chronicled in the Kram book, converting the story line from "Ali Returns" or even

"Christian versus Muslim" to "Black Hero against the Gorilla, the Uncle Tom." Instead of the old standby Great White Hope narrative line, we were dished up a politically tinged Black Brother fight. And Ali's trash talk injected a measure of spite between the two men that may have never truly disappeared.[23]

What struck me most forcefully about the fight was not the glitter of the celebrity crowd, garnished with an amazing display of fur-coated drug dealers, or the brilliantly and designer-dressed women, or the sea of rhetoric evoked in almost every journalist and writer who could snare a ticket, or even the Great Return, in which I could justly claim a significant role. No, the contest itself transcended the glamour surrounding it. The physical battle was furious. I had never seen a fight in person before and never wanted to see one again, but it was clear in a moment why so many of the writers quite lost themselves in effusion. Frazier was a force of nature. He just kept coming; nothing stopped him. Ali was his imaginative self, jabbing as he moved back and to the side to escape the full force of Frazier's blows, quickly sliding in his own. He was, as always, full of grace.

But Ali had been rusted by the years of inactivity and was not yet truly fit. Frazier was relentless, dedicated to his task despite the costs to his body. After fifteen brutal rounds he was justly awarded the decision.

Then as Ann and I stood around the Garden afterward, unable like many others to leave and too stunned by the impact of the fight to say much, I remembered my father's rule and realized that though this fight was certainly not fixed, once again he would have had the winner. Because Frazier had won, there would certainly be a rematch, and then another. The money would flow and all the clever gamblers would be happy.

The Complex World of Law Reform

W ITH schools finally being desegregated in the Deep South and a range of innovative court decisions across the social horizon, change through large-scale litigation still had its luster in the final years of the civil rights decade. Soon, however, such lawsuits would come under scrutiny for their limited impact on persistent patterns of poor schooling and for supposedly providing a costly distraction from the political work to be done in local communities, even as they became an effective tool for other groups demanding full inclusion in a society many felt kept them marginalized. Organized women's rights advocates, Hispanics, Native Americans, the disabled, welfare recipients, environmentalists, and consumers all began to use the courts and administrative agencies to enhance the rights of their constituents with remarkable frequency.

Lawyers for the poor, first funded by the new Office of Economic Opportunity (OEO) as part of Lyndon Johnson's War on Poverty, and suddenly aggressive welfare rights groups took on an epic struggle through administrative and court challenges to cause a crisis in the philosophy and funding of public assistance. Following the reasoning of the lawyer and teacher Edward Sparer, who has often been called "the father of poverty law," the tactic was to make government respect its own definitions of adequate support throughout the country, an approach it was thought would require either serious reform of the system or massive infusion of cash to the poor. As the first legal director of New York's Mobilization for Youth community organization and later when he founded the Welfare Law Center at Columbia University, Sparer sought to get rid of "tests for aid and exclusions from aid . . . unrelated to need" and ultimately win an entitlement—support on the basis of need.[1] At the same time, local welfare rights groups founded the feisty

148

and irreverent National Welfare Rights Organization (NWRO), led by George Wiley, a former civil rights official at CORE. The NWRO program broke with the past, arguing that its mostly black and Hispanic female members were entitled as a matter of right—not as a gift from a beneficent state—to guaranteed income and treatment with respect, whether or not they were working, because they were Americans. Surprisingly, this position had a libertarian cast: the multiple behavioral and job-seeking conditions attached to benefits might lead to desirable personal outcomes but, according to the NWRO, whether to abide by them was the business of the women, not the state.

The Supreme Court docket suddenly filled with cases brought by lawyers for Neighborhood Legal Services programs on behalf of welfare recipients, many dealing with the procedures government had to follow in dealing with the poor. "The establishment of OEO and nationwide federal funding initiated explosive growth in law reform work." In the eighty-nine years before the OEO, not one legal aid attorney took a case to the U.S. Supreme Court. In the first nine years of federally funded legal services, program attorneys "sponsored 164 cases" before the Court and won a majority of those accepted for review.[2]

The number of victories was significant, but the poverty lawyers badly misread the temper of the country and perhaps the nature of the problem. The Court eased the harshness of the welfare system, but the prize of converting public assistance benefits into a guaranteed income free of minute intrusion by the state would soon recede from view. The Supreme Court decisively rejected the goals of welfare rights in 1970 when the justices refused to enlarge the maximum grant available to a family when the number of children in the family increased. Then the Court ruled that a welfare recipient could be denied benefits if she refused to permit a caseworker to inspect her home and a year later decided that a state could pay a smaller benefit to children (disproportionately Hispanic and black) than to recipients who were aged, blind, or disabled (disproportionately white).[3] As welfare recipients (the term was fast becoming code for black or Hispanic, although the majority were white) made demands, white voters pushed back. Pejorative welfare-related imagery was commonly employed in public discussion, and Governor Ronald Reagan of California and the Nixon administration began a successful campaign that would continue for the rest of the century to starve poverty lawyers and emasculate their power to challenge the structure of government programs through class-action litigation.

A central feature of public assistance programs was the division in the public mind between government benefits for children, most of whose recipients resided in households headed by young women, which were "hated," as Linda Gordon puts it, "by the prosperous and the poor," and generally approved government help to the elderly, disabled, and other "worthy" groups.[4] Lawsuits could help diminish the gap between these two views of the world by contributing to the sense of crisis necessary for change. They could also raise basic issues of respect—the folly of granting benefits to children only if no adult male lived with them; of giving caseworkers general authority to search recipients' homes as a condition of support. But if, as students of poverty argued, only a systemic or structural fix would work, litigation, valuable as it could be, was a sideshow. Whether you believed the best way to fight poverty was, as most of Lyndon Johnson's Great Society programs assumed, to provide support services—job training, community organizations, legal resources—or it was better to end welfare by providing income transfers, as promoted by Richard Nixon's never-enacted Family Assistance Plan, lawsuits were clearly ancillary. Yet many lawyers, LDF staff among them, felt more comfortable in a role that privileged court challenges rather than designing legislative strategy or organizing a movement. It is not that these roles weren't filled but that too few people were available to play them. One of the unplanned consequences of the civil rights movement's amazing courtroom record of success was that such activity became what good lawyers aspired to do, even when, as with antipoverty policy, they might be more effective doing other things.

Raising the visibility of law reform or impact litigation, as it was sometimes called, naturally provoked public debate over its efficiency and political impact. Republican criticism of public funding for the legal services lawyers who sued government agencies would become a staple of the Washington budget season. On an organizational level, widespread use of rights-assertion techniques employed by African Americans inevitably made the black civil rights cause seem less exceptional and historically blessed. A muted rivalry for media attention and funding would follow. On the other hand, the wider application of movement strategies promised an America that would come to terms with the boundaries, economic, social, and cultural, that made many people feel victimized. Greenberg's efforts during the late 1960s to found ethnically oriented defense funds for Mexicans, Puerto Ricans, and Asians on the LDF model should be viewed in this light, but—a sign of the times—each group would soon go its own way and struggle to create a viable identity.

At the same time, less visible but perhaps more significant, politicians, policy makers, and bureaucrats were suddenly faced with decisions about how best to allocate limited resources among various groups clamoring for new government programs and vigorous enforcement of preexisting commitments. Title VI of the Civil Rights Act of 1964, for example, prohibited discrimination on the basis of race and national origin in programs receiving federal financial assistance. When this act was joined by similar legislation (and rights-creating court decisions) intended to eliminate discrimination on the basis of gender, age, and disabilities, the federal government was suddenly faced with a series of frustrating and politically sensitive decisions about how to spend limited enforcement dollars. Sharing the stage with other groups that perceived themselves as rights-deprived created tensions for me and other civil rights advocates who had invested in a powerful vision of the exceptional character of racial victimization. An analysis of the federal government's Title VI efforts would later find its effectiveness seriously hampered by random patterns of enforcement and by an absence of clarity about where to place priority in allocating resources.[5]

But the micro problem of rivalry over priority among groups of rights claimants was trivial compared to the macro problem that even as the use (and users) of reform litigation multiplied and achieved some success, it began to hit a wall of resistance. The undeniable sense of crisis that gripped the nation in the late Johnson and Nixon years was hardly conducive to a continuation of domestic liberal reforms. Deeply troubling was the growing recognition that changes in the laws, whether brought about through litigation or otherwise, would often fail to be reflected in changed economic and social circumstances. Johnson's War on Poverty programs would have many positive effects, but it would be difficult to conclude that they significantly enriched the poor. Indeed, the most powerful force for ending poverty would be across-the-board programs that did not target blacks, such as those aimed at the elderly.

One measure of the malaise was the reception given what became known as the Moynihan Report, written for the Department of Labor. Daniel P. Moynihan, who would later become a leader of the U.S. Senate while representing New York State, argued that the Negro family was collapsing, failing at its basic duty to ensure stability and socialize the young under the strain of single-parent households, almost all of them headed by unmarried women dependent on welfare. He urged a national effort to support the Negro family structure by developing a set of aggressive strategies; for example, tackling black unemployment and promoting the levels of educational achievement necessary to reduce it, both of which he linked to family stability.[6]

But the report was taken not as a call for action, as Moynihan intended it, but as an assault on black people. Criticism of its author was matched by vilification of the social science that produced it. William Julius Wilson concluded that the reaction to the report kept analysts, especially white scholars, from studying the ills of the inner city for over a decade.[7] At LDF the report prompted intense but informal debate. Some of the staff thought it unfair to locate in the black family problems that were the products of structural forces beyond its control, such as wage and employment policy. Others thought it tactless or actually bizarre to focus on the instability of black families at a time of high divorce rates among whites; they pointed to the strengths of the black family, such as solid kinship ties and religious affiliation. It was remarkable, others said, how when we were suing against discrimination we cited its pernicious effects, but we found the same destructiveness hard to talk about when it was clothed in policy analysis that was said to characterize the family. Too close for comfort to racist claims of inherent inferiority. It was as if, I thought in a flight of humor that I did not share with my colleagues, someone were insulting your mama.

Moynihan had pointed out the growing divergence of the poor and the middle class in the black community—an observation that today is taken for granted—but as the 1960s waned, it was urban riots, rising crime rates, a vast drug culture, and the assassinations of Dr. King, Malcolm X, and Robert Kennedy that were emblematic of domestic crisis; the war in Vietnam dwarfed even these tragedies with its capacity to divide, distract, and worry. Settled arrangements were flying apart and it was far from clear where the pieces would land. Like almost everyone else on the left, LDF played dumb when it came to the Moynihan Report and explicitly advancing its policy goals. I was unable, for example, to find any reference to it in the index to Jack Greenberg's comprehensive history of LDF.[8]

Despite the constricting impact of national events and the influence of black separatism as a potential polarizing force on the staff, in one way working at LDF during those years was surprisingly calming. Some long-sought goals were in sight, such as the beginning of real school desegregation in Alabama and Mississippi and the opening of white-collar jobs for African Americans in corporate America. Those of us who thought the war an immense blunder beyond our capacity to alter dug deeper into work for a vision of social justice. We were involved in many of the major policy conflicts of the day, trying to trump with the rule of law patterns of

discrimination, urban decay, and racial conflict. By August 1969, for example, more than eighty-five LDF employment discrimination suits were
pending in the federal courts against major corporations (General Electric,
Georgia Power, Reynolds Metals, Kaiser Aluminum, Cone Mills) and
powerful unions (the United Mineworkers and the United Steelworkers).[9]
So long as cases against major corporations and unions opened opportunities for jobs, they promised a chance of breaking the cycle of poverty.[10]

The cases pursued by the welfare rights lawyers to improve the status of
persons receiving public assistance were important efforts to provide minimum support to those Americans most susceptible to long-term poverty and
the disastrous living conditions and social dislocation that it produced. In
addition to a long docket of traditional civil rights cases, LDF lawyers
worked on more than sixty cases that were similar to those handled by the
new public-interest lawyers. They commonly intervened in potential and
actual riot situations, feeling the emotional highs and lows similar to hospital emergency room work. In December 1969, a staff report counted eight
cases of discrimination against Indians and migrant workers. Inspired by
Michael Davidson, a specialist in land use, another eight challenged conditions in public housing from Georgia to San Francisco. Two cases sought to
develop for the first time a remedy for unequal allocation of municipal services such as garbage collection, fire protection, and street repair. In others,
LDF represented consumers and prison inmates as well as poor neighborhoods struggling to fend off destruction from urban renewal.

Even within the small world of law reform, however, life became more
complicated. No longer did the wider community of friends, colleagues,
and surrounding voices we respected agree on the course LDF was taking
the way they had universally condemned southern racism. On the eve of
trial, an expert witness I had retained to testify about the validity of police
practices in taking eyewitness identifications wanted to drop his assignment when he decided our client might be guilty, despite having concluded that the procedures in question were likely to lead to mistaken
identification. Lawyers doing our kind of work soon found themselves in a
universe where clarity of principle and a perception of national responsibility for social dislocation were in short supply. Suddenly, what at least
some of the time people in authority had been able to accept as a moral imperative to compensate for historic wrongs against a devalued racial group
became a series of questions turning on cost-benefit analysis, balancing
conflicting views and a coming to terms with multiple interests and market forces. Of course, we'd lived before with indeterminacy, uncertainty,

conflict, and resistance—core elements of a litigator's life—but now they became harder to struggle with.

Elizabeth Bartholet and I encountered the shift in attitude when we wrote a friend-of-the-court brief supporting lower bail in a case against Black Panther Party members charged with planning to blow up New York department stores. We weren't supporting urban violence but arguing that while the state might detain the accused before trial for valid reasons of public safety, the decision whether or not to release them before trial should never depend on how much money they could raise. The day after the brief challenging the high bail was reported in the *New York Times,* the well-known theologian Reinhold Niebuhr stopped a contribution check and fired off a telegram resigning from membership on a committee of key LDF supporters.[11]

No longer was everyone we sued a racist, everyone we represented a pure victim. Of course, race was always a factor in American life, though often it was masked, but how much and what kind of historical victimization should the law recognize? And with what remedies?

The New York City school system had failed many minority youths, but did that warrant control of the schools by untrained local groups subject to intense political pressure from a few activists?

Welfare payments often failed to ensure subsistence to recipients. They were administered arbitrarily by a vast and costly paper-driven bureaucracy that often ignored its own admittedly dense rules and standards. But was the strategy of sequential test lawsuits then being mounted by the new federally supported legal services offices for the poor and often supported by LDF co-counsel the best way to go? Was it likely to produce a minimum national standard of living or merely contribute to temporary inflation of the welfare rolls and ultimate election of hostile politicians because of a backlash from voters who were disproportionately not poor? Or would defeat be worth it if it energized welfare clients?

In similar backlash fashion, would court decisions bringing the level of due process protection for defendants prosecuted by the states in line with the procedures thought fair by the federal courts and criminal law experts actually reduce the excesses of law enforcers or end up facilitating a new set of punitive policies—for example, an exploding prison population, longer sentences for nonviolent offenses, and intense coercive pressure for guilty pleas instead of trials?

How far should we go in demanding integration of a school system if the predictable result was white (and middle-class black) flight to suburbs and private schools, leaving public schools with a large black and Hispanic majority and a tiny minority of mostly poor and immigrant white students and politically weak parents? Was what some critics referred to as just "moving bodies around" worth this result?

If an employer maintained a workforce with significantly few minority workers, was that fact enough—without proof of actual racial bias—to merit governmental intervention? Should it be a defense to such a discrimination suit that the employer thought business success, including creation of jobs, required continuation of present employment practices?

Would large-scale efforts to reform inhumane and antiquated state custodial facilities for the mentally ill and prisons for convicted criminals significantly improve the institutions or merely encourage deinstitutionalization of the former and privatization of the latter?

What was the role of an organization such as LDF if the black community was split, some members preferring higher-quality local schools, if they could get them, to integrated schools outside the neighborhood?

Finally, when a black neighborhood erupted in riot after a police shooting—the most common precipitating event—should LDF represent accused looters who claimed innocence? Sue to impose better guidelines covering encounters between police and community? Stay away unless civil rights laws had clearly been violated?

These and dozens of other context-specific questions did not bother us when we were suing Birmingham's Bull Connor, defending students trying to buy a hamburger at Woolworth's, challenging explicit segregation statutes, or protecting Dr. King's right to demonstrate. The movement's turn to the North and West required a different set of goals and strategies, even if litigation was still a prime tactic. And many of these vexing questions had a technical legal dimension not easily conveyed to lay observers. How should we decide, for example, just who our clients would be? Even when a decision was made to go ahead in a particular case, how was proof assembled? Which side in a dispute that went to court had the responsibility of first presenting evidence—carrying the burden of production, as lawyers would say—and then of ultimately persuading judges and juries? An aspect of LDF litigation not much appreciated by laymen was how much non–civil rights doctrine and technical lawyer labor was involved in cases that were generally known for their lofty arguments of principle.

While LDF lawyers had to be technically proficient when they framed legal issues for the courts, they were also promoting a view of justice—a set of moral and legal values—asking that they be accepted as part of a set of national norms and applied in an active, transformative way to change behavior and status. This is why the riots that began in the Watts neighborhood of Los Angeles in 1965 and continued for years in city after city marked the beginning of the end of an expansive civil rights vision, even though paradoxically they undeniably stimulated short-term legal and economic reforms such as Lyndon Johnson's Great Society programs.

The peaceful and abused southern marchers who demonstrated for basic rights had forced many whites actually to see black people for the first time and had seduced them to abandon their customary resistance or indifference. Suddenly just as white Americans were coming to terms with images of sympathetic victims of racial oppression, those images were replaced in the public imagination by pictures of fire bombers and looters bent on creating chaos. African Americans were coming to be seen less as unique victims than as just another self-interested group clamoring for a bigger piece of the pie. The result was polarization: greater efforts to bring about a change in basic economic and social arrangements and greater resistance to those efforts. As the civil rights era began to close in this country, LDF continued to devote most of its by now several million plus annual budget to rights implementation (with heavy concentration on school desegregation and employment discrimination suits), but lawyers' time was increasingly spent on interventions geared to issues with a class as well as a racial component that ultimately assumed that the interests of blacks to a large extent overlapped the interests of the poor.

It would soon become obvious that regardless of how entrenched were perceptions of white superiority and black inferiority, whether Americans were able to acquire a good education and decent housing depended largely on their wealth or lack of it. In 1966 the Ford Foundation, America's leading source of funds for liberal causes, made it clear that it regarded poverty and racial progress as intertwined. For the first time offering significant support to a civil rights organization, Ford appropriated $1 million for a National Office for the Rights of the Indigent, a paper office within LDF. NORI, as it was called, was intended to advance the rights and opportunities of the poor through legal action; an internal Ford report accurately called NORI a back door into the civil rights field. Foundation policy had shifted with the arrival of a new president, McGeorge Bundy. As the report put it, "Viewing the idea of equal opportunity as 'the leading moral imperative' of the times, Bundy gained trustee support to make civil rights and the needs of disadvantaged minorities the Foundation's top domestic priority."[12]

There were ironies in the gift: though by 1970, 40 percent of the foundation's annual giving would go to minority rights work, up from 2.5 percent in 1960, in 1966 Ford still needed a cover story because it thought making a large grant supporting an organization with NAACP in its name too controversial.

Under Bundy's leadership the foundation soon blocked out a range of concerns—welfare administration, urban renewal, inner-city evictions, inequality in the criminal justice system, the need to train a cadre of lawyers for the poor—that would soon become the subject of widespread policy intervention by Ford-sponsored advocates at LDF and many, many other groups. Bundy linked progress in civil rights to advances against poverty. There was "a real chance," he said, that "what had been learned in the struggle for Negro rights can be put to the service of other Americans as well."[13]

Money went to the Lawyers' Committee for Civil Rights under Law, which initially funneled lawyers in big northern firms to Mississippi and Georgia, to new legal groups representing Chicanos, Native Americans, and Puerto Ricans, and to law schools willing to place students in clinics serving the unrepresented urban poor. In the 1970s Ford broadened the scope of its philanthropy to promote organizations that sought to influence the federal government's decision making on the environment, communications, education, prisoners' rights, gender discrimination, and drug policy. Other foundations followed with substantial grants. Law offices, policy groups, advocacy projects grew like kudzu. By 1974 the ACLU had 275,000 members in 49 state affiliates and 375 state chapters. Its legal director, Melvin Wulf, estimated that five thousand volunteer attorneys supplemented a legal staff that included thirty-four full-time staff attorneys in nineteen local offices and eighteen lawyers in the ACLU national office. I remembered that in 1961, when I was looking for my first job, I asked about work with the ACLU and was told to forget it—the national office already had a lawyer.

Despite the hostility to law reform of substantial segments of the nation, there seemed to be no stopping the government and foundation-subsidized march to the courthouse. One night my wife and I went to Greenwich Village to see the touring San Francisco Mime Troupe present what was billed as a contemporary political satire of a commedia dell'arte play by the eighteenth-century Italian playwright Carlo Goldoni. The play had something loosely to do with the comings and goings of steamy illicit lovers, but soon enough the Mime Troupe left the conventional plot behind, converting the story into a vicious attack on American involvement in Vietnam. The troupe hammed it up, to the glee of the audience, while making a serious point about the stupidity of so much that was said in support of the war.

But the obvious appreciation and loud applause was too much for the theatrical anarchists of the Mime Troupe. They affected outrage and suddenly filled the stage with swordplay; several velvet-doublet-clad warriors moved menacingly toward the audience, blades drawn.

"All right," the swordsmen demanded firmly, "everyone here supported by the Ford Foundation stand up."

Wagging their prop-closet blades under the noses of the New Yorkers in the first row, they persisted: "Come on, grantees, no holding back." When no one rose, they shouted, "Cowards!" did a little dance, and withdrew offstage. Again the theater erupted.

To survive, the troupe had itself taken Ford Foundation money, like so many others, but at least it could convert the fact that it was on the goodworks dole to entertainment.

I was never sure whether the million for NORI allowed us to do things that would have been beyond our capacity or whether we would have done them anyway. Certainly some projects, such as a court challenge to the money bail system and the campaign to eliminate capital punishment, were in progress before we saw the Ford money. Just a few years later both LDF and Ford could dispense with the NORI cover story; Ford money would flow directly to LDF, as it still does. But Ford grants may have provided the fiscal cushion that permitted Greenberg to hire more lawyers and move forcefully in new areas.

One of those projects was particularly bold, even unprecedented. It also makes clear that as hard as it is to win civil rights lawsuits, redistributing wealth and challenging settled economic arrangements are harder. This would also be the fate of Ford- and later government-financed efforts to ensure a significantly higher level of financial support for welfare recipients and of litigation to establish a federal constitutional right to equally financed public education.

In the second half of the 1960s, a new staff member, Philip Schrag, began bringing test cases to challenge commercial practices that he thought unfairly affected urban poor and unrepresented consumers. Just out of Yale Law School, he combined the confidence of a mature lawyer with the energy and quickness of a teenager. With Greenberg's blessing for what was essentially an experiment in changing the terms of common but troublesome economic relationships through litigation, Schrag went to the New

York State courts to sue deceitful salesmen, overcharging merchants, and finance companies that purchased installment contracts from retailers and enforced usurious payment conditions. His low-income clients were just making ends meet; they had been lied to, sold inferior merchandise at high interest, and denied critical information about the transactions. But at almost every step Schrag found himself thwarted. Lawyers for the defendants took unnecessarily lengthy depositions, made motions whose only purpose could be delay, and played procedural games that avoided resolution of the legal issues Schrag wanted the courts to decide.

The New York judiciary catered to these defense tactics and paid superficial attention to Schrag's legal papers. Judges were so busy that they never actually saw many of the motions he filed; they regularly let law clerks decide most of them. Though he had some victories, as when the U.S. Supreme Court established (in a case brought in Wisconsin, not New York) the constitutional principle that debtors were due a hearing before their salaries could be garnished, Schrag learned some grim lessons in how difficult it could be to win a test case in an area of law where racial impact is indirect and commercial interests and market habits dominate. Even though his approach to the cases was novel, he thought the manifest injustice of his clients' treatment would produce reform. He learned "that the lower state courts were neither friendly nor hostile to law reform. Instead, they are totally indifferent."[14] He had thrown himself into the fray, after having been given an opportunity to bring just six cases a year, so few that no legal office serving the poor could afford to have a lawyer with such a small caseload, and still he had failed to make a dent.

Hardened by the bullying and stubbornness of New York civil lawyers, Phil Schrag would go on to become the official consumer advocate of the City of New York. He later served the United States as a nuclear disarmament negotiator before beginning a distinguished career as a Georgetown law professor. In the 1970 he and I would write lawbooks and articles together and found Morningside Heights Legal Services, Columbia Law School's neighborhood law clinic. Under our supervision, the clinic gave law students the opportunity to represent clients in court and before New York City administrative agencies, allowing me to vicariously correct a defect in my own education by seeing to it that my own students would not be sent out into the world innocent of the perils of law practice.

If Schrag's experience with the New York State courts was a lesson in how difficult it would be to tackle poverty with techniques that had often been successful when the issue was race, LDF's involvement in prison reform was a frustrating success. For years the federal courts had taken the view that what went on in state prisons was not only primarily but almost exclusively a matter for correctional officials. Despite prisoners' allegations of wholesale violation of basic standards of decency in the manner in which officials employed segregated (solitary) confinement, failed to provide adequate medical care and food, and displayed their indifference to overcrowding, judges evolved something called the "hands-off doctrine" as a means of protecting the courts from having to deal with thousands of troublesome prisoner complaints. But such was the power of the basic 1960s message, that attention must be paid to the rights of disadvantaged groups, no matter how despised, that the doctrine had begun to erode. Even though each year the courts would decide the ultimate issues in more of these cases—in one of mine a southern federal court ruled that banned reading material of interest to African American inmates, such as *Ebony* and *Sepia* magazines, was subject to First Amendment protection[15]—it was still very difficult to challenge prison conditions.

In 1967 the influential federal court of appeals for the New York area, the Second Circuit, rejected the argument that federal courts had no role to play in seeing to it that certain constitutional principles were honored in state prisons.[16] The court ordered a hearing on a handwritten complaint from a life-sentenced inmate named Lawrence Wright setting out "disturbing conditions" about his solitary confinement at Dannemora Prison, near the Canadian border. When the case returned to the trial court, Wright was joined by Robert Mosher, another resident of the segregation unit, who had been hauled off to solitary because he refused to sign a safety sheet in a prison workshop. Judge James T. Foley appointed an LDF lawyer, William Bennett Turner, as Mosher's attorney, joining another public interest lawyer, Betty D. Friedlander, who represented Wright. In October 1968 the case went to trial—one of the first prison-conditions cases in American history to go to a full trial. The record of the case, including 1,566 pages of testimony from wardens, guards, physicians, corrections experts, and inmates, painted such a vivid picture of confinement that even a judge as skeptical as Judge Foley was shocked.

Inmates in the segregation unit were kept naked for days at a time, even in winter near the Canadian border. They had to eat all their food from a single bowl with a spoon. Cells contained no furnishings but toilet and sink; inmates slept on a cement floor without a mattress and they were often deprived of toilet articles. Only a two-minute weekly shower was permitted. Prisoners were told they had to stand at attention at the door whenever a guard passed. Eyeglasses were taken from them. One warden claimed he could hold an inmate who didn't meet the "criteria" he wanted in these conditions for his whole term of imprisonment.

Given the powerful testimony before him, Judge Foley ordered the state to promulgate new rules governing the segregation unit if it wanted to use it in the future. He made provision for basic health care, heat, and ventilation, prohibited enforced nudity as a disciplinary measure, and provided a number of protections for the two men before him, such as restoring hundreds of days of "good time" credit that Mosher had lost because of being held in segregation. As a result of Foley's judgment, the state abandoned many of the practices of which Mosher and Wright complained, promulgated guidelines prohibiting punitive or degrading confinement, and promised to permit personal hygiene items and allow regular showers and exercise.

Judge Foley had been a reluctant convert to the role of prison monitor. Turner soon found himself dealing with a very different judicial attitude. A few years later, having been made head of LDF's small West Coast office, he set off for a sabbatical of mountain climbing in Nepal. Returning to his Katmandu hotel one day, he found a thick package from William Wayne Justice, a federal judge in East Texas, where two large prisons were located. Like his predecessor on the bench, Judge Justice had been receiving numerous letters of complaint and scrawled, barely literate motions from prisoners alleging the familiar abuses: lack of decent medical care, "grotesque overcrowding," arbitrary discipline, excessive physical punishment. In Texas the guards were often unregulated inmates called "building tenders." As he wrote later, the prisoners were being subjected to the "same crowding experiment ethologists have performed on the common gray rat . . . and the experiment was having the same result."[17]

But all the judge had when he wrote Turner was a series of allegations with the ring of truth from convicts, prisoners who had neither the opportunity to collect evidence nor the legal skills to present their claims in court. Justice had heard Bill Turner speak at a legal conference and knew he had worked on some Texas prison cases. Would Turner come to East Texas and take over the case of several inmates whose claims were typical of the grievances of the larger prison population? The judge promised he would bring the U.S. Department of Justice into the case as friend of the court and get the FBI to provide access to evidence that would be hard for a lawyer representing inmates to get. Turner contacted Greenberg, who committed LDF to what would be over two decades of struggle.

Judge Justice later unapologetically explained the activist stance he had taken. He had only three choices: he "could have continued to hear large numbers of prisoner petitions . . . with full knowledge that such petitions were destined to fail"; he "could have attempted to right the balance in the hearings," in effect tried to play two conflicting roles, advocate and umpire; or he "could find some means of classifying and consolidating the complaints and seeking out an attorney with resources to present the prisoners' case adequately."[18]

By bringing LDF and later the Department of Justice into the case as an intervener, the judge facilitated a massive lawsuit that the state of Texas would concede twenty years later "transformed its prison practices and policies." During this period the American Civil Liberties Union would also make a major impact on inhumane conditions of confinement with a national reform project. But while Texas expressed "sincere" gratitude for "court guidance" and consented to major changes in prison administration, the state never stopped fighting the judge's orders.[19] The trial in the Mosher case had been novel and impressed insiders who knew the courts' hostility to such suits. It had lasted seven days. The trial in the Texas case raised eyebrows. It took 159 days. The court had admitted 1,565 exhibits into evidence. A court-appointed "special master" would monitor compliance with the judge's numerous orders and the consent decree for years. While the case dragged on, the Texas prison system grew from 25,000 inmates in 1972 to 140,000 in the late 1990s. Its budget grew accordingly.

By 2001, Judge Justice was still trying to cajole Texas into doing better. He had previously held that the prisons were grossly overcrowded; that sanitation, health care, and recreational facilities were wholly inadequate; that health care had to be overhauled; that hearing procedures for discipline and access to courts for complaints were inadequate; and that fire safety and sanitation standards were in violation of state law and the Constitution. Despite great changes in the administration of the prisons and elimination of many of these practices, he concluded that "constitutional violations persisted . . . in three major areas: conditions of confinement in administrative segregation, the failure to provide reasonable safety to inmates against assault and abuse, and the excessive use of force by correctional officers."[20] He ordered injunctive relief to continue until he was barred from further action by passage of a massive procedural reform statute that clipped the wings of federal judges in dealing with prison conditions. The Prison Litigation Reform Act, signed into law by President Clinton in 1995, imposed filing fees, limited damage awards, and required inmates to navigate bureaucratic obstacles before filing suit against prison officials; it also made it more difficult to continue in effect consent agreements between officials and inmate representatives.[21] Once again, an apparently successful set of reforms had produced a countereffort to minimize its impact.

As harsh drug laws and new federal and state sentencing guidelines sent a flood of new arrivals into correctional institutions, Alvin Bronstein, a leading reformer and the former director of the ACLU's National Prison Project, pointed to a dilemma facing any group trying to change a set of deep-rooted and practically necessary institutional arrangements: "For years we have wrestled with the question of whether our [attempts and successes at] improving prisons [are] really part of the problem. . . . By making [prisons] better, are we really insulating them from a more important policy review? . . . We have abolished 19th-century dungeons in this country. At the same time, the last few years have been very depressing for me, because I see us going back 25 years, if not more."[22]

Schrag and Turner's work was the sort of innovative and costly litigation LDF designed and pursued from the late 1960s on while at the same time still trying to enforce basic civil rights protections for African Americans in education, employment, and voting rights. In seeking to secure protections for low-income consumers and prisoners, not explicitly for racial minorities, Schrag and Turner relied on the same techniques that had led to victories in race cases in larger and more inclusive economic and human rights contexts. In both instances, success would have disproportionately aided African Americans while still enhancing the rights of everyone affected. But while the relative record of success and failure with cases of this sort was decidedly mixed, it was plain that the structural defects in American social services, education, and patterns of wealth distribution remained largely untouched. To attribute the persistence of these lacks to the limits of litigation, however, is like blaming a nurse for the blunders of the surgeon. Sometimes litigation works and sometimes it doesn't. It is certainly true that the more systemically complex and interconnected the cluster of issues confronting the courts in any particular subject area, the greater the need for judicial action to be linked closely to targeted action by other institutions and branches of government.

Of course, for every law reform or impact case or campaign that LDF seriously contemplated filing, several never got off the ground. One particular example stands out for me as a source of frustration, one that also illuminates the limits of litigation and the sort of situation that LDF as an organization was not suited to address.

The Reverend Milton Galamison, a Presbyterian minister and former leader of the Brooklyn NAACP, had been advocating greater integration in city schools for years. Aggressive and persistent, Galamison burst on the scene in 1950 as an opponent of conservative Presbyterian church leaders who wanted to spend money to build a church in the all-white Long Island suburb of Levittown. Later he co-founded a citywide coalition of civil rights groups working to improve educational quality and turned it into a personal power base; grown frustrated by lack of support from national organizations and by the famously bureaucratic recalcitrance of the Board of Education, he would ultimately use this power to paralyze the schools by organizing massive student boycotts.

Unlike the black nationalists who flocked to the banner of local control, Galamison never abandoned his faith in integration and actually believed a decentralized, segregated system would ultimately lead to an integrated system.[23] But from 1966 to 1968, when he left the fray, Galamison became a vocal public supporter of a movement dominated by the demand for each school district's self-determination. When Anthony Amsterdam and I met with him in a Brooklyn church vestry, he was thought to be the city's most powerful force for local control. I have been unable to document the precise circumstances that brought us to visit Galamison. It was, however, an unusual assignment for both of us. Tony Amsterdam (a Philadelphian who only became a New Yorker some years later) provided vast and invaluable pro bono service to LDF in an array of civil rights cases, but the decentralization dispute involved little law and a great deal of both educational policy and New York City politics. I wasn't much better suited to the task. While a native New Yorker who had attended city public schools and a veteran of school desegregation cases in the South, I had few New York political credentials. Both of us were whites coming into an area where the races had been polarized.

Decentralization, however, had been a pet project of the Ford Foundation president, McGeorge Bundy, and Mayor John Lindsay. Perhaps someone at Ford or City Hall realized there had been a gross miscalculation and asked LDF to try to save the situation or at least to see what was up.

Galamison was exceedingly polite and reserved. Albert Shanker, head of the United Federation of Teachers, had painted him as a dangerous extremist, but he hardly seemed the firebrand who had said he would rather see the New York schools "destroyed" than continue unintegrated. Galamison's base was local, not national, and he had to produce visible change in the Brooklyn communities where his constituency lived. While he led boycotts that had closed down the schools, he had failed to wrestle enough from stonewalling school administrators to satisfy his followers. His luck with the black elite wasn't much better. There was a history of struggle over tactics with such NAACP officials as Roy Wilkins and the national CORE leader, James Farmer, though not with CORE's more radical Brooklyn branches. Relations with Wilkins, never good, had turned poisonous when indications surfaced of anti-Semitism, which was totally inconsistent with NAACP policy and was bound to affect its fund-raising. At the time we met with Galamison, he may have just lost his leadership role to more militant, violent, and racially exclusive competitors. At any rate, he indicated he had no use for our services.

Some years earlier, in 1964, Galamison had told the novelist Robert Penn Warren that he was for integration but only if it was a two-way street:

[Only] one construction can be put on the kind of attitude which says, "It's all right for Negro children to transfer into my community, but I will not have my children transfer or travel to a . . . Negro school." The construction that I would put on this is just race arrogance. This is all it is. That and . . . an assumption that integration is completely to the benefit of the Negro without realizing that there are many other values apart from academic values which would accrue to the white child in a situation like this, you see.[24]

Every LDF lawyer, regardless of race or political point of view, would have endorsed this statement, but just a few years later the man who made it would become the emblem for a kind of "Either integrate the schools or give them to us" politics that led to less integration, fewer white students, fewer able teachers, and a city whose school hallways were given over to shouting of racial epithets and worse. The result was a chaotic educational environment, accelerated middle-class flight to suburbs and private and parochial schools, and too many districts with a small contingent of poor white students.

It was probably a good thing that Galamison wanted no part of us. I'm not sure what LDF would have offered to a black community so deeply divided, some members making it clear they preferred higher quality local schools if they could get them (and it was far from clear they could get them) to geographically farther removed integrated schools, while others deeply longed for a less confrontational educational environment and were frightened by the threats against teachers and nonconformist parents from the militants. But LDF had no clout in Brooklyn and never had an opportunity to confront these issues. We were of Manhattan, literally and figuratively, and decentralization leaders saw us as irrelevant. But at least we did no harm of the sort so many others seemed to induce in the boiling cauldron of decentralization politics. As Tamar Jacoby, the former *Newsweek* law reporter, put it in *Someone Else's House,* her scathing indictment of the experiment in decentralization in the Ocean Hill–Brownsville neighborhood, "Nothing the city, the Ford Foundation or the central board could do seemed to appease the anger in Ocean Hill—and no amount of vituperation or even violence seemed likely to stop the Manhattan establishment from granting ever more power to the district's militants."[25] There was, of course, plenty of anger outside of Ocean Hill too.

The efforts to decentralize portions of the New York schools (and the bloody battles to change the schooling in a number of northern cities like Boston and Detroit) mark a critical failing of the civil rights movement because they drove home the lesson that southern strategies were virtually useless in the urban North. At LDF, the crisis at first occasioned very little official comment. We had plenty of other things to do as the nation exploded and at times imploded in conflict during the late 1960s. The lawyers made their own judgments on the issues, their own identifications, and often a separate peace. But as the controversy deepened, it eventually presented an example of an issue that divided the staff as it divided New York City, stimulating a few heated arguments and sarcastic exchanges. These were less symptoms of some racial malaise than markers of the almost trigger-fast relation of LDF lawyers to events in the mad world around them.

But it took years for the New York schools to recover from the controversy. The school system had a well-deserved reputation for providing an education that had opened the gates of true social mobility to the poor, the lower middle class, and recent immigrants, but had recently failed many minority children under pressure from an unruly and rebellious youth culture and more southern migrants than it could absorb in a short time. The struggle of minority communities to control local districts and ultimately oust teachers of whom it disapproved, most of them Jewish, embroiled the liberal Republican administration of Mayor John Lindsay, school officials, the state legislature, black nationalists, the Ford Foundation, and the United Federation of Teachers in one battle after another. Until 1969, when a watered-down local-control statute enacted by the legislature briefly eased frustrations if not criticism, anti-Semitic and antiblack talk appeared everywhere, though it was often wrapped in code. "Welfare queens" were said to be ruining the city; public school staff and teachers had "a plantation mentality." Some teachers thought minority students hopeless. In turn, they were accused of not knowing how to do their work. The teachers saw a power grab by untrained local groups subject to intense political pressure from a few demagogues. Sometimes the racism of both sides was out in the open. A black teacher read an anti-Semitic poem on the radio. White teachers had been assaulted; many were fearful. Those who supported the new local boards were subject to abuse from their peers. Parents saw only schools that were failing them. Many but certainly not all were black.

One can sense the pressures that LDF was operating under in this period from the fact that it made only modest efforts to intervene in the controversy, and those failed, though one could hardly imagine a more important mission for the organization than resolving the tensions that beset the nation's largest public school system. Partly this was a matter of will (LDF was still fully engaged in the South and moving into more cases in the rest of the country) and partly it was inability to see a solution. As the number of boycotts grew and the firings and violence against teachers escalated, it became apparent that no one else did, either. Mostly, however, the problem was that LDF had no community base or credibility with the parents of children who attended the New York City public schools. It angered me that we could litigate in New Orleans, Little Rock, Miami, and Nashville—though soon enough similar problems with community engagement would emerge in Atlanta and other cities—but our expertise seemed useless in the five boroughs. There was a sense of resignation in the office but no formal recognition that only a crash program to improve the quality of schools that were likely to remain largely segregated offered a chance to change the downward educational cycle in places such as Ocean Hill.

A few years later, however, LDF was approached to bring change in New York's schools by a route that was more congenial to its methods of operation. The limited objective was to further the decentralization cause and simultaneously to bring blacks and Puerto Ricans into the almost entirely white ranks of school principals and assistant principals. The named plaintiffs, Boston M. Chance and Louis C. Mercado, were both former teachers who had been working for the city school system for over a decade. They had been hired as acting elementary school principals by community boards acting under the state's new decentralization law, but although they were state-certified for the posts, they could not obtain permanent principal positions unless they also passed tests given by the Board of Examiners, the agency empowered to clear supervisory personnel for hiring.

The case illustrates what litigation can and can't do. As proof accumulated, it demonstrated the role played by the examination system in excluding blacks and Puerto Ricans from supervisory positions: they failed the exams disproportionately, and the exam's reputation functioned to deter many teachers from taking it in the first place. A court-ordered statistical survey covering some six thousand applicants (analyzed by a federal judge, Walter Mansfield) showed that the likelihood that the pass-fail ratio of minorities to whites could have occurred by chance alone was less than 1 in 10,000.[26]

As Elizabeth Bartholet, the LDF lawyer who brought the case, argued, the tests used placed "a premium on familiarity with organizational peculiarities of the New York City school system which, while having little to do with educational needs, are largely gained through coaching and assistance from present, predominately white, supervisory personnel." Challenging the tests for over six years consumed Bartholet and the team of lawyers and consultants she assembled. When her investigations began, she was a junior LDF staff attorney; then she became the director of the Legal Action Center, a new Ford-supported public interest group that focused on fairness in drug and penal policy; before the case was finally concluded, she joined the Harvard Law School faculty, eventually the school's second female tenured professor.[27] Before it was over, *Chance v. Board of Examiners*, as the case was called, had been heard by three district court judges who had sat through dozens of hearings.[28] Eight times the parties appealed to the court of appeals and twice (unsuccessfully) asked the U.S. Supreme Court to intervene. LDF's files on the case, stored at the Library of Congress, amount to over twelve feet of paper.

In the end a new interim system gave local boards the power to make provisional appointments on the basis of education and experience, and then to grant permanent licenses on the basis of on-the-job performance evaluations, entirely bypassing the testing procedure. The courts also awarded seniority rights to applicants who could show that they had failed to apply for or take one of the rejected examinations because it was discriminatory and unrelated to job performance. By 1985, a dramatic change in demographic composition had taken place. From a negligible number a decade earlier, 28 percent of the principals and 16 percent of the assistant principals were black or Hispanic; seventeen years later the percentages had climbed to 42 percent of the principals and 41 percent of the assistant principals.[29]

Why had LDF been successful in *Chance* but not in its earlier foray into decentralization? One key element had to be that *Chance* was an integration case, not an effort to reconfigure the structure, management, and finances of a whole school system. Success was relative; satisfied as they were by the outcome, Bartholet and her team had no illusions that they were curing the sickness of the New York City school system. Another reason highlights the opportunities as well as the constraints of using the courts. Even if Reverend Galamison had wanted to go to court, no attractive legal theory was available to assist him. Parents could dictate local school policy only if the legislature or local officials had granted them such powers. The angry parents and activists in Brooklyn may have controlled small enclaves, but other groups in both educational circles and the black community opposed them. Galamison and his supporters faced a classic political problem: they had been unable to get the changes they wanted by complaints to the authorities or by negotiation; as a distinct political minority, they felt the only hope was in the power of disruption. While they could mobilize a set of angry local residents, they held too few legal and political cards to make the courts listen.

In contrast, members of the school board and black educators—a discreet middle-class client group—supported the challenge to the practice of testing applicants for principalships. In the end only the union representing sitting principals and assistant principals opposed the new system of selection. With a respectable legal theory, a unified middle-class client base, and a goal of empowering professionals, it was unnecessary to deal with a rowdy and contentious mass movement. Despite these factors, *Chance* was hardly an easy case to win. Its outcome was a product of the extreme persistence of the team of lawyers and educational consultants headed by Bartholet and LDF's willingness to support the case for years. Even then it took cumulative evidence and imaginative legal argument to persuade the judges. There was no time in the case's long history when the result was certain.

LDF's expertise, reputation, and approach had been crafted in intense battles against blatant racial classifications. As the explicit signposts marking racial separation came down and the boundary between race and poverty grew fuzzy, the odds that LDF could continue to use its arsenal of major law-reform interventions successfully grew longer. Ironically, just as the prospects for large-scale litigation campaigning faded for race lawyers, techniques honed in the civil rights movement gained wide acceptance among an array of organizations and their lawyers, conservative as well as left-leaning, seeking to influence virtually every aspect of public policy through the courts.

Litigation: Means of Choice or
Last Resort?

M
AY 17, 2004, was the fiftieth anniversary of *Brown v. Board of
Education,* the most pronounced effort ever by a court to change
the basic conditions under which Americans live. It was also the
day the first homosexual couples were married in Massachusetts, an event
that would have been unthinkable a generation before.[1] Both the end of le-
galized racial segregation and the expansion of the right to marry to gay
couples fifty years later were the results of controversial court decisions en-
suring equality to defamed groups, rather than of electoral politics; they
reflected the unique role litigation has come to play in resolving policy disputes, changing norms and values, and creating an arena for public debate
and education as well as for political retribution. The reasons why this nation, with a racially, ethnically, religiously, and economically diverse and
dispersed population, relies so heavily on a judicial process to resolve disputes and set policy lie deep in our political culture. It's clear, however, that
so long as we do so, the role of the courts will be contentious. Both decisions were resisted by angry demonstrators who railed against changes in
basic law that had not been put to a legislative vote. Yet both also were
greeted by enthusiastic supporters who declared renewed faith in a legal
process that could deliver a measure of justice.

An examination of LDF's Web site and a survey of its annual reports between 1997 and 2004 reveals abundant signs of an organization that still believes in the vitality of litigation.[2] It continues to be a major player in cases
defending affirmative action plans; because many foundation funders insist
on collaboration between grant recipients, LDF often appears in these
cases with a coalition of public interest litigators and pro bono lawyers. Behind the scenes, LDF has quietly attempted to preserve race-conscious

compensatory remedies by encouraging targeted foundation financial support for African American students and sponsoring workshops for university admissions officers.

LDF could be seen acting in concert with other groups in efforts to change practices that disfranchised African Americans in the 2004 presidential election; in suing government agencies (the New York City Parks Department) and major corporations (Abercrombie & Fitch) over their treatment of minority workers; in challenging state legislative efforts to draw electoral district lines that eliminated districts in which blacks predominated; in negotiating an agreement with the University of California to consider an applicant's entire record, not just scores on standardized tests, when making admissions decisions; in efforts to gain release for Wilbert Rideau, an award-winning prison journalist who had been imprisoned over forty years after what the federal courts now say was an illegal conviction; and in persistent efforts to win greater educational resources for the public schools of Hartford, Connecticut, where 95 percent of the students are minorities. Many of the more than seventy school desegregation cases (half in Alabama, a good number in rural communities) are kept alive more as leverage to enable LDF to seek remedies for particular abuses, say in hiring or disciplinary policy, than as vehicles for major reform. The courts no longer issue many orders requiring racial balance or busing, and African American parents are not aggressively pushing for them.

While the LDF Web site and publications still give pride of place to its role in *Brown v. Board* and past association with Thurgood Marshall, the docket includes cases that suggest a readiness to tackle issues with a negative impact on blacks whenever they occur. An example is LDF's role in exposing the false testimony and suppression of evidence by law enforcement that led to the baseless convictions of dozens of people on trumped-up drug charges in Tulia, Texas. On August 22, 2003, thirty-five defendants were fully pardoned by Texas's governor, Rick Perry.

With a workload of over a hundred cases, a staff of some seventeen lawyers, a professional and support staff twice that large, offices in New York, Los Angeles, and Washington, and impeccable political and charitable foundation connections, LDF still defines the contours of civil rights law. It is particularly noticeable that despite the ebb and flow of events and changes in leadership, the organization has generally maintained its level of financial support despite some lean years for civil rights funding. Nevertheless, LDF could not remain immune to trends in public and political opinion. "Let's face it," says Norman Chachkin, "civil rights litigation is no longer sexy." Foundation money to support LDF's core work is also harder to come by because so many competing organizations now seek funding for a wide variety of causes. As a result, LDF has become reluctant to take on new cases until older ones are concluded. At the same time that LDF is pinched for money, the buildup of conservative judicial appointments from Reagan and both Bush presidencies has led to a host of technical rules that make traditional civil rights litigation more difficult to bring. During the years of the Rehnquist Court, the justices consistently narrowed the range of discrimination claims that could be brought in federal court by private individuals.

LDF's docket once featured ambitious plans to initiate large changes in the way the law treated poverty, criminal justice, and provision of public services and public education; judicial hostility and political resistance now is thought to make such efforts unrealistic. Much of the caseload looks defensive and reactive, as if LDF were under threat and its priorities set elsewhere. But, Chachkin explains, plans for new "litigation campaigns really depend on raising new funds." For example, LDF is investigating "the close connections between the lack of educational opportunity for black youth and the explosive increase in the juvenile offender population, including the failure to provide appropriate educational services for youth who are deemed to be delinquent,"[3] but before this sort of exploratory research ripens into serious litigation and policy initiatives, money will have to be found to pay for expert witnesses and cooperating counsel. While from a historical perspective LDF's budget has grown substantially, in today's much more costly environment, available civil rights dollars are severely limited.

In the 1970s, Greenberg conceded, neither LDF nor others were "very successful at redistribution of economic opportunity through the courts."[4] In the 1980s Julius Chambers set one of his most talented lawyers, Jack Boger, the task of trying to mount a campaign for the poor modeled on the *Brown v. Board of Education* approach. It never got off the ground. An inquiry into how our health-care system fails to serve the needs of blacks produced a trenchant report in the 1990s but little in the way of actual followup. The staff no longer includes a lawyer whose major responsibility is intervention into racial or class bias in health-care policy. Certainly one does not see in the LDF caseload overwhelming recognition that one of the key issues for black America is the persistence of the underclass. Only a dozen cases deal with economic justice, and while these are important cases, they are the sort that will help primarily to improve the educational or employment opportunities of the middle class.

In the past LDF felt fully empowered to start on its own a major litigation campaign if it decided it met a pressing need. The sense was that the money would come. Long before anyone expected a statute as strong as the 1965 Voting Rights Act, for example, Greenberg packed me off to the District of Columbia to research a way to implement what seemed to be one of the deadest letters in the Constitution. Section 2 of the Fourteenth Amendment provides for reducing the basis for apportionment for the House of Representatives in states that wrongly exclude voters. It was an impractical innovation of hard-line radical Republicans after the Civil War and it is not surprising that it has never been implemented. But after a few brainstorming sessions with Professor Abram J. Jaffe of Columbia University, an expert on the census, we thought we had enough of a case to justify a court order to collect the necessary statistics—a move that might at least scare southern legislators into supporting some sort of bill that would help black registration.

So I spent days in an immense container-filled government warehouse in southeastern Washington that resembled the place where the Ark of the Covenant ends up in the Indiana Jones movie. For company I had a civil servant minder who thought I was seriously disturbed and boxes of census background papers that had never been published and never would be. Perhaps, I wondered idly, no human hand had touched them before mine. The case we finally brought was audacious: our argument implied that a judge should start a process that might end by ordering southern congressmen home. The court took so long to decide the appeal that the Voting Rights Act of 1965 became law; even then judges sent us away with a reservation that the client group we'd assembled from ten states could come back if progress in removing barriers to the vote were not forthcoming.[5] It seems unlikely that federal judges today would be so considerate, but I can't imagine LDF now initiating a case with such long odds and high stakes because the open, even eager judiciary necessary to take such transformative litigation seriously no longer exists.

LDF spends in the vicinity of $9–10 million yearly and runs a substantial deficit. Comparisons with the American Civil Liberties Union are of limited value because ACLU, but not LDF, is a membership organization with 300 dispersed chapters and between 300,000 and 400,000 members. But though both started from humble origins, ACLU has expanded while LDF has not. With fifty-three staffed affiliates in major cities, the ACLU claims to handle nearly six thousand court cases annually. While it was once thought to be concerned exclusively with the First Amendment, for some time it has maintained a presence across the range of public interest concerns—from increasingly important national security issues to reproductive rights, from AIDS policy to protection of immigrants. Concerns over the impact on civil liberties of antiterrorism practices are likely to continue to keep the ACLU at center stage and swell its war chest.

The shift from innovative and even adventurous litigation aimed at social change to a reactive, even defensive posture is no fault of LDF's legal staff but rather a product of changing civil rights fortunes. The number of large class-action challenges to the racial employment policies of major businesses has declined. Corporations have responded to Title VII and earlier litigation with more benign general practices; employment discrimination cases today are far more likely to involve individual disputes of the "he said, she said" type. Decades of increasingly restrictive court decisions, such as the blocking of suits by private individuals to enforce certain antidiscrimination rules even when government refuses to act, have taken their toll. For years LDF has lived pragmatically by the case. It lived well when victory was in the air and has trimmed its sails when faced with more variable political and legal winds. In the short term, at least, there is little hope for a return to the more powerful role litigation played in the past. But that doesn't mean it is irrelevant. Given the composition of the courts and the changing nature of the issues, the question is how much value litigation has as a means for substantial reform.

Traditionally, the utility of litigation as a means of altering major institutions and government policy was understood to be extremely limited. Judges look back to earlier decisions for guidance, a means to find governing principles, which usually commit them more to social order than to social change. Nevertheless, from the earliest days of the Republic litigants who did not believe they could prevail otherwise sought leverage by drawing the courts into disputes over major issues of power and policy. Both *Marbury v. Madison* (1803) and *Plessy v. Ferguson* (1896) were test cases— the former a move in the struggle for dominance between the nation's first two political parties, the latter a last-ditch effort to reverse the tide running against full implementation of the post–Civil War amendments.[6] The parties who brought both suits lost, but as influential court rulings with discernible impact *Marbury* and *Plessy* have few peers.

Still, most litigation is far from grand, relating to disputes between private individuals and businesses rather than public concerns. Government, of course, was often a party, but it behaved more like any other litigant raising issues over property, accidents, and employment relations than might be expected. But no matter who actually came out ahead, in the vast majority of cases litigation or the threat of litigation commonly resulted in a negotiated settlement primarily affecting only the parties to the dispute. In effect, the parties and their lawyers viewed the lawsuit as a contest over something that had happened in the past, the main issue being who would carry the burden of paying damages or providing some other remedy closely related to the legal claim that had led to the dispute. The parties to the case controlled the pace of litigation; submitted the legal questions to a supposedly neutral decision maker, an often noninterventionist judge who would decide the issues identified by the litigants and, subject to appeals correcting error, end the controversy.

But with LDF's campaign against segregation and the subsequent explosion of public interest cases in the late 1960s and 1970s, a new vision began to emerge. In describing and supporting law reform of the sort LDF had spawned, two leading law scholars, Abram Chayes of the Harvard Law School and Owen Fiss of Yale, made an effort to describe the activity that by then had been adopted by lawyers for the poor, prison reformers, environmentalists, mental health advocates, and many others as being composed of new and potentially revolutionary elements. At the time, LDF lawyers wondered in their youthful arrogance where the academics had been. Was this news? Maybe not to insiders, but Chayes and Fiss marked the contours of the work in a way that authoritatively defined the profile of the novel form litigation had taken and, in turn, justified the efforts of the new organizational players who came to use it.

In contrast to the traditional lawsuit, the approach Chayes charted was not "a dispute between private individuals about private rights but a grievance about the operation of public policy." Before the courts were groups or individuals who stood in for a large class of interested parties. The cases were framed by group interests; the lawyers who brought them were not neutrals hired for the occasion but players with an agenda often kindred to their clients'. Judges didn't just passively listen to arguments and decide questions of law but, like Judge Justice in Bill Turner's Texas prison case, pushed the parties toward broad settlement arrangements and played a role in "organizing and shaping the litigation to ensure a just and viable outcome." They would often seek the help of outside experts and governmental agencies in the effort. In these cases, the courts looked to influence or even to manage a host of issues having to do with the operation of important social organizations—schools, hospitals, prisons, public assistance programs, national parks. The list was as long as the concerns of the modern state. Because courts would be engaged in engineering change in complex bureaucracies, they would consider larger factual patterns and general behaviors, not just resolve a narrow controversy and end it but continue to oversee the administrative arrangements they had either facilitated or created.[7]

"This type of suit is one in which a judge," according to Owen Fiss, "confronting a state bureaucracy over values of constitutional dimension, undertakes to restructure the organization to eliminate a threat to those values posed by the present institutional arrangements."[8] A former clerk of Justice Marshall's, he pointed out that judicial engagement in structural reform originated in the *Brown v. Board of Education* decree that separate school systems be transformed into "unitary, nonracial school systems." That decree required concrete changes in every aspect of institutional life and "reallocation of resources among schools and among new activities." By the second decade after *Brown,* judges had increasingly become managers of large institutions under their jurisdiction. The claims that were the basis of a lawsuit could often be summarized in a paragraph, but proof of the case, management of the defendant institution, and figuring out how to compensate victims seemed to take forever, even when the parties decided that it was in their interest to work out a settlement.

Such operations shared certain organizational characteristics, but the ACLU, LDF, the new Washington-based public interest firms, and a raft of specialized advocacy organizations were hardly identical in purpose or style.

A critical characteristic of the work was a decent-sized permanent staff organized to monitor governmental institutions, develop expertise in certain subjects, and nurture long-term relationships with clients, allies, and the press. Although from the beginning a New York–based LDF used cooperating attorneys to find and service local clients and cases, central control was another key aspect of its organizational model. *Brown v. Board of Education* was choreographed nationally though at first it was performed locally. As important as it was to have a central leadership assembling strategies, coordinating cases, raising money, and dealing with the federal government, the relation between LDF's central office and its cooperating lawyers was never totally without tension. The ACLU, relying on scores of local branches and volunteer lawyers as well as paid staff, was even more susceptible to conflict between the national office and its affiliates. Many of the new Washington-based public interest organizations were too small to have satellite offices; those that did were too close-knit to worry about excessive autonomy.

Fund-raising was a common need. This was subsidized lawyering—it required financial support to compete in court with government or the lawyers of paying clients. The money came from contributors (LDF, ACLU, Environmental Defense Fund, etc.), membership dues (ACLU, NAACP, Sierra Club), foundation grants (virtually all public interest firms), government (neighborhood legal service programs), or fees awarded to lawyers who won certain cases when counsel fees were authorized, an option that became increasingly available after Congress began to include authorization for payment in civil rights statutes but that recently has met with disfavor in the courts.

As was early recognized, subsidized litigation often required a tight budget, pushing the lawyers to structure cases around manageable legal issues rather than bring multiple cases involving complex facts and long trials. Nevertheless, at times elaborate and costly proof was essential. When LDF tried to prove that the death penalty was disproportionately paid by blacks, it brought before the courts sophisticated statistical evidence gathered by researchers in numerous field locales like courthouse file rooms across the South and later analyzed by top-flight academic specialists, such as the leading criminologist Marvin Wolfgang of the University of Pennsylvania and David Baldus of the University of Iowa. When in the 1970s LDF sued many corporations for racial hiring and skewed promotion patterns, the cases required us to prove patterns of behavior throughout the many departments of a large company. The arrival of the jet airplane once had permitted LDF lawyers to move quickly from one case venue to another; now law reformers seized upon the computer to marshal proof, "analyzing," as Jack Greenberg put it, "black and white jobs, seniority, previous experience, salaries, hires, layoffs, terminations, overtime, promotions, and pay, and to demonstrate disparities explainable only by race that surprised even defendants."[9]

Litigation also has some obvious advantages. Its very focus on a particular controversy allows problems to appear manageable even if general across-the-board solutions prove elusive. The new public law cases that dealt with long-term management or monitoring of large institutions and government bureaucracies presented serious administrative challenges, but the courts were often able to bring other branches of government into pattern-changing negotiations. The federal courts, for example, were able to use new federal government desegregation guidelines promulgated in the mid-1960s to speed enforcement in the South as the Office of Civil Rights had used earlier court decisions as models for these antidiscrimination standards.

Once sued, government agencies regularly displayed their own self-interest in presenting plans for wide-ranging change in operations along with notice that because some operations had been declared in violation of law, they would seek increased funding from Congress or a state legislature. Though they rarely did so, courts could make up their own minds in a manner that defied the popular attitudes of the day. Factual records could be assembled and employed to educate. Bureaucrats could be held accountable for actions that otherwise would remain invisible. In a crude way courts could offer to satisfy hopes that would otherwise descend into bitterness and antisocial conduct. And judges could say no to certain policies in the name of the Constitution, forcing reevaluation, reconsideration, and amendment of policy.

But the limits as well as the potential of law reform were well understood by activist lawyers, even if they did not always deter them from suing. Abram Chayes famously emphasized the potential of public law litigation but he also warned, "What experience we have with administrative resistance to intrusive court decrees is not particularly encouraging."[10]

Would-be reformers confronted a host of institutional factors that made use of the courts difficult. Litigation can be painfully slow and remarkably costly. Trial lawyers gather information through tedious and constrained testimonial methods, and their relative isolation from politics often fails to translate into superior methods of policy analysis. Even well-thought-out, carefully planned actions usually dealt with a slice of a problem as viewed from the perspective of a particular class of litigants. Case-by-case decision making can point the way to new and imaginative solutions to nagging social problems, but there is no doubt that court orders require political and administrative support to change widespread behavior. Yet submitting issues to the courts may paradoxically change their shape and inhibit other approaches to change.

The steps available to judges to implement a decision are often defined by the traditional forms used by the law and thus may not be flexible enough to remedy novel claims. Court orders can lead to government spending on compliance, but appropriation of funds is generally the business of legislators. Courts have to be imaginative in acquiring assistance from others—finding deep enough pockets in the parties or in government—because they simply do not have the power of the purse or the personnel at hand to support the monitoring and administration required by the more complex arrangements they may order.

These and other limits on the power of judges were built into our mind-set at LDF. They were constraints that operated to limit what we could accomplish even if we won courtroom battles over the meaning of the law. Elected officials generally saw themselves as heeding the interests of the organized majority and of course were susceptible to expectations of financial support that might lead to reelection; despite court orders, civil servants did not yield to minority claims that required them to change their behavior without clear directives and firm pressure from above. They were experts at sitting on their hands. In short, LDF, ACLU, and their progeny went to court because they had to, not because litigation was a superior means of ending white supremacy or protecting old-growth forests or challenging censorship or opening up job categories from which blacks had been barred or inhibiting overaggressive police conduct. Filing suit might look like a knee-jerk response but a court order was often the only chance for change. And patience was required; it was not work for anyone who couldn't delay gratification.

Political adversaries who oppose the social goals of the public interest litigators often argue that law reform through the courts is undemocratic — though groups from the right of the political spectrum have increasingly decided there is good reason to create defense funds and litigation arms to promote their views. Spurred by remarks made in 1971 by Lewis Powell before he became a justice of the Supreme Court, property and business interests organized well-funded groups such as the Washington Legal Foundation, the Pacific Legal Foundation, and the Mountain States Legal Foundation to advance a market-based, private-property agenda much the way LDF fought for equal protection and the ACLU defended the First Amendment. Today such activity is also carried on by groups with goals to affect the way the law views social issues arising from religion, family status, and immigration. When I hear politicians or activists complain that judges appointed by elected officials are not democratically chosen but have no quarrel with the proposition that elected legislatures controlled by seniority or a few powerful leaders and heavily influenced by lobbyists reflect pure Jeffersonian principles, I ask myself whether the speaker is likely to talk in the same vein when the courts rule his or her way.

Academic critics also have a long record of questioning the use and general effectiveness of litigation; with the spread of public interest law and claims for its value from highly respected analysts, a new series of challenges emerged. Surprisingly, much of this criticism would be directed at *Brown v. Board of Education,* previously thought to exemplify successful reform litigation. In part the critics were reacting to the positive reviews Chayes, Fiss, and others were giving to a broadened judicial role, but they were also moved by a desire to examine the mythmaking praise that the media had heaped on *Brown*.

In 1977, a year after Chayes mapped the contours of public law litigation, the lawyer and political scientist Donald Horowitz published a book-length critique of judges' capacity to promote effective social change. He emphasized that constitutional rights are limited, judges are both cautious and deferential, and legal culture resists change. Courts as currently structured are poor at distinguishing the facts of individual from the general run of cases, impatient with "protracted litigation," and have "limited ability to monitor the consequences of their action." When it comes to forecasting the impact of their decisions, Horowitz gives judges failing grades. Closely examining four major lawsuits, he concludes that even if litigators win in court, in implementation victories often turn out to be worth very little.[11]

Nineteen seventy-seven was also the year of the founding of the Critical Legal Studies (or CRITS) movement, a loose collection of academics mostly from elite schools whose widely disseminated intellectual message was a direct attack from the left on the "legal liberalism" that LDF stood for. Of course, the details of that liberalism as civil rights lawyers and the CRITS understood it were in dispute, but by casting doubt on the conventional forms of "progress" the movement had a dramatic effect on legal scholarship and on the inner life of many law schools. Because the CRITS consumed vast quantities of ink in challenging the sincerity of judges' justifications, they caused no end of apoplexy in academic colleagues but had little effect on mainstream politics.

This is not the place to go into the full story of the lively project mounted by Critical Legal Studies, the subject of hundreds of lengthy articles, critiques, and countercritiques, many of them so heavy with the kind of writing that gives Marxists a bad name that the text loses focus. I shall only note that its intellectually quite diverse membership is as one in arguing that law is both a sham discourse (a narrative behind which power has its way) and a means of preserving the hierarchical order that those in power wish to see in place. To the CRITS' way of thinking, liberals were duped into believing that the operation of legal processes (especially judicial processes) could or did produce social justice. In fact, the CRITS treated liberals far worse than those they considered conservatives; indeed, the CRITS shared major criticisms of liberals with the right—both thought that case victories, antidiscrimination laws, and mainstream social programs were wildly overvalued and generally ineffective.

It was obvious that the tide was turning against those who believed that test litigation by public interest lawyers was the engine of social progress.

Horowitz's work had earned its share of laudatory references from academics, not by any means just from the members of the Critical Legal Studies movement, but it took a 1991 book by the political scientist Gerard Rosenberg, *The Hollow Hope,* to spread the anti-*Brown* gospel widely through the community of legal analysts who pursue such questions. Derrick Bell had thought *Brown* ineffective; in 1976 he too questioned the value of litigation and insisted that it would take action from the black community to achieve educational equity. But he still believed that what courts did mattered, if only they would do the right thing. Rosenberg, for his part, tried to make the case that courts played almost no significant role in bringing about the liberal reforms. He sought signs of any impact of constitutional cases in periodicals, poll results, statistical summaries, legislative debates, and the speeches of activists and politicians.[12] While he focused on references to *Brown,* Rosenberg found similar results when he looked at the elimination of restrictions on abortion ordered by *Roe v. Wade*[13] as well as court decisions on environmental regulation, reapportionment, and criminal law.

With respect to segregation, he contended that news coverage of the decision, speeches given by civil rights leaders, textbook references to the case, and other sources indicated that *Brown* was not much on the minds of either white elites or the black community, much less those who actually engaged in sit-ins, freedom rides, and other demonstrations in the early 1960s.[14] Cass Sunstein of the University of Chicago Law School, an admirer of the *Hollow Hope* thesis, called attention to a core premise of the "*Brown* didn't matter" school when he wrote, "It was not until 1964, when Congress and the executive branch became involved, that widespread desegregation actually occurred." Sunstein added that litigation may have "diverted attention from more productive alternatives" such as political activity and education efforts.[15]

The Virginia law professor Michael Klarman developed a closely related view, that *Brown*'s major import was stirring resistance that quickly defeated moderate politicians in the South and by its excesses eventually produced a pro–civil rights consensus in the rest of the country. Klarman asks whether there was a link between judicial decisions and the civil rights legislation of 1964 and 1965. He concludes that court victories inspired both Negroes and their opponents to grow assertive; the conflict featured vivid images of fire-bombed churches, racist cops, attacks on children, and brutal beatings. National politics, not the courts, decided who won.[16]

The historian David Garrow replied directly to Rosenberg and Klarman that *Brown* clearly conveyed a sense of hope and dignity that propelled the civil rights movement forward. Garrow claims that statements calling attention to *Brown* by key leaders such as Dr. King were minimized.[17] (Certainly Rosenberg is off the mark to the extent that he fails to acknowledge Dr. King's growing reliance on legal advice and litigation tactics after such debacles as the early demonstrations in Albany, Georgia.) Others pointed out additional flaws in the *Hollow Hope* approach such as the absurdity of expecting *Brown* to accomplish integration of schools on its own when *Brown II* was crafted to employ delay as a way of gaining the support of other government actors as well as to disable hostile, violent portions of the public. The "*Brown* wasn't important" thesis also fails to take full account of the interaction between the decision and subsequent events that occurred only because of *Brown,* such as the struggle over integration of the Little Rock schools. In 1958 a reluctant President Eisenhower was forced to take action that conveyed unmistakably that the federal government would back the courts if they were defied.

Moreover, many of the legislative and executive proposals that ended up protecting civil rights came from lawsuits that may have had limited effect on their own but developed principles that traveled. The *Simkins* case, which declared the Hill-Burton Act's "separate but equal" clause in respect to grants made to hospitals unconstitutional, held that the grantees were subject to the Constitution even if they were private entities because they took federal money with regulatory strings attached.[18] The principles laid out in Judge Simon Sobeloff's opinion in the court of appeals was an authoritative assertion that equality must travel with federal money. *Simkins,* therefore, helped pave the way for Title VI of the Civil Rights Act of 1964, the provision that followers of *The Hollow Hope* describe as really responsible for progress in desegregation. In the end, no matter how thought-provoking the arguments over *Brown's* effects, the variables are so numerous and so difficult to measure that they are impossible to settle.

Two months after the Civil Rights Act of 1964, the president signed the Economic Opportunity Act; the following year, in addition to the Voting Rights Act, amendments to the Social Security Act created Medicare and Medicaid. Time has exposed the flaws in the compromises that went into these legislative initiatives, but they dramatically altered the plight of many poor Americans, black and white; they are generally understood to be products of an era focused on stimulating government to create a more equitable social system. *Brown* and its progeny were essential parts of the spirit that produced such legislation.

From my point of view, that of a lawyer who arrived on the civil rights scene during the period that Rosenberg was using to measure *Brown*'s impact, his labors established only the slender truth that activists did not walk around actively citing *Brown* as Scripture. It was obvious, to me at least, that during these years anyone who worked with and seriously talked to blacks and whites who cared about integration and looked for a totally different set of relations between the races would conclude that belief in the possibility of change in status and law were radically different before and after *Brown*. It is easy enough to disparage this sort of testimony as "anecdotal," yet so many people active at the time had this sense of things that perhaps there is some wisdom to it, "conventional" or not.

The most important of the positive accomplishments of the civil rights movement was facilitating a general sense of black pride and legitimate expectation of betterment. The *Brown* Court relied on the premise that segregation hurt the self-esteem of Negro children. Putting aside whether integration of schools was a remedy for that condition, the Court's rejection of subservience with its finding of inherent inequality boiled down to an official body blow to beliefs in caste inferiority. Once that line was crossed, it was only a matter of time before the arrival of "black is beautiful."

With hindsight we can identify the events that led us to *Brown*. The service of blacks in the World Wars, the Truman administration's integration of the military, and the growing importance of African American voters were just some of the factors that led some of the Supreme Court justices who heard the case to believe the status of black Americans had changed dramatically. But while the decision itself, as Klarman puts it, "was unnecessary for educating blacks to condemn segregation, it unquestionably motivated them to challenge it." Ironically, the civil rights activists who share most aspects of the *Hollow Hope* perspective are those whose disappointment with the United States' reaction to *Brown* and bitterness at its limited transformative power lead them to devalue it. As interesting as the pros or cons of this debate is the respectful attention the question of *Brown*'s impact has stirred among experts. Peter Schuck of Yale Law School, for example, virtually whacks Rosenberg's methods, most significantly in claiming to answer "unanswerable questions" about what caused complex events. Nor does Rosenberg take the measure of the interaction of judicial decisions with other institutions; he pays too little attention to the actual reform goals of litigators. (I would add that he doesn't show what might have happened if *Brown* had been decided differently.) But despite all these negatives, Schuck also thinks Rosenberg has been "resourceful, imaginative and pointed" in marshaling evidence and that he has cast "serious doubts on the common understanding" of *Brown*.[19]

It's possible that *Brown* has been so overpraised and its impact so taken for granted that scholars are merely engaged in their usual function of not allowing oversimplified explanations of important events to go unquestioned. Certainly *Brown* has iconic status. Its anniversary is the occasion for self-congratulatory events, but many recent celebrations, especially the fiftieth anniversary, have been marked more by sober reflection on *Brown's* mixed message and ambivalent legacy than by flag-waving. Much of this commentary has been devoted to measuring *Brown* as a true disappointment because it left thousands of students in segregated inferior schools. Worse, it did so under cover of a right to equality that was held out as a new reality but in fact was only partial.

But there is more to Rosenberg's argument than deflating self-interested hype or even arguing, in the fashion of Derrick Bell, that *Brown's* integration formulation, whatever its original utility, has long since proved inadequate to provide equal educational opportunity. His contention does not depend on whether *Brown* was doctrinally flawed but rather asserts that whatever the message of the decision, it was not a significant force in subsequent history; that is, court decisions simply do not produce social change or attitudinal shift. He makes the same point about other major Supreme Court decisions. The conclusion is general: courts are inconsequential; they rarely matter.

Rosenberg asks, "Can courts bring about social change?" One observer has answered amusingly, "Sometimes yes, sometimes no."[20] Whatever the empirical evidence in support of *The Hollow Hope*, this is certainly the attitude that LDF lawyers carry into their work. But the book and its reception raise other important questions. One was posed by the University of Chicago's Cass Sunstein, a scholar of deserved reputation, who surprisingly employs Rosenberg's conclusions without serious examination. Rosenberg says he wants to help lawyers decide when and whether to devote resources to litigation; following him, Sunstein comments that litigation "may have diverted attention from more productive alternatives."[21] He is surely correct in general, but in the particular such pronouncements are nothing more than wishful thinking unless a practical political alternative to judicial action exists that the lawyers and clients can explore.

With respect to *Brown,* there is little evidence that such an alternative was available. It is an exercise in science fiction to imagine that legislative action in a Congress dominated by southern segregationists or in Jim Crow state legislatures would have ended white supremacy. Presidential power had in theory integrated the military and could have influenced other federal policy, but it could go just so far, even assuming a president who was on a mission (as was not the case with Dwight Eisenhower). Other options one can imagine hardly inspire confidence in even middle-term social change. Education about racism is critical, but there is no easy way to convert it into practical results. The educational value of Supreme Court decisions is real but regularly overrated, but then so is the educational value of political debates, classroom lectures, and advertising campaigns.[22]

Of course, political action would have been preferable to a Supreme Court decision. Litigators for the NAACP and LDF knew how to deal with politicians if politics would get them where they wanted to go. The fact is that except in times of great public turmoil, no one can predict how political action of the sort critics imply should take the place of litigation will affect minority interests. Only occasionally do civil rights proponents or advocates for the poor have the votes they need to advance their cause. Ancillary to political action, grass-roots fieldwork is also important but also of limited impact—it is dangerous, it is hard to do, and too often it yields only isolated, unpublicized local victories that are not usually translated into regional or national policy. The NAACP's Clarence Mitchell lobbied Washington lawmakers with great effect during the civil rights era, but even a magician like Mitchell required a visible national framework, the political support of white officials, and at least passive acceptance from their primarily white electorates for the success of his legislative proposals. Not incidentally, Mitchell loved to quote court decisions to bolster his arguments to key legislators.

Taking on the issue of alternatives to litigation seriously would require both a rigorous investigation into the moribund state of the activities and leadership of civil rights organizations in recent decades and an inquiry into what, if anything, could be done about it. Few students of litigation in the academy will go near these topics because they involve greater intimacy with messy practical intervention than with textual analysis. As for asking the civil rights world to engage in a review of this sort, unfortunately, it probably takes a leader of Dr. King's stature to shake people out of their habits. Finally, it is evident that too many Americans, black as well as white, are currently indifferent to the racial and class issues that concern civil rights actors, a matter with vast political implications. In short, there is nothing accidental in the strong tendency of LDF and others with a public policy agenda to think about courts first.

Perhaps one shouldn't ask scholars to do more than play their own role. In this respect, the essential point of *The Hollow Hope*'s reception is the unwillingness of numerous reviewers and analysts to develop the territory lying between, on the one hand, the common idea that courts sometimes accomplish useful reform but sometimes inhibit it and, on the other, the conclusion that as vehicles for reform they are virtually worthless. While Rosenberg appears at times to give credence to both views, again and again he suggests that if there are truly effective reformist court decisions out there, he has yet to find them.

No civil rights lawyers or activists that I know of claimed that *Brown*-stimulated court orders directly produced significant school desegregation in the decade after the decision was announced. From a civil rights advocate's perspective, however, *Brown*'s statement of principle had to be interpreted broadly and urged adamantly until a critical mass of political forces brought about an end to segregation. The idea that *Brown* might produce massive results given the limited terms of *Brown II*'s "all deliberate speed" formulation computed only in the narrow sense that many moves toward an end to segregation reinforced each other and that a decision by a government institution as respected as the Supreme Court, speaking in the name of the Constitution, carried weight in some quarters. Americans had lived with slavery and segregation for hundreds of years; why does the fact that serious school desegregation took ten to fifteen years suggest that the Supreme Court decision played no significant part in the changes that took place in the 1960s and 1970s?

Much like the Fourteenth Amendment of 1868, whose "equal protection" language it construed, *Brown* has become a mythic text as well as a mythic event, one with disputed and multiple foundational meanings that tell us more about our contemporary perspective than its original understanding. While changing patterns of employment, military service, and government policy encouraged civil rights activity before 1954, and sit-ins, marches, and legislative victories accelerated progress thereafter, continued efforts to come to terms with its legacy remind us that *Brown* remains the movement's imaginative center.

Brown was good because it fostered integration and condemned a detestable racial system. It was bad because the Supreme Court, instead of insisting on immediate compliance, diluted its decision to take account of the racism of its opponents. It was bad because it failed to make clear that the constitutional goal was educational equity and that desegregation was just one means to that end, resulting in a system of integrated and superior education for black families who could afford to live where middle-class whites lived and inferior and segregated education for those who couldn't. *Brown* created a vast middle class, multiplied the numbers of high school and college graduates, and greatly bolstered black income. *Brown* divided the black community along class lines. It produced hardly anything except resistance to its terms, which, ironically, did lead to progress—but ultimately, with respect to education, to a great deal of resegregation.

We should honor it; we should lament it.

It is certainly true that LDF attempted to squeeze *Brown* for all it was worth in subsequent cases; sometimes this was an effective tactic and at other times not, but at some point other branches of the federal government had to say that segregation was unconstitutional and act accordingly for progress to be made in ending second-class citizenship and fantasies of white superiority. A court decision can go just so far under the best of circumstances. But a movement needs a name, a rallying cry, and benchmarks of progress; *Brown* supplied them for a time, as well as legal precedent. It is passing strange that because *Brown* didn't do everything, it should be held up as doing nothing. The effort to demonstrate this is no more convincing than the effort of those scholars who over a hundred years ago foolishly sought to identify a single cause for the fall of the Roman Empire.

The real story about *The Hollow Hope,* I think, is why it has been taken so seriously as a metaphor for the limited powers of the judiciary and why so little analysis has been given to the concrete options and practical alternatives to using the courts. The American legal scene has always been populated by prominent lawyers who have preached the limits of litigation as a strategy for social reform. The left complains that too little has changed—court decisions have had so little effect after raising hopes for dramatic structural change. The right agrees. It strives to support legislation that trims judges' wings and complains about lawyers who scuttle settled social arrangements and judges who hold business to cost-inefficient regulatory standards. The talk of how little litigation can matter moderates conservatives' fears. Finally, the intellectuals who point to institutional factors that make the courts' role marginal at best in many areas and largely exhortative in others have never been blind to its obvious shortcomings. They seemed pleased to have empirical evidence available that appears to support what they firmly believed anyway.

By contending that courts are basically flawed when it comes to controversial reform, those who rely on the *Hollow Hope* thesis are also obviously innocent of any accusation that they favor undemocratic means of decision making. More important, they can point to a preference for means of accomplishing major social change other than "foolish" reliance on litigation. But aside from generalities about supporting legislation, education of the electorate, or further research, neither Rosenberg nor those who follow him have much to say on this subject. The result is a diagnosis that can easily be understood to undermine one of the few accessible modes of reform available to the disempowered while providing nothing but bromides in its place.

It is fascinating that many of the academics who accept Rosenberg's conclusion that *Brown* did little, if anything, to bring about change in racial patterns call attention to and teach about Supreme Court cases as if they were events of great importance. American legal education is overwhelmingly concerned with discussion of legal cases and their implications. All American lawyers are educated as if litigation must be studied carefully, especially constitutional litigation, and that other means of resolving disputes, such as legislative bargaining tactics and administrative action, negotiation. and arbitration, while of obvious significance, need be dealt with only at the educational margins.

This circumstance gives a sharp edge to Stephen Carter's comments on *The Hollow Hope*. If Rosenberg is correct, Carter says, there is a basic "misreading of the relationship of the Supreme Court to the civil rights movement [that] has combined with the typical elite impatience with ordinary politics to lead an entire generation of scholars into a dubious effort to explain how a wide variety of rights are already in the Constitution—as though," and here is the heart of Carter's flamboyant point, "should the courts agree, the social changes that the scholars seek would, like magic, come to pass." Carter concludes that if courts cannot bring about "major social change, then the great bulk of contemporary constitutional theory," and implicitly the work of many of his colleagues, "which assumes otherwise, is a waste."[23]

But notice the leap Carter makes—from "dubious" claims that "rights" are in the Constitution to the conclusion that *if* Rosenberg is correct, court decisions could not "bring about major social change." In short, if you are *against* attributing those "rights" (privacy, for example) to the

Constitution and *against* the "major social change" that might follow from doing so, Rosenberg is a truly welcome visitor.

Given their dependence on litigation, the difficulty of determining the impact of judicial power in particular cases and classes of cases, and the ideological currents that tangle objectivity, American lawyers are ambivalent about the powers and influence of courts. They are deeply committed to attending to what courts say while at the same time they know that the more significant the public law ruling, the more likely it will be assailed as antidemocratic by the losers. Once it is understood that the impact of litigation will be variable even if it is successful, it may be easier to accept that some battles must be fought in the courts because no other forum is available. As Charles F. Sabel and William H. Simon put it in a *Harvard Law Review* essay published thirteen years after *The Hollow Hope*—evidence of the longevity of such concerns—courts can destabilize or "unsettle and open up public institutions that have chronically failed to meet their obligations and that are substantially insulated from the normal processes of political accountability."[24] By intervening, as in the prison and principal-hiring cases, lower courts brought about budget changes, negotiation over policy, and outside monitoring of bureaucracies that would not have taken place otherwise. Litigation still has enormous value in the proper setting and can be a frustrating diversion in others. The ability to know the difference in advance is art, not science. Yet as we move into a world where broad claims of terrorism will be used to justify intrusions on liberty, invasions of privacy, and restriction of personal freedom, the ability to go to court may be all that keeps a massive government accountable.

In 2005 the debate over the impact of reform litigation moved from the law reviews to a mainstream political controversy over the role of the courts. Demands for change arose from distress over Supreme Court resolution of abortion and gay rights issues. Bolstered by surprising claims that the Court is hostile to religion, the attacks came from those who feel their interests have not been recognized by adverse decisions and who believe legislative and executive branches present more favorable opportunities to influence policy. When joined with efforts to change the manner in which federal judges are confirmed by the Senate, the implications for the traditional understanding of judicial review in a system of representative democracy with built-in checks and balances are significant.

Attacking the scope of the judiciary's power is as old as exercise of that power. More recently, in the early twentieth century, progressive voices were raised against a Supreme Court that thwarted economic regulation; then it was the turn of the conservatives to rail against the rights-creating activism of the Warren Court. Today groups angry with particular results are joined by opponents of judicial review who assert high-minded concern for proper democratic values.

The basic contention is that giving the courts final authority to review certain legislative acts for constitutionality is a betrayal of public opinion. Justification for change proceeds from notions aptly captured by the title of a book recommending them, *The People Themselves,* by Stanford Law School dean Larry Kramer. While noticeably vague about what would replace the current system, proponents like Kramer imply judicial review should be narrowed or conditioned on approval of Congress or state legislatures. According to Kramer, in the eighteenth century judicial review was not authoritative; the people themselves, directly or via elected representatives, controlled basic decision making, and should once more. It is unclear what such historical reconstructions, assuming they are more than mythology, tell us. The country was new; it was populated only by a few million, and its franchise was limited to a homogenous, property-owning elite, excluding of course women and African American slaves. Communication and transportation were rudimentary.

Mark Tushnet relies less on history and more on axioms—true self-government requires political not judicial decision making on constitutional issues. Tushnet proposes doing away with review of statutes entirely; he asserts faith that basic rights and constitutional values would be protected by the public operating through the electoral process and by those judicial powers that would remain.

Critics have pointed to some of the apparent defects in such proposals. They short-weight the democratic control of how judges are selected. Institutionally developed patterns of reasoning and case-focused decisional processes should be seen as essential parts of a multifaceted and multifunctional government, not viewed alone and in the abstract. Whether having an institution committed to impartiality that must give reasons for what it does and works from a settled record is undemocratic depends on how one defines the democracy one wants.

At the same time, the democratic glories of legislatures are overstated. Proposals for "popular democracy" often ignore questionable districting and elections excessively influenced by campaign contributions. These legislatures are often controlled by a few senior members, influential lobbyists, and a rigid committee structure. In some cases, they are explicitly unrepresentative—as in the U.S. Senate—and in others at most they reflect less "the people" than controlling segments of the voting population.

The behavior of congressional leadership in deciding the medical care that Terri Schiavo would have wanted exemplifies the worst abuses of a legislative body attempting to resolve individual disputes. Courts also have their record of abuses; perhaps the best protection the public has in a polarized nation is multiple centers of power. In truth, this debate is not between democratic and nondemocratic decision making but over how democracy should be defined and understood.

Proposals to restrict or abandon judicial review are intimately if confusedly connected to the thesis of *The Hollow Hope.* On the one hand, popular constitutionalists, pointing to Rosenberg, say that courts do not really protect minority rights; they tell critics not to get upset because what courts do is not that important. On the other hand, paradoxically, the basic assumption of their project is that courts have grabbed too much power from the people and that, therefore, major surgery is called for. It is a measure of the changes at work in the nation since the civil rights era that supposedly liberal theorists can put forth ideas that offer no serious assurance that minority interests in speech and expression, fair trial procedures, and, of course, equality will be given much protection. These scholars seem to wince when forced to consider how *Brown v. Board of Education* would have been decided under their system. Here Kramer and Tushnet rely on what civil rights lawyers will regard as a truly naive belief in miracles: because the courts have taken on the obligation to protect civil liberties and rights, it is claimed, Congress and the president have abdicated their responsibilities; if only the judicial power is diminished, they will assert themselves to assure constitutional protections.

Legal Killing Revisited

ONE issue dominated my last years at LDF and continues years later to hold me in its grip. To the amazement and sometimes consternation of staff members past and present, LDF is also still absorbed after forty years by its role in opposing capital punishment. The longevity of the issue is all the more surprising when one realizes that save for its significant racial dimension, civil rights advocates never dreamed as the 1960s began that capital punishment would become a consuming concern, much less that LDF would come agonizingly close to eliminating it permanently.

In 1972, in an unexpected and startling decision, the Supreme Court was to rule 5 to 4 that state death-penalty sentencing laws had produced such arbitrary and capricious results as to amount to cruel and unusual punishment, in violation of the Eighth and Fourteenth amendments.[1] At first there was a profound sense of vindication at LDF. The press and many of the justices themselves believed that the decision in *Furman v. Georgia* meant an end to execution, bringing national policy in line with diminishing domestic support and abandonment of capital punishment in the rest of the world. But *Furman* was followed quickly by a powerful citizen backlash: hostile poll numbers, public rejection of the Court's position in a key California referendum that reauthorized the death penalty after it had been judicially abolished by the Supreme Court of California, and the prompt passage of new laws in thirty-five states—nineteen by 1973— aimed in various ways at restoring state power to kill by mending the flaws pointed out by *Furman*.[2]

Four years later, the Court shifted course from looking toward abolition to promoting regulation of decisions to execute; it approved several of the new laws on the assumption that states had narrowed their scope by identifying specific aggravating factors that would make a murder so serious it could support a death sentence rather than life in prison. The Court also endorsed a separate sentencing hearing at which evidence of mitigating as well as aggravating circumstances could be presented and implied that state appellate courts should play a key role in reducing capricious death sentencing by carefully reviewing the consistency of trial courts' sentencing practices.[3]

So much for theory. In literally hundreds of subsequent decisions the justices have added to and subtracted from this basic system, producing a complicated hodgepodge of hard-to-understand rules, tendencies, and approaches that seem to reflect more the tensions of case-by-case institutional management of death than any effort at consistent lawmaking.[4] The Court waited twenty-five years to ban execution of the retarded and in 2005 finally ruled out killing juveniles.[5] It has told states to narrow the range of death-eligible cases, held that rape or robbery cannot be a justification for execution, required rules that encourage a due sense of responsibility on the part of sentencing juries, and set aside numerous judgments of lower courts for constitutional error.

On the other hand, the Court has refused to require state supreme courts to review death sentences for consistency, set a high bar for those claiming innocence, declined to intervene in eliminating racial disparities, found acceptable virtually all state definitions of aggravating circumstances, raised concerns about the finality of lower court judgments above fears of wrongful conviction, and narrowed to the point of occlusion the range of options open to federal courts considering new claims of constitutional violation. The Supreme Court has, of course, declined to review far more cases, many of which have ended in execution, than it has actually considered.

There were 655 men and women on death row in 1972; as of the winter of 2004–5 the number was 3,455.[6] The way the system now operates has few defenders, but if Americans are told that its defects are so great that they might justify abolition, a majority will still adamantly prefer capital punishment (though by a somewhat smaller margin than in the past) and may vote against any politician who disagrees with them. The number of executions trended up in the early 1990s, and given the large death row population, it may eventually climb higher unless changes are made in the basic law governing the penalty—even though the average number of death sentences has been cut by a third in the last four years. Depending on your point of view or values, we are either too slow to punish or too careless in investigating critical facts, spend too much money to bring about an execution or are too chary to spend what is needed on adequate defense lawyers. Death row houses too many people whose crimes, while serious, do not justify a death sentence but does not contain enough of those who should die, if anyone should. Capital punishment pressures defendants to plead guilty; that outcome is either good (it is efficient) or bad (it catches people who are fearful but not guilty rather than the truly guilty). Capital punishment is selective; no, it is unequal. And so on.

A seemingly endless series of doubts about the reliability, fairness, and effectiveness of over thirty years of post-*Furman* death sentencing covering the entire political spectrum have led some observers to question efforts to rid the country of the death penalty. According to the law professors Jordan and Carol Steiker, "One could argue that the Court's attempt to dismantle segregation was more intrusive (and more fated to fail) than its rejection of the death penalty in that segregation was a pervasive and deeply rooted social practice as compared to merely an alternative penal sanction that was used only rarely even in its heyday." The Steikers believe, however, that such a contention "ignores the popularity of the death penalty, the genuine outrage that was voiced at its purported abolition by the Court, and its significance as a symbol of social hatred of and power over violent crime." The Steikers ultimately reject the conclusion that the courts had no role to play in scrutinizing the legality of the death penalty and implicitly that it was a mistake for LDF to ask them to intervene: "Unlike the desegregation context and many other settings of institutional reform, in the context of capital punishment, the 'institution' subject to reform was the legal process itself—the criminal justice system. . . . The administration of capital punishment is much more court-centered than the education of children. . . . When the Supreme Court speaks to the reformation of the legal process, it speaks with special experience and legitimacy."[7]

Another complaint finds that the LDF rushed "ahead in advancing its arguments [against the death penalty]," spending too much time and money on capital cases and too little on educating the public, distracting LDF from the legitimate claims of noncapital litigants and benefiting "nearly as many whites as blacks" by advancing legal arguments that had no "necessary connection with racial issues." According to this view voiced by Eric Muller, a North Carolina law professor who interviewed Greenberg, Nabrit, and me when he was a law student, under the pressure of representing so many men at risk of dying LDF failed to exercise sufficient control over the cases by bringing the issue before the Supreme Court without first creating a supportive political consensus. The organization's decisional process was insufficiently "clinical" in that it did not balance the demands of winning a legal campaign "with the emotion inherent in capital representation." Muller speculates that had the Fund waited to bring cases like *Furman* until after "the 1977 case that eliminated the death penalty for crimes that did not take life," the Supreme Court might have produced a coherent Eighth Amendment condemnation of the death penalty, attracting a majority rather than just two votes for per se abolition.[8]

After LDF moved from a campaign to eliminate the racially discriminatory application of the death penalty for rape to challenging the arbitrariness of all death-penalty laws, claims were occasionally made that costly litigation against the death penalty should not have been placed so high on the civil rights agenda. While aware of the criticism, we concluded with little discussion of competing needs for the money that racism pervaded death cases and the only way to fight it effectively was to check the death penalty in general. When LDF believed it had the means to save lives, its next step was predictable—the staff was not constituted of people likely to engage in cost-benefit analysis of life-and-death issues.

It is difficult, however, to be sure exactly what lies at the heart of Muller's complaint. The literature describing the Supreme Court's actions in those capital cases brought to it in the 1960s and 1970s makes clear that it was not LDF lawyers representing men who might be executed who set the pace for the Court or controlled the way it acted. LDF brought the cases in quantity but the justices themselves were responsible for the jagged movement toward, away from, and then toward and again away from significant restriction of the death penalty. In the LDF case *Maxwell v. Bishop*,[9] for example, the Court had an opportunity to test out public attitudes by taking a measured step toward abolition, but it shied away, only to be faced with a more extreme choice in *Furman*.

The Court could then have imposed procedural requirements that might have set the stage for determining how pronounced and intractable was the arbitrariness claimed for capital sentencing. A preliminary vote of the justices after *Maxwell* was argued revealed that a majority supported requiring a separate hearing on sentencing at which the defendant could present evidence to the jury as to why he should be allowed to live. But then Justice Abe Fortas resigned from the Court and the judge who replaced him, Harry Blackmun, recused himself because he had written the lower court opinion in Maxwell's case. As a result, the conviction was overturned, but on a limited ground; when the separate-hearing issue was presented again the following year, Justice John Harlan changed his vote, leading the Court to reject the procedural arguments that might have postponed the ultimate confrontation with the constitutionality of execution.[10]

LDF had raised doubts about how death was selected by sentencing juries because every American state that permitted execution did so without setting out any principles to guide the life-or-death decision, and most made it difficult for a defendant to offer evidence of mitigating circumstances. Jurors were being told to act like Roman emperors giving thumbs up or down in the Coliseum. We believed this absence of law produced enough freakish results to render the death sentence unconstitutional, but LDF also challenged the laws for strategic purposes—to give the Court an opportunity short of abolition to force the states to reexamine the death penalty. LDF's framing of issues was an important part of the lawmaking process but it obviously could not control the Court's understandable ambivalence about what to do with the cases brought to it. Once one realizes that on many issues the High Court is really nine separate courts operating in a less than optimal and not always integrated manner, the conclusion is inescapable that the justices themselves had no consistent or coherent idea about what to do with the death penalty.

Nor could LDF keep death cases from the Court until it had assurance of success. There were too many cases and too many lawyers with typewriters in their offices, but even if we had represented every death row inmate in the United States we would not, of course, have let them die without a judicial appeal.

Another Muller objection—that LDF ended up spending a great deal of time and money on capital punishment when it offered to represent anyone on death row, regardless of race or crime—is factually accurate but ultimately strategically shortsighted and morally obtuse. LDF decided that its best chance to persuade Americans as well as the Court that the nation had rejected the death penalty was to try to stop its use. This task required us to influence the thinking of as many lawyers and judges as possible in any case, rape or murder, regardless of the race of the defendant or victim. LDF and the lawyers who followed its lead were able to postpone enough executions by pointing to the very litigation campaign that was sending all the major issues to the Supreme Court for resolution. By 1972, no one had been executed in the United States in five years. Five of the group of 655 whose lives were saved by *Furman* were thought to have been demonstrably innocent of the charges against them.

When *Furman* was decided, the Court's ruling went as far as LDF lawyers could have realistically hoped and farther than they expected, but the fragmented and divergent character of the five majority opinions gave powerful evidence that the justices had been unable to reach common ground. The decision of the Court was actually a few lines setting out the result. But the nine individual opinions themselves appear to have covered more pages in the official law reports than any other case in Supreme Court history. A matter of importance that might be lost on those who weren't close observers of the Court was that none of the opinion writers in the majority joined in the opinion of any of his fellows. This fragmentation was a rarity and, more significant, it would become a source of a good deal of the criticism that *Furman* was confusing and obscure in not telling lawyers what lay ahead. Though it hardly compensated for the uncertainty, there was a virtue in each justice's writing a solo opinion: each thus took personal responsibility for a particular point of view.

Robert Burt, Muller's teacher at Yale Law School, has contrasted the "disarray" of the Court's behavior in *Furman* with the Warren Court's record of unanimity in school desegregation cases, where in case after case for two decades the justices put aside differences to shape the message they thought the country needed, that integration was here to stay. Burt complained that the Court failed to link *Furman* to "the recent history" of its capital-punishment decisions or "even to link one Justice to another." The "isolation" of the justices from their "shared institutional history" and from one another, he found, abandoned the pursuit of the common ground necessary for society's faith in the rule of law.[11]

This charge of poor leadership by the Court reflected a growing division in the population. The civil rights movement promised changes in society greater than it had produced, but it had accomplished enough to create a backlash. LDF defined its capital-punishment campaign as an extension of the movement, highlighting the connection between black aspirations and white fears of black criminality. The justices, in Burt's view, had failed to meliorate the social divisions that beset Americans, but the public response to *Furman* revealed that the society itself was "divided by implacable hostilities." The death penalty did not fully define this conflict but it was a powerful metaphor—a signpost that the country was moving away from a liberal understanding of human nature and finding that a

Hobbesian view better fitted the facts; the ultimate penalty would become a highly visible marker of this shift.[12]

If the justices' venture in abolition had not fallen apart and we were no longer a death-penalty country or if capital punishment had been implemented in a way that justified confidence that life was being taken in a manner that comported with a consensus of national values, few doubts would be raised about the origin and strategy of litigation against the death penalty. It is only because the post-*Furman* death penalty has produced a costly, muddled, and dangerously unreliable legal and ethical universe that criticism has been directed toward the behavior of lawyers and judges associated with capital-punishment litigation. Earlier I discussed the criticism addressed to LDF and other public interest organizations that have attempted to use the courts as agents of social change. To consider these objections in the context of the death penalty requires us to go back to the beginnings of the modern movement to end capital punishment.

In the early 1960s I was about as prepared as the rest of the Legal Defense Fund staff to become an anti-capital-punishment lawyer; in other words, poorly. For years, LDF had joined with its cooperating attorneys in the South to represent men who had been sentenced to death in circumstances that indicated racial discrimination or a failure to use procedures required by the Constitution that would have protected African American defendants. While criminal lawyers had long been aware that the federal courts were likely to define and apply constitutionally required procedures more liberally when life was on the line and when black defendants were involved, the courts had stayed away from airing doubts about the legality of state-imposed death itself. Almost no legal precedent was available for attacking the death penalty in court. Until 1965, even the American Civil Liberties Union did not think capital punishment itself, as opposed to the way it might be administered in particular cases, amounted to a violation of civil liberties.

In the 1949 case against the defendants known as the Martinsville Seven, the NAACP had participated through key Virginia cooperating attorneys and later by an unsuccessful petition to the Supreme Court written by Jack Greenberg, challenging the commonwealth's record of sending only black men convicted of raping white women to death. Since the early years of the century, fifty-five black men and no whites had been executed for rape in Virginia. Before the Civil War, Virginia, like most southern states, maintained a system of dual penalties for rape: whites could be sentenced to a maximum of twenty years but blacks could be put to death.

After the ratification of the Fourteenth Amendment in 1868, Virginia and virtually every other state in the region accomplished the same dual sentencing result by eliminating explicit racial designations but giving trial juries discretion to choose between prison and execution. Overwhelmingly white southern juries didn't need to have anything written in lawbooks to tell them what to do when rape charges were brought before them. One explanation put forth to justify the practice had a bizarre twist: a common defense in intraracial rape cases was consent, but any black defendant who claimed before a Virginia jury that a white woman had agreed to intercourse doomed himself by doing so. In a gruesome execution scenario, all seven defendants in the Martinsville case were ultimately put to death.[13]

In another set of 1949 interracial rape cases, Florida charged four blacks in Groveland with rape of a white woman under circumstances that made the story extremely suspicious. Mob violence dominated the trial in rural Lake County and local police badly beat two defendants and actually killed a third one, claiming he resisted arrest. The trial led to death sentences, but the Supreme Court ordered a new hearing because of blatant exclusion of blacks from the jury system. Before a second trial took place, events so horrific occurred that Greenberg would later say they prepared him to fight the death penalty for rape when an occasion presented itself.[14] First, Ku Klux Klan members threatened the lawyers. Then, on the eve of trial, two defendants were shot by a Lake County sheriff on what appeared to be a pretext as they were being transported to the county seat from prison. One died; he was the second of the four accused to be killed by law enforcement officers. Walter Irvin, who survived, was badly injured. He was eventually tried anyway, this time in another segregated Florida county, and was convicted and sentenced to death on the basis of what turned out to be faked tire impressions and shoeprints. These events were so embarrassing to the state that the governor later commuted the death sentence.

In the following years southern black lawyers made sporadic efforts to raise equal-protection challenges to rape prosecutions; they all failed. In 1961, when I joined the staff, I knew only the flimsiest version of the nightmarish history of race and sexual assault in the South, most of it from law school reading about the cases generated by the infamous Scottsboro prosecutions in the 1930s, so similar to the Groveland case that it was called the Little Scottsboro case. Of course, I was familiar in a bookish way with the South's history of lynching, and while in college had followed the chilling story of Emmett Till, a fourteen-year-old boy who was kidnapped, mutilated, and then shot to death in 1955 because he had whistled at a Mississippi white woman. I'd also read a number of Supreme Court opinions in coerced confession cases. These were staples of the law school courses that dealt with issues of criminal law; many of these cases featured black defendants charged with capital crimes, white law enforcement officers, and gruesome accounts of violence and intimidation. Like many attorneys before and after me, I began to question the death penalty when I recognized the obvious racial patterns that emerged in such case reports—blacks excluded from juries, given inadequate trial counsel, making questionable statements to hostile and often physically brutal interrogators, cases reviewed by elected state appellate judges who too often rationalized a harsh and unreliable criminal justice system. At LDF I would move from skepticism to fierce opposition by direct contact with the cases of men on death row.

Within a month of my arrival, it became part of my job to read a share of the piles of letters that reached LDF every week from prisoners requesting legal assistance. These letters were easy to recognize from the envelopes: they were addressed, often in pencil, to "NAACP, New York" or "Lawyer Marshall," with a post office box in some rural town as return address. The letters themselves were usually scrawled on lined paper and all too often incoherent. The prisoners had no law libraries and most had such a weak grasp on literacy that they couldn't have taken advantage of lawbooks if they had been available. Not all of the writers were mentally competent; statistics indicate that almost 20 percent of the death row population suffer from some degree of retardation. Many of the letters were also addressed to the White House or J. Edgar Hoover and even the pope.

The prisoners listed their grievances: constitutional rights disregarded; conviction because of race despite innocence of all charges. They told confused, partial stories of how a lying codefendant or bad cop or bigoted judge or sleazy lawyer was responsible for their incarceration; often the facts were so tangled it took imagination to grasp what the inmate was really complaining about. Most of the letters were pathetic attempts to find reasons to upset jury verdicts of conviction, long sentences, or condemnation to death.

More often than I expected, though, I heard a ring of truth in these allegations. If I sensed something worth investigating, I wrote the prisoner. Eventually I was able to get delivery of court files. Most of the time the trail ended here. The inmate's first letter had been misleading or overstated or had omitted crucial facts or had just plain lied about what had happened or told a painful set of truths for which there was no legal remedy. By writing to a prisoner, though, I had caused my name to pass though the system, and I was secretly proud when I got mail addressed to me personally, along with J. Edgar Hoover, the pope, and the president.

Sometimes, however, the claim checked out and I found myself in Jack Greenberg's office, asking him to let me or some other staff lawyer add the case to our load. He raised some pointed questions but almost always let me pursue the matter if he glimpsed signs of a legal issue of any substance. Once or twice every few years the process produced a winning case and a feeling on my part that no matter what else happened, my life as a lawyer was worth the cost. In 1967, for example, I started getting marginally coherent letters from a Tennessee prisoner, a former mental patient, who complained that his conviction for murder had been based almost wholly on a statement he gave to two newspaper reporters. After some digging, I learned that the police had improperly taken a statement from the suspect and, realizing they could not use it as evidence, brought the journalists into the suspect's jail cell and let them seek incriminating answers. Tony Amsterdam and I wrote a pauper's petition to the Supreme Court, and to our amazement, the Court reversed the conviction without even hearing argument.[15]

I worked with Tony on many cases from 1963 on. Although he is better known as the chief architect of capital-punishment strategy, his contribution to vast numbers of important civil rights cases has gone largely unappreciated beyond the circle of LDF insiders. I mark the hours spent in his company as the highest points in over forty years of lawyering. He combined overwhelming brainpower across the disciplines and true compassion for the underdog with vast energy packed in his rail-thin body. Amsterdam could have accepted the easy life of a celebrated scholar; instead, he dedicated himself to using his knowledge in action—to protect values he cherished and clients he thought oppressed.

Amsterdam's work habits were fascinating. When I first met him we were only in our twenties, but he conveyed the accumulated legal wisdom of a much older man. His office was located inside the library of the University of Pennsylvania Law School, where he went to teach in 1962 after clerking for Justice Frankfurter and serving briefly as an assistant United States attorney. It was easy to playfully imagine legal principles being piped into the office from some central intellectual furnace room in the library basement. I thought I worked hard, but it was immediately clear that compared to him, I was a part-timer. He sat behind a mountain of lawbooks of every description and every recent decision—thousands a year—reached by the federal courts of appeals. Regularly sleeping but a few hours a night, he left the impression of having at least skimmed them all and also of rarely leaving the premises.

Because he found it hard to say no to requests for assistance, Tony had to adopt a set of quietly evasive tactics to get time to do his work—his day job as a law teacher and prolific scholar, lead lawyer in LDF cases he had volunteered to take on, and a never-ending list of phone calls seeking a "brief" consultation. As far as I know, he never took a fee for any of this work. Carrying drafts of legal documents and what must have been dozens of red pens, he might disappear and be unreachable for several days, then materialize early one morning to smack down on my desk a revised version of a brief or pleading.

In 1973, when I was completing a book in which I described him in glowing terms, my famously skeptical editor, Joe Fox of Random House, looked up from paging through the manuscript and deadpanned, "Does this guy have any faults you know of?"

"Well, you know he has a degree in art history" was all I could come up with, "and he actually likes those ridiculous sixteenth- and seventeenth-century European Mannerist paintings." Joe looked at me longer than I liked, deeply inhaled one of the Camels that ultimately killed him, and then turned the page.

The personal satisfaction of victories such as the Tennessee appeal was real but also deeply frustrating. For each such case there must have been dozens no one ever heard of. Such cases hinted at major flaws in the picture most Americans held of criminal justice. Only systemic change could fix them, and that seemed unlikely. When due process vied with the promise that punishment would ensure our security, it usually came in second.

Other death cases were sent to us by busy cooperating lawyers who had taken matters as far as they could in state courts. The case files arrived at 10 Columbus Circle with little fanfare unless an execution date was imminent. At such times, the atmosphere at LDF grew tense until an application for a stay of execution was prepared and dispatched to the higher courts. All too often death cases came from lawyers with little more information than might be gleaned from an inmate's scrawled letter. One such file referred to me in 1962 involved a young black man from rural Greene County, Alabama, named Johnny "Big Time" Coleman. Johnny had been convicted of the capital murder of a white man called Screwdriver Johnson, whose nickname came from the constant companion that hung from his belt. There were no witnesses to the fight that led one man to death and the other to death row; just how the all-white jury conjured up a death sentence for my client was unknown.[16]

Unfortunately, innocence or a claim of self-defense was not then and is not now an easy point to win on appeal once a jury has come back with a guilty verdict. Nor was it practically possible then to argue to an appellate court that even if Coleman was guilty, this was not the sort of extreme case that deserved execution.

At the same time that I was being initiated into the mysteries of prisoner mail and trying to pick the best strategy to use in Coleman's case, Professor Bickel was including a passage about the death penalty in what would prove to be his most influential book. "Unfortunately," he wrote, "from the point of view of one who disbelieves in legal killing . . . the Court has missed or has willfully passed up its most signal opportunities to shape and reduce the issue. No sort of colloquy can be said to be in progress and barring spectacular extraneous events, the moment of judgment is therefore a generation or more away."[17] Bickel was reacting to the Court's lackluster performance in the appeal of the convicted atom spies Julius and Ethel Rosenberg; its acquiescence in the execution of a notorious inmate in California, Caryl Chessman, for a crime that state law no longer deemed worthy of death; and its refusal to intervene when two men of dubious sanity were put to death. As a teacher and scholar, Bickel could be provocative, but where the Court's institutional competence was concerned, he instinctively exercised caution—it is no accident that he called the book in question *The Least Dangerous Branch.* His frustration that the Supreme Court had not reached out in the 1950s to set in motion principles that might bring down the death penalty was, to say the least, surprising, and hinted at a personal connection to the issue. No less surprising, however, was that the "spectacular extraneous events" he had no hope of actually occurring were but a year away.

It would take two trips to the Supreme Court of the United States to get Johnny Coleman a new trial before a jury from which blacks had not been excluded. I was afraid that the new trial would lead to another death sentence, but at that trial, as if to thumb his nose at the far-off court in Washington, the local white prosecutor empaneled an all-black jury, one of the first to sit in Alabama since Reconstruction. Coleman was acquitted.

On the way to the Supreme Court we had to surmount technical hurdles set up by the Alabama courts; to meet them I had to read several decades' worth of opinions written by justices of the Alabama Supreme Court in capital murder and rape cases. Sitting in the dreary windowless library at the Legal Defense Fund's offices, surrounded by a growing pile of lawbooks, I discovered to my horror that dozens of these cases had been bungled. I felt like a pathologist doing autopsies that revealed lethal malpractice. The lawyers in these cases had either not raised at all or not raised properly legal claims that should have resulted in new trials. It was not difficult to conclude, for example, that the juries had been unconstitutionally selected because even after only a year or so at LDF I was aware of the racial practices of the counties in question. The local white defense attorneys had not dared to risk the ostracism that would follow a demand for a racially integrated jury process. In too many other cases, the representation ran from mediocre to poor.

It was a big leap from these disturbing cameos of the law at work to the abstract manner in which capital punishment was discussed—when it was—in those days. A few tiny anti-death-penalty organizations distributed literature and sponsored debates about the ethics of government-sponsored killing. When a particularly egregious case surfaced, they would gain adherents and press legislators to change the law. In New York, a gory 1963 double murder charge against a nineteen-year-old black man named George Whitmore Jr.—later exonerated—would ultimately play this role. In Boston, Herbert Ehrman, once a lawyer on the defense team for the anarchists Nicola Sacco and Bartolomeo Vanzetti, who had been executed in 1927, and his wife, Sara, worked tirelessly to gain supporters, but they had failed to make abolition a part of mainstream political activity. Delaware, Hawaii, and Alaska abolished capital punishment in the late 1950s, but the Delaware legislature reversed itself three years later.[18] Twelve other states had working abolitionist committees, but sincere as their efforts were, there was little chance they would succeed.

Hopeful about the future but paradoxically unable to take an optimistic view of human nature, I decided I was a different kind of abolitionist. Most abolitionists talked philosophically about deterrence and retribution, the vengefulness of "an eye for an eye," the logic of "just deserts," and the potential for rehabilitation of convicted murderers. I didn't so much disagree with their positions as find myself unmoved by the academic and abstract quality of such discourse. The problem for me was that all sorts of crimes made me feel the killer deserved to die; after all, I told myself, the Nazis had almost taken over the world. It's "extreme and repellant crimes," as Scott Turow put it years later, "that provoke the highest emotions" and are the greatest obstacles to efforts to dispense with capital punishment.[19]

When my work on the death penalty began, it took a while to learn that I could feel repulsion and acknowledge the wish for retribution without having to conclude that my feelings should be written into law. Capital punishment had to be seen as a system that operated generally, not as a means of gratifying the wish to rid the world of an evildoer. Still, I knew where the impulse to pay back came from and found it anything but alien; even if I ended up in the same place as the organized abolitionists, I couldn't talk about legal death the way they did. I would forever be hung up on the way the law did it—which was obviously racial, slanted, inept, on the cheap, and even lazy. And my education had just begun.

While I was working my way through the reports of forgotten Alabama death cases, the lawyer in the next office was also working on a capital case. Frank Heffron, another white lawyer overlooked by Judge Motley in her autobiography, had been asked to look into the case of an Arkansas death row prisoner named William Maxwell. An intruder had forced his way into a house occupied by a thirty-five-year-old woman and her aged father in Hot Springs. The Arkansas courts found that she fought and struggled to defend herself against the rapist, to no avail. When the intruder forced his hand over her mouth to silence her screams, she bit his finger. Her father tried to aid her, but was struck and left bleeding. The victim identified Maxwell as the rapist.

He vehemently denied the charge, but though the evidence against him wasn't overwhelming, it was enough to convict him. A previous lawyer had unsuccessfully challenged the way some of it had been obtained, by a warrantless search of Maxwell's house, as well as exclusion of Negro jurors from Maxwell's jury. LDF agreed to look at these claims, but Greenberg ultimately decided that Heffron's main task was to develop proof of racial bias in the imposition of the death sentence for rape. Government statistics indicated that of the 3,334 persons with a known race who had been executed for murder in the United States since 1930, 1,664 were white and 1,630 black; of the 455 persons executed for rape, 48 were white and 405 black. It was a matter of public record that since 1913, twenty-one men had been executed for rape in Arkansas; nineteen of them were black and one or two white. All the victims were white.[20] To establish that these obviously racially skewed results were no fluke, Heffron and an Arkansas lawyer (later a federal judge), George Howard, sought to submit questions to prosecutors or court clerks in seventy-two counties inquiring into the facts of rape prosecutions in the state over the previous ten years. LDF had no time to conduct its own study of the working of the Arkansas legal system in rape cases; Heffron's hope was that either sufficient evidence would emerge from the request or that if it were denied by the trial court, a higher court would postpone the execution to permit the necessary gathering of facts.

The state's lawyer told the court that he thought most of the information Heffron and Howard sought was unavailable, but ultimately the judge permitted the testimony of officials from three counties on a "trial basis." This evidence showed that blacks committed fewer rapes than whites; the same number of blacks and whites had been convicted of rape; and of the three men sentenced to death in these counties since 1954, two were black and one white.[21]

Obviously, these fragmentary results added little to Maxwell's claim of disparate sentencing; the two federal courts that considered the case found his proof of discrimination insufficient. But because everyone knew the nature of the prevailing racial practices in Arkansas rape cases, the opinions had an *Alice in Wonderland* quality. While it was true that scientifically acceptable proof of discrimination required more of a showing that similar phenomena were being compared—that blacks, for example, could not be said to be sentenced differently because they had used more force or killed for hire or participated more in felonies that led to death—the courts still would not confront the implications of racial sentencing clearly raised by the state's sentencing patterns.

The judges, including Harry Blackmun, who much later was to undergo a conversion in regard to the death penalty just before he ended his service as a Supreme Court justice, wiggled (certain issues hadn't been raised properly) and evaded (the court would not look beyond the county in which Maxwell's crime had taken place) and belittled (there had been only two references to "nigger" at the trial [only one by a prosecuting attorney], and both were out of the hearing of the jury) and even sounded quite dimwitted (they deemed it important that prosecuting attorneys called to testify stated under oath that they had prosecuted all cases, including rape cases, without regard to race). It would have been news only if the prosecutors had actually admitted they went out of their way to send African Americans to their deaths.

Two years later, Maxwell would be back before Blackmun with a full record of evidence pointing to racial sentencing gathered from court records by law students we hired for the summer and analyzed by the United States' leading criminologist. But the judges remained unmoved: the evidence, they found, failed to substantiate racial discrimination. By virtue of legal errors, Maxwell, who had come within four days of dying in

1964 and within twenty-four hours in 1966, would ultimately escape death, but the federal courts would never be able to bring themselves to announce that in the second half of the twentieth century Americans still engaged in racial sentencing. A lay observer might be surprised that judges would find it so difficult to characterize as racial discrimination a practice that so plainly continued historical patterns going back to the days of slavery, but lawyers were familiar with judges' ability to avoid knowing in court what they understood very clearly elsewhere.

In October 1963, Heffron's efforts on Maxwell's behalf acquired another dimension. At the behest of the newest justice of the Supreme Court, Arthur Goldberg, three justices indicated, in a dissent from a decision to deny review of two capital rape cases, that grounds such as lack of proportionality between crime and punishment were substantial enough to persuade them to vote to have the Court consider the possible unconstitutionality of the death penalty for rape. The opinion, signed also by Justices William J. Brennan and William O. Douglas, was totally unexpected—most of all it must have surprised the defendants' lawyers (who were unknown to LDF), as they had not even raised the issue—but the *Rudolph* opinion, as it was called, would play a key role in energizing LDF's then very modest anti-capital-punishment campaign.[22] Goldberg's main goal was to invite lawyers to develop arguments and proofs to challenge the death penalty, because, as Alex Bickel had written the year before, if ultimately a "broader judicial judgment" on the constitutional arguments for abolition were to emerge, the evolutionary lawmaking process had to begin.[23]

The aspect of the *Rudolph* opinion that most shocked the three junior attorneys who dealt most with death cases at that time (Heffron, Leroy Clark, and I) was the failure of the justices even to mention the strongest argument against the death penalty for rape—the overwhelming evidence that southern states virtually reserved it for African Americans convicted of raping white women. Justice Goldberg and his law clerk Alan Dershowitz would have included racial discrimination in cases of black male defendants and white female victims in the enumeration of potential issues; but with the Court at the center of a host of racial controversies, from legally difficult sit-in cases that commanded the front pages to implementation of *Brown v. Board of Education*, Chief Justice Warren pressured Goldberg to narrow his opinion.

Dershowitz later told a Harvard law student, "I think Goldberg had a big argument among the Justices . . . he came in and told me . . . 'you are going to be very disappointed; Bill [Justice Brennan] and I have decided that we have to do a much shortened version of this—it would have to be a more cryptic opinion.'"[24]

In 1972, when the Court decided to set aside death sentences for murder and rape because they were arbitrarily applied, race was mentioned in several of the opinions but did not rise to the level of a central decisional factor. The most pronounced use of race was in Justice Douglas's finding that the death penalty was cruel and unusual when procedures were employed that gave "room for play" of prejudice based on "race, religion, wealth, social position or class," and by Thurgood Marshall's discussion of racially skewed execution statistics. In his history of the death penalty, however, Stuart Banner explains what was generally agreed at the time, that in *Furman* "randomness became in effect a code word for discrimination." The key swing justices, Byron White and Potter Stewart, "could fight racism while claiming to fight only case by case inconsistency."[25] Decades later Clarence Thomas, who had few qualms about the death penalty, characterized the 1972 decision as driven by concerns about racial discrimination that he thought were no longer fully legitimate and used this argument to justify his opposition to the Court's efforts to craft more reliable procedures in death cases. Even Justice John Paul Stevens, who had a very different view of how the Court should deal with appeals in death cases, agreed with Thomas that *Furman* was driven by concern about race.[26]

But then how does one explain the Supreme Court's unwillingness to rest any of its decisions against the death penalty on racial grounds despite LDF's persistence in presenting statistical evidence of racial effects on death sentencing? In 1977, when the Court got around to ruling in *Coker v. Georgia* that death was a disproportionate punishment for rape, it even then refused to refer to the blood shed in the service of condemning physical contact between black men and white women.[27]

The explanation certainly wasn't weakness in the legal theory. As I have mentioned, unequal, race-based sentencing was a characteristic of southern law before the Civil War, and abolishing such discrepancies was a specific purpose of the Fourteenth Amendment, ratified in 1868. A number of elements combine to explain the Court's reluctance to act here, in contrast to its willingness to find discrimination in virtually every other corner of American public life. The explanations often given for the Court's avoidance of the issue just don't add up. One is that proof of discrimination was based primarily on statistics. True, but the courts have often relied on statistics as a mode of proof. American courts are not so guided by know-nothingism as to disregard empirical data. How could they otherwise regulate a modern economy? One could plausibly point out that empirical research required the analysis of many variables, but surely doubt occasioned by such complexities was a technical question about particular studies. It did not rise to the level of general condemnation of statistical proof.

Arkansas had argued in *Maxwell* that statistics didn't tell whether a death-sentencing jury had actually been impelled by racial animus. Aside from the obvious fact that not all discriminators know or will admit their own bias, this objection totally misconceived LDF's claim of discrimination, which was not that every juror in every interracial rape case acted with bias but that the states had created a system of law and practices that one way or another produced racial results that could not have come about by chance alone. Indeed, when one factors into the equation that without statistical proof there could be no proof at all—unless prosecutors and jurors were to testify that they decided a man should be executed because of his race—the failure to accept overwhelming statistical proof is easily understood as a judicial cover story. In the beginning the Court just was unwilling to adopt a position that would have been understood as based on the assumption that thousands of private citizens practiced racial discrimination during their jury service. There was nothing new in the justices' belief that little would be gained by explicitly blaming southerners. At the time of *Brown v. Board of Education,* Chief Justice Warren cautioned his brethren on the Court that the opinion must be "non-accusatory."[28]

A second and equally important concern had to do with remedy. The courts considering the racial issue just did not believe they had a comfortable response to discrimination in death sentencing. One could use it as the premise for total abolition, but unless the Court was willing to take that giant step, the obvious rejoinder to discrimination would be an unacceptable form of "integration"—execute more whites. The Court's uncertainty about the protective procedures available to it if it acknowledged that the clear racial disparity was unconstitutional is, I find, the only explanation for the 1977 decision in the *Coker* case, where the Court finally decided that death was a constitutionally excessive penalty for rape but did so on the grounds of proportionality, without mentioning the penalty's racial history.

If LDF were to wait until the Court was ready to confront overtly the role of race in capital sentencing, as Eric Muller suggested, it would still be waiting. When the study directed by David Baldus was presented to the Court in 1987 in the Georgia case of *McCleskey v. Kemp,* it showed that, except when evidence of serious "aggravating" factors was either overwhelming or almost totally absent, people who kill whites receive death at a significantly greater rate than those who kill minorities. But the Court simply could not face up to the numbers and disparaged their importance. Although "defendants charged with killing white victims in Georgia are 4.3 times as likely to be sentenced to death as defendants charged with killing blacks," Justice Lewis Powell refused to require the state even to present evidence explaining or justifying the numbers. The results were not strong enough, he concluded, echoing the fiction that in this area one could assume that southern justice was neutral.[29]

A year after *McCleskey,* Randall Kennedy of Harvard Law School observed that the "justices have made the violations they are willing to recognize dependent upon the remedies they are willing to provide. They have tailored declarations of rights to fit their perceptions of acceptable remedies." This focus on what it might have to do blinded the Court, according to Kennedy, to facts that confirmed *McCleskey's* claim that only race could explain Georgia's pattern of capital sentencing. At most, the Court concluded, the Baldus study indicates "a discrepancy that appears to correlate with race." According to Kennedy, Justice Powell reduced *McCleskey's* arguments concerning the history of racial discrimination in criminal law to a footnote and dismissed it summarily. And while Kennedy saw a violation of the Constitution where the Court saw none, he cared less about protecting the cop-killer Warren McCleskey than about protecting the "black communities whose welfare is slighted by criminal justice systems that respond more forcefully to the killing of whites than the killing of blacks."[30]

Several years later, when Thurgood Marshall's Court files were opened, it appeared that one justice in the majority, Antonin Scalia, had, initially at least, forcefully indicated that his problem was not with the level of proof offered by Professor Baldus and LDF but with the fact that in his view racial discrimination by juries was "ineradicable." Rather than offer an argument favoring McCleskey, however, Scalia indicated in an unpublished memorandum to colleagues that he did not "share the view" that "an effect of racial factors upon sentencing" would require reversal of the death sentence. Although he promised to write an opinion expressing his views, Scalia ultimately signed on to the Powell opinion silently, making the fifth decisive vote. Scalia's memo was subject to a variety of interpretations that made it seem less than consequential, but an exhaustive study of its terms and context by one scholar makes such a conclusion unlikely. If Scalia's view was sincerely held, he was ultimately arguing that he would rather send a man to his death in part on the basis of race than have no death penalty at all.[31]

Lost in the shuffle was the fact that Georgia gave its prosecutors largely unregulated discretion to seek or not to seek the death penalty. The state could have defined eligible capital cases in a manner that restricted them to offenses in the highly aggravated circumstances where Baldus had found no evidence of racial taint. It had chosen not to do so. Despite LDF's argument for such a course, the Supreme Court could see only "intolerable" potential outcomes such as abolition or a need to find more killers of whites to execute.

In his dissenting opinion, Justice Brennan challenged the majority's flip dismissal of *McCleskey*'s historical account of Georgia racism as "actions taken long ago": "Evaluation of *McCleskey*'s evidence cannot rest solely on the numbers themselves," Brennan argued. "We must also ask whether the conclusion suggested by those numbers is consonant with our understanding of history and human experience.[32]

McCleskey thus marks another chapter in the Court's unwillingness to rely on either history or the implications of large statistical disparities when it was called on to cope with a race-based challenge to the death penalty, even as history and statistics were credited when other civil rights issues came up for decision. There was also troublesome language in Justice Powell's opinion, the subtext of which was "No matter what you show or argue on this point, you will lose." Powell, for example, defended the *McCleskey* outcome because "racial bias" might not be restricted to capital cases. But even the distressing suggestion that racial death sentencing would be tolerated because otherwise the law would have to deal with equally serious discrimination throughout the rest of the criminal justice system paled before the greatest fault of the judgment—its tolerance of a system that weighed one set of lives more heavily than another set for reasons of race alone. If the taking of life by the state had sufficient value to be constitutional, then didn't that value have to be a benefit shared by all? One would think the legal acceptance of differential valuations of life the very essence of the white supremacy condemned by the Civil War amendments.

Powell did try to pass the buck by suggesting that a remedy might be found in Congress or the state legislatures. Shortly thereafter, legislation called the Racial Justice Act was introduced in Congress, requiring the courts to reverse a death sentence when an unexplained racial sentencing disparity was found, without regard to proof of intentional discrimination.

It passed the House in 1990 and 1994 but was never approved by the Senate. It has not been heard from since.[33]

Unlike most legal principles, the Eighth Amendment's prohibition of cruel and unusual punishment, which is at the heart of the constitutional controversy over the death penalty, is closely linked to public attitudes. If enough people think a punishment is barbaric or wildly disproportionate, it will eventually be set aside, if not by legislation, then by the courts. While reading of the public will is tricky, the fate of the Racial Justice Act hardly suggests overwhelming concern about racial differentials in capital sentencing. It seems easier for the general public to identify with victims of the criminal justice system's incompetence and mistakes. Hence a version of the Innocence Protection Act first proposed by Senator Patrick J. Leahy (D-Vermont), which will facilitate DNA testing, was enacted in 2004.[34]

Some penalties, of course, hide their inequality and wantonness by radically uneven administration aimed at the outsiders or powerless among us. Anthony Amsterdam's theory about why capital punishment was unconstitutional harked back to seventeenth-century English law, which made hundreds of crimes subject to death; but while many were condemned, many were also pardoned. Putting so many in jeopardy and then letting them live operated as a social-control device and allowed influential landowners and merchants to play favorites. Amsterdam asserted that in its modern form the American way of death operated in a similar manner. It was only by arbitrary administration that the cruelty of the death penalty was masked, thereby encouraging public support for execution it would not have garnered if the facts of inequality were fully known or if the penalty had been evenhandedly implemented. This theory prevailed in *Furman* but only in *Furman;* its failure thereafter was not one of litigation tactics, organizational limitations, or even judicial shortsightedness, but ultimately of national values and electoral politics.

In their 1992 book *The Supreme Court and Legal Change,* the political scientists Lee Epstein and Joseph F. Kobylka also take Amsterdam and LDF to task for poor tactics. Their book carefully describes litigation moves, briefs, and arguments submitted to the Supreme Court with a view to challenging what the authors describe as the "conventional wisdom" among political scientists that major shifts in legal doctrine are largely the results of changes in Court personnel. Though they concede that turnover through strategic use of the political process "can, and often does" result in change, they conclude that "other important instances [of change] . . . cannot be explained by the appointment of the Justices." Appointments "standing alone" cannot, for example, explain the results in *Brown v. Board of Education* or the presidential tapes case, *United States v. Nixon*, decisions that did not reflect the views of the presidents who appointed the justices who decided the cases. They reach a similar conclusion with regard to the importance of public opinion, actions by the legislatures, and the executive branches of the state and federal governments, the behavior of interest groups, and the "climate of the times."[35]

Epstein and Kobylka conclude it is "the law and legal arguments grounded in law [that] matter, and they matter dearly . . . it is the arguments they [the justices] hear and make that—at least in the early stages of a doctrinal and decisional shift—seem to influence most clearly the content and direction of legal change that results." Judges, they conclude, are constrained and guided "at least to some extent" by law; they are not purely political actors.

To illustrate their thesis, that legal arguments and the justices' response to them shape to a large degree the paths the Court takes, they zero in on Amsterdam's 1976 oral argument, most prominently in cases known collectively as *Gregg v. Georgia*,[36] decisions that had the effect of reinstituting the death penalty. Even more precisely, they focus on Amsterdam's answer to a question by Potter Stewart, the key swing justice, about the argument that the Court must reverse death sentences meted out by a system honeycombed with discretionary decision makers who had produced clearly arbitrary results.

Stewart pointed out how much discretion existed throughout the criminal law. He asked Amsterdam:

> STEWART: And if a person is sentenced to anything as the end product of that system, under your argument, his sentence, be it life imprisonment or five years' imprisonment, is cruel and unusual punishment because it is the product of this system. This is your argument, isn't it?
>
> AMSTERDAM: No.
>
> STEWART: And why not?
>
> AMSTERDAM: It is not. Our argument is essentially that death is different. If you don't accept the view that for constitutional purposes death is different, we lose that case, let me make that very clear.

Epstein and Kobylka think Amsterdam and LDF have "misread the doctrinal glue" that held the *Furman* majority together by continuing to advance an absolute abolitionist position to a Court that, as *Gregg* would clearly show, was no longer supportive of such an approach. Death was different for LDF and Justices Brennan and Marshal but not for the rest of the Court. Amsterdam and LDF "were blinded to the necessity of strategic backtracking by the tyranny of absolutes, the belief that to win the big one is to establish for all time the precedential base for future victories." *Gregg* was lost because "defenders doggedly clung" to their understanding of earlier victories. "This fatally constrained their ability to shift grounds when those victories came under threat."

In *Gregg* and its companion opinions in cases from Texas and Florida, the Court reversed the direction of its anti-capital-punishment doctrine and set in motion the events that were to dominate the issue for the next three decades. If the 1976 shift can be ascribed to a blunder, if LDF should have employed a different strategy, one that "made use of carefully constructed and layered arguments that could have spoken to all potential members of a favorable majority," then Epstein and Kobylka would have gone far in advancing their thesis that what lawyers say in argument is decisive. In short, the authors use the oral argument to make their case for what causes shifts in Supreme Court decisions: if only Amsterdam had denied that "death was different" and come up with some solution, probably procedural, short of arguing for abolition, all might very well have turned out differently.

My first reaction on reading this analysis was to laugh. Could Epstein and Kobylka really believe that with politicians and public loudly demanding a return of the death penalty, a new mix of justices would abandon a pronounced disposition because of a few words from counsel? These scholars, I thought, must think that the justices decide major constitutional issues solely for the reasons they give in their opinions. They must see opinions as transparencies rather than crafted narrative acts. Had the authors been able to read studies such as Jerry Kang's analysis in "Deny Prejudice: Internment, Redress, and Denial," published in the *UCLA Law Review*, they might have come to a different conclusion.[37] It tells the story of how the Court and lower federal courts pretended to decide the legality of placing more than 100,000 Americans of Japanese extraction into concentration camps during World War II and how they actually did it.

More important, Epstein and Kobylka do not give the slightest indication of another convincing answer to Stewart's question that Amsterdam might have offered. They advance only a general claim that other arguments could have been raised to give the Supreme Court a different set of choices. But what were they?

On the way to *Furman* the Court had rejected the major extant procedural challenges to the way juries were instructed when they were to consider death. The claims that were left were the products of the particular formulation of the post-*Furman* statutes, and they depended on linking the discretionary decision making authorized by the new statutes with the fact that human life hung in the balance. Stewart was voicing the fear that seriously attacking such discretionary decision making could undermine the criminal law, which at all levels depends on it.

As difficult as would be a decision that flew in the face of popular, as well as legislative and executive branch, hostility to abolition, the fallout would be small in comparison with the predictably passionate and vituperative response to a decision that undermined the sense of safety conveyed by the entire criminal law.

The new death laws, moreover, were basically untested; if the Court was unwilling in 1976 to go along with a "death is different" approach, it could still one day take a different view if prosecutorial charging authority, plea bargaining, and the standards used by juries and judges in determining guilt under the laws produced arbitrary results. But cutting back on the death penalty required that a line be drawn between capital punishment and the rest of the criminal law. To argue otherwise would have been suicidal.

The more one thinks about the "death is different" approach, the more necessary it seems not to abandon it. The aggravation-mitigation formulation that the Georgia and most other "guided discretion" statutes adopted were all forms of the options set out by the American Law Institute (ALI) and its prominent director, Herbert Wechsler, in the 1950s. Wechsler was a foe of the death penalty, but he realized he could not get the institute to agree to recommend abolition. To have even a small chance of winning *Furman* and the cases that preceded it, LDF had to point to the refusal of the states to adopt the ALI formulation. Failure to do so would almost have been malpractice, not to mention that it would require us to urge the most absolute of positions on the Supreme Court—abolish the death penalty even though you haven't tried to tighten procedures in death cases because there is no alternative for the law to explore. Such a strategy might be likened to the idea of suggesting to the Court in 1920 that it was time to overrule *Plessey*.[38]

Once *Furman* was decided, however, on a basis and in a manner no one could have predicted, and the states, prompted especially by Chief Justice Warren Burger's dissent, enacted their various versions of the basic ALI formulation, the only thing to do was to challenge those formulations. LDF had to present them as riddled with potential abuse on the basis of both their texts and the states' experience in administering a criminal procedure with the attributes of the new laws. Given the presence of similar elements of discretionary decision making throughout the entire criminal law, arguing that death is different becomes a necessity, not some pleader's choice. Despite the fantasies of some right-wingers, there was no way that the Supreme Court was going to allow itself to be viewed as disabling the criminal law.

"Death is different" also had something going for it doctrinally that Epstein and Kobylka fail to plug into their "law counts" approach. It was a classic intermediate premise, a limiting principle—if the Court wanted to use it—that would enable judges in the future to justify resisting the pressure to extend a move against discretion to the rest of the criminal law. The Court is always aware that the logic of its decisions can be pushed farther than a particular majority wishes, and therefore is on the lookout for rational-seeming barrier principles. It is no accident that when the Court in 1987 once again encountered an overwhelming statistical showing that race continued to infect capital punishment, Justice Lewis Powell shot it down in these terms: "If we accepted *McCleskey's* claim that racial bias has impermissibly tainted the capital sentencing decision, we could soon be faced with similar claims as to other types of penalty."[39]

In the post–World War II United States, there have always been justices who thought executions stupid and unnecessary. The problem for them was to find a way to justify this conclusion in legal terms that did not damage the Court, contradict their sense of how law should be made, or usurp the rights of the people. Harry Blackmun was one such justice. Even before his judicial papers were opened in 2004, the evidence strongly suggested that as an individual he always rejected capital punishment. His law clerks let us know so sotto voce in the 1960s, during the *Maxwell* litigation. Still as a judge he supported it again and again until shortly before his retirement in 1994 he declared opposition with his famous "I shall no longer tinker with the machinery of death" statement.[40]

In the 1960s, Potter Stewart was the most important of the justices who rejected execution, and in his opinions he often, though not always, supported efforts that might bring abolition closer. In the *Witherspoon* case, he crafted a process that he hoped would significantly narrow the death penalty by widening jury service to include persons who tended to oppose capital punishment.[41] It was clear that he thought or expected or hoped that by clearing death rows, the ruling would give the states a fresh chance to decide they did not need the death penalty.

Stewart's approach, one that I believe influenced Justice White, was high judicial art. It pushed the country toward a result but hardly commanded it. The justices, led by Stewart, gave the political process a chance to follow or to oppose the Court, but did so in a manner that gave the voters a set of principles that might guide their thinking. If Stewart thought the political process would produce the outcome he wanted, however, he was to be proved wrong. When that became clear, as it quickly did, he retreated to the cautious and institutionally protective stance he usually took, which was also attractive to other justices, especially the newly arrived John Paul Stevens. Stewart simply believed that contemporary standards of decency as they affected the death penalty had changed over the four years since *Furman*.

Amsterdam and LDF could do no more than give the Court a workable theory, as they had done in *Furman*—if the justices were of a mind to make it work. What they could not do and what no one could have done in 1976 was overcome an aroused public opinion, one that could damage the Court's credibility with relative ease, as the referendum vote to rewrite California's constitution showed.

A final reservation about LDF's approach in the years shortly after 1976, when capital punishment was reestablished, comes from the charismatic southern attorney Millard Farmer. A pioneer of aggressive efforts to persuade trial juries not to vote for execution, Farmer thought abolitionist lawyers devoted disproportionate money and attention to appeals and challenges to death sentences and too little to defending capital cases at trial.[42]

Farmer, who apparently is no longer doing death-penalty work, had compiled an admirable record in capital cases in the 1980s and early 1990s. When his group, called Team Defense, became involved in a case, it devoted thousands of hours to it, often aiming to put the local justice system on trial. A hallmark of the Team Defense approach was thorough investigation and making prosecutors work very hard for every conviction and death sentence by filing a plethora of legal motions.

John Charles "Jack" Boger, LDF's former chief death-penalty lawyer, is a great admirer of Farmer's lawyering, but Boger thought the Team Defense model simply "impossible to replicate on a national level, with several thousand death row inmates, all of whom needed representation, without lawyers ready to expend tens of thousands of uncompensated hours." Boger questioned Farmer's assumption of infinite resources. "Yes—if we had hundreds of willing lawyers with thousands upon thousands of available hours, strategies that focus on the individual flaws in our clients' cases would be ideal. But, of course, we didn't, and couldn't. Given these limitations, its obvious that cases have to be brought with potential to affect groups of defendants as well as individuals." Still, even after 1976, LDF's approach spared literally hundreds of lives, and even when systemic challenges did not ultimately succeed in court, they accomplished something. According to Boger, Farmer's complaint also failed to credit "delays spawned by the judicial need to consider carefully the LDF systemic issues (which gave years of life to many inmates and provided the time in which many other individual claims were brought to light)."[43] One might add that on certain issues the Supreme Court could eventually reverse itself, as it did in regard to the eligibility of juveniles for execution and to the defense of mental retardation.

My great teacher Alexander Bickel believed that to do any good and play its role in government, the judiciary had to protect its credibility by avoiding overbroad and untimely decisions and by not assuming legislative functions. But he also made clear that courts had an essential role to play in protecting us from ourselves, even if it proved costly to "what was good for the Court." In a sense, that is what the Constitution itself does. By putting certain issues at a remove from the popular will, it slows things down, provides the stability in which true liberty thrives, and allows us the political time and space to manage passions that might otherwise consume us. The Court majority in *Furman* believed that with its encouragement the death penalty would wither away. The justices' prediction was mistaken but their aim was worthy. Capital punishment is a heavy burden to carry, and someday, probably with the help of LDF or the groups with which it is now allied, the justices will figure out a way to put it down.

The Future of the Death Penalty

AFTER 1976, when the *Gregg v. Georgia* set of decisions made clear that the death penalty would again become a staple if a no less contentious part of American life, LDF could have greatly reduced its role in the abolition campaign. Responding to questions from the LDF board of directors, Greenberg estimated that "less than 20% of our energies [go] into the capital punishment program, probably more in terms of manpower and less in terms of money."[1] Something like 20 percent was actually an enormous investment, especially in view of the fact that LDF would never raise enough money to pay fully for its death-penalty work. The board continued to support the campaign but felt "discomfort" at such a large commitment. Some of it was eased by increased success in obtaining foundation funds to pay for a few test cases under the new generation of death laws and criminological research into racial sentencing patterns. Ford would grant LDF several million dollars over succeeding decades for general support, a portion of which went to pay for capital cases.

The staff initially grumbled that perhaps LDF had for too long put money and time into representing a constituency composed largely of violent criminals. Would the money be better spent bringing, say, more employment-discrimination cases? It was plain, however, that the more closely the lawyers attended to criminal justice issues, the more tragic faults they found—not only the wrongly convicted but signs of racial infection often no less obvious to them for being difficult to prove.

Tony Amsterdam's willingness to remain as the campaign's spiritual leader, strategic planner, and primary litigation resource made Greenberg's decision to maintain LDF's presence in the field much easier, as did the series of remarkable young lawyers who for a time took over in-house responsibility for cases testing the new laws before moving on to other public interest organizations, teaching, partnerships in law firms, and government positions. These lawyers—among them Peggy Davis, David Kendall, Joel Berger, Deborah Fins, Jack Boger, Richard Burr, and George Kendall—handled their own capital cases but were also the crucial links to Amsterdam, who had taken up residence on the NYU law faculty.

Until the late 1980s LDF had been involved directly or as a friend of the court in almost every important Supreme Court capital case, but the demands of an increasing number of death row trials and appeals began to tax its resources, as well as those of the few organizations that provided post-sentence legal assistance—the Southern Center for Human Rights, Millard Farmer's Team Defense project, and a number of ACLU-affiliated defenders. It soon was apparent that divided public opinion, the steady beat of vicious murders, and the fears of politicians that they might be called "soft on crime" operated to ensure that prolonged contests over the wisdom and legality of state-imposed death were not going to wither away. In *McCleskey* the Supreme Court had rejected one of the last on a list of high-impact systemic issues that could have cut back on the death penalty significantly without abolishing it. The era that followed would be characterized more by case-by-case combat than by the few claims that affected large numbers.

With almost forty states holding prisoners on death row, LDF was no longer able to exert control over prosecutions and appeals of capital cases. At a time when it became obvious that it couldn't manage the rising tide of death row cases by itself and that sheer numbers were forcing the courts to appoint inexperienced lawyers to do trial service, another set of anti-death-penalty lawyers, only some of whom had LDF connections, entered the scene or increased their efforts. Bryan Stevenson and Stephen Bright, media-savvy, sophisticated lawyers, directed effective public interest law firms in the South, where most executions took place; by demonstrating that capital cases could be won at the trial level, Millard Farmer focused attention on the paucity of trained counsel available to most accused; Barry Scheck and Peter Neufeld founded a revolutionary law clinic at New York's Cardozo Law School, the model for many others, which used DNA analysis as well as more traditional techniques to determine if innocent men where in danger of execution.

A number of major law firms took on individual cases in states that had a shortage of lawyers. Death Penalty Resource Centers, set up in the early

1990s and then defunded by Congress after they proved surprisingly efficient at finding legal errors that courts had previously ignored, attracted experienced defenders such as David Bruck of South Carolina and trained a cadre of death-case attorneys. (Bruck not only won a number of capital cases before an increasingly hostile Supreme Court but was instrumental in saving the life of Susan Smith, who drowned her children by driving her car into a lake.) Some states, such as New York, North Carolina, and Florida, would set up their own capital defender projects, occasionally bolstered by private money.

The very rough outlines of a career path emerged. Lawyers might shift from LDF or government-sponsored defender work to standard private criminal law practice or to teaching or to coordinating the pro bono activity of a large firm or to working as trainers for government agencies that had to see to it that knowledgeable capital defenders were available for court-appointed trial work. They might shift from any one of these roles to any other. Many of them earned reputations as charismatic capital defenders, among them Mark Olive, who is currently of Florida but has handled death cases in nine states; John Blume, who commutes between Cornell Law School and the southern courtrooms; Judy Clarke, a federal capital defender who volunteered to represent Susan Smith and would later broker a life sentence plea bargain for serial bomber Eric Rudolph; Denise Young, former director of the Arizona Capital Representation Project; and Kevin McNally, veteran of more than fifty capital trials.

George Kendall and Richard Burr, both former directors of the LDF project, are still linked closely to its legal strategy. A recent LDF listing of pending cases, for example, names Kendall as counsel in several, though he is also senior counsel in the New York office of the law firm of Holland & Knight. Burr (along with Bruck, McNally, and Michael Burt, an experienced defender from San Francisco) recruits and trains lawyers appointed by the federal courts in capital cases under a program established in 1992 by the Administrative Office of the United States Courts. Burr represents several of the young men who were affected when the Supreme Court changed its mind about permitting the execution of sixteen- and seventeen-year-olds.[2] Ronald J. Tabak coordinates pro bono activity at the large firm of Skadden, Arps and plays an important role in American Bar Association support of abolitionist positions.

The continuity of abolitionist roles despite changing employers is illustrated by Deborah Fins's career. An LDF attorney assigned to work on capital cases upon her graduation from Columbia Law School in 1978, she eventually moved on to other work in the 1980s. After stints teaching law and in private practice, she became the director of training at New York State's highly regarded Capital Defender Office, created when the state reinstituted the death penalty in 1995. By the end of the decade, she found herself back at LDF, writing briefs and responsible for the authoritative quarterly statistical report *Death Row USA.*

As the death row population grew into the thousands, the impact of contested homicide prosecutions exerted extreme influence on the lives of the lawyers, their clients, and the families of victims. One defender, Michael Mello, was so affected by the wealth of relationships, ironies—he lost one client to execution and then a unanimous Supreme Court reprieved a former client on the basis of the very same issue it had rejected in the earlier case—and sheer caprice found in the capital punishment system that his writings mix legal analysis with a Joycean sensibility, full of literary detours, "true stories generated by Florida's culture of the condemned," and personal letters to friends.[3]

The most impressive trait displayed by these lawyers is tenacity. A death case is a high for an ambitious litigator. A second capital case gives attorneys the opportunity to test what they've learned in the first. But the cases can go on for years. They are extraordinarily demanding and stressful, requiring great technical skill in virtually every aspect of trial and appellate work as well as personal balance and steadiness; they don't bring in much money. After a few years of this, only dedication and character keep one going. The lawyers who campaigned against the death penalty in the 1960s were sustained by the optimism of the era and their success in stopping all executions for almost a decade; they had reason to believe the public was moving closer to their view of the world. Today's advocate, by contrast, confronts a field of law grown treacherous in its complexity, where lawyers' mistakes are potentially fatal. A lawyer, for example, can wrongly waive a good legal claim, but unless his behavior fails to meet minimum professional standards, the client loses the claim and perhaps his life because of the error.

In the 1960s, a moratorium on executions lasted nine years; today, not only does the public seem hopelessly and permanently divided over the death penalty, but many judges, including several Supreme Court justices, have turned hostile to the very idea of a persistently vigorous defense in a capital case.

LDF has reshaped its abolitionist agenda with the times. The loose network of independent front-line defenders keeps in touch with cases of national import, such as the Supreme Court ruling barring the death penalty for the retarded and its holding that a jury must find aggravating circumstances before a judge can impose a death sentence. Trends in case-related research are addressed at an annual LDF conference on the death penalty. The problems confronting the advocates are highly contextual. Texas, the national leader in number of executions, has a few excellent defenders, but the state appoints many attorneys in death cases who have no experience with the issues involved in a capital trial; whereas California has a highly qualified group of capital defense lawyers but its law is so broad that there are more than 600 men and 14 women on death row. Still, for both political and legal reasons, California has executed only 12 as of this writing, whereas the Texas total is 345.

New York State's Capital Defender Office is so capable—winning appeals that removed the death penalty from state law—that LDF lawyers focus their attention elsewhere, on states where finding counsel to take a death case is difficult. But then LDF resources are not what they were when Greenberg told his board that death-penalty work amounted to around 20 percent of the workload. Once a separate project within LDF, the work has been combined with other criminal justice cases. When lawyer hours are counted up, LDF is investing about two full-time lawyer slots to death-penalty work; they work formally on a dozen or so death cases but consult on numerous others.

Another change has to do with visibility. Closely identified with a relentless litigation campaign that ultimately fell short of its larger objectives but forced many judges to take public responsibility for sending men to their deaths, LDF and Amsterdam in particular became the objects of occasional judicial hostility.[4] It is hard to resist the conclusion that, as a consequence, LDF has decided to reduce publicizing its role in contemporary litigation. Crafting arguments for use by others, doing its best to send supportive friend-of-the-court briefs to the Supreme Court from unusual sources such as prosecuting attorneys, and stimulating primary research are all ways in which LDF influences litigation without directing a movement or appearing to take credit for its role. Some cases, of course, naturally affect the agendas of scientific researchers who don't need to be prodded: the case that decided the unconstitutionality of executing juveniles included neurological research findings about the state of juvenile brain development and capacity for judgment.[5]

While publicity once tended to find Amsterdam, he was not the sort of person who sought it; now he appears to keep himself even more in the background. He has consistently made his skills available to capital defenders but no longer appears regularly in court or puts himself in situations in which he could be viewed as the dominant courtroom voice of a movement. "By the mid-1980s," he has written, the justices "came to view the Fund's lawyers as abolitionist zealots, embarked on a crusade against the death penalty for its own sake"—they viewed LDF's claim of racial discrimination in *McCleskey*, for example, as "a mere tool or tease of abolitionist design."[6] Plainly, Amsterdam thinks too noticeable a role may not serve his clients well. But he is still a major force, writing articles—one contrasted the Supreme Court's interventionist use of the equal protection clause of the Fourteenth Amendment to overrule a state court and make George W. Bush president in 2000 and its quite different attitude when faced with state court rulings in capital cases—teaching a celebrated legal clinic where law students work on capital cases and offering immense legal expertise to most comers.

I was reminded of the work habits of the man I first encountered in the early 1960s when I was told that after a bout with Lyme disease several years ago, Amsterdam complained that the effects of the disease had forced him to sleep more than a few hours a night.

The continuation of conflict over the death penalty, given the social and legal context in which it is enforced, has exposed some of the most glaring weaknesses in the American judicial process. *McCleskey* was a grim reminder that the value attached to a person's life can depend on his race. Investigation of wrongful convictions led to the discovery of police and prosecutors who had suppressed evidence, as well as a host of shoddy investigative practices. With life on the line, defenders have started to challenge the way police take the statements of witnesses and suspects and the suggestive manner in which they present suspects to eyewitnesses.

The main reason why LDF has stayed with its campaign is the deeply held abolitionist beliefs of many of its lawyers. These views are bolstered by powerful evidence of the impact of race on the exercise of discretion by prosecutors in death cases, but any evaluation of the contemporary death penalty must also take the measure of the justice system, of which capital punishment is an integral part in most jurisdictions.

It is plainly in a ragged state, kept from citizen condemnation by a relative invisibility (coupled with a fear of criminals) that protects it from examination. Even educated Americans get their sense of criminal justice from often sensationalized television news and dramas. But while today we seem quite capable of processing more people than ever before, filling new prison space with record numbers of inmates—over a million Americans are now incarcerated—concerns of fairness and reliability continue to trouble anyone who cares enough to look closely.

Critics decry the wholesale imprisonment of drug offenders—one in four or five inmates—and that too little attention is paid to the actual extent of their danger to the public; the vast overrepresentation of young African American males in the prison population; and a system that increasingly abandons trials and public determinations of guilt for highly leveraged plea bargaining, which takes place without real scrutiny and regulation by judges. Despite promises of equal access to legal services, both the number and the quality of defense attorneys available to persons who are not affluent is grossly inadequate. With about 90 percent of all cases disposed of by bargaining, prosecutorial discretion has become the single most powerful force in determining results.

During the summer of 2003, Attorney General John Ashcroft issued orders to federal prosecutors calculated to make already heavy sentences even harsher. Ashcroft required prosecutors to appeal sentences they thought lenient and to keep records on judges who granted "downward sentencing departures" for reasons such as crediting defendants who took responsibility for their crimes. He required United States attorneys to lodge the most serious charges they could prove and seek his approval before agreeing to plea bargains.[7] When Congress and many state legislatures set up rigid sentencing guidelines (now under intense legislative review) and increasingly authorized mandatory minimum sentences, judges had less opportunity to consider individual circumstances in sentencing. Control of a defendant's fate was left largely in the hands of prosecutors. Their influence is neither new nor inappropriate, but unconfined and unregulated by the judiciary it leads us inexorably toward unaccountable administrative decision making and an overaggressive adversary system. Legislative oversight means little when it is politically perilous for legislators to oppose any demand of law enforcement. What is true of the mundane prosecution is even more true when the death penalty is involved.

Since 1976 we have learned much about the American way of state-imposed death. Capital punishment is still sometimes debated as if it were an abstraction. For example: On what basis do we justifiably claim the right to kill? Is it ethical to execute a person in order to discourage another from killing? But much of the commentary on the death penalty is now geared to the way it operates; I do not include the sound-bite-sized mentions the topic gets from candidates for election. This change moves discourse from religious and philosophical terrain, where positions are notoriously resistant to change, to consideration of particulars, which at least holds out the hope, faint though it may be, that information will shift opinion.

In the real world of capital punishment, the evidence for what James Liebman of Columbia calls a "broken system" is overwhelming.[8]

Reversals. The number of condemned persons ultimately exonerated continues to grow: 122 is the last number I have seen for the period 1973–2005, though some prosecutors consider that figure too high. The average number of years between sentence and exoneration is 9.3. Many of these individuals have been proved wrongly convicted by conclusive DNA tests, but a majority of them were simply the victims of bias, shoddy police work, overzealous prosecutors, and overvalued eyewitness identification testimony.[9]

Looking at the overall reversal rate from 1973 to 1995, Liebman, the nation's leading death-penalty scholar, reported that the courts found "serious reversible error" in 68 percent of capital cases appealed, indicating that even supporters of the death penalty are skeptical of the reliability and fairness of what goes on in capital trials. The reversal rate will probably decline with time, but it is likely that it will remain higher than average in states where executions are numerous and the black population is disproportionately large.

Liebman and his associates step back and take a good look at the whole capital-punishment system, from arrest to execution, and what they see is chaos. The way things work—in part because of differential incentives motivating police, prosecutors, defense lawyers, anti-death-penalty specialists, and lower court and appellate judges—is that the trial part of the criminal process places far more defendants in jeopardy of death than will end up executed. The numbers tell the story: of the 6,912 under sentence of death from 1977 to 2002, only 12 percent were executed.

Bowing to local pressure to show themselves "tough on crime," prosecutors obtain convictions and death sentences in the knowledge that many will be set aside; and since few people outside the legal system pay attention to reversals by appellate courts, the prosecutors have no inducement not to seek a sentence of death. In the same vein, Scott Turow describes how he and other members of the state Commission on Capital Punishment shifted their views after intense study of Illinois cases led to doubts of the reliability of death-case convictions and sentences.[10] The commission's recommendations influenced George Ryan, the governor of Illinois, to commute the sentences of all death row inmates, the largest such commutation in American history. In 2002 Judge Jed Rakoff concluded that "the best available evidence indicates that, on one hand, innocent people are sentenced to death with materially greater frequency than was previously supposed, and that convincing proof of their innocence often does not emerge until long after their convictions." Rakoff declared the federal death penalty unconstitutional because the risk of convicting the innocent was great and execution made the mistake irreparable, but his ruling did not survive appeal: it was overturned by a higher federal court on the ground that the Supreme Court has upheld capital punishment despite the risks of wrongful death sentencing.[11]

Trial Lawyers. Many lawyers who are appointed to represent defendants in capital trials have little experience at this sort of work and are paid trivial amounts, often just a few thousand dollars. Judges are so resistant to regulating the capital trial bar that they have been known to argue over how much time a lawyer must have to sleep to have his work declared constitutionally inadequate.

The performances of some of these lawyers are truly shocking. According to the Death Penalty Information Service, one court-appointed lawyer was so drunk during a 1989 trial that he was held in contempt and sent to jail. The next day, both client and attorney came out of the cell block and the trial resumed. But being drunk in court was just the tip of the iceberg. The same lawyer failed to present hospital records showing that the defendant was a battered spouse, a key factor in her defense.[12] Many other women have successfully appealed the death penalty on the grounds of such abuse.

A Georgia defendant was represented at his capital trial by a husband-and-wife team who had never read the state's death-penalty statute. The lawyers apparently "never visited the crime scene or interviewed the state's witnesses, made no attempt to discover the state's evidence" (they were "too busy"), and hardly ever spoke to their client.

Severe mental illness may have led another defendant to plead guilty to a crime he did not commit. His attorney spent a total of fifteen hours on the case, including only seven hours of investigation. He never requested or received the previous attorney's file, never obtained his client's medical records or military files, and made no inquiry into his psychiatric background. As a result, the attorney had "no idea that his client had been on psychotropic medication, had undergone 81 shock treatments, or had been diagnosed as psychotic by three different psychiatrists."

In one oft-cited Texas case, the entire argument offered by an attorney for his client at a capital sentencing consisted of these words: "You are an extremely intelligent jury. You've got that man's life in your hands. You can take it or not. That's all I have to say." The defendant was executed in 1992.

A 1997 American Bar Association (ABA) study found numerous un- qualified lawyers "who have nothing like the support necessary to mount an effective defense" in capital cases. The need for skilled counsel is so great that the ABA has a Death Penalty Representation Project whose head, Robin Maher, scours the country looking for lawyers willing to volun- teer.[13] Under current law, there is no right to state-financed counsel after a first appeal.

Liebman and his team at Columbia ended up studying the error rate in 4,578 appeals; they found the most common causes of reversal were the in- competence of defense lawyers, who "didn't even look for—and demon- strably missed—important evidence the defendant was innocent or did not deserve to die," and the suppression of evidence by police or prosecu- tors.

Numbers. We spend millions of dollars to execute a criminal—the Florida estimate is $3.2 million; in Texas it's $2.3 million per execution— and we do it many years after the crime. The national waiting average is around eleven years—in Florida, forty-nine inmates have been on death row more than twenty-five years; in Texas, the state that has carried out the most executions since 1976, twenty-five convicts have been on death row more than twenty-five years. Except for a few celebrated inmates, by the time we kill an offender almost everyone but the immediate families has forgotten the events that gave rise to the execution.[14]

The extraordinary qualities of some of these legal odysseys is illustrated by the case of William Neal (Billy) Moore, who pleaded guilty to murder, waived a sentencing jury, and received a death sentence in Wrens, Georgia, in June 1974. A day before his scheduled execution in August 1991, his sen- tence was finally commuted to life imprisonment; he was paroled the fol- lowing year. According to his longtime volunteer lawyer, Daniel Givelber, during Moore's seventeen years on death row, "his case was reviewed by the Georgia Supreme Court four times, the United States District Court twice, a United States Court of Appeals five times, and by the United States Su- preme Court six times." Virtually all this litigation concerned not whether Moore deserved to die but whether he had forfeited his opportunity to have a court consider his claims at all. The appeals court twice found in his favor but the decisions were set aside. The second time the court's person- nel had changed and Moore lost by one vote. Ironically, the fact that Moore had never had an opportunity to present most of his legal claims to any court was one of the factors relied upon by the Board of Pardons and Parole in its rare decision to grant clemency.[15]

Despite some unevenness based on court rulings, the number of death row inmates continues to climb. With 3,500 death row inmates, if we were to kill 100 individuals a year, a significantly greater number than our average of 72 in the four years from 2000 to 2004, it would take more than thirty-five years to execute the backlog; of course we would be putting a hundred or so more on death row while we were doing it. So there would be no change in the number on death row after thirty-five years of executions.[16]

Another way to look at our practices starts by acknowledging that death sentences amount to at most 2 percent of first-degree homicides and that we can execute fewer than 10 percent of the people we sentence to death. Those numbers make it obvious that the reasoning behind the American way of death is far removed from that which guides governmental programs aimed at applying explicit inducements to encourage or discourage particular sorts of behavior. Rather than systematic initiatives, death cases are in the nature of sacrificial events that keep alive the social knowledge that the death penalty is an option.

Moreover, well over half of all executions take place in a few southern states, states with traditionally high murder rates. Such a system is unlikely to deter potential killers elsewhere or even to support for very long the belief that we are dealing seriously with evil. It would be slightly more comforting, I suppose, if we could believe that instead of picking a few to represent the whole, we were being selective—that everyone executed was a Timothy McVeigh or Jeffrey Dahmer—but for every monster who dies there are several (Ted Kaczynski, Eric Rudolph) who don't. When you are dealing with a wide range of behavior and relationships, dozens of states and thousands of jurors, attorneys, and judges, consistency is impossible. Indeed, no matter what juries decide, plea negotiating with individual prosecutors ensures ad hoc death sentencing. Of the 381 defendants reviewed by the Justice Department, 103 were approved for capital punishment; many avoided a trial by bargaining, but at this writing the specific characteristics that led the attorney general to agree to a lower sentence haven't been revealed.[17]

Deterrence. When I worked on death cases in the 1960s, many debates about the death penalty featured claims that it was or was not marginally more effective than life imprisonment at deterring murder. Justice Stephen Breyer observed in 2002 what has become generally accepted—that evidence of deterrence is, "at most, inconclusive."[18] The same statement could have been made thirty years ago, even though the federal government cited a deterrence study in 1976 to support the return of the death penalty. The research was savaged by critics and is no longer credited. Death penalty debaters today emphasize the heinousness of the crime, the rights of the victim, and the nature of the judicial process that charges, convicts, selects a sentence, reviews the case, incarcerates, and then kills. But emerging econometric studies using sophisticated computer models are invigorating arguments that the death penalty deters. They suggest that for every execution lives are saved (some claiming as many as eighteen), and contend that if one values life, capital punishment is morally required. The research is subject to the same withering criticism over methodology as in the past: contradictory findings in different jurisdictions, and debate about the ethics and utility of killing a specific person to save the lives of indeterminate unknowns. Nevertheless, proponents of the death penalty will plainly seize upon these studies in an effort to counter criticism of the growing record of wrongful convictions.[19]

Closure. Most Americans get to learn what they know about the death penalty through media reports or film versions of individual cases. Historically, professionals in the legal system have resisted the impulse to personalize crime and punishment so they could maintain some control over pending litigation free of the volatile emotions generated by criminal violence, but now our law privileges the families of victims by giving them an opportunity to participate directly in the capital sentencing process. Rather than providing the psychological, medical, and other services they may need to ease the burden of losing a loved one, the law usually affords them only a right to testify. The families of victims have always influenced prosecutors' exercise of discretion to seek or not to seek the death penalty and governors' exercise of clemency, but participation was rarely formalized. Now state law often confers a right to enter the process. Family members regularly claim that a death sentence will bring "closure," and often deride lethal injection as insufficiently painful in comparison with the way the victim died.

At the same time, whether because of the delays attendant on execution or recognition that a death sentence doesn't sufficiently heal a damaged family, my internet review of hundreds of news stories suggests that a good number of participants in the criminal process soon decide that an arrest and a quick guilty plea or a sentence of life without parole provide as much resolution as the law can offer. Nevertheless, the emotional freight of intense family participation moves the capital trial jury perilously close to becoming a stand-in for the family rather than acting as a community instrumentality that supposedly determines the best outcome for society.

Such developments challenge the very capacity of the modern state to regulate clan violence. Difficult as it may be for persons who have suffered a grievous loss to accept, society does not confer enormous powers on jurors and judges to punish primarily to comfort a family but to advance public safety. To do otherwise is to sentimentalize and sensationalize a decision that even under the best of circumstances enters a mysterious realm of moral nuance. Justice for the victim does not capture the full meaning of justice.

Finally, the testimony of family members on the choice of life or death can undervalue the interests of persons who have no one to speak for them. Regardless of their culpability, killers who had the misfortune to take the life of members of an articulate or politically connected family will obviously be less likely to win merciful treatment than those whose victims' families have no such connections. Of course, the jury need not listen to the grieving family, but just as politics writ large makes it unlikely that many politicians will oppose the death penalty, the more intimate politics surrounding the impact of the killing as reported by the family and friends is bound to affect who is selected to live and who to die.[20]

Carol and Jordan Steiker begin their exhaustive 1995 study of two decades of Supreme Court regulation of the death penalty by reporting that "virtually no one thinks that the constitutional regulation of capital punishment has been a success." While proponents generally avoid endorsing how the death penalty is administered, they respond that death is a just and proportionate response to murder, that racial discrimination is rare and better lawyers are being appointed in death cases, that the innocent are never executed, and that in any event more lives are saved by capital punishment than lost through mistaken enforcement. But after 48 closely reasoned pages supported by 390 footnotes, the Steikers basically found the Supreme Court's capital punishment jurisprudence unnecessarily incoherent, producing a system that both upholds death sentences when it shouldn't and acts leniently in too many cases where one might expect the absolute penalty. The present system seems trapped by contradictory goals of narrowing the range of conduct that might serve as the predicate for the death penalty while expanding the information available to the sentencing jury.[21]

Why, then, is there so little interest in abolishing the death penalty? Why such a great reluctance to acknowledge that we are not only out of step with other Western democracies but apparently in a state of denial about the obvious imbalance of costs and benefits?

As a member of an Illinois study commission, Scott Turow concluded that "the cases that seemed to present the most compelling facts favoring execution proved, under scrutiny, to have elements that raised second thoughts." But Turow also observes that "sometimes a crime is so horrible that killing its perpetrator is the only correct response."[22] Some version of this sense of "moral proportion" is why most Americans still support the death penalty. However, if fear of the brutality or randomness of criminal violence serves to maintain the death penalty, capital punishment has not led to significant investment in prevention of violence.

Remarkably, efforts to discover and fill those gaps in social policy that encourage lethal violence are not a feature of the American political scene. Gun manufacturers, for example, have even failed to make design changes—childproofing and disabling weapons when the magazine is removed—that would plainly save lives. While promising, electric shock stun guns and various forms of pepper pellet projectiles involve serious risks themselves.[23]

In contrast, attention is directed to the often operatic tale of justice performed in three acts: the apprehension of the killer, the murder trial, and the struggle over the death sentence. Actual events and media representation of this set of encounters, often implying that most murders are the products of studied choices and planning by rational actors, spill over into the little space left for contemplation of how public policy might reduce occasions for violence. Paradoxically, the death penalty, with its capacity to engage powerful emotions, to sensationalize criminal justice, and to focus attention, operates as a major distraction to exploring ways to reduce murder. As long as we are tinkering with the machinery of death we are not in a mode or mood to confront the difficult options, some fraught with unknowns, necessary to reduce killing.

There are, moreover, more powerful reasons why our political leaders may prefer to keep our eyes on the capital punishment drama. And why we let them. Homicide rates are linked to the availability of guns, a perennial electoral hot potato. They are associated with poverty, but Americans have declined to endorse a consistent national antipoverty policy. The dealing, acquisition, and use of drugs produce their share of violent deaths, and here we have a national policy; the only problem is that it is the wrong one, too greatly favoring enforcement of criminal law over prevention and treatment. Race is a factor in the way guns, poverty, and drugs are related to violence. In addition, community policing, neonatal services, treatment of alcoholism, interventions aimed at reducing domestic violence, meaningful parole services—all these and other violence-reduction programs are not only expensive but of undemonstrated efficacy.

Thus the alternatives to the death penalty, expensive as it is, are unsure, costly, and most of all controversial. Not only do we avoid them, we avoid rigorous study of these and other approaches government might take to reduce violence.

Moreover, the confusing, fragmented, and costly death penalty system has several dubious distinctions. Of particular concern is that it provides a sense to the public that there is something rational and orderly about the process when ultimately jurors and other system actors are making subjective moral decisions to take or not take life. In the old pre-*Furman* days the jury was basically told to look to its conscience and decide if a defendant should live or die. This was a terrible legal regime that left jurors uninstructed and prone to express their prejudices, whatever they were, in the verdict. At LDF we always assumed that any new regime of capital punishment would require the state to set forth narrow standards for the choice of life or death. But rather than a clear statement of policy in response to *Furman,* the new laws mostly provided laundry lists of factors that would guide the jury. The state abdicated; the courts have acceded. The result is that today's death penalty mimics the same arbitrariness that led to partial abolition in 1972.

The new laws did, however, produce a revealing shift in eligibility for execution, ultimately a window into the fears of the public, at least as lawmakers perceived it. Before *Furman,* capital murder was defined by deliberation and premeditation. Once these elements of the crime were established, jurors determined whether to sentence to death. It was the selection practice from the pool of potential condemned created by this system that led the Supreme Court to find unconstitutional arbitrariness and to insist, for a time seriously, that the net be cast more narrowly. The primary means of accomplishing this narrowing of the availability of the death penalty was requiring jurors to find aggravating circumstances as a precondition to a capital sentence. But the states were given almost total freedom in defining aggravation. What they did was to do away with the requirements of premeditation and deliberation, substituting a list of factors, the most potent of which made it sufficient for a killing to take place in the course of a felony—say robbery, burglary, rape, or arson—to supply circumstances sufficiently aggravating to warrant death.

Daniel Givelber has shown that this "new law of murder" shifts attention from "those killings in which the murderer has thought about ending the victim's life," say murder of a lover or spouse, to the murderer's behavior in committing an offense when the victim is more likely a stranger or bystander. Other common aggravating circumstances can serve as predicates for a death sentence—killing a member of a designated class such as a police officer, killing for hire, a second murder conviction, and in some states a killing that involves torture or a prolonged death—but killing during the commission of a felony is the circumstance most commonly used.[24]

Some of the consequences of this shift make clear why trying to select only the worst offenders for execution is an exercise in tail chasing but also how particular legislative decisions can serve to keep the death penalty politically palatable. In the first place, a domestic killing does not qualify as an aggravated circumstance. Take a murder that the Supreme Court found justified a death sentence in 1971. The defendant, James Crampton, killed his wife with a .45 caliber revolver while she was using the toilet in her home. They had been married only four months at the time, and he recently had been hospitalized for alcoholism and drug addiction. Crampton made a number of threatening calls to his wife before the murder; she had sought and received police protection. Under Ohio law he was found guilty of murdering his wife "purposely and with premeditated malice."[25]

Today, however, Crampton would be ineligible for a death sentence because his killing doesn't fit the state's list of aggravated circumstances. In those states that use "heinous" or "cruel" murder as an aggravator the jury might be able to sentence Crampton to death, but such a vague standard is always open to question. Murder is almost always cruel. To avoid arbitrariness, the states were supposed to narrow the reach of their death statutes to the worst offenders. A broad definition of torture and prolonged death flies in the face of that edict.

In sharp contrast to the fate of defendants such as Crampton is the robbery codefendant whose partner shoots and kills a victim during a scuffle. Under the new murder laws, he will be charged with "felony murder" and be eligible for death even if he had no intent to kill, had no knowledge of the gun, and started to run away or was in police custody when the victim began to resist. Who is more culpable, the defendant in this all-too-common scenario or Crampton? At this point many people who are trying to sort out their beliefs about capital punishment will understandably want to head for the exit.

One thing is clear: the new laws at best maintain and at worst exacerbate the racial element that has always plagued capital punishment in this country. Despite the Supreme Court's decision not to find the results unconstitutional, few Americans doubt that people who kill whites are more likely to receive a death sentence than those who kill blacks. This risk that white lives will be more highly valued than black lives is enhanced when felony murder becomes the touchstone of capital murder because felony murder involves strangers more often than murders in many other circumstances. According to Givelber, it is the "murder most likely to involve African American perpetrators and white victims." So the shift in law is away from treating "with maximum seriousness" people who had an opportunity "to reflect upon what they were doing and chose to do it anyway" to aiming the death penalty apparatus at the sort of behavior the public associates with black criminality.[26]

There is also something painfully complicated about the legalities of the death penalty, something so morally perplexing about the specifics of selecting and actually killing murderers that it breeds political resignation. The sordidness of the subject matter contributes to the difficulty. It is unpleasant, for example, to realize that there is no escape from a flawed selection process that forces us to live with unintended and unequal consequences of this sort unless the death penalty is made truly mandatory (currently considered unconstitutional) or abolished (currently opposed by both the public and the judges).

We have, for example, a legal system that engages in wrangling over whether it is permissible to force medication on an inmate to rid him of the psychosis that keeps us from killing him.

Or take the problem faced by Washington State law enforcement professionals. They permitted the Green River Killer, Gary Ridgeway, to plead guilty and disclose the facts of forty-eight killings in return for a life sentence and information desperately wanted by the families of victims and supposed victims. The prosecutors knew they were opening themselves up to comments such as those of this writer of a letter to the *Seattle Times:* "What a disgrace for this state to allow a man who has killed 48 women, or more, to make a 'deal' so he won't die. Wow! I wonder if he gave those women and girls a 'deal' before he killed them and threw them out on the side of the road around the Green River. Shame, shame on this state."[27]

Ridgeway calmly admitted he wanted to murder as many prostitutes as he could. He left dead bodies in roadside clusters and enjoyed driving by the killing sites to recall his handiwork. Ridgeway's plea deal not only demonstrates the impossibility of satisfactory selectivity in capital punishment but underscores how much power it places in the hands of police and prosecutors—when they can threaten not to ask for a death sentence, they can even get an admission to forty-eight murders. Unfortunately, even an innocent man is subject to the same pressure as a psychopathic killer such as Ridgeway.

Such dilemmas agitate abolitionists and leave supporters unmoved. The pragmatic middle-of-the-roaders and the undecided tend to throw up their hands. Although a majority of Americans continue to say they favor the death penalty, a different result follows when the sentence of life without parole is presented as an alternative. A 2004 Gallup Poll showed support for the death penalty had dropped to 50 percent of respondents and 46 percent preferred life without possibility of parole. "When Americans were asked the same question in 1997, the gulf was much wider—with 61% favoring capital punishment and only 29% preferring life without parole." But the volatility of the issue was demonstrated by a 2005 Gallup Poll that found the country moving once again toward support of the death penalty.[28] But to date, no death-penalty state has adopted such a system; they have simply enacted laws covering life without parole while retaining execution.

The case-by-case decision making that is part of our common law heritage has proved itself a failure in bringing coherence to death sentencing. Our beloved adversary system has failed here too, as the need for plea bargaining, the inadequacy of the skills of many defense lawyers, and the vast superiority of prosecutors' resources have stood in the way of just treatment of individuals. If legislators could have devised a persuasive policy indicating who should live and who should die, the courts might have done better, but leadership on this set of moral issues has not been evident. Indeed, as the clearest signal the public has given is that it will hold pronounced movement away from the death penalty against any elected official who flirts with it, a political solution to the mess is unlikely until it gets worse, much worse.

To a certain extent the capital punishment wars are being fought for the minds of future generations. The cultural critic Austin Sarat has written that "a society now unwilling to see the links between poverty, neglect and the death penalty may, 'a hundred years from now,' be more receptive to that structural narrative."[29] Attention has shifted from an almost total focus on the more formal aspects of the legal process to efforts to understand the cultural meaning of death penalty practices. Part of this change flows from the postmodern interest in stories. When a matter of life and death is before the courts, the legal process presents a struggle to define good and evil and the level and origins of victimization. Racial imagery has played a key role here, presenting a choice of stories: some assert a black proclivity for crime, others focus on violence against the blameless black child who in turn becomes a killer, and still others tell of the innocent black male wrongly identified as a criminal by whites. Recently it has been innocence, substantiated by science, that drives many of the narratives.

It is doubtful that any of the abolition-minded critics who help us ponder the meanings we invest in the death penalty will be satisfied if their efforts do not bring change for a hundred years, but their perspective reflects a keen sense of impotence about the present. The public continues to support the death penalty, if with diminished enthusiasm; fears of terrorism contribute to an atmosphere that is not conducive to calm, equitable decisions about how to deal with crime. In the United States we are awash with stories of violence (often against children), of crime and punishment, of incompetent and unreliable systems of judgment, but we are fearful of abandoning the comfort supplied by the existence of the maximum penalty.

When you have a major public health problem (homicide) and hold public ceremonies (the capital trial) that permit life to be taken, you are dealing with emotionally loaded encounters, subjects powerful and evocative enough to make consistent rational thought difficult and informed more by literature, morality, and culture than by law and statistics. Much ink has been spilled in deconstruction of the narratives that detail the usual violent crime, the subsequent trial, and then the drama surrounding punishment. Cultural critics debate what it would mean to televise executions. Is it fabricating the experience of execution, as Wendy Lesser suggests?[30] Or justly requiring us to know what is being done in our name, as Sarat argues? Or a matter that should be decided by applying the First Amendment, as urged by my former colleague Bill Turner, the lawyer for the public television station KQED in the case that unsuccessfully sought to televise California's 1992 execution of Robert Alton Harris?[31]

I hope analysts who believe that the public is learning more about the risks in a death penalty system and is less seduced by the claims made for it are right, but in the end my skepticism rules. There is ample evidence that unless a major Supreme Court decision snarls the process, always possible if not probable, our muddled system will soldier on. I used to think that only intimacy with bureaucratic death, in effect a strong dose of government killing, would end the death penalty. But I no longer expect reform so long as execution is presented sensationally as a response to monstrous evil, so that many people see it as simple justice, as in the case of a murderous dictator, a terrorist, or a serial killer, rather than a complicated and error-filled system of social control.

It is very difficult to concentrate on assigning individual blame, as media coverage does, and then expect the public to evaluate the death penalty on the basis of the social costs it incurs. Nevertheless, if change comes it is more likely to begin with the nonprofessionals who cast their opinions on the penalty of death as jurors. The most promising Supreme Court decisions in recent years may be those preserving the power of juries to reflect attitudinal shifts in determining guilt and punishment.

Still we live in a fearful time when it is difficult to resist the promise of security so often linked to the greatest punishment. At present no national political leader is willing to point out that a primary function of the death penalty is to mask many of the social and economic causes of violence and dysfunction. Under the pressures of a dangerous world, we may have allowed the qualities and costs of our own violence to remain beyond full awareness because we are engaged in legitimate self-protection. As a society, we both nurture and fight crime, but we have become largely indifferent to the cruelties inflicted by the process we have created in the good name of personal security. The cruelties of perceived "defensive" violence may seem necessary and, even when regretted, distant and forgettable.

Epilogue

WITH the exception of time spent earning a state license as a marriage and family therapist and later directing a writing program at the Harvard Law School, I've spent the years since I left LDF and Columbia at Northeastern Law School (NULS), teaching criminal and constitutional law. For five of those years, I also served as the law school's dean. Friends thought my work at a community health clinic in Somerville, Massachusetts, was leading to a career change, but family therapy was a way of continuing, though on a smaller scale, the kind of client problem-solving that had given me so much satisfaction as a practicing lawyer.

NULS's way of training practicing lawyers is unique: it grants degrees only to students who successfully complete four clerkships or "co-ops" with lawyers or sitting judges. The program attracts an assertive band of students who believe they learn best by incorporating work experience with academics. The school is also unusual for an atmosphere of left-leaning political ferment reminiscent of an earlier era, perhaps best described by a former student who complained to me that at NULS New Deal Democrats were the right-wingers.

At times Northeastern law students are so politically active that they remind me of LDF's protester-clients in the 1960s. Trying to relate the legal world of the movement era to the present concerns of these students keeps me thinking often about the yin and yang of American legal history over the last forty years. Many of my cases have been overruled or disregarded by later courts, brushed aside as if they never were; yet others have been woven tightly into the fabric of the law. After a recent conversation with a filmmaker who hoped to make a documentary about the obstacles confronted by black physicians and their patients under segregation, I was reminded that many of my clients and most of the southern black lawyers we worked with at LDF have passed from the scene. On the other hand, LDF and other organizations that focused on civil rights are still coping with some of the same basic frustrations that emerged after the passage of the 1964 and 1965 Civil Rights Acts—getting past a focus on antidiscrimination litigation to find effective interventions that move toward greater economic and educational equality.

Despite similar obstacles, in the movement era civil rights activists floated on waves of hope. We were primed to act and act often, foreseeing generally positive, if also limited, results. We had a feeling of slow but inevitable progress, built on confidence in the justice of what we were doing, reinforced by widespread public support and the belief that a majority of federal judges agreed with us. Some LDF cases asserted the rights of particular individuals to fair treatment but others were significant systemic interventions that aimed to open up areas for subsequent political development or establish cherished first principles. I think here of securing the right to counsel fees for litigants who established that their treatment had been unconstitutional, barring jail sentences for poor defendants who could not afford to pay fines, efforts to equalize shameful misallocation of such municipal services as garbage removal and street paving, fighting the practice of dumping toxic waste in poor communities, challenging interstate highways planned to bisect black neighborhoods, and the many, many more that fit the mold. Win or lose, such efforts were rewarded by professional attention and general interest as well as by a measure of success.

Much of the high we experienced was possible only because we usually could not weigh the long-term consequences of our actions. Thurgood Marshall could not have known in 1954, for example, that the freedom rides and sit-ins would lead to the integration of much of the South. In the mid-1960s LDF lawyers could not predict how or when the long series of legal disputes over school segregation would end or what detours lay ahead—the idea that LDF would have more than seventy such cases on its docket by 2005 or that many black parents would be said to suffer from integration fatigue would have been unimaginable.

In a related sphere, one of the great victories of the 1960s was the Supreme Court's ruling in *Gideon v. Wainwright* that ability to defend oneself required appointment of counsel for indigents accused of state felonies.[1] At the time it was easy to predict that lawyers were also needed to ensure fair trials in misdemeanor cases, but that logical step would not come for nine years. More significant, it was clear in 1963 that the actual value of a right to counsel would depend on the training and financing of the lawyers who would serve the poor. But this idea was an abstraction, to be fully grasped only after years of cases, experimentation with various defender programs, successful and failed financing schemes, and political collisions—many of which are still going on. Lawyers of the 1960s are rightly praised for their skill, but the hard work of making rights concrete was down the road. LDF, by the way, is still trying to ensure that the *Gideon* ruling is enforced in Mississippi.[2]

Both my small law school and the larger environment have changed in significant respects. When I came to NULS, 45 percent of its graduates took public interest jobs and half of those became lawyers for the poor. But twelve years of Reagan-Bush hostility to legal services would greatly advance trends already in the making—student debt levels would rise, poverty law jobs would be cut, and student interest slowed as poverty lawyers were starved for funds and then robbed of the authority to bring cases with a potential for structural change. The courts increasingly constricted civil rights protections. The legacy of the 1960s and 1970s is the continued makeover of a dying caste system into the diffuse patterns formed by a growing black middle class and a much larger underclass as well as a move in white society from explicit to implicit racial differentiation. These social forces dictate that the continued inequalities that plague the nation are much harder to see and to treat. People doing my kind of work today do not have an enviable lot.

During the Reagan-Bush years and in the two Clinton terms the strategies of Johnson's Great Society were replaced or altered by a hodgepodge of budget cutbacks, shifts in program control and in allocation of funds through block grants to the fifty states, forays into privatization, and termination of entitlements. "Urban programs and urban policy had become deeply associated with African Americans and thus were primed for a political backlash," wrote Georgia Persons. The backlash was expressed by white flight from integration and inner-city crime to suburban enclaves, a process that was reinforced by law the way segregation itself was legally encouraged in the late nineteenth century: by the refusal of the Supreme Court to order interdistrict segregation remedies, for example; by "federal spending on highways; [by] decades of racist implementation of Federal Housing Administration . . . housing subsidy programs which froze African-Americans out."[3]

The backlash produced a shift in political power and national policy, whether the presidency was in Democratic or Republican hands, which doomed the promise of the Johnson programs. Those programs had their flaws, of course—emphasis on providing services rather than income to the poor seems to have been largely ineffective in ending poverty—but at least the Great Society put inner-city ills on a national To Do list; no coherent set of urban policies has replaced it.

The result of political movement away from the concerns of the poor has left us with racial disparities in every category of social measurement—educational attainment, earned income, adequate housing, incarceration, public health. Take health: "African American infants are more than twice as likely as white infants to die before reaching their first birthday; African American women are three times more likely to die in childbirth than white women; life expectancy for African American men is eight years shorter than for white men; and African American women have a life expectancy nearly six years shorter than white women." Civil rights advocates have no doubt that the "disparity in health status reflects, in part, the widespread continuation of discriminatory . . . practices in the provision of medical services." Evidence also shows that the health burdens falling on lower-class children dramatically affect their school performance.[4] But inquiries into the precise mixture of race-based and poverty-associated factors in public health and other disparities are of limited use. The more critical question is how long and under what circumstances such disparities will be permitted to continue.

Except in the crafting of detailed remedies, it shouldn't matter whether the situation confronted is predominantly economic or racial, or de jure or de facto, but rather whether a society that accepts gaps in life chances and outcomes that it is capable of altering is acting immorally or whether the costs incurred in maintaining the status quo are greater or less than what it will take to change it. Because men are not angels, the answer will depend on the perceived interdependence of the good life as Americans perceive it and the dismal condition of the underclass. It is beyond dispute, in this country at least, that government will more readily address social problems when they not only afflict the poor (especially the minority poor) but either affect the rest of us too or threaten to do so.

The most successful intervention since the Johnson years, for example, the earned income tax credit (EITC), can be discussed in nonracial, nonurban terms that stress the "worthy" working poor. Enacted into law in 1975 and enlarged several times thereafter, with votes from both parties, the credit refunds taxes primarily to low-wage families with children; the benefit is not generally counted as taking eligibility away from other federal programs such as food stamps and Medicaid. EITC is a prime example of what analysts call "stealth" urban policies, those that address major problems associated with cities through "program initiatives" that are "not perceived as directing benefits toward cities" and are sold as targeting low-income people without being race-specific.[5] The political reality is that finding more racially inclusive means to fight disadvantage makes implementing reform measures more acceptable.

Developing government programs that make a serious dent in poverty rates is difficult under any circumstances; you can get a glimpse of the complexities by considering one of the invisible transactional costs that plague such programs as the EITC: despite its aim to funnel money to the poor, because of the way the program is organized, recipients have to pay hundreds of millions to profit-making tax preparation companies to claim their EITC benefits.[6]

EITC aside, when lack of political strength requires that new programs mask their true purpose or adopt approaches to promote tangential political ambitions, the result is convoluted, ad hoc policy making. An instance of how such considerations shape efforts supposedly aimed at the poor is George W. Bush's Faith-Based Community Initiatives (FBCI), a series of still not fully defined efforts to stimulate local religious institutions to engage in social service work while advancing the Republican Party's interest in courting churchgoers. Putting aside the serious church–state constitutional issues raised by the administration's proposals (including approval of religious tests for hiring and breach of the wall separating program delivery and religious proselytizing), it is far from clear how local congregations, few of them organized around consistent delivery of services, will reach their own parishioners, not to speak of the large number of impoverished without church or religious affiliation. FBCI is geared to inputs—sending money to local religious institutions—not to specific outcomes for the poor.[7]

Urban inequality was once attributed primarily to race; it is now as often tied to class-related and general economic factors. Of course, racial discrimination and racial privileging have not gone away, but "the problems of the truly disadvantaged," as William Julius Wilson put it, "may require *nonracial* solutions such as full employment, balanced economic growth, and manpower training and education training."[8] Wilson's message about the declining influence of race is controversial, but it is beyond serious debate that the greatest challenge of the postmovement era is the series of seemingly intractable social and economic issues in which poverty, race, and nonracial concerns merge.

Many of these issues are matters of distribution, not of basic access or principle, which call for the best advocacy to be done by lobbyists and program designers; dealing with these issues effectively requires accommodation, compromise, and ultimately tracking of administrative implementation over time. Often the only viable intervention is local, based on detailed knowledge of conditions that have uncertain impact elsewhere. It is disheartening, however, that public interest advocates apparently could not see to it that mainstream political discourse during the 2004 presidential campaign included discussion of the vacuum in urban policy or that as of late 2004 LDF's Economic Justice program consisted of eleven cases, all traditional employment discrimination suits that might help individual or small groups of employees but no longer seemed capable of narrowing differentials in the wages and occupational status of white and black workers.[9] None of the cases was targeted at an issue of critical concern to the underclass. Given suburban control of the political balance of power, the obstacles to a refocus on the inner city are formidable and likely to remain so unless the demographics change later in the century or circumstances encourage an effective form of direct action.

Given such a political universe, my students often ask, what is the wisest course to follow? If civil rights lawyers were to have a business plan, what should it look like?

With a change in leadership at LDF in 2004, the inquiry is timely. Though the Legal Defense Fund is now just one player on a broad public interest landscape, it remains the primary organization concerned with the rights of African Americans; clearly LDF must continue to be available to challenge racial discrimination where it finds it.

My response—that I am not expecting major changes—is self-protective: I don't want to play Pied Piper to young lawyers who are prodding themselves into doing good. Fortunately, most of the students I see at Northeastern have made up their own minds about the professional life they want to lead. They are surprised, however, that my first comment about the future role of civil rights lawyers seems drawn more from the arts than from the law. I emphasize uncovering operative social facts and relationships that people would rather not see; connecting the dots when events in black America are presented as if they happen in a land remote from life in the white suburbs—a fortress in our midst. The job here is to make news out of stories that are ignored and to develop the hidden racial dimensions buried beneath sanitized narratives. Legal academics are deeply engaged in this activity. The ultimate goal for the practitioner is to assemble factual records capable of persuading larger constituencies that political and legal intervention is justified. The need to connect superficially contingent but actually linked experiences is ever present: when the Iraq prisoner abuse scandal became public in 2004, how many Americans were aware that they were being shocked by practices that had close parallels in what occurs in domestic correctional institutions?

Civil rights lawyers have been playing versions of this role for decades, but they and their allies have a special responsibility to do the necessary work to identify and reveal to a hostile or indifferent public the suppressed interdependence of rich and poor, black and white. In this respect they are the legatees of the goals left unrealized at Martin Luther King's death. I both admire and pity these lawyers, social scientists, and politicians and the activists with whom they work. They have a just cause to work for but they must proceed without Dr. King's overwhelming and comforting presence—not for nothing was he sarcastically but affectionately called "De Lawd" in movement circles. Rightly celebrated as the symbol of a national commitment to eliminate second-class citizenship, he is less well remembered for attempting to redirect the civil rights movement toward a successful attack on the ills of poverty. He began his fumbling efforts in that direction just a few years before he was assassinated. Much of value has happened since his death in 1968—jobs created, improved African American educational achievement, successful government income-transfer programs, and the emergence of a strong black middle class—but the progress has been overwhelmed by escalating rates of drug use and incarceration for violation of drug laws among African American men and continued substandard housing, gang activity, educational failure by students from low-income families, unemployment and underemployment of inner-city residents, homelessness, and public transportation that is inadequate to the needs of inner-city job seekers.

The portrait of the United States sketched here is not of malevolent bigots run amuck but of widespread self-deception or disassociation with regard to the implications of color. Contemporary American culture reflects only the most superficial knowledge of the nation's history of violence and subordination with respect to Native Americans, Asians, and Hispanics as well as blacks. Of course, a vague general sense of past unfair treatment is a staple of textbooks and media portrayals of historical events, but the particulars only fitfully have enough currency to drive contemporary public policy. It is generally conceded, for example, that the Supreme Court's approval of affirmative action in limited circumstances was a concession to the needs of leadership, of elites, for the legitimacy that diversity confers, not a principled approval of a remedy that might repair the past by changing the future.

It's a matter not of knowing little about African American history but of a failure to incorporate the racial meanings found there into American history—of which of course it is a part—and to acknowledge in practice the role those meanings play in shaping everything from our sexual mores to concepts of masculine identity to taste in music to the spoken language to the face we paste on fear of crime to land use, welfare policy, and national politics. Most white Americans simply do not know any black person well, much less are able to say anything concrete about the divisions of class, culture, gender, and behavior that operate within communities of color. Black actors report that when they show up for an audition they are often told to "act black"—by which the director apparently means like a hoodlum, addict, or bundle of incandescent emotion. In short, the specifics of life in an African American subculture with its own divisions and alliances are terra incognita for most white Americans.

Even Justice Antonin Scalia (no friend of affirmative action) concedes that government can *sometimes* act on the basis of race to undo past discrimination, but if this backward-looking inquiry is to accomplish much in the way of social change, it must be broad enough (contra Scalia's view) to eradicate the present effects of race-based subjugation.[10] This depends on making connections, historical or contemporary, that are congruent with the systemic interdependence of modern life. So, for example, to challenge the Supreme Court's deceptive unwillingness in the name of local control to permit interdistrict transfers to minimize racial isolation in the public schools, it is necessary to make visible the wealth of cross-over arrangements in derogation of localism that characterize American government—regional hospital and school compacts, water and historic districts that cross county lines, court jurisdictions that include various cities and towns, regional planning boards, area development authorities, and highway commissions. Reminders of interdependence in other spheres may not persuade committed opponents, but eventually evidence of this sort is bound to have an impact on public discourse.

A second step, I tell my students, is to concede without fully accepting that lawyers' activity on behalf of the poor is important even if very little of it ends up generating significant structural change. Macro issues, of course, are exquisitely demanding even when they aren't intractable. In a 2004 column in the *New York Times,* Henry Louis Gates Jr., chair of the

Epilogue

Afro-American Studies Department at Harvard University, wondered tongue in cheek (quoting liberally his friend Franklin Raines, then CEO of the Fannie Mae Corporation) whether blacks could even catch up to the level of inequality experienced by white Americans. Raines estimated that an improvement to that modest level would mean 2 million more high school diplomas, 2 million more college degrees, 3 million more professional and managerial jobs, 3 million more homeowners, $200 billion more in stock market equities, $120 billion more in retirement savings, and $80 billion more in the bank accounts of black Americans. Gates asked: "Has the average really become too much to ask for?" Apparently the answer is yes, because after canvassing the (modest) remedies proposed— better transportation from the inner city to job sites; public service jobs for employees in transition; more job training and more money to poor school districts—he concludes "there just isn't the political will, in either party," to provide the changes that would allow us to find out.[11]

But a host of smaller issues affect the lives of the poor and of more Americans considered middle class than is generally supposed. Policy intervention here requires patient monitoring, surgical intervention, fund-raising, and mobilizing of constituencies. These challenges to public interest lawyers are far different in kind from the larger issues Gates mentions or the basic dignity concerns that were at the heart of the civil rights movement:

- A federal law passed in 2003, the Medicare Modernization Act, offered $1 billion over four years to subsidize hospital emergency room services, but only if the hospitals in question were willing to collect information about immigrants, data that might lead to deportation. The federal government claims the information would be used only to ensure that the money is used correctly; hospitals and immigrant-support groups are wary, worrying that the net result will be to deter people from seeking health care.

- In 2004 the Bush administration proposed to deal with the increasing costs of the federal Section 8 housing subsidy program for low-income earners by distributing money in block grants to housing authorities rather than by establishing a set number of vouchers. Did this proposal ensure that there would be more homeless Americans, or was it a carefully planned way of encouraging local housing authorities to control costs and serve more families? Or did it matter not at all if Congress rejected the proposal because then federal budget writers would merely be reducing the gross amount of Section 8 funds available to the Department of Housing and Urban Development?

• "Medicare pays for about 40 percent of all hospital and physician services," according to Charles D. Baker, the president and CEO of a large private health insurance company. But the fees paid out are not made public, so that it is extremely difficult to ensure competition to hold down the escalating costs of health care.

• New York State has a food stamp program for needy legal immigrants, mostly children and the elderly, but the program as set up keeps about ten thousand potential recipients ineligible by barring those who have moved from one county to another since 1996 or traveled out of the United States for more than ninety days.

The very successes of the 1960s and 1970s produced a host of such problems; it is as hard to spot and to evaluate them as it is to know the best action to take in the circumstances. Even wins and losses become hard to calculate. The examples listed above are, of course, just a tiny fraction of those that surface every day in Washington and state capitals; each necessitates constant scrutiny of the small print by lawyers and policy analysts.

In the absence of proof that the operation of a market economy can do more than privilege a minority of a minority, how should the present-day work of civil rights be conducted? A third element of postmovement civil rights legal strategy looks toward more extensive support for grass-roots interracial cooperation. Only by forming alliances with others was the movement I joined in 1961 able to move closer to a true integration of American life. It was part of Dr. King's genius that he saw that support for economic justice and peace in Vietnam, controversial as they were at the time, held the makings of a bridge to white communities that rested on shared interests rather than a merely transient identification with the black cause. Our only viable course is to convey the message that racial and economic reform is not a black issue but a general social issue.

A model for organized biracial action might be found in the activities of the Association of Community Organizations for Reform Now, or ACORN, the nation's largest advocacy group for poor and middle-income families with some eight hundred chapters in sixty-five cities. ACORN promotes issues of importance to moderate-income earners by building community organizations; it also supports living-wage campaigns sponsored by local labor and religious groups. Living-wage advocates seek wage and benefit increases and in some instances seek to pass local ordinances requiring private businesses that benefit from public money to pay their workers enough to live decently. The concept has attracted increasing attention as the plight of the underemployed emerged as a key issue after changes in the public assistance system sent more women and recent immigrants into low-income jobs. One idea behind the campaign is that "limited public dollars should not be subsidizing poverty-wage work. When subsidized employers are allowed to pay their workers less than a living wage, taxpayers end up footing a double bill: the initial subsidy and then the food stamps, emergency medical, housing and other social services low-wage workers may require to support themselves and their families even minimally."[12]

The syndicated columnist Robert Kuttner has described living-wage campaigns as "the most interesting (and underreported) grassroots enterprise to emerge since the civil rights movement . . . signaling a resurgence of local activism around pocketbook issues."[13] Living-wage activity and the work of ACORN chapters illustrate how racial and economic concerns can merge in communal expression, but despite some local successes, the campaigns have not fully blossomed into effective national political action. What is lacking in these diverse local campaigns is not coordination with similar moves in other communities but a national identity and transformative presence of the sort that the civil rights movement ultimately achieved. Bringing the energy of the living-wage campaigns to the national stage is a tactical challenge worthy of the attention of the entire public interest bar.

A final entry on the wish list I give my students is examining the benefits of new and different legal interventions in public education. Here, because of its role in *Brown*, LDF has a special interest and expertise; though the payoff may be years away, education issues connect as none others with social and economic mobility.

The grim truth is that general dissatisfaction with school performance has not been put to rest by any of the forces driving for improvement. Desegregation (limited as it has been) has gone about as far as it can go in improving educational quality. At any rate, courts no longer order it and black parents no longer yearn for it or tolerate the long-distance busing that would be necessary to bring it about. Increased school financing has probably helped improve achievement, but the feeling in many communities, North and South, is that more than money is necessary and that amounts large enough to make a difference will never be made available. The premise that public schools are still failing to provide adequate education to many children is rarely challenged. The result is a search for grand solutions, as well as efforts to farm out school problems to private management systems or charter school programs or even to evade them with voucher programs.

The current centerpiece of school reform is the federal No Child Left Behind Act (NCLB), which Congress passed with support in both parties in 2001.[14] The heart of the act is a mandated articulation of academic standards and requirements for high-stakes testing as a predicate for accountability. NCLB does not focus on individual achievement but rather holds schools, districts, and states accountable for the academic progress of their students. Under the NCLB, schools and districts must "(1) bring all subpopulations of students up to a state-defined level of educational adequacy and (2) improve the performance of those subpopulations at a threshold rate defined by state law; and states are routinely required to (3) divide those institutions into similarly situated cohorts (ones with racially and socioeconomically comparable student bodies), and (4) publicly identify the institutions in each cohort that do and do not satisfy those adequacy and improvement requirements."[15]

Potential sanctions for failing schools include the right of parents to transfer children to a school that performs better, requirements for supplemental educational services, and, theoretically, a cut-off of funds. After four years of failure, school districts must take corrective measures such as replacing staff or implementing a new curriculum. After another year of substandard performance schools can be taken over by the state or converted to charter schools. Once schools are found to be failing under NCLB, agencies of the state education department are required to submit a plan to eliminate deficiencies. NCLB deals explicitly with race only by telling educational planners to take preexisting desegregation plans into consideration and to seek their modification if appropriate, but because children in failing schools are accorded an opportunity to transfer out of them, NCLB holds out the possibility that underserved populations will find a higher level of educational attainment by attending schools with presumably different demographics.

Analysts see no shortage of problems in the NCLB approach. The University of Virginia law professor James E. Ryan points to the act's "perverse incentives"—by measuring absolute achievement (which will favor affluent school populations) instead of gains in achievement (which will measure the progress of the disadvantaged) the act rewards "relatively affluent schools" and punishes "relatively poor ones."[16] With standardized test failures associated with low-income minority students, administrators have an incentive to find ways to exclude students who will bring scores down and for teachers to avoid schools whose students have low test scores. Even more significant, the most obvious way to avoid NCLB sanctions and the ignominy of administering or teaching at a failing school is for education officials to water down testing standards. State departments of education are given broad discretion in setting standards, and past performance suggests that the U.S. Department of Education is unlikely to exert pressure on the states to implement the law rigorously.

The most attractive aspect of NCLB for those concerned with equal educational opportunity is the right to transfer, which comes into play after a school has failed to reach its achievement goals. Unfortunately, the promise of transfer to more affluent and perhaps integrated schools may be illusory. Even if state law permits such transfers, movement of significant numbers of students cannot just be willed. As Ryan says, "Saying that space is not a constraint does not make it so."[17] The Harvard education professor Richard Elmore holds that to the extent that schools meet their NCLB targets only by teaching the tests or "because the law is based on a faulty theory that improvement occurs in equal annual increments, while actual improvement moves in a much different pattern," we can expect a continuation of the frustration that accompanied every healing nostrum proposed in the last fifty years.[18]

In a larger sense, the political forces that restricted integration are unlikely to disappear just because integration is labeled "school choice." It is no accident that the NCLB does not contemplate transfer from one district to another.

For too long the debate over the education of minority children has pitted supporters of educational reform against those who saw desegregation as the most effective available reform. Critics argued that the vast sums spent on desegregation should have been invested in educational reform; civil rights groups responded that giving isolated minority children access to better schools is an educational reform. Battered by judges' resistance to integration and by black parents who increasingly explore vouchers or independent schools in their frustration at defective public school systems, LDF has now moved toward combining the two approaches.

In 2003 LDF's education staff issued a highly critical report rejecting key provisions of the NCLB approach. While endorsing standards that would help to equalize the resources available to schools and school districts, access to advanced curricula, and better physical facilities, the staff labeled as "misguided" the hope that testing will improve "the quality of public education, including school accountability and student performance." Testing associated with punitive consequences, the staff recommended, should be challenged in court, one theory being that often minority students aren't given the instruction that would enable them to pass.

The report argued that such testing led to marginalization, pushed students out of school, and stood in the way of "broader academic and skill development." The tests have never been shown to have predictive validity; they measure a "narrow conception of individual merit" and can facilitate tracking arrangements that segregate black students within school walls. Test results can also have a huge impact on an entire system. Most attention has been directed to the prospect of teachers' "teaching for the test" and not for learning, but "teacher bonuses, state funds for schools, and even the control of a particular school or school district can all be affected by the results of the standardized tests."[19]

In a departure from decades of intense focus on court-ordered desegregation, instead of supporting NCLB the staff recommended broad efforts to deal with social policies that affected educational achievement—residential segregation that keeps blacks educationally isolated and the "school-to-prison pipeline"—using harsh disciplinary methods and incarceration instead of providing education. The report urged litigation over group tracking by ability and excessive labeling of black children as in need of special education classes and restrictive educational settings. Finally, it calls for LDF to deploy a consultant and a policy analyst to monitor national education developments, as well as for a much greater investment in informing the public.

But is LDF making a crucial mistake in ignoring the possibilities of accepting and exploiting NCLB? James Liebman, not content with his towering scholarship on the death penalty, and Charles Sabel, his colleague at Columbia, see enormous potential in NCLB. Fully aware of the skepticism that will greet them, Liebman and Sabel predict that public education is on the verge of a dramatic breakthrough. Their optimism is rooted in two apparently contradictory trends: (1) the creation of state accountability systems that they say establish for the first time local responsibility and significant consequences for school outcomes; and (2) what they claim is the increasing ability of creative principals, teachers, and civic organizations to develop successful urban schools from the bottom up. Out of the synthesis of these centralizing and decentralizing trends Liebman and Sabel see a new model for education governance in which states articulate high standards of performance and then give school districts and schools the autonomy to develop strategies to meet those goals.[20]

Another expert, Gordon Whitman, associate director of Temple University's Center for Public Policy, found NCLB promising because it may deal with perhaps "the greatest injustice in American public education . . . that low-income and African-American and Latino students are disproportionately taught by teachers who have limited teaching experience, lack certification and are not educated in the subject areas they are teaching." NCLB requires that school authorities take steps to ensure that poor and minority children are not taught at higher rates than other children "by inexperienced, unqualified, or out-of-field teachers." But Whitman issued a warning:

> The broader lesson . . . is that it is difficult for accountability systems to work under conditions of severe inequality. It is not just that poorer school districts lack the absolute resources to meet standards, but that they are unable to effectively compete. . . . It is not unusual for economically disadvantaged students . . . to enter school without pre-school experience, to be retained in the early grades without any special help in reading, to attend classes with 30 or more students, to lack counseling and needed social services, and to be exposed to a curriculum in which important courses are not taught and materials are inadequate and outdated.[21]

An assessment of the potential of NCLB also implicates larger issues. According to a report by two university researchers, Roland Fryer and Steven Levitt, black and white students basically enter school in the same educational place but performance rapidly diverges. Surveying 20,000 children who entered kindergarten in the fall of 1998, Fryer and Levitt found that the "leading explanation for the worse trajectory of black students in our sample is that they attend lower quality schools." This explanation made much more sense to Fryer and Levitt than the impact of the poverty rates of black children or factors such as family culture—whether and how much parents read to their children or the time the students devote to homework. "Black pre-kindergarteners," for example, "are now more likely than their white peers to be taught letters, words, or numbers in their homes three times a week."[22]

But Richard Rothstein argues that no matter how ambitious the school reform agenda, it will be undermined if economic and social disparities are not vigorously challenged. Unless we deal with a whole array of inequalities—children's physical health, inadequate family income, cultural valuation of learning, availability of books—we are just kidding ourselves about real progress. Rothstein believes there are stark class differences in the way middle- and lower-class parents read and talk to their children. Because of the home the child comes from and goes back to every day, even skilled teachers and programs at good schools, Rothstein insists, cannot be effective unless we tackle class-based issues.[23]

If the views of critics such as Ryan, Whitman, and Rothstein prevail, NCLB will be just another failed educational reform nostrum. For reasons I have discussed above, however, on the national level the only short-term prospect for any serious change must target schools, not urban economic and social inequality. The Liebman-Sabel thesis assumes that if NCLB is consistently and strictly enforced, it is probable that large numbers of children of color will have the opportunity to transfer to schools with higher test rankings and a less pronounced racial imbalance. To the extent that desegregation for reasons of explicit nonracial performance meets the same resistance as desegregation itself encountered and litigation challenges are blocked, the impetus for enforcement will have to come from parent groups and community activists around the nation. "The key need," urges the longtime civil rights lawyer William Taylor, is for every community to establish a group that will "inform and counsel parents about the opportunities provided by the transfer program and will contest unneeded restrictions in the way the program operates."[24]

No organization compares to LDF in having the interest and credibility, if not at present the money, to explore the possibilities of NCLB and meliorate its flaws. The 2003 staff report identified some of those flaws and sought to chart a sensible course focused on both school resources and broader environmental sources of educational disparity. Like it or not, however, NCLB is the only source of significant change in national educational patterns on the horizon; only marginal good is likely to come from LDF's current docket of mostly holdover (and nonurban)desegregation cases. Despite understandable skepticism, LDF cannot afford to ignore its potential. There is at least a chance that successful implementation could redress racial and economic disparities that have plagued reform efforts, halting or reducing the steep levels of resegregation that are a legacy of the post-*Brown* decades. The costs of NCLB's failure, however, are extreme enough to justify efforts to make the act work even if the odds are long. Moreover, LDF lawyers are masters at overcoming the sort of technical obstacles that could be used to block nongovernmental oversight; they would not hesitate to challenge in court a statutory scheme that places great and unreviewable powers in the hands of educational bureaucrats. At the other end of the spectrum, using the promise of NCLB as an organizing tool and community education stimulus is an obviously promising move that (if money to fund it can be found) will allow LDF to develop a local NCLB monitoring network.

It turns out that in the end what I learned at LDF had a lot to do with legal doctrine and litigation but more to do with a way of thinking about my country. The black experience may be no easier to apprehend authentically by outsiders than that of any group with a rich, bloody, tangled history; it may be especially difficult in a land with a major racial hang-up that creeps silently into the thought and actions of even the best intentioned. But civil rights are not the property of any one group, even one whose victimization and its repair often define those rights for everyone. The world is full of populations that find it agonizingly difficult to live together nonviolently. Ultimately, the highest calling of civil rights activity is to increase the prospects for a common ground, chances that, say, once blacks gain sufficient power to feel that integration will not spell annihilation and once whites learn the costs of keeping an underclass, enough Americans will grasp that a regime of rights means respect for everyone who has less than he or she needs to thrive.

Of course, it would be utopian to think something like this will ever happen. The odds are certainly against it. But then, the movement I worked in brought about amazing transformations of outsiders into stakeholders, and someday, with or without the help of LDF-type lawyers, the poor of all hues may yet find the way.

After I delivered the manuscript for this book, the devastation caused by Hurricane Katrina and the inept response to the disaster by the Bush administration appeared to have forced reconsideration of a host of government policies—for example, those concerning wetland management, evacuation planning, tax and spending priorities, and even the lines demarking military and civilian, state and federal responsibility to protect citizens and to allocate the costs of property damage to nonvictims. But, driven by searing media images of death and misery, nothing quite compared to the rediscovery of the thousands of poor—mostly the black poor—left unaided and unassisted in the floodwaters of New Orleans. Almost immediately, old arguments over how to treat poverty erupted: Were more social supports or more entrepreneurial initiatives called for? Was it sensible for the administration to focus on faith-based and similar initiatives whose purpose was to make the poor more "responsible" in the face of indifference to a rising poverty rate and United States Census figures showing five straight years of decline in household income?

It is unclear how long or how steady is the sudden determination of the Bush administration to help the poor, media commitment to report on the plight of the underclass, and voter attention to fighting poverty over the long haul.

So close in time are we to the passions of a national crisis, about all that is certain is that crises often force upon us shifts in understanding and that there is in this set of dramatically unsettling events an opportunity for a civil rights movement to reform and reconstitute itself and the society it once served so well.

Appendix

So You Want to Be a Lawyer

WHY practice law? Most of the law students and young lawyers I have taught and worked with thought they knew the answer, at least for themselves: the respect conferred by professional status; political ambition; the prospect of making a good living; love of strategic thinking, debate, or competition; even the expected rush of the courtroom. They might have encountered a role model in a family member or friend who was an attorney or even learned early the pleasures of helping to solve other people's problems or playing a public role in work that advanced prospects for a more just society.

Of course such reasons still carry a great deal of weight and will probably do fine for law school applications, job interviews, and cocktail-party chitchat. But after identifying the why of lawyering, these days the would-be or beginning attorney needs to focus on some details that have much to teach about the evolution of a professional life. It is more important than ever to know something about the legal world you will enter. Trash talk about lawyers, even (and sometimes especially) by people who rely on them, has almost acquired the status of a national sport. Fragile egos will be easily punctured. Law school costs big bucks. The average graduate leaves school these days well over $50,000 in debt; despite law schools' subsidies of loan repayments, for years I've watched student dreams of a life in public service evaporate in the harsh reality of debt schedules.

Moreover, the days of a staid, predictable professional career are gone. Recent graduates encounter more bottom-line-oriented law firms than the more stable ones of years gone by. Despite fashionable addresses and the latest in technology, many firms are engaged in deadly competition with peers or with the growing legal firepower of international accounting firms for their very existence. In the first five years of practice, the average law graduate will hold two or three jobs. Firms that once hired for life now expect attrition. Once new hires realistically hoped for partnership though not all, of course, got it. Hiring partners who used to look for grand generalists or potential superstars among recent graduates now extend job offers knowing full well that most associates will spend much of their time with the firm doing the legal equivalent of hourly piecework: writing memos, coding documents, summarizing depositions. Training and supervision are generally limited, geared to match these different task expectations and patterns of firm loyalty. At the "best" firms, the new lawyer may work for several years before being in the same room as a client.

Television and movie melodramas, seemingly obsessed with the easy good-vs.-evil plot devices that can be stuffed into an adversary system formula, frame the popular understanding of lawyering. They may not have elevated the always-shaky level of esteem the profession occupies in the public mind, but by slicking up the work with full portions of sex, danger, good clothes, and power politics while avoiding the often tedious necessities of study and reflection, the media have made lawyering entertaining enough to encourage large numbers of young people to give law school a try. Admissions officers have long been secretly delighted by the increased numbers of applicants attributed to *LA Law*, the O. J. Simpson trial (a "true-life" melodrama), and even *Ally McBeal*.

Thus competing and overlapping clusters of imagery seem to define the prospects for the would-be lawyer. Most of them, however, seriously distort what lies ahead—whether your goal is to make a lot of money fast or be a full-time public interest lawyer or build a commercial practice that also includes a decent component of civil rights, civil liberties, or similar humanitarian work even though you are not working directly for a nonprofit organization.

If you can't make your peace with long hours of reading, writing, or meetings that accomplish little more than put players together in a room, then a legal career may not be for you. Naturally, you aren't going to see a great many frames on cable television of lawyers sitting pensively in front of computer monitors or sifting for hours through piles of documents or getting home night after night after the kids have gone to bed. The stillness surrounding much legal work and the delays encountered before one actually enters a courtroom are often shocks to the system of a high-energy, upwardly mobile, assertive young attorney.

Recently I spent four years directing a program at the Harvard Law School that attempted to train first-year students in the legal writing and research protocols they would need to survive as newly hired associates. Many immediately grasped the importance (as well as the dreaded grayness) of these skills but just as many were incredulous. They believed that because they had attended worthy undergraduate institutions, scored high on standardized tests, and were experts at operating computers, cell phones, iPods, and instant messaging devices, they were endowed with innate talent to master elaborate research tasks requiring them to dig cost-effectively into obscure sources. Or perhaps they didn't really understand—because the time students spend searching for data on computer sites is free—that someone would be paying excessively for their labor if they did it badly or inefficiently.

I pitied the sober, dedicated librarians and Harvard First Year Lawyering Program instructors who too often were treated by their charges—after all, *they* were on course to become the future leaders of the free world—like nagging parents who were insisting that they eat all their spinach. Of course, every summer when the students were handed research assignments for real clients who were usually paying top dollar to highly regarded firms for advice, the students besieged their former trainers with urgent phoned-in questions and belated thank-you letters.

In the *Harvard Law Review* a particularly perceptive Harvard student told what happened to many of his fellow students who on admission to law school thought themselves the truly elect: "Far from brimming over with personal and intellectual self-confidence, by the second (2L) year, a surprising number of Harvard Law students come to resemble what one professor has called 'the walking wounded': demoralized, dispirited, and profoundly disengaged from the law school experience. What's more, by third (3L) year, a disturbingly high number of students come to convey a strong sense of impotence and little inclination or enthusiasm for meeting the world's challenges head on."[1]

The source of this malaise is superficially legal education itself, with its emphasis on adopting a neutral detached perspective on clients' personal problems and pressing social issues; students who are trained to argue any side of any issue become "alienated from their former ideals" of social change.[2] David Wilkins, a former colleague of mine at Harvard, has emphasized that law schools have also failed to convey a realistic portrait of what lawyers actually do and the settings in which they do it.[3] Law professors, many of whom are ignorant of both the blunt and fine points of practice, prefer to analyze rules and dissect judicial reasoning, a task they usually do brilliantly.

In a recent "state of the school" address, the dean of Harvard Law School (where at most 5 to 10 percent of graduates take public interest jobs) expressed amazement at widespread criticism of the school for its lack of commitment to public service; she held students responsible for taking "appropriate ownership of your career and your choices." A dissident student replied that the school's program was geared to "providing fresh bodies to replace burned-out or retiring corporate lawyers" and urged the dean to take "appropriate ownership to ensure that as few students as possible suffer the same fate."[4]

A major portion of the responsibility for students' alienation, however, flows from a circumstance neither schools nor students created—from the recognition that, at least at Ivy League institutions, admission is more important to career success than school performance, except at the far extremes of exceptionally high or low grades. The law firms descend on such institutions en masse, eager to snap up students with at least an easily earned B average to staff the ranks of new associates. These legal foot soldiers will soon bill in amounts that reflect their salary more faithfully than their skill and as a result help keep the firms hugely profitable; senior partners will be paid handsomely by the firm's clients for capping primary research and drafting tasks completed by bright but green associates. Some recruits will thrive and eventually become officers themselves in these legal armies, but most will operate pretty much as mid-level corporate functionaries unless they take affirmative steps to reshape their work lives.

Unfortunately, those who are not able to find their own career paths or who are in firms that take little interest in growth and development of the newly minted lawyers (after all, a new crop of hires is coming up next year) still suffer from what the Harvard student describes as characteristic of many 3Ls: "resignation, confusion, and a loss of their capacity to chart their own futures or make things happen."[5] But if law school can be infantilizing and law firms disappointing, the practice of law still provides so many material benefits and opportunities to shine that many law graduates a few years out generally accept their situation. The student commentator labels them a docile lot, but if their larger ideals have been thwarted, it is at least a general condition—they aren't alone in this fate—and they are well paid, working for powerful organizations, and likely to find a new employer without much trouble if need be.

A great deal more would have to be said to fully explicate the way the law schools and firms socialize their fledglings into work roles and how the economics of practice plays back to define both what people do and how they feel about what they do: how the schools ration professional knowledge, for example, by privileging doctrinal analysis to the detriment of client-centered and other dimensions of practice, and how they tell students little about the sociology and history of the profession; on the other side of the ledger, how hard the schools try (with only marginal success) to stem the rush toward private practice by hiring public interest job coordinators (Harvard's and Northeastern's are exemplary), setting up loan-forgiveness schemes, and bringing public servant role models to campus.

From what I've said so far, you may understandably suspect that I have my doubts about the prospects for both the legal profession and public interest lawyering. And you would be partially right. But only partially because, win or lose a particular battle, mine was an intense love story of work and workplace, a serendipitous journey through the heart of what was for the legal profession the best of times. There is no reason to believe those times will not come again. It is in this spirit that I want to underscore how the changes in civil rights or public interest practice relate to the also shifting attributes of the law schools and the profession and to suggest how these developments affect the lawyer contemplating a career that includes at least some public interest work.

These suggestions, as will be obvious, are far from comprehensive; indeed, they are intended to help create a context where you can learn how to learn rather than a laundry list of dos and don'ts. They are impelled by a dangerous shift at the intersection of private practice and public service. From the founding of the Republic to the present day lawyers have moved from roles in the private sector to roles in government or vice versa. Thomas Jefferson, Alexander Hamilton, Daniel Webster, Abraham Lincoln, Louis Brandeis, Felix Frankfurter, and Archibald Cox were all on that very long list. Traveling this route certainly helps the careers of the lawyers. They gather in money or praise derived from the knowledge and prestige acquired by combining public and private connections. There are serious risks of opportunism here because, for a short time at least, insider information or influence available in one sector may be brought to and hoarded by those in the other, but, abuse aside, combining public and private roles helps broaden the perspective of both government official and private practitioner. In a loose way creating a group of citizen–public servants allows government to keep in touch with its ultimate constituency and non-governmental players to share in the responsibilities of governance.

But the problem for the new lawyer is that the practice of law has become so hectic, so ruled by financial concerns, and so cutthroat in competition that opportunities to advance in the firm while playing a significant pro bono publico role have diminished. There are many exceptions—firms that take public service seriously and reward associates who make pro bono a significant part of their workload—but there are many more that pay only lip service to a public role or deter it by conveying the message that advancement will depend solely on bringing in or working on highly remunerative business.

The first rule, then, is *take responsibility for learning what you need to learn to do what you want to do.* Many young lawyers have chosen their careers with the expectation that they will get to court, interrogate witnesses, address jurors, and argue to judges. If this is the work you want to do, it is likely that you will have to pursue the necessary skills and experience wherever you can find them; the firm or agency you work for may provide a few training days and mock exercises, but trial work requires confidence, and confidence rests on having been there. One problem for the would-be litigator is that trials are far fewer as a proportion of case filings than they were in the past; as a consequence, both experienced trainers and training opportunities are in short supply. Even criminal defense work, once the easiest way to get trial experience, nowadays is mostly plea bargaining. Take advantage in law school of any courses that provide front-line experience. Once you've graduated, try to volunteer for second or third chair whenever you get a chance or just hang around a litigated case. Don't for a minute restrict yourself to opportunities available where you work. If you can't find someone to let you play even a minor role in a litigated case, just turn up in court and watch; if you can't find time to watch, check out as many books as you can that describe actual trials and, even better, read trial transcripts from law office files.

What applies to litigators also applies to transactional lawyers—those who see themselves as primarily working on deals, counseling clients, mediating between the parties to a dispute, negotiating. Baseball experts who observed the efforts of the basketball superstar Michael Jordan to become a major-league player noted that despite his superb athleticism he had just started too late; in short, to become a successful major-league hitter you have to have taken thousands of swings even if you are Michael Jordan. The same principle holds for counselors, mediators, and negotiators as well as courtroom examiners. You need to get started doing the work when you are young. While the guidance of a decent theory is always useful—it will contain valuable task-orienting generalizations—to be a successful negotiator you must negotiate and negotiate and negotiate some more. Now that many law schools and continuing education programs offer what are called for some reason "alternative" dispute-resolution workshops and the vast majority of both civil and criminal cases are being settled by the parties rather than decided by judges, there should be plenty of opportunities to begin to learn this essential part of the lawyer's trade.

Of course, an aggressive personal agenda to shape your own career path requires not only sacrifice but knowing what your goal is. Unfortunately, resolving conflicting aims may be more difficult than moving toward a goal once it is determined. If you are at all like me, it will take some experience with the workplace itself to define what you really want. Many young lawyers find it painful to discover that law teachers do not impart the skills most valued by practicing lawyers, such as effective oral communication, clear writing, and the ability to inspire confidence in others. As a result, completing (and repeating) even relatively simple tasks in real cases under professional guidance can provide more powerful socialization into the profession than the most elegant analytic lecture.

This brings me to my third precept: *Pay careful attention to the culture of the place where you work and the people you choose to work with; understanding both will have a critical impact on how you come to see your work.* This is the case whether you work for a large or small firm, a government agency, a court, or a nonprofit advocacy group. The fact that the organization fits with your politics and does the sort of good you want to do or pays the kind of money you want to make doesn't necessarily mean it is the kind of place where you can learn, grow, and come into your own. Just as the best classroom teachers can hold opinions you roundly reject, so the best supervisors and mentors can have belief systems you do not share. It is essential to find or to create a place where you can acquire what you haven't learned in law school or elsewhere, and this means knowing what makes both you and the places where you work tick.

My experience at LDF gave content to such general beliefs and ethical tendencies as I carried into adulthood. I came to think American society would always be dysfunctional until it fully exposed and dealt with its racial pathologies, and that much in national life was randomly but persistently organized to avoid confronting these realities. To join in the task of uncovering these hidden lethal tumors was to realize that the people involved, whether white or black, had more interests in common than issues that divided them. It's an oversimplification to say so, but for the African American or indeed the member of any minority group, legal rights have a special importance that may at times be difficult for the person who has not experienced a system of subordination to grasp. And obviously when both the black advocate and her client can take advantage of rights the law yields, they are more likely to identify with each other. Fighting for your people casts a light on events that even a treasured visitor may not see. But if the black lawyer combines personal interest and natural group identification, the white civil rights lawyer represents something of great value for a social movement that in the end must be inclusive to realize its goals.

The presence of white advocates is obviously important tactically, in the narrow political sense that you need votes if you are just one group among many. But as I hope this book has shown, it also resonates in a broader and more long-lasting ethical sense—down the road a just society can't only mean one group coming up to the level of another; it requires a system of respectful and equitable encounter, interaction, discourse, exchange, and growth.

All of these considerations bring me to my last exhortation: *Take charge of your professional life.* No one else will do it for you. Recognize the trap of debt, dependence, and detachment and do what you can to avoid it. I escaped from it serendipitously. In the 1960s civil rights lawyers had no time for dependence—you either acquired the knowledge you needed or you drowned. I could get through law school with only a modest student loan of $2,000 plus part-time work. Alas, my personal constitution made it clear early that a stance of cool detachment was not an option. The challenge is far greater for today's lawyer entering a crowded, overheated, and exorbitantly priced universe that sometimes seems to make it impossible to pick the fruits of professional satisfaction—displaying competence, serving others, and caring about the communities of which you are a part.

But if things are more demanding now, that too has its rewards. I was startled to find out my 1960s LDF colleague, the late Norman Amaker, had been the only black person in his college and law school classes, a circumstance that caused him pain if not solemnity; encountering classmates years later, he would slyly ask, an innocent expression on his face, if they remembered him.

Norman could be a tough and hardened warrior when he had to be; most of all, he had learned from his sometimes lonely journey who he was. The 1960s anthem wasn't "We Shall Overcome" for nothing.

ACKNOWLEDGMENTS

It is a pleasure to thank those who have assisted me, discounted by concern that the helping hands have been so numerous that inadvertent omissions are inevitable. I am fortunate to have been able to use the facilities of the Library of Congress (LOC) Manuscript Division; I am particularly grateful for the assistance of Adrienne Anna Cannon, David Kirby, and Ernest Emrich. David Wigdor of the LOC provided valuable advice during the years in which the files of the NAACP Legal Defense and Educational Fund (LDF) were off limits.

As many professional historians are aware, LDF donated files covering case-and office-related materials from the 1940s until 1968 to the LOC in the late 1980s but failed to permit outside researchers, with the apparent exception of the journalist Carl Rowan, to examine any of those million or so documents. Elaine Jones, LDF director-counsel, took the position that the files potentially contained privileged material that should be screened for confidentiality before it could be disclosed.

In 1995 I sought access to files in connection with cases in which I had been the responsible attorney during the decade I was an LDF staff counsel, offering to take on the task of determining whether my own files (and others if requested) contained privileged material. My offer was declined; at the same time, a request to open the files from a group of eminent historians, including three Pulitzer Prize winners, was also rejected. In 2000 LDF assigned a retiring staff member the task of examining the files. Two years later, I learned that the files had been opened to a federal judge and former staff member, Robert L. Carter; I renewed my request for access, which Ms. Jones finally granted on September 5, 2002.

The Harvard Law School Library and the Northeastern University School of Law Library responded to my every request. Deanna Barmakian and the staff of the Faculty Research and Information Delivery Assistance (FRIDA) program at Harvard and Dennis Turner and Sharon Persons at Northeastern went out of their way to assist me in locating hard-to-find materials. Alan Divack and Anthony Maloney facilitated my use of the Ford Foundation archives. The staff of the Rare Books and Manuscript Library at Columbia University made my donated papers on capital punishment available on short notice. I thank Gary Smith and Paul Stoop and the talented group they work with at the American Academy of Berlin for offering me a residence, financial support, and essential peace and quiet at a critical time in the writing process. Kathy Alberts was a knowledgeable guide to the city and its research facilities. Support for additional research-related travel was provided by the Mark DeWolfe Howe Fund under the direction of the Harvard law professor John Mansfield.

Former and present staff members freely shared their views about LDF's history, present environment, and prospects. I am particularly grateful to Margaret Burnham, who trusted me enough to unpack a set of difficult memories; Derrick Bell, who alerted me to developments that ultimately facilitated access to files that had long been off limits to researchers; Jack Boger; Leroy Clark, whose recollections have proved more than usually evocative; Norman Chachkin, LDF's director of litigation, whose civil rights service goes back to his law school days in the 1960s; Deborah Fins; Frank Heffron; James M. Nabrit III; Charles Stephen Ralston, who scrutinized LDF files so that they could eventually be examined by scholars. Elizabeth Bartholet and William Bennett Turner were kind enough to read portions of the text dealing with impact litigation they had conducted.

Dennis Roberts and David Harris freely shared moving recollections of C. B. King. Joseph Claxton helped me understand the life and legacy of Senator Augustus Octavius Bacon. Liz Benedict, Robert Belton, Brian Britt, Matt Berger, Dan Coquillette, Leslie Epstein, Mark Ferber, Stanley Fisher, Lawrence Friedman, Daniel Givelber, Josh Hauser, Jessie Meltsner, Molly Meltsner, Alan Jay Rom, Harry Subin, and Elizabeth A. Wilson generously made recommendations, answered questions, or sent me books and references. I suspect many of them have forgotten the precise shape of their support, but I have not. I was assisted by the research of law students Nicole Branch, Sunu Chandy, Linda Ireland, Pantea Yashar, and Emily Waldman, and by the secretarial work of Tom Potter, Evelyn Wiley, and Jan McNew, staff members at Harvard and Northeastern. I've been kept aware of developments in constitutional law by the remarkable case investigation and reports produced by Columbia and Northeastern law student members of a seminar in constitutional litigation, a course I have enjoyed teaching since its creator, the late Telford Taylor, initiated me into its mysteries more than thirty years ago.

The chapter "Me and Muhammad" was published with minor changes in 12 *Marquette Sports Law Review* 583 (2002) and is reprinted here with the permission of Marquette University.

Elizabeth Bartholet, Lincoln Caplan, Geoff Cowan, Ed Davis, Tom Holzel, Jill Kneerim, Sanford Levinson, and Holly Cowan Shulman at various points helped me maneuver through the minefield of today's publishing world, allowing me to get to the point where I could take advantage of talented editors, Richard Holway and Ellen Satrom. I greatly appreciate the support and flexibility extended by the Harvard deans Robert Clark and Todd Rakoff and by Professor Peter Murray, which permitted me to make progress on this book while engaged in a difficult academic assignment. My wife, Heli, put her own work aside to offer encouragement, computer advice, and countless book-enhancing suggestions.

As even a casual reader will grasp, I've been fortunate to work with and learn from men and women of enormous skill, dedication, and stamina. They were both gifted and, more important, giving. I thank them.

NOTES

Macon, Georgia

1. Text and images charting the development of the park can be found in the original cases record, Records and Briefs 2B, *U.S. Sup. Ct. Rpts.*, 396 (on file in the Harvard Law Library). For a photograph of Senator Bacon and a brief biography as well as comments on his role as a legislator, see *J. of So. Legal History* 5, nos. 1 and 2 (1997).

2. The Macon park litigation began in 1963 with the filing of a lawsuit in state court by the Board of Managers of Baconsfield to remove the city as trustee and transfer title of the land to new trustees appointed by the court, *Evans v. Newton*, 220 Ga. 280, 138 S.E. 2d 573 (1964), *rev'd* 382 U.S. 296 (1966).

3. In the second Baconsfield case, *Evans v. Abney*, 224 Ga. 826, 165 S.E. 2d 160 (1968), *aff'd* 396 U.S. 435 (1970), the Supreme Court ruled that the Georgia court's construction of the will passing the property to the senator's heirs did not violate the U.S. Constitution.

4. Compare Richard Posner, *Economic Analysis*, 482 (3d ed., 1986), with Jonathan R. Macey, "Private Trusts for the Provision of Private Goods," 37 *Emory L. J.* 295 (1988). As a young lawyer in the office of the solicitor general of the United States, Posner had taken the position, despite the objection of the Civil Rights Division of the Department of Justice, that the government should file a brief with the Supreme Court in an important housing case urging that a Reconstruction statute authorized action against privately as well as publicly supported discrimination. Richard A. Posner to Ralph S. Spritzer (acting solicitor general), memorandum, Sept. 26, 1967, regarding *Jones v. Alfred H. Mayer Co.*; David L. Norman (of the Civil Rights Division) to Spritzer, memorandum, Oct. 6, 1967 (copies in possession of the author). The acting solicitor general ultimately authorized government amicus participation.

5. The classic treatment is Clement B. Vose, *Caucasians Only: The Supreme Court, the NAACP, and the Restrictive Covenant Cases* (1959). The key decision was *Shelley v. Kraemer*, 334 U.S. 1 (1948), a Missouri case involving a covenant providing that non-Caucasians could not occupy the property concerned. Treated as a companion case by the Supreme Court was a decision from Michigan, *Sipes v. McGhee*, 25 N.W. 2d 638 (1947), pursued by the NAACP because of feuding over timing and arguments between Thurgood Marshall and the St. Louis lawyer in charge of the *Shelley* case, George Vaughn. The Court used a federal statute to reach a similar result in the District of Columbia, *Hurd v. Hodge*, 334 U.S. 24 (1948), *Urciolo v. Hodge*, 332 U.S. 749 (1948). In both cases, it was enforcement, not the racially exclusive agreement, that the Court found illegal. Five years later the justices prohibited a state award of money damages against a white property owner who had sold to an African American, in effect ruling that a white defendant could

269

raise the racial defense of a black purchaser, *Barrows v. Jackson*, 346 U.S. 249 (1953). Although *Shelley* is not often relied upon today, it was a critical case pointing toward the decision in *Brown v. Board of Education* six years later. As important as the legal result, the United States filed a brief in support of overturning the covenants. Three justices— Stanley Reed, Robert Jackson, and Wiley Rutledge—recused themselves from sitting on the case because they owned property subject to racial covenants. See Del Dickson, ed., *The Supreme Court in Conference (1940–1985)*, 697–99 (2001).

6. "The third significant aspect of the 1970 decision in *Abney* is that it did not take into account the Court's 1968 holding, in *Jones*, that section 1982 prohibits private as well as public discrimination": Florence Wagman Roisman, "The Impact of the Civil Rights Act of 1866 on Racially Discriminatory Donative Transfers," 53 *Ala. L. Rev.*, 463, 483–84 (2002).

7. Telephone interview with Frank C. Jones, summer 2003.

8. For examples of this genre see Dinesh D'Souza, *The End of Racism* (1995); Abigail & Stephan Thernstrom, *America in Black and White: One Nation, Indivisible* (1997).

9. Jerry Kang, "The Trojan Horses of Race," *118 Harv. L. Rev.* 1489, 1528 (2005).

10. "Met Life Faces Trial in Discrimination Suit; Insurer Allegedly Denied Blacks Fair coverage," *N.Y. L. J.*, June 27, 2001; "Met Life Plans to Take 250 Million Charge," *New York Times*, C8, Feb. 8, 2002; "Met Life Will Pay Missourians $4.8 Million as Part of Discrimination-Suit Settlement," *St. Louis Post-Dispatch*, 4, Nov. 2, 2002.

11. See Ian Ayres, "Fair Driving: Gender and Race Discrimination in Retail Car Negotiations," 104 *Harv. L. Rev.* 817, 821–22 (1991); "Further Evidence of Discrimination in New Car Negotiations and Estimates of Its Cause," 94 *Mich. L. Rev.*, 109 (1995).

12. http://www.racematters.org/blackspaymorefornissans.htm. Mark Cohen of Vanderbilt University examined more than 300,000 auto loans arranged through Nissan dealers from March 1993 to September 2000. His statistical study showed that in thirty-three states black customers paid more for auto loans than white customers with identical credit ratings. In 2002 another researcher, Debby A. Lindsey, found that African Americans who financed their cars through General Motors Acceptance Corporation were charged higher interest rates than similarly situated white customers; see http://www.consumerlaw.org/initiatives/cocounseling/impact.shtml. GMAC settled the case two years later: "GMAC Agrees to Settle Racial-Basis Lawsuit; Lender Accused of Charging Blacks More," *Washington Post*, E1, Jan. 31, 2004. See also "Judge Rules against Ford in Discrimination Lawsuit," *New York Times*, 3, Mar. 17, 2005.

13. "Spectre of Racism in Health and Health Care: Lessons from History and the United States," 316 *British Medical Journal*, 1970, June 27, 1998; "The Ghosts of Medical Atrocities: What Next, after the Unveiling," *New York Times*, F6, Dec. 23, 2003. An Internet documentary resource on the Tuskegee Study is http://www.dc.peachnet.edu/~shale/humanities/composition/assignments/experiment/tuskegee.html.

14. Glen C. Loury, *The Anatomy of Racial Inequality*, 103 (2002).

15. C. M. Steele & J. Aronson, "How Stereotypes Influence the Standardized Test Performance of Talented African American Students," in *Black-White Test Score Differences*, ed. C. Jencks & M. Phillips (1997), and "A Threat in the Air: How Stereotypes Shape the Intellectual Identities and Performance of Women and African-Americans," 52 *American Psychologist*, 613–29 (1997); Claude Steele, "Thin Ice: 'Stereotype Threat' and Black College Students," *Atlantic Monthly*, 44, Aug. 1999.

16. Telephone interview with Joseph E. Claxton, summer 2003.

How I Went to Work for Thurgood Marshall

1. The act was signed by President Johnson on July 2, 1964, but the equal employment provisions of Title VII did not go into effect until a year later. In anticipation, LDF sent a dozen or so students to the South to identify potential discrimination cases and develop facts necessary to file large numbers of them as soon after July 2, 1965, as possible. The goal was to spread the word about the new law and to convince the federal government of the need to add to the powers of the Equal Economic Opportunity Commission (EEOC) and devote substantial resources to enforcement of Title VII. "Panel to Press Job Rights Cases," *New York Times*, 32, July 2, 1965. The first suit was settled quickly, before it came before a judge. *Brinkley v. The Great Atlantic and Pacific Tea Co.*, unreported, filed Oct. 18, 1965 (E.D.N.C.). Unfortunately, the EEOC had been underfunded and was soon overwhelmed by its new responsibilities; it was several years before a stable and trained staff could reduce the backlog of complaints.

2. "Bush Heckler Fired from Job," *Pittsburgh Post-Gazette*, A-9, Aug. 22, 2004; *Dixon v. Coburg Dairy, Inc.*, 369 F. 3d 811 (4th Cir. 2004).

3. *Life*, 35–36, Jan. 22, 1945; 32–37, May 7, 1945.

4. For a discussion of the treatment of Jews in the fiction of the times, see Ruth R. Wisse, *The Schlemiel as Modern Hero*, 72–78 (1971). Hobson's best-selling novel, inspired by an anti-Semitic speech on the floor of the House of Representatives by a Mississippi congressman, was made into a successful 1947 film directed by Elia Kazan and starring Gregory Peck and Dorothy McGuire.

5. The Josephine Baker incident is retold in Martha Biondi, *To Stand and Fight: The Struggle for Civil Rights in Postwar New York City*, 186 –90 (2003).

6. New York's alternative daily, started by Ralph Ingersoll in 1940, closed on June 22, 1948. *PM* leaned much to the left. During most of its existence it refused advertising. It was perhaps best known for Crockett Johnson's irreverent comic strip "Barnaby."

7. For the influence of this humanitarian philosophy see, e.g., Holly C. Shulman's "Recollections of Polly Spiegel Cowan" in the Jewish Women's Archive: http://www.jwa.org/discover/inthepast/recollections/cowan.html.

8. Lubell's novel analysis of party politics and voter behavior based on in-depth interviews was followed closely by the political world in the 1950s. His most influential book was *The Future of American Politics* (1962). There is no shortage of works on the McCarthy period. See Richard Rovere, *Senator Joe McCarthy* (1959); Robert Griffith, *The Politics of Fear: Joseph R. McCarthy and the Senate* (1970); Thomas C. Reeves, *The Life and Times of Joe McCarthy: A Biography* (1982); Richard M. Fried, *Nightmare in Red: The McCarthy Era in Perspective* (1989). See also 131 *Cong. Rec.* S11, 920 –26 (Sept. 23 1985) (Senator Robert Byrd).

9. Arthur Liman, *Lawyer: A Life of Counsel and Controversy*, 3–14 (1998). According to Mark Tushnet, the formative experience for left activists in the legal professorate of the time was "the law's half-hearted defense of civil liberties against McCarthyism, not the civil rights movement," Mark Tushnet, "Critical Legal Studies: A Political History," 100 *Yale Law Journal* 1515, 1535 (1991).

10. Laura Kalman, "The Dark Ages," in *History of the Yale Law School*, ed. Anthony T. Kronman, 162 (2004). See also Laura Kalman, *The Strange Career of Legal Liberalism* (1996). Bickel published *The Least Dangerous Branch* in 1962. He died prematurely in

1974, having packed what seems like several lifetimes of achievement into his forty-nine years. For more on his career see David Adamy's contribution to *The Oxford Companion to the Supreme Court of the United States*, ed. Kermit L. Hall, 8–69 (1992); Robert A. Burt, "Alex Bickel's Law School and Ours," 104 *Yale L. Rev.* 1853 (1995); Richard Kluger, *Simple Justice*, 654–55 (1975).

11. Greenberg tells his salary story in *Crusaders in the Courts: How a Dedicated Band of Lawyers Fought for the Civil Rights Revolution*, 27–29 (1994).

12. See, e.g., Deborah L. Rhode, "A Tribute to Thurgood Marshall: Letting the Law Catch Up," 44 *Stanford L. Rev.* 1259 (1992); Martha Minow, "A Tribute to Thurgood Marshall," 105 *Harv. L. Rev.* 66 (1991).

13. Jack Greenberg, *Race Relations and American Law*, 59–61 (1959). Though forgotten today, the Supreme Court's 1958 refusal to review a state court decision upholding a "private" college's policy of excluding Negroes was a source of great dismay to civil rights activists at the time.

14. Ibid., 34–37; Greenberg, *Crusaders in the Courts*, 58–59. In *Thurgood Marshall: American Revolutionary*, 75–76 (1998), Juan Williams quotes Marshall as recalling the Margold Report as recommending an all-out attack to enforce the "equal" in *Plessy v. Ferguson*'s 1896 "separate but equal" formula. In a key passage Margold wrote: " . . . if we boldly challenge the constitutional validity of segregation if and when accompanied irremediably by discrimination, we can strike directly at the most prolific sources of discrimination. . . . And the threat of using adjudication as a means of destroying segregation itself, would always exert a very real and powerful force at least to compel enormous improvement in the Negro schools through voluntary official action."

15. *Brown v. Board of Education*, 347 US 483 (1954); *Brown* II is reported at 349 U.S. 294 (1955).

16. *Cooper v. Aaron*, 358 U.S. 1 (1958). For a sample of writing about Marshall see Greenberg, *Crusaders in the Courts*; Mark Tushnet, *Making Civil Rights Law: Thurgood Marshall and the Supreme Court, 1936–1961* (1994); Randall W. Bland, *Private Pressure on Public Law: The Legal Career of Justice Thurgood Marshall, 1934–1991* (2d ed., 1993); Carl T. Rowan, *Dream Makers, Dream Breakers: The World of Justice Thurgood Marshall* (1993); Michael D. Davis & Hunter Clark, *Thurgood Marshall: Warrior at the Bar, Rebel on the Bench* (1992); Roger Goldman & David Gallen, *Thurgood Marshall: Justice for All* (1992).

17. For the influence of the Bronx High School of Science see Stokely Carmichael with Ekwueme Michael Thelwell, *Ready for Revolution: The Life and Struggles of Stokely Carmichael (Kwame Ture)*, 83–109 (2003).

18. "A Colloquy with Jack Greenberg about *Brown*: Experiences and Reflections," 14 *Const. Commentary* 347, 364 (1997). When the *New York Times* announced his appointment as director-counsel under the headline "N.A.A.C.P. Names a White Counsel," he was disappointed that "the *Times* chose to focus on the least relevant aspect of my persona." Greenberg, *Crusaders in the Courts*, 296–97.

19. Quotations here and in the following paragraphs are from Norman Podhoretz, "My Negro Problem—and Ours," 35 *Commentary*, 93 (1963). For Podhoretz's views thirty years later see http://www.reportingcivilrights.org/perspectives/podhoretz.jsp: "Yet if I did the right thing from the perspective of intellectual coherence and literary fitness, I was wrong to think that miscegenation could ever result in the elimination of color 'as a fact

of consciousness,' if for no other reason than that (as Ralph Ellison bitingly remarked to me) the babies born of such marriages would still be considered black."

20. Randall Kennedy, *Interracial Intimacies*, 157 (2003).

21. *Loving v. Virginia*, 388 U.S. 1 (1967). See also Phyl Newbeck, *Virginia Hasn't Always Been for Lovers: Interracial Marriage Bans and the Case of Richard and Mildred Loving* (2004).

What They Didn't Teach Me at the Yale Law School

1. Laura Kalman, "The Dark Ages," in *History of the Yale Law School*, ed. Anthony T. Kronman, 169 (2004). The quote is from J. L. Pottenger, a clinical professor at Yale Law School, 42 *Yale Law Report* 6 (Spring 1996). One of the ways the legal realist school of the 1920s and 1930s sought to challenge prevailing educational models was to bring the factual context of practice into the law schools. In the short run the movement's success in stimulating empirical research was at best fair; as far as introducing the actual training of practitioners went, it was an abject failure. Still, Frank and others took a stance toward professional education that would influence the thinking of those who sought to introduce clinical legal education into the curriculum several decades later. See also Laura G. Holland, "Invading the Ivory Tower: The History of Clinical Education at Yale Law School," 49 *J. Legal Educ.* 504 (1999).

2. Thomas I. Emerson was a New Dealer and early First Amendment theoretician but also a practicing civil libertarian. He was a founder and president of the National Lawyers' Guild, the politically left bar association that LDF lawyers were warned to steer clear of. Finding the American Civil Liberties Union too tame, Emerson co-founded the Emergency Civil Liberties Committee (ECLC) during the McCarthy era. He was also a moving force behind the litigation that voided the Connecticut law that made it a crime to counsel married couples in the use of contraceptives. The case, *Griswold v. Connecticut*, 381 U.S. 479, was decided in 1965, but Emerson, other Yale faculty, and Planned Parenthood of Connecticut had been working to craft a suit during the years I attended the Yale Law School. See *Buxton v. Ullman*, 147 Conn. 48; 156 A. 2d 508 (1959), a case later argued, as *Poe v. Ullman*, 367 U.S. 497 (1961) (appeal dismissed) in the Supreme Court by my torts professor, Fowler Harper. *Griswold* would provide the doctrinal impetus for *Roe v. Wade*, 410 U.S. 113 (1973), and an important line of cases describing a zone of personal autonomy into which government could not intrude.

3. Daniel J. Givelber et al., "Learning through Work: An Empirical Study of Legal Internship," 45 *J. Legal Educ.* 1, 10 (1995). There have been some changes, but law professors, according to a prominent legal historian, still "know very little about the structure of practice" and believe it has "no solid theoretical structure": "In any case, the practice of law as we [future law teachers] experienced it was just one boring job after another, with occasional modest but finely grained differing details. We did not want to live out our lives in such a world": John Henry Schlegel, "But Pierre, If We Can't Think Normatively, What Are We to Do?" 57 *U. Miami L. Rev.* 955, 963 (2003).

4. On Sept. 25, 1958, President Eisenhower federalized the Arkansas National Guard, authorizing use of regular Army troops to force compliance with the federal court order to end segregation at Central High School in Little Rock. Four days later the Supreme

Court denied the request of the Little Rock school board to postpone implementation of the integration plan.

5. Richard C. Donnelly, Joseph Goldstein, & Richard D. Schwartz, *Criminal Law* (1962); Joe Goldstein is eulogized at 19 *Yale L. & Policy Rev.* 5 et seq.(2000).

6. *Louisiana ex rel. Francis v. Resweber,* 329 U.S. 459 (1947). See also Barrett Prettyman Jr.'s pioneering study *Death and the Supreme Court* (1961). For the Supreme Court's conference on the case see *The Supreme Court in Conference (1940–1985),* ed. Del Dickson, 604–6 (2001).

7. *Louisiana ex rel. Francis,* 464.

8. Ibid., 476.

9. *Arizona v. Youngblood,* 488 U.S. 51 (1988). See Jim Dwyer, "No DNA Test Can Correct Court's Crime," *New York Daily News,* 30, Jan. 21, 2001.

10. Deborah Denno, "When Legislatures Delegate Death: The Troubling Paradox of State Use of Electrocution and Legal Injection," 63 *Ohio St. L. J.* 63, 137 (2002).

11. *Louisiana ex rel. Francis,* 470–72.

12. William M. Wiecek, "Felix Frankfurter, Incorporation and the Willie Francis Case," 26 *Supreme Court History* 53, 64 (2001).

13. *Naim v. Naim,* 197 Va. 80, 87 S.E. 2d 749 (1955), vacated by 350 U.S. 891 (1955), adhered to, 197 Va. 734, 90 S.E. 2d 849 (1956).

14. *Loving v. Virginia,* 388 U.S. 1 (1967).

15. For the origins of the clinical movement see Philip G. Schrag and Michael Meltsner, *Reflections on Clinical Legal Education,* 3–14 (1998).

16. Personal communication. The power of even narrowly conceived and indifferently supervised student practice in law school may be gathered from the fact that both of my roommates and I later ended up spending significant time representing indigents in criminal cases.

17. Kalman, *History of the Yale Law School,* 170.

On-the-Job Training

1. Before 1925, the Court felt obliged to decide every case brought to it. As a result, its time was taken up by disputes that should have been finally settled in the lower courts; the Court's docket of undecided cases grew unmanageable. After a lobbying effort led by Chief Justice William Howard Taft, Congress broadened the Court's discretion to accept or reject cases and its control over the docket was made virtually total by the Supreme Court Case Selection Act, Public Law no. 100–352, 102 Stat. 662 (1988) (codified as 28 U.S.C. §1254 [1994]).

2. *Edwards v. South Carolina,* 322 U.S. 229 (1963).

3. His youth in a family headed by a civil rights lawyer and law teacher is described in "A Conversation with James M. Nabrit III," *Washington Lawyer,* July/Aug. 2001. See also "Law Man," *Bates Magazine,* http://www.bates.edu/x57054.xml (Summer 2004).

4. *Simkins v. Moses H. Cone Memorial Hospital,* 323 F. 2d 959 (4th Cir. 1963), *cert. denied,* 376 U.S. 938 (1964). The Hill-Burton Act of 1946 provided federal subsidies to hospitals that participated in community planning of hospital expansion. The act stimulated a multibillion-dollar construction program shaped in part by state planning and licensing laws. 42 U.S.C. §291(f) authorized "separate facilities" for "separate population groups"

so long as "the [state's] plan makes equitable provision for each group." Because the LDF senior staff (only three lawyers) was so overwhelmed with cases in 1962, I was able to conduct the trial after only a year of practice; Greenberg argued and won the all-important appeal before the Fourth Circuit Court of Appeals in Richmond.

5. The story of civil rights work in the South and the Kennedy administration's mostly reactive policies is well documented. Among the best sources are Taylor Branch, *America in the King Years:* vol. 1, *Parting the Waters, 1954 – 63* (1988) (Branch describes *Americus* at 864 – 66; C. B. King and his remarkable family, 524 – 25), and vol. 2, *Pillar of Fire, 1963 – 65* (1998); David J. Garrow, *Bearing the Cross: Martin Luther King and the Southern Christian Leadership Conference* (1986) and *The FBI and Martin Luther King , Jr.* (1981); Fred Powledge, *Free at Last? The Civil Rights Movement and the People Who Made It* (1991); Harvard Sitkoff, *The Struggle for Black Equality, 1954 –1992* (2d ed., 1993); Diane McWhorter, *Carry Me Home: Birmingham, Alabama: The Climactic Battle of the Civil Rights Revolution* (2001). A particularly readable account is Pat Watters and Reese Cleghorn, *Climbing Jacob's Ladder: The Arrival of Negroes in Southern Politics* (1967); for views on the judiciary and the administration's policy of intervention see 210 – 42; for the Americus crisis, 136. See also Michael Meltsner, "Southern Appellate Courts: A Dead End," in *Southern Justice,* ed. Leon Friedman (1965). No one can do serious research on this period without consulting the twenty-volume set of key documents and facsimiles, *Civil Rights, the White House, and the Justice Department,* ed. Michael R. Belknap (1991). See especially Louis Martin to Ted Sorenson, May 10, 1961, 13 : 5; Harris Wofford's aspirational speech to civil rights leaders on Mar. 23, 1961, in 1 : 293; Burke Marshall's report to Attorney General Kennedy that "many lawyers in the South feel that the Administration has affirmatively 'egged on' the Negro to defy local law and court decrees against demonstrations and violence": 9 : 105; Robert F. Kennedy's report to his brother the president on Jan. 24, 1963, trumpeting "great progress" in civil rights "in large measure because of the responsibility and respect for law displayed by the great majority of the citizens of the South": 1 : 423. Samples of thoughtful journalism of the period are reprinted in *Pursuing Dignity through Three Tumultuous Decades, Reporting Civil Rights,* pt. 1, *American Journalism, 1941–1963;* and pt. 2, *American Journalism, 1963 –1973,* ed. Clayborne Carson et al. (2003). For a review of the selection of articles in these volumes that finds insufficient coverage of women, lawyers, progressives, and others, see the review by Peter Jan Honigsberg, 44 *Santa Clara L. Rev.* 335 (2003).

6. In 1964 Burke Marshall concluded that the Justice Department's seven-year campaign of voting suits had failed to make "significant advances" in ending discrimination against black would-be voters "in Mississippi, large parts of Alabama and Louisiana, and in scattered counties in other states": Watters & Cleghorn, *Climbing Jacob's Ladder,* 213. For an appreciation of Burke Marshall, see Diane McWhorter, "Marshall's Law," *Legal Affairs* 61 (Sept. /Oct. 2003).

7. Victor S. Navasky, *Kennedy Justice,* 137–55 (1972). See also David Garrow, *The FBI and Martin Luther King, Jr.* (1981); McWhorter, *Carry Me Home,* 139– 40, 259– 60, 274–75, 310 –11, 316, 468 –72.

8. Navasky, *Kennedy Justice,* 122.

9. Ibid., 137–55.

10. Meltsner, "Southern Appellate Courts," 152.

11. *Rabinowitz v. United States,* 366 F. 2d 34 (5th Cir. 1966). For Branch on the Albany Nine, see his *Parting the Waters,* 866 – 68.

12. C. B. King's beating is told in Branch, *Parting the Waters*, 622–24. For the King family see http://georgiaencyclopedia.org/nge/Article.jsp?id=h-2552. Regarding Carol King, personal communication Sept. 16, 2004, from Elizabeth Vorenberg, who as a foundation executive funded her project.

13. *Aelony v. Pace*, 8 *Race Relations Law Reporter* 1355 (N.D.Ga. 1963), enjoining the prosecution of plaintiffs under Georgia's "insurrection" statute.

14. Richard Wasserstrom, "Lawyers as Professionals: Some Moral Issues," 5 *Human Rights* 1, 8–9 (1975).

15. *Spaulding v. Zimmerman*, 263 Minn. 346, 116 N.W. 2d 704 (1962).

16. For a summary of the Sarbanes-Oxley Act of 2002, see http://www.aicpa.org/info/sarbanes_oxley_summary.htm.

17. Wasserstrom, "Lawyers as Professionals," 14.

18. Calvin Trillin, "State Secrets," *New Yorker*, May 29, 1995.

19. The restaurant case was *Adams v. City of New Orleans*, 208 F. Supp. 427 (E.D.La. 1962).

20. William Gaddis, *A Frolic of His Own*, 11 (1994).

A Sense of the Work

1. Constance Baker Motley, *Equal Justice under Law*, 172 (1998).

2. "Civil Rights Division Association Symposium: The Civil Rights Division at Forty," 30 *McGeorge L. Rev.* 957, 967 (1999).

3. Derrick Bell, *Confronting Authority* (1994).

4. Mark Tushnet, *Making Civil Rights Law: Thurgood Marshall and the Supreme Court, 1936–1961*, 311 et seq. (1994).

5. *Plessy v. Ferguson*, 163 U.S. 537 (1896).

6. Del Dickson, ed., *The Supreme Court in Conference (1940–1985)*, 644 et seq. (2001).

7. Justice Brennan to Justice Clark, Dec. 2, 1964, memorandum, re "*Hamm v. City of Rock Hill*, 379 U.S. 306 (1964), and *Lupper v. Arkansas*," in Papers of William J. Brennan, Library of Congress, pt. I, box 116, folder 4. Other sit-in cases are *Bell v. Maryland*, 379 U.S. 226 (1964); *Barr v. City of Columbia*, 378 U.S. 146 (1964); *City of Columbia v. Bouie*, 378 U.S. 347 (1964). The admiralty case is *United States v. Schooner Peggy*, 5 U.S. (1 Cranch) 103 (1803).

8. For reactions to the demonstrations, see Michael Klarman, *From Jim Crow to Civil Rights*, 372–81 (2004).

9. Anthony Lewis, *Portrait of a Decade: The Second American Revolution*, 92 (1964).

10. Pat Watters and Reese Cleghorn, *Climbing Jacob's Ladder: The Arrival of Negroes in Southern Politics*, 164–68 (1967).

11. Taylor Branch, *Parting the Waters*, vol. 1 of *America in the King Years*, 620 (1988).

12. Samuel Eliot Morison and Henry Steele Commager, *The Growth of the American Republic*, 1:537–39 (4th ed., 1955).

13. *Dred Scott v. Sandford*, 60 U.S. (19 Howard) 393 (1856); *The Civil Rights Cases*, 109 U.S. 3 (1883); *Plessy v. Ferguson*, 163 U.S. 537 (1896). In 1905 the Supreme Court invalidated a maximum-hour law for bakers in *Lochner v. New York*, 198 U.S. 45 (1905). See also *Adair v. United States*, 208 U.S. 161 (1908) (overturning a conviction for firing a worker

for belonging to a union); *Coppage v. Kansas,* 236 U.S. 1 (1915) (invalidating a law banning contracts forbidding workers to join unions). In 1923 the Court struck down a law establishing a minimum wage for women and children, *Atkins v. Children's Hospital of the District of Columbia,* 261 U.S. 525 (overruled by *West Coast Hotel v. Parish,* 300 U.S. 379, 400 [1937], a reflection of political changes brought on by the Depression and subsequent change in the membership of the Court). See also Cass R. Sunstein, *"Lochner's* Legacy," 87 *Columbia L. Rev.* 873 (1987).

14. Dickson, *Supreme Court in Conference;* Lee Epstein & Joseph F. Kobylka, *The Supreme Court and Legal Change: Abortion and the Death Penalty* (1992).

15. The Charlotte case is *Swann v. School Board of Charlotte-Mecklenburg Board of Education,* 402 U.S. 1 (1971); the Atlanta case is *Calhoun v. Cook,* 332 F. Supp. 804 (N.D. Ga. 1971), *aff'd* 522 F. 2d 717 (5th Cir. 1975). For the brilliant scholarship of Tomiko Brown-Nagin on the Atlanta case see "Race as Identity Caricature: A Local Legal History Lesson in the Salience of Intraracial Conflict," 151 *U. of Pa. L. Rev.* 1913 (2003), concluding that judges ignored controlling Supreme Court precedent, that the plaintiff class was split into two factions, and that serious allegations of conflict of interest and misrepresentation went uninvestigated.

16. Risa L. Goluboff, "We Lives in a Free House Such as It Is: Class and the Creation of Modern Civil Rights," 151 *U. of Pa. L. Rev.* 1977, 1989, 1998–2001, 2007–18 (2003).

A White Civil Rights Lawyer

1. Greenberg, *Crusaders in the Courts: How a Dedicated Band of Lawyers Fought for the Civil Rights Revolution,* 293–98 (1994); Louis Lomax, *The Negro Revolt,* 180 (1962).

2. Constance Baker Motley, *Equal Justice under Law* 154 (1998).

3. Jack Greenberg interview with the Columbia Oral History Project as quoted in Juan Williams, *Thurgood Marshall, American Revolutionary,* 260 (1998).

4. Report of a meeting of the [NAACP] liaison committee with the Fund board, Apr. 6, 1962 (purporting to set out the views of Adrian B. DeWind and asserting that tax law considerations "do not appear" to interfere with LDF financial support of NAACP legal programs), in Records of the NAACP, container III, box A237, Library of Congress, Manuscript Division, Washington, D.C.

5. Williams, *Thurgood Marshall,* 259–62, 272, 295, including Robert Carter's subsequent criticism of Jack Greenberg's selection and Marshall's motives for selecting him.

6. Robert L. Carter, *A Matter of Law,* 140–47 (2005); Greenberg, *Crusaders in the Courts,* 294.

7. Example of gift transmittal from the NAACP files: Roy Wilkins to Lenore G. Marshall, July 1, 1964 (NAACP not in competition with LDF "in any sense whatever" but NAACP faces $250,000 deficit, so "at some future time, you might mention to interested friends and foundations our new tax deductible . . . Fund"). See also Sam Winn, president, United Hatters, Cap and Millinery Workers International Union, to National Association for the Advancement of Colored People, contributing $165 to the "Freedom Riders Fund," Oct. 31, 1961. The letter contains an initialed note, probably from John Morsell, second in command at the NAACP: "Advise send to Inc. Fund which is handling the bulk of the Freedom Ride Cases." These communications are in Records of the NAACP, "Contributions 1960–65," container III, box A237; see also Records of the

NAACP Legal Defense and Educational Fund (Accession 20,038) (unprocessed), in Library of Congress, Manuscript Division.

8. Carter–Greenberg correspondence in the NAACP files at the Library of Congress. See also Carter to Greenberg, Feb. 16, 1962 (complaining about a planned LDF meeting "with a number of N.A.A.C.P. lawyers"); Greenberg to Carter, Feb. 20, 1962 (asserting that Carter is misinformed: not just NAACP lawyers were invited); Carter to Greenberg, Jan. 30, 1964 (expressing dismay at the LDF's policy of paying certain expenses and fees incidental only to cases it litigates); Carter to Greenberg, July 1, 1964 (renewing requests that LDF pay lawyers); Greenberg to Carter, July 21 1964 (expressing willingness to pay for and "cooperate" on pending South Carolina and Mississippi cases: "We only ask that we have responsibility for and power over their conduct"). Carter, *A Matter of Law*, 143–44.

9. *NAACP v. NAACP Legal Defense & Educational Fund, Inc.*, 753 F. 2d 131, 137 (D.C. Cir. 1985).

10. Lewis Steel, "Nine Men in Black Who Think White," *New York Times Magazine*, Oct. 13, 1968.

11. *Deal v. Cincinnati Board of Education*, 369 F. 2d 55 (6th Cir. 1966), *cert. denied*, 389 U.S. 847 (1967); *Downs v. Board of Education*, 336 F. 2d 988 (10th Cir. 1964), *cert. denied*, 380 U.S. 914 (1965); *Bell v. School City of Gary*, 324 F. 2d 209 (7th Cir. 1963), *cert. denied*, 377 U.S. 924 (1964).

12. As one federal judge put it in dissent: "The Negro children in Cleveland, Chicago, Los Angeles, Boston, New York, or any other area of the nation which the opinion classifies under de facto segregation, would receive little comfort from the assertion that the racial make-up of their school system does not violate their constitutional rights because they were born into a de facto society, while the exact same racial make-up of the school system in the 17 Southern and border states violates the constitutional rights of their counterparts, or even their blood brothers, because they were born into a de jure society. All children everywhere in the nation are protected by the Constitution, and treatment which violates their constitutional rights in one area of the country, also violates such constitutional rights in another area": *United States v. Jefferson County Board of Education*, 380 F. 2d 385, 397 (5th Cir. 1967) (Gewin, J., dissenting).

13. *Jackson v. School Board of Lynchburg*, 201 F. Supp. 620 (W.D. Va. 1962); 203 F. Supp. 701 (W.D. Va. 1962).

14. Lawrence Tribe, *American Constitutional Law*, 1502–21 (2d ed., 1988).

15. *Regents of the University of California v. Bakke*, 438 U.S. 265 (1978); *Grutter v. Bollinger*, 539 U.S. 306 (2003); *Gratz v. Bollinger*, 539 U.S. 244 (2003).

16. *Griggs v. Duke Power Co.*, 401 U.S. 424 (1971).

17. U.S. Department of Justice, Civil Rights Division, Introduction to Federal Voting Rights Laws, at http://www.usdoj.gov/crt/voting/intro/intro.htm.

18. *South Carolina v. Katzenbach*, 383 U.S. 301, 328 (1966).

19. *Green v. County School Board of New Kent County*, 391 U.S. 430 (1968); *Alexander v. Holmes County Board of Education*, 369 U.S. (1969); *Swann v. School Board of Charlotte-Mecklenburg Board of Education*, 402 U.S. 1 (1971); *Keyes v. School District No. 1, Denver, Colo.*, 413 U.S. 189 (1973). These decisions led to significant desegregation, especially in rural areas and small southern cities, but this pattern was never matched in large cities, where the majority of youngsters attend school.

20. The unwillingness of the Court to approve an interdistrict remedy in *Bradley v. Milliken*, 418 U.S. 717 (1974), sealed the fate of mostly black inner-city school systems; but of even greater weight than a particular Court decision was the social fact that in northern city after city white parents were moving to the suburbs or enrolling their children in parochial or private schools. For a summary of these events, see Derrick Bell, *Race Relations and American Law*, 149–96 (5th ed., 2004).

21. See generally Eleanor P. Wolf, *Trial and Error: The Detroit School Segregation Case* (1981).

22. 20 U.S.C. §§ 1228, 1652 (1978). The Justice Department, however, was still able to enforce the rights of minorities in court cases.

23. Alan Freeman, "Antidiscrimination Law: The View from 1989," in *The Politics of Law: A Progressive Critique*, ed. David Kairys, 121, 124–26 (1990).

24. *City of Richmond v. J. A. Crosson Co.*, 488 U.S. 469 (1989).

25. *McCleskey v. Kemp*, 481 U.S. 279 (1987).

26. *Wards Cove Packing Co. v. Atonio*, 490 U.S. 642 (1989).

27. Derrick Bell, "Serving Two Masters: Integration Ideals and Client Interests in School Desegregation Litigation," 85 *Yale L. J.* 470, 487–88 (1976).

28. Derrick Bell, "Reinventing *Brown v. Board of Education*," in *What Brown v. Board Of Education Should Have Said*, ed. Jack M. Balkin (2001).

29. Gary Orfield & Susan Eaton, "Back to Segregation," *The Nation*, Mar. 3, 2003. The Harvard study, which was conducted by the university's civil rights project, found "a pervasive pattern of racial separation" in public schools. See also *New York Times*, A24 (Jan. 27, 2003).

30. Todd Gitlin, *The Sixties* 109 (1987).

31. Steven Phillips, *No Heroes, No Villains* (1977).

32. Quoted in *Chicago Tribune*, 2, Sept. 5, 1995. Kuntsler's obituary appeared also in *Chicago Sun-Times*, 31, Sept. 5, 1995. For Constance Baker Motley's critical assessment, see her *Equal Justice under Law*, 139.

Greenberg and Bell

1. Derrick Bell, *Confronting Authority*, 113, 114–15, 148 (1994).

2. Leroy D. Clark, "A Critique of Professor Derrick A. Bell's Thesis of the Permanence of Racism and his Strategy of Confrontation," 73 *Denver U. L. Rev.* 23, 27 (1995).

3. Derrick Bell, "The Space Traders," in *Faces at the Bottom of the Well*, 158 (1992).

4. Clark, "Critique," 27.

5. Conversation with William Robinson, Nov. 15, 2003.

6. Norman Chachkin, Interview, Mar. 20, 2003.

7. Diane McWhorter tells the story of Louis Burnham's work in *Carry Me Home: Birmingham, Alabama: The Climactic Battle of the Civil Rights Revolution*, 58, 63–64, 73, 76 (2001). In 1946 Burnham led "fifty black veterans to the Birmingham courthouse to assert their voting rights under a banner reading 'Join Us to Register—Bring Your Discharge Papers.'"

8. For Jack Greenberg's version of these events see his *Crusaders in the Courts: How a Dedicated Band of Lawyers Fought for the Civil Rights Revolution*, 402–7, 410–11 (1994).

9. *Davis v. Lindsay,* 321 F. Supp. 1134 (S.D. N.Y. 1970).

10. Bettina Aptheker, *The Morning Breaks: The Trial of Angela Davis* (1999). Margaret Burnham gave her version of these events in an interview with the author, spring 2004.

11. Panther letter (undated) in the author's possession.

12. Greenberg, *Crusaders in the Courts,* 410–11.

13. Bell's comments appear in "Serving Two Masters," 85 *Yale L. J.* 470 (1976). See Derrick Bell's letter to the editor in 3 *Civil Liberties Rev.* 7 (1976).

14. For relations with the guild, see Taylor Branch, *Pillar of Fire: America in the King Years, 1963–65,* 273–74 (1998); Greenberg, *Crusaders in the Courts,* 349–53; James Forman, *The Making of Black Revolutionaries,* 380–81 (1997).

15. Greenberg, *Crusaders in the Courts,* 406.

16. Derrick Bell, "*Brown v. Board of Education* and the Interest-Convergence Dilemma," 93 *Harv. L. Rev.* 518, 524 (1980).

17. For quotations regarding the Harvard Law School controversy see Greenberg, *Crusaders in the Courts,* 502–4; Bell, *Confronting Authority,* 46–47; Randall Kennedy, "Racial Critiques of Legal Academia," 102 *Harv. L. Rev.* 1745, 1756–60 (1989); Robin Barnes, book review, 101 *Yale L. J.,* 1631, 1655 (1992) (protest not against Greenberg but in support of Bell); Jonathan Feldman, "Race-Consciousness versus Colorblindness in the Selection of Civil Rights Leaders: Reflections upon Jack Greenberg's *Crusaders in the Courts,*" 84 *Calif. L. Rev.* 151, 154 (1996). See also in Harvard Law Library Special Collections File on Randall L. Kennedy, "Racial Critiques of Legal Academia," containing articles and commentary on the boycott, including material from *Harv. L. Record* and a letter to *Time* by former *Harvard Law Review* editor.

18. Norman Amaker, *Civil Rights and the Reagan Administration* (1988).

19. Christopher Edley Jr., "The Boycott at Harvard: Should Teaching Be Colorblind?" *Washington Post,* A23, Aug. 18, 1982.

20. The exchange of letters between Bell and Chambers can be found in the Harvard Law Library Special Collections File on Randall L. Kennedy.

21. Quoted in Helen Hershkoff & David Hollander, "Rights into Action: Public Interest Litigation in the United States," in *Many Roads to Justice: The Law-Related Work of the Ford Foundation Grantees around the World,* ed. Mary McClymont & Stephen Golub (1998).

Me and Muhammad

1. Thomas Hauser, *Muhammad Ali: His Life and Times* (1991); David Remnick, *King of the World: Muhammad Ali and the Rise of an American Hero* (1998); Mark Kram, *Ghosts of Manila: The Fateful Blood Feud between Muhammad Ali and Joe Frazier* (2001).

2. Bob Woodward and Scott Armstrong, *The Brethren,* 137 (1979).

3. *Clay v. United States,* 397 F. 2d 901, 918n. (5th Cir. 1968), vacated sub nom. *Giordano v. United States,* 394 U.S. 310 (1969).

4. Ibid., 918–19.

5. Watchtower Bible and Tract Society of Pennsylvania, *Jehovah's Witnesses: Proclaimers of God's Kingdom,* 119 (1993).

6. *West Virginia State Board of Education v. Barnette,* 319 U.S. 624, 642 (1943).

7. *Clay v. United States,* 397 F. 2d, 917.

8. Hauser, *Muhammad Ali,* 170.

9. *Ali v. Division of State Athletic Commission,* 308 F. Supp. 11, 14 (S.D. N.Y. 1969).

10. *Clay v. United States,* 397 F. 2d., 906 –7.

11. Ibid., 914.

12. See Hauser, *Muhammad Ali,* 155; *Clay v. United States,* 397 F. 2d., 914.

13. *Clay v. United States,* 397 F. 2d., 914, 916 –17, 924.

14. *Giordano v. United States,* 312.

15. *United States v. Clay,* 386 F. Supp. 926, 930 –32 (S.D. Tex. 1969), *aff'd* 430 F. 2d 165 (5th Cir. 1970), *rev'd* 403 U.S. 698 (1971).

16. President's Commission on Law Enforcement and the Administration of Justice, "Task Force Report: Corrections" (1967).

17. Higher Education Act of 1998, 20 U.S.C. §1091(r)(1) (1999); Debbie A. Mukamal & Paul N. Samuels, "Twelfth Annual Symposium on Contemporary Urban Challenges: Statutory Limitations on Civil Rights of People with Criminal Records," 30 *Fordham Urb. L. J.* 1501 (2003).

18. *Ali v. Division of State Athletic Commission,* 316 F. Supp. 1246, 1253 (S.D. N.Y. 1970).

19. *Clay v. United States,* 403 U.S. 698, 702 –3 (1970) (per curiam).

20. Woodward & Armstrong, *Brethren,* 137–38. Thurgood Marshall had been solicitor general of the United States during earlier phases of the case and recused himself.

21. Hauser, *Muhammad Ali,* 239.

22. Ibid., 218 –19.

23. See generally Kram, *Ghosts of Manila,* esp. 129; see also Hauser, *Muhammad Ali,* 220 –23.

The Complex World of Law Reform

1. See Edward V. Sparer, "The Right to Welfare," in *The Rights of Americans: What They Are, What They Should Be,* 66 – 67 (1971); for a critique of the emphasis on legal rights see Mary Ann Glendon, *Rights Talk* (1991).

2. Susan E. Lawrence, *The Poor in Court: The Legal Services Program and Supreme Court Decision Making,* 9, 21 (1990).

3. For the more disappointing defeats see *Dandridge v. Williams,* 397 U.S. 471 (1970); *Wyman v. James,* 400 U.S. 309 (1971); and *Jefferson v. Hackney,* 406 U.S. 535 (1972). For the tension between service to individual clients and structure-changing litigation, see Deborah J. Cantrell, "A Short History of Poverty Lawyers in the United States," 5 *Loyola J. of Public Interest Law* 11, 27 (2003). See also Martha F. Davis, *Brutal Need: Lawyers and the Welfare Rights Movement, 1960 –1973* (1993).

4. Linda Gordon, *Pitied but Not Entitled,* 2 (1994).

5. The emergence of a multitude of claimants for enforcement of Title VI of the Civil Rights Act is acutely described in an undeservedly ignored scholarly gem, Stephen C. Halpern's *On the Limits of the Law,* 284 –94 (1995).

6. Daniel P. Moynihan, "The Negro Family: The Case for National Action" (Office of Policy Planning and Research, U.S. Department of Labor, 1965).

7. William Julius Wilson, *The Truly Disadvantaged: The Inner City, the Underclass, and Public Policy,* 20 (1987).

8. Jack Greenberg, *Crusaders in the Courts: How a Dedicated Band of Lawyers Fought for the Civil Rights Revolution* (1994).

9. Docket Report, NAACP Legal Defense and Educational Fund Inc., 31–42, Aug. 1969 (on file with the author).

10. Research into subsequent developments suggests that the racial pay gap narrowed only between 1965 and 1975 and that thereafter Title VII–type litigation had limited impact on general patterns. See John J. Donohue III & James Heckman, "Re-Evaluating Federal Civil Rights Policy," 79 *Geo. L. J.* 1713, 1729–35 (1991).

11. The brief was filed in *United States ex rel. Shakur v. Commissioner of Corrections George F. McGrath,* 303 F. Supp. 299 (S.D. N.Y. 1969).In total, ten Panthers had bail set at $100,000, two at $50,000, and one at $25,000. For Greenberg on Niebuhr, see his *Crusaders in the Courts,* 407 (the theologian was "shocked" by LDF's action).

12. For the Ford Foundation's move into civil rights see Dorothy J. Samuels, "Expanding Justice," 20–26 (1984); Robert B. McKay, "Nine for Equality under Law: Civil Rights Litigation" (1977). For its support of public interest law, see "The Public Interest Law Firm: New Voices for New Constituencies" (Ford Foundation, Feb. 1973); "Public Interest Law: Five Years Later" (American Bar Association, Special Committee on Public Interest Practice/Ford Foundation, Mar. 1976). These reports are on file in the Ford Foundation Archives, New York.

13. See Samuels, "Expanding Justice," 20–22.

14. Philip G. Schrag, "Bleak House 1968: A Report on Consumer Test Litigation," 44 *NYU L. Rev.* 115 (1969).

15. *Jackson v. Godwin,* 400 F.2d 529 (5th Cir. 1968).

16. *Wright v. McMann,* 387 F. 2d 519 (2d Cir. 1967).

17. *Ruiz v. Estelle,* 503 F. Supp. 1265 ((S.D. Tex. 1980), *aff'd* in part, vacated in part, 679 F. 2d 1115 (5th Cir. 1982); William W. Justice, "The Origins of *Ruiz v. Estelle*," 43 *Stanford L. Rev.* 1 (1990).

18. Justice, "Origins of *Ruiz v. Estelle*," 11.

19. *Ruiz v. Johnson,* 37 F. Supp. 2d 855, 860–61 (S.D. Tex. 1999).

20. *Ruiz v. Johnson,* 154 F. Supp. 2d 975 (S.D. Tex. 2001).

21. The Prison Litigation Reform Act (codified in scattered sections of 11, 18, 28, and 42 U.S.C.A.) makes it more difficult to file claims against prison officials and to continue in effect consent agreements negotiated under court supervision between officials and inmates' representatives.

22. See Harvey Berkman, "Proud and Wary, Prison Project Director Bows Out," *National L. J.,* A12, Jan. 8, 1996, as quoted in Dean Hill Rivkin, "Reflections on Lawyering for Reform: Is the Highway Alive Tonight?" 64 *Tenn. L. Rev.* 1065, 1068n (1987).

23. Clarence Taylor, *Knocking at Our Door* (1997).

24. Galamison interview with Robert Penn Warren, University of Kentucky oral history program, June 17, 1964.

25. Tamar Jacoby, *Someone Else's House* (1998).

26. *Chance v. Board of Examiners,* 458 F. 2d 1167, 1170 (2d Cir. 1972).

27. Interview with Elizabeth Bartholet, Jan. 14, 2004.

28. Among the key opinions are *Chance v. Board of Examiners,* 330 F. Supp. 203 (S.D. N.Y., 1971), *aff'd* 458 F. 2d 1167 (2d Cir. 1972); 496 F. 2d 820 (2d Cir. 1974).

29. Statistics provided in an e-mail in author's files from New York State Department of Education, Feb. 2, 2004.

Litigation: Means of Choice or Last Resort?

1. In *Goodridge v. Dept. of Health,* 440 Mass. 309, 798 N.E. 2d 941 (2003), the Supreme Judicial Court held the restriction of the right to marriage to heterosexual couples unconstitutional under the Massachusetts constitution, setting in motion a series of steps that led to authorization of same-sex marriages.

2. Docket Report, NAACP Legal Defense and Educational Fund Inc., 31–42, Aug. 1969 (in author's files). See also http://www.naacpldf.org. Norman Chachkin interview, Mar. 20, 2003.

3. "*Brown* Post-50: The Opportunity to Learn Initiative," 8 (LDF Education staff's recommendations, Nov. 17, 2003).

4. Jack Greenberg, *Crusaders in the Courts: How a Dedicated Band of Lawyers Fought for the Civil Rights Revolution,* 439 (1994).

5. The voting case was *Lampkin v. Conner,* 360 F. 2d 505 (D.C. Cir. 1966).

6. *Marbury v. Madison,* 5 U.S. 37 (1803); *Plessy v. Ferguson,* 163 U.S. 537 (1896).

7. Abram Chayes, "The Role of the Judge in Public Law Litigation," 89 *Harv. L. Rev.* 1281, 1302–3 (1976). For Jack Greenberg's formulation see "Litigation for Social Change: Methods, Limits, and Role in a Democracy," 29 *Record of the Association of the Bar of the City of New York* 320 (1974).

8. Owen Fiss, "The Supreme Court 1978 Term: Foreward: The Forms of Justice," 93 *Harv. L. Rev.* 1, 2 (1979).

9. Greenberg, *Crusaders in the Courts,* 421.

10. Chayes, "Role of the Judge," 1309.

11. Donald Horowitz, *The Courts and Social Policy,* 264–65, 284 (1977). For the political science literature on the difficulties of policy implementation see Peter Schuck, "Public Law Litigation and Social Reform, *The Hollow Hope: Can Courts Bring About Social Change?*" 102 *Yale L. J.* 1763, 1765 (1993).

12. Gerard Rosenberg, *The Hollow Hope: Can Courts Bring About Social Change?* 111–56 (1991).

13. *Roe v. Wade,* 410 U.S. 113 (1973).

14. Rosenberg, *Hollow Hope,* 140–45.

15. Cass R. Sunstein, "Symposium: Civil Rights Legislation in the 1990s: Three Civil Rights Fallacies," 79 *Cal. L. Rev.* 751, 765 (1991).

16. Michael Klarman, "*Brown,* Racial Change, and the Civil Rights Movement," 80 *Va. L. Rev.* 7 (1994), and *From Jim Crow to Civil Rights* (2004).

17. David J. Garrow, "Hopelessly Hollow History," 80 *Va. L. Rev.* 151, 151–57 (1994) (Garrow replies to Klarman and finds Rosenberg's analysis "wholly unpersuasive"). See also Mark Tushnet, "The Significance of *Brown v. Board of Education,*" 80 *Va. L. Rev.* 173 (1994).

18. *Simkins v. Moses H. Cone Memorial Hospital,* 211 F. Supp. 628 (M.D. N.C. 1962), *rev'd* 323 F. 2d 959 (4th Cir. 1963), *cert. denied* 376 U.S. 938 (1964).

19. Schuck, "Public Law Litigation and Social Reform," 1773. Rosenberg also makes no effort to compare the general impact of what legislatures accomplish with the activities

of courts; indeed, his treatment of legislative impact is subject to the same charge of using anecdote and impression that he lodges against supporters of judicial action.

20. Mark Tushnet, "'Sir, Yes, Sir!': The Courts, Congress, and Structural Injunctions; Democracy by Decree: What Happens When Courts Run Government," 20 *Const. Commentary* 189, 202 (2003).

21. Sunstein, "Three Civil Rights Fallacies," 765.

22. For the educational potential of Supreme Court decisions, see Klarman, *From Jim Crow to Civil Rights,* 464.

23. Stephen Carter, review of Rosenberg, *Hollow Hope,* 90 *Mich. L. Rev.* 1216, 1221 (1992).

24. Charles F. Sabel & William H. Simon, "Destabilization Rights: How Public Law Litigation Succeeds," 117 *Harv. L. Rev.* 1015, 1020 (2004).

25. Larry D. Kramer, *The People Themselves: Popular Constitutionalism and Judicial Review* (2004); Mark Tushnet, *Taking the Constitution Away from the Courts* (1999). See also Richard D. Parker, *Here the People Rule: A Constitutional Populist Manifesto* (1994). Commentary on efforts to limit judicial review include book review, "Popular? Constitutionalism?" 118 *Harv. L. Rev* 1594 (2005); Norman R. Williams, book review, "The People's Constitution," 57 *Stan. L Rev.* 257 (2004); Erwin Chermerinsky, "In Defense of Judicial Review: The Perils of Popular Constitutionalism," 2004 *Ill. L. Rev.* 673; Mark Tushnet, "Democracy versus Judicial Review," *Dissent* 59 (Spring 2005); Lawrence G. Sager, *Justice in Plainclothes: A Theory of American Constitutional Practice,* 198–207 (2004), and "Theories of Taking the Constitution Seriously Outside the Courts: Courting Disaster," 73 *Fordham L. Rev.* 1361 (2005).

Legal Killing Revisited

1. *Furman v. Georgia,* 408 U.S. 238 (1972).

2. Stuart Banner, *The Death Penalty,* 267–71 (2002).

3. Ibid., 273–84; *Gregg v. Georgia,* 428 U.S. 153 (1976); *Jurek v. Texas,* 428 U.S. 262 (1976); *Profitt v. Florida,* 428 U.S. 242 (1976). See also *Roberts v. Louisiana,* 428 U.S. 325 (1976); *Woodson v. North Carolina,* 428 U.S. 280 (1976).

4. Intense criticism of the Court's record, not all of it by any means from an abolitionist perspective, has been frequent. See, for example, Robert Weisberg, "Deregulating Death," 1983 *Sup. Ct. Rev.;* Randall K. Packer, "Struck by Lightning: The Elevation of Procedural Form over Substantive Rationality in Capital Punishment Proceedings," 20 *NYU Rev. L. & Social Change* 641 (1993/94); Robert Burt, "Disorder in the Court," 85 *Mich. L. Rev.* 1741, 1764 (1987).

5. *Atkins v. Virginia,* 536 U.S. 304 (2002); *Roper v. Simmons,* 125 S. Ct. 1183 (2005), (affirming *State ex rel. Simmons v. Roper,* 112 S.W. 397 3d [2003]).

6. *Death Row U.S.A.* (Winter 2005), a quarterly report by the Criminal Justice Project of the NAACP Legal Defense and Educational Fund Inc.

7. Carol Steiker & Jordan Steiker, "Sober Second Thoughts: Reflections on Two Decades of Constitutional Regulation of Capital Punishment," 109 *Harv. L. Rev.* 355, 406–7 (1995).

8. Eric Muller, "The Legal Defense Fund's Capital Punishment Campaign: The Distorting Influence of Death," 4 *Yale L. & Policy Rev.* 158, 164 (1985). At times scholarship is

a blood sport. Muller reported (in 1985) that Jack Greenberg told him (in an interview) that my description (in a 1972 book) of how (in 1963) three staff lawyers persuaded him "that a staff attorney should be assigned to investigate the possibility of proving the existence of racial sentencing in rape cases" was "nonsense" because LDF had "debated" challenging the death penalty fifteen years earlier. The lack of connection between my description of 1963 events and the reasoning attributed to Greenberg (both my statement and his were true) was so stark that I could only assume it reflected the way Muller had conducted the interview. (Though he cited his earlier interview of me eleven times, he did not ask me to comment on the response before publication of his article.) I pointed out the disconnect to Greenberg when he interviewed me for his 1994 LDF history; after citing my book (*Cruel and Unusual*), he went on to write only that "there are a few points on which our perceptions differ": *Crusaders in the Courts: How a Dedicated Band of Lawyers Fought for the Civil Rights Revolution*, 596 (1994).

9. *Maxwell v. Bishop*, 369 U.S. 711 (1969).

10. Bob Woodward & Scott Armstrong, *The Brethren*, 205–6 (1979).

11. Robert A. Burt, "Disorder in the Court," 85 *Mich. L. Rev.* 1741, 1761–62 (1987).

12. Ibid., 1771.

13. Eric W. Rise, *The Martinsville Seven: Rape, Race, and Capital Punishment* (1995).

14. Greenberg, *Crusaders in the Courts*, 99–102, 133–35, 140–49.

15. *Robinson v. Tennessee*, 392 U.S. 666 (1968)

16. *Coleman v. Alabama*, 377 U.S. 129 (1964); see also 389 U.S. 22 (1967), described in Michael Meltsner, *Cruel and Unusual: The Supreme Court and Capital Punishment*, 16–18 (1973).

17. Alexander Bickel, *The Least Dangerous Branch*, 240–43 (1962)

18. Herbert L. Cobin, "Abolition and Restoration of the Death Penalty in Delaware," in *The Death Penalty in America*, ed. Hugo Adam Bedau, 359–73 (1964).

19. Scott Turow, *Ultimate Punishment*, 34 (2003).

20. Meltsner, *Cruel and Unusual*, 75, 77, 90; *Maxwell v. Bishop*, 257 F. Supp. 710, 724 (E.D. Ark.).

21. See *Maxwell v. State*, 236 Ark. 694, 370 S.W. 2d 113 (1963); *Maxwell v. Stephens*, 229 F. Supp. 205 (E.D. Ark. 1964), *aff'd* 348 F. 2d 325 (8th Cir. 1965), *cert. denied* 382 U.S. 944 (1965).

22. *Rudolph v. Alabama*, 375 U.S. 889 (1963).

23. Bickel, *Least Dangerous Branch*, 243.

24. Alex Gordon, "Nothing Less than the Dignity of Man: The Eighth Amendment Jurisprudence of the Warren Court" (unpublished paper on file with the author).

25. Banner, *Death Penalty in America*, 255–66.

26. *Graham v. Collins*, 506 U.S. 461, 479–84, 500–501 (Justices Thomas and Stevens); Justice Blackmun in *Callins v. Collins*, 510 U.S. 1141, 1145 (1994) (dissenting from denial of certiorari).

27. *Coker v. Georgia*, 433 U.S. 584 (1977).

28. Sanford Levinson, "The Rhetoric of the Judicial Opinion," in *Law's Stories: Narrative and Rhetoric in the Law*, ed. Peter Brooks & Paul Gewirtz, 187, 198 (1996), quoting Joseph Goldstein, *The Intelligible Constitution*, 58 (1992), quoting a memorandum from Warren to his fellow justices.

29. *McCleskey v. Kemp*, 481 U.S. 279, 287 (1987).

30. Randall Kennedy, "*McCleskey v. Kemp:* Race, Capital Punishment, and the Supreme Court," 101 *Harv. L. Rev.* 1388, 1394 – 95, 1414 (1988). (Powell wrote: "Although the history of racial discrimination in this country is undeniable, we cannot accept official actions taken long ago as evidence of current intent.") See also John C. Jeffries Jr., *Justice Lewis F. Powell, Jr.,* 450 – 53 (1994). After retiring, Powell called *McCleskey* one of two major decisions he regretted, and in 1990 he said that if he had been a legislator, he would have voted against capital punishment.

31. Justice Scalia's memorandum is authoritatively discussed in Dennis D. Dorin, "Far Right of the Mainstream: Racism, Rights and Remedies from the Perspective of Justice Antonin Scalia's *McCleskey* Memorandum," 45 *Mercer L. Rev.* 1035 (1994).

32. *McCleskey v. Kemp,* 340 – 44.

33. The Racial Justice Act (RJA), H.R. 4092, 103d Cong., 2d sess.; Title IX (1994), in 140 *Cong. Rec.,* H2655-56 (Apr. 25, 1994). In 1994 the House of Representatives approved it, but it was later dropped from the Crime Bill in conference with the Senate. A 1990 version had met with the same fate. The RJA would have permitted defendants to present data that raised an inference that the death sentence was imposed with a racial motivation. It also provided for rebuttal of the inference, but if the government was unable to offer such rebuttal, imposition of the death penalty was prohibited. See also U.S. General Accounting Office, *Death Penalty Sentencing: Research Indicates Patterns of Disparities* (Report to Senate and House Committees on the Judiciary) 5 (Feb. 1990).

34. The Innocence Protection Act, H.R. 4167, 106th Cong. 201–3 (2000), was enacted as part of the Justice for All Act, Pub. L. no. 108 – 405 (2004).

35. The quotations here and in the following paragraphs are from Lee Epstein & Joseph F. Kobylka, *The Supreme Court and Legal Change: Abortion and the Death Penalty,* 106 –15 (1992).

36. *Gregg v. Georgia,* 428 U.S. 153 (1976).

37. Jerry Kang, "Denying Prejudice: Internment, Redress, and Denial," 51 *UCLA L. Rev.* 933 (2004).

38. See Meltsner, *Cruel and Unusual,* 21–23.

39. *McCleskey v. Kemp,* 315.

40. See n. 26 above.

41. *Witherspoon v. Illinois,* 391 U.S. 510 (1968).

42. Millard Farmer's views can be found at hhtp://www.goextranet.net/Seminars/BlackHole/DeathRowUSA.

43. Jack Boger's comments are in an e-mail to the author, Dec. 29, 2003.

The Future of the Death Penalty

1. Jack Greenberg, *Crusaders in the Courts: How a Dedicated Band of Lawyers Fought for the Civil Rights Revolution,* 454 (1994).

2. *Roper v. Simmons,* 125 S. Ct. 1183 (2005).

3. Michael Mello, "A Letter on a Lawyer's Life of Death," 38 *S. Tex. L. Rev.* 121, 216 (1997). The number of death cases is so great and the lawyers involved so many that I have hesitated before supplying what must perforce be but a partial listing.

4. Justice Blackmun's view of Amsterdam illustrates how frustrating certain justices find the long line of death cases waiting at their door. According to David von Drehle in

the *Washington Post,* "his death penalty files are salted with irritated and condescending asides concerning the now-legendary lawyer. ('I suspect I am too far removed from academic days to understand the professorial mind,' he wrote after reading one Amsterdam brief. Years later, he complained in his bench notes that Amsterdam's 'voice squeaks' during oral argument, and later still, Blackmun jotted a one-word note while listening to Amsterdam argue a case: 'Ugh')": "Death Penalty Divide Frustrated Blackmun," 4, Mar. 15, 2004. See Lee Epstein & Joseph F. Kobylka, *The Supreme Court and Legal Change: Abortion and the Death Penalty,* 110 (1992)("some [including justices] say [Amsterdam] had not been at his best" in 1976 argument). See also Edward P. Lazarus, *Closed Chambers,* 114 (1998) (Justice Powell thought him a "nut" for opposing death for a nuclear bomber); Bob Woodward & Scott Armstrong, *The Brethren,* 209 (1979). (Justice White held Amsterdam's 1972 argument to be the best he had ever heard.) At one Supreme Court death case argument that I observed early in Blackmun's tenure as a justice, he asked Amsterdam a question about Minnesota capital case legal procedures. Amsterdam garbled his response, apparently willing to appear stupid rather than to embarrass the justice by pointing out his state had abolished capital punishment in 1911. See also Linda Greenhouse, *Becoming Justice Blackmun* (2005).

5. *Roper v. Simmons,* 125 S. Ct. 1183 (2005).

6. Anthony G. Amsterdam & Jerome Bruner, *Minding the Law,* 198 (2000).

7. Marc L. Miller, "Domination and Dissatisfaction: Prosecutors as Sentencers," 56 *Stan. L. Rev.* 1211, nn. 151–63 (2004).

8. The quotations here and in the following paragraphs are from James S. Liebman et al., "A Broken System: Error Rates in Capital Cases, 1973–1995" (June 12, 2000), at http://www2.law.columbia.edu/instructionalservices/liebman. See also James S. Liebman, "The Overproduction of Death," 100 *Colum. L. Rev.* 2030 (2000); James S. Liebman et al., "A Broken System, Part II: Why There Is So Much Error in Capital Cases and What Can Be Done About It" (Feb. 11, 2002), at http://www2.law.columbia.edu/brokensystem2/index2.html (an examination of the overall reliability of capital-punishment systems on a national scale). For more on Liebman and his collaborators' work see sources collected in Bryan Stevenson, "Close to Death: Reflections on Race and Capital Punishment in America," in *Debating the Death Penalty,* ed. Hugo Bedau and Paul Cassell, 102 n9 (2004). For one state's experience, see Stanley Z. Fisher, "Convictions of Innocent Persons in Massachusetts: An Overview," 12 *Boston U. Public Int. L. J.* 1 (2002).

9. http://www.deathpenaltyinfo.org/article.php?scid=6&did=110.

10. Scott Turow, *Ultimate Punishment,* 39–40, 123–24 (2003).

11. *United States v. Quinones,* 205 F. Supp. 2d 256 (S.D. N.Y. 2002), *rev'd* 313 F. 3d 49, 63 (2d Cir. 2002). In reversing, the court of appeals relied on a Supreme Court decision holding that it would not overrule a lower court "based solely on a statistical or theoretical possibility that a defendant might be innocent." The Court also concluded that the nation has accepted capital punishment despite the risk of executing the innocent and that Congress, before enacting the Federal Death Penalty Act, heard "extensive evidence in support of the argument that innocent individuals might be executed" but passed the law anyway.

12. This account and those in the following paragraphs are in Richard C. Dieter, "With Justice for Few: The Growing Crisis in Death Penalty Representation" (Oct. 1995), http://www.deathpenaltyinfo.org/; Stephen B. Bright, "Counsel for the Poor: The Death

Sentence Not for the Worst Crime but for the Worst Lawyer," 103 *Yale L. J.* 1835 (1994). The consensus among specialists in the field is that improved training has ameliorated but hardly ended a grave shortage of lawyers skilled in handling capital cases.

13. American Bar Association Section of Individual Rights and Responsibilities, Report with Recommendation 107, Approved by the ABA House of Delegates, Feb. 3, 1997.

14. An overwhelming number of capital cases clog the dockets of U.S. courts, state and federal. One study noted that between 1987 and 1994 an average of 28.6 percent of all opinions published by the California Supreme Court each year were capital cases; see Gerald F. Uelmen, "The Lucas Court's Seventh Year: Achieving a Balanced Menu," *Los Angeles Daily Journal,* June 8, 1994, *Res Ipsa* (magazine), 8, table 1, as cited in Alex Kozinski & Sean Gallagher, "Death: The Ultimate Run-On Sentence," 46 *Case W. Res. L. R.,* 1, 32 (1995). At one time the Florida Supreme Court spent about a third of its time on death cases; see Robert Sherrill, "Death Row on Trial," *New York Times Magazine,* Nov. 13, 1983. "There are something like 186 cases that could be prosecuted as capital cases, potential capital cases, that are in the docket right now of . . . Harris County, Houston, Texas, which if it were a state, it would have the second largest number of executions in the United States, second only to the rest of the State of Texas." "The Death Penalty in the Twenty-first Century," 45 *Amer. U. L. Rev.* 239, 265 (1995). "In an era when the number of published opinions from the Supreme Court has dwindled, the Supreme Court continues to issue a regular stream of opinions in death cases." Kozinski & Gallagher, "Death."

15. Personal communication from Daniel Givelber, Oct. 28, 2004.

16. For the base figures see *Death Row U.S.A.,* Winter 2005, a quarterly report by the Criminal Justice Project of the NAACP Legal Defense and Educational Fund Inc. But see "Fewer Death Sentences Being Imposed in U.S.," *New York Times,* A14, Sept. 15, 2004; "Death Sentences Hit 30-Year Low in U.S.," *Washington Post,* A2, Nov. 15, 2004.

17. A Department of Justice panel prescreens death-eligible defendants and makes recommendations to the attorney general; Kevin McNally, "Race and the Federal Death Penalty: A Nonexistent Problem Gets Worse," 53 *DePaul L. Rev.* 1615, 1619–20 (2004).

18. *Ring v. Arizona,* 536 U.S. 584, 614–15 (2002) (Breyer, J., concurring).

19. See, e.g., Cass R. Sunstein and Adrian Vermeule, "Is Capital Punishment Morally Required? The Relevance of Life-Life Tradeoffs," Working Paper 05–06, Mar. 2005, AEI-Brookings Joint Center for Regulatory Studies; Richard Berk, "New Claims about Executions and General Deterrence: Déjà Vu All Over Again?," 2 *J. Emp. L. Stud.* 203 (2005); Ted Goertzel, "Capital Punishment and Homicide: Sociological Realities and Econometric Illusions," *Skeptical Inquirer* (July–Aug. 2004).

20. Matthew L. Engle, "Due Process Limitations on Victim Impact Evidence," 13 *Cap. Def. J.* 55 (2000); Alix M. Karl, "A Symposium on Capital Punishment in Virginia since *Furman v. Georgia:* Suggestions for Capital Reform in Virginia," 12 *Cap. Def. J.* 123 (1999).

21. Carol Steiker & Jordan Steiker, "Sober Second Thoughts: Reflections on Two Decades of Constitutional Regulation of Capital Punishment," 109 *Harv. L. Rev.* 355, 421–25 (1995).

22. Turow, *Ultimate Punishment,* 63 (2003). See also Scott Turow, "To Kill or Not to Kill: Coming to Terms with Capital Punishment," *New Yorker,* 40, Jan. 6, 2003.

23. Craig Lambert, "Death by the Barrel," *Harvard Magazine* 53 (Sept./Oct. 2004): http://www.harvardmagazine.com/on-line/090433.html; "Claims over Tasers' Safety Are

Challenged," *New York Times*, C1, Nov. 26, 2004; "A Stun Gun Maker Struggles to Shake Off Safety Concerns," *Wall Street Journal*, 1, Mar. 25, 2005.

24. Daniel Givelber, "The New Law of Murder," 69 *Ind. L. J.* 375, 403–4 (1994).

25. *Crampton v. Ohio*, 402 U.S. 183 (1970).

26. Givelber, "New Law of Murder," 417.

27. *Seattle Times*, D3, Nov. 9, 2003.

28. "Death Sentences on Decline as Public's Skepticism Grows," *Los Angeles Times*, A28, Dec. 14, 2004; Samuel R. Gross, "Symposium Update: American Public Opinion on the Death Penalty—It's Getting Personal," 83 *Cornell L. Rev.* 1448, 1452–55 (1998). See also Richard Morin & Claudia Deane, "McVeigh's Execution Approved, While Principle Splits Public," *Washington Post*, A9, May 3, 2001. (In a 2001 poll, 46 percent favored the death penalty over life without parole, while 45 percent favored life without parole—up from 38 percent two years earlier.) "Parties Split on Nation's Morals," *Washington Times*, A06, May 17, 2005.

29. Austin Sarat, "Representation and Capital Punishment: Bearing Witness and Writing History in the Struggle against Capital Punishment," 8 *Yale J. L. & Human.* 451, 61 (1996), and *When the State Kills: Capital Punishment and the American Condition*, 324 (2001).

30. With respect to whether executions should be televised, Sarat notes and disagrees with Wendy Lesser's argument that televised execution is indecent and voyeuristic. See Wendy Lesser, *Pictures at an Execution*, 171 (1993).

31. *KQED, Inc. v. Vasquez*, 1991 U.S. Dist. LEXIS 19791; WL 489485, 18 *Media L. Rep.* 2323, 2324 (N.D. Cal. 1991).

Epilogue

1. *Gideon v. Wainwright*, 372 U.S. 335 (1963), was not an LDF case.

2. See http://www.naacpldf.org/landing.aspx?sub=11.

3. Georgia A. Persons, "Race, Politics, and Community Development in U.S. Cities," 594 *Annals* 65, 68 (July 2004).

4. Marianne Engelman Lado, "Breaking the Barriers of Access to Health Care: A Discussion of the Role of Civil Rights Litigation and the Relationship between Burdens of Proof and the Experience of Denial," 60 *Brook. L. Rev.* 239, 242 (1994).

5. Persons, "Race, Politics, and Community Development," 68.

6. 26 U.S.C. §32; "Low-income workers often turn to tax preparation services and costly refund loans to access their government tax refund check under the Earned Income Tax Credit (EITC)," Michael S. Barr, "Banking the Poor," 21 *Yale J. on Reg.* 121, 123 (2004).

7. Thomas W. Ross, "The Faith-Based Initiative: Anti-Poverty or Anti-Poor?" 9 *Geo. J. Poverty Law & Policy* 167 (2002).

8. William Julius Wilson, *The Truly Disadvantaged: The Inner City, the Underclass, and Public Policy*, 147 (1987).

9. NAACP Legal Defense and Educational Fund Inc., case docket, 62–68 (July 2004)(in the author's possession).

10. *City of Richmond v. J. A. Croson Co.*, 488 U.S. 469, 520–28 (Justice Scalia concurring) (1989).

11. Henry Louis Gates Jr., "Getting to Average," *New York Times,* sec. 4, p. 11, Sept. 26, 2004.

12. See http://www.acorn.org/index.php?id=42.

13. As quoted in *Multinational Monitor,* 14, Jan. 1, 2001.

14. The No Child Left Behind Act of 2001, Pub. L. no. 107–110, 115 Stat. 1425 (2001) (codified as amended in sections of 20 U.S.C.A.).

15. James S. Liebman & Charles F. Sabel, "Symposium: What Are the Likely Impacts of the Accountability Movement on Minority Children?: The Federal No Child Left Behind Act and the Post-Desegregation Civil Rights Agenda," 81 *N.C. L. Rev.* 1703, 1744 (2003).

16. James E. Ryan, "The Perverse Incentives of the No Child Left Behind Act," 79 *N.Y.U. L. Rev.* 932, 935 (2004).

17. Ibid.

18. Richard F. Elmore, "Response: Details, Details, Details," 28 *N.Y.U. Rev. L. & Social Change* 315, 317 (2003).

19. "*Brown* Post-50: The Opportunity to Learn Initiative," LDF Education Staff Recommendations Nov. 17, 2003.

20. James S. Liebman & Charles F. Sabel, "A Public Laboratory Dewey Barely Imagined: The Emerging Model of School Governance and Legal Reform," 28 *N.Y.U. Rev. L. & Social Change* 183 (2003).

21. Gordon Whitman, "Response: Making Accountability Work," 28 *N.Y.U. Rev. L. & Social Change* 361, 366–67 (2003).

22. Roland G. Fryer Jr. & Steven D. Levitt, "Understanding the Black–White Test Score Gap in the First Two Years of School" (American Bar Foundation, May 2002).

23. Richard Rothstein, *Using Social, Economic and Educational Reform to Close the Black–White Achievement Gap* (2004).

24. William L. Taylor, "What Are the Likely Impacts of the Accountability Movement on Minority Children? The Federal No Child Left Behind Act and the Post-Desegregation Civil Rights Agenda," 81 *N.C. L. Rev.* 1751, 1760 (2003).

Appendix

1. "Making Docile Lawyers: An Essay on the Pacification of Law Students," 111 *Harv. L. Rev.* 2027 (1998).

2. Ibid., 2030.

3. David B. Wilkins, "Symposium on Civic and Legal Education: Two Paths to the Mountaintop? The Role of Legal Education in Shaping the Values of Black Corporate Lawyers," 45 *Stan. L. Rev.* 1983, 2017–25 (1993). See also Steven Lubet, "Artificial Intelligence," *American Lawyer,* 146, Mar. 4, 2005.

4. "HLS to Blame for Corporate Career Path," letter from Noah Lewis 3L to *The Record,* Oct. 7, 2004.

5. "Making Docile Lawyers," 2030.

INDEX

Index

Index

Goldstein, Abraham, 42–43, 44
Goldstein, Joseph, 42–43, 44–45
Goluboff, Risa, 97
Goodridge v. Dept. of Health, 283n1
Gordon, Linda, 150
Grauman, Lawrence, 139, 140
Greenberg, Jack: as adviser to King, 88;
  Ali's boxing license case and, 145; on
  analysis and statistics, 177; on Carter's
  request for funds, 103–4; civil rights law
  course of, 131–36; Angela Davis case
  and, 123–27, 129; death-penalty cases
  and, 194, 198, 201, 205, 219–20; on de
  facto school desegregation cases, 105; on
  economic justice, 172; ethnically oriented defense funds of, 150; later career
  of, 135; LDF growth under, 117–18, 158;
  as LDF leader, 92, 95–96, 98, 99–103,
  112, 115, 129–30; prison reform cases
  and, 161; on race, 37, 99–100, 122,
  272n18; *Race Relations and American
  Law,* 32–33; reputation of, 30; on salary
  issues, 31–32
Greenberg, Sema, 103
Greene, Harold, 63
Greensboro (N.C.): hospital discrimination case in, 59–60, 182, 274–75n4
Gregg v. Georgia, 213–14, 219
Griggs v. Duke Power Co., 108
Griswold, Erwin, 8, 142
Griswold v. Connecticut, 273n2
Grooms, Hobart, 68
gun manufacturers, 232

Hamilton, Alexander, 261
Hampton, Fred, 124
Harlan, John, 146, 196
Harper, Conrad, 123
Harper, Fowler, 42
Harris, Paul, 73
Harris, Robert Alton, 237
Harvard Law Review, 259
Harvard Law School: case method at, 44;
  controversy over Greenberg and Cham-
  bers's course at, 131–36; faculty hiring at,
  80, 81–82, 168; legal writing and re-
  search protocols course at, 239, 259;

public interest law and, 260, 261; repu-
  tation of, 131; Yale's approach distin-
  guished from, 45
Hastie, William, 80
Hauser, Thomas, 138
Hawaii: capital punishment abolished in,
  204
health: insurance for, 247, 248; racial dis-
  parities in, 242
Heffron, Frank, 205–7
Hegland, Kenny, 73
Hemingway, Ernest, 23
Henry, Patrick, 38
Herndon, Angelo, 67
Hershey, Lewis B., 141
Hicks, Jim, 99
Hill-Burton Act (1946), 59, 182, 274–75n4
Hobson, Laura Z., 23, 271n4
Holland & Knight (firm), 221
Holmes, Oliver Wendell, 44
Holocaust, 23
Holtzman, Elizabeth, 73
Hoover, J. Edgar, 24, 62, 64, 126, 200, 201
Horowitz, Donald, 180, 181
Hot Shoppes Corporation, 77–79
housing: conditions in public, 153; munici-
  pal ordinances on, 9; racial discrimina-
  tion in, 61, 105–6, 109; restrictive cov-
  enants cases and, 9–10, 269–70n5,
  270n5; Section 8 subsidies for, 247–48
Houston, Charles Hamilton, 32, 33, 118
Howard, George, 205–6
Howard Law School, 56, 60
Hurd v. Hodge, 269–70n5

Illinois: death-penalty cases in, 226–27,
  232. *See also* Chicago (Ill.)
Illinois Commission on Capital Punishment, 226–27, 232
impact litigation. *See* law reform litigation
Indiana: school desegregation cases in, 105
Ingersoll, Ralph, 271n6
Ingraham, Joe, 141, 142, 145
Innocence Protection Act, 212, 286n34
institutional reform: complexities of, 155;
  litigation's utility in, 174–78. *See also*
  death-penalty cases; law reform litiga-

Index

Mansfield, Walter, 144–45, 168

Marbury v. Madison, 174

Margold, Nathan, 33, 272n14

market capitalism, 77. *See also* consumers; poverty

marriage: interracial, 38, 39, 51; same-sex, 170, 283n1

Marshall, Burke, 60, 61, 63, 275n6

Marshall, Lenore, 103

Marshall, Thurgood: background of, 32, 240; *Brown II* and, 82–83; Carter's relationship with, 101, 102–3, 112; characteristics of, 34–35, 83; on citizenship tests, 67; classmates/colleagues of, 56, 60; death-penalty cases and, 210–11, 214; on direct action, 86–87; on execution statistics, 208; Greenberg chosen by, 99–103, 112; Greenberg compared with, 92; judicial appointment for, 63, 82; as LDF leader, 28, 31, 89, 93; legacy of, 101, 118; on NAACP, 104; prisoners' letters to, 200; reputation of, 33–34; restrictive covenants cases and, 269–70n5; rumors about, 126

Martinsville Seven, 198–99

Maryland: lunch counter sit-in cases in, 85–86

Massachusetts: same-sex marriage in, 170, 283n1; school desegregation cases in, 105

Mathews, Z. T. (Zeke), 88–89

Maxwell, William, 205–7

Maxwell v. Bishop, 195–96, 205–7, 209, 216

McCarthy, Joseph, 25, 26–27, 271n9

McCleskey, Warren, 210

McCleskey v. Kemp, 111, 209–11, 216, 220, 286n30

McGuire, Dorothy, 271n4

McNally, Kevin, 221

McVeigh, Timothy, 229

McWhorter, Diane, 123

media: on capital punishment as closure, 230; color as depicted in, 245; on Hurricane Katrina, 255–56; Jewish people as depicted in, 23, 271n4; justice as depicted in, 232–33; lawyering as depicted in, 258; on protest demonstrations, 88–89

Medicaid, 182–83

medical experiments, 13–14

Medicare, 182–83, 248

Medicare Modernization Act, 247

Mello, Michael, 222

Meltsner, Heli, 27, 56

Meltsner, Ira D.: antidiscrimination advocacy of, 18–19; boxing bets of, 137, 147; character of, 22–23; employment struggles of, 17, 19–20, 21–22, 29, 77; job applications of, 20, 21

Meltsner, Jessie, 6

mentally ill and retarded people: ban on executing, 193, 218, 223; death-penalty case and, 201, 202, 203; guilty plea and, 227

Mercado, Louis C., 167–68

Mercer University Law School, 15–16

Meredith, James, 61

Metropolitan Life, 12

Michie, Thomas, 107

Michigan: school desegregation in, 110–11, 279n20

Miller, Arthur, 134

Miller, Zell, 73

Minnesota: death penalty abolished in, 287n4; motor vehicle negligence case in, 69–70

miscegenation, 38–39, 51

Mississippi: judiciary in, 62–63; legal assistance for civil rights workers in, 115–16, 126; right to counsel in, 241; voting rights suits in, 61

Mitchell, Clarence, 93, 185

Mobilization for Youth (N.Y.), 71, 148

Moissant International Airport, 76

Monocle (magazine), 85

Moore, Alvin, 49

Moore, Howard, 141

Moore, William Neal (Billy), 228–29

Morgan, Charles, 141

Morningside Heights Legal Services (Columbia Law School), 54, 126, 129, 130, 159

Morrison, Samuel Eliot, 89–90

Index

Moses, Bob, 36
Mosher, Robert, 160–61, 162
Motley, Constance Baker, 80, 100, 105
Mountain States Legal Foundation, 179
Moynihan, Daniel P., 151–52
Moynihan Report, 151–52
Muhammad, Elijah, 127, 138, 142
Muller, Eric, 194–95, 196, 197, 209, 284–85n8
Murphy, Frank, 48

NAACP (National Association for the Advancement of Colored People): founding of, 34; funding of, 93; Galamison and, 165; lawsuits of, 94; LDF distinguished from, 31, 34; LDF separated from, 99, 101–2, 116; LDF's rivalry/conflict with, 103–4, 112; Martinsville Seven case of, 198–99; members of, 81; prisoners' letters to, 200; school desegregation approach of, 105, 109–10, 114–15; SNCC disdain for tactics of, 88; special counsel of, 32
Nabrit, Jackie Harlan, 56
Nabrit, James, Jr., 55–56
Nabrit, James "Jim," III: background of, 55–56; Bacon's trust cases and, 7–8; on Angela Davis case, 123; death-penalty cases and, 194; King's Selma march and, 91; school desegregation cases and, 105, 107; work habits of, 55, 56–57
National Conference of Black Lawyers, 126
National Lawyers' Guild, 25, 126, 273n2
National Office for the Rights of the Indigent (NORI), 156–57, 158
National Welfare Rights Organization (NWRO), 149
Nation of Islam: Ali as minister of, 138–39, 140, 141–42; fear of, 144
Navasky, Victor, 61, 62, 64, 85
negotiation and mediation, 45
Negro: use of term, ix. See also African Americans; civil rights; race
Neighborhood Legal Services, 149
Neufeld, Peter, 220
New Haven (Conn.): public defender in-

ternship in, 51–53
New Haven Railroad (Boston), 21
New Orleans (La.): school integration case in, 95
Newton, Huey P., 125
New York City: consumer advocate of, 159; criminal courts in, 13; growing up in, 24, 25, 27, 36, 37, 39–40; school decentralization and local control issues in, 163–67
New York State: capital defender project in, 221, 222, 223; consumer cases in, 158–59; death-penalty cases in, 204; death penalty reinstituted in, 222; food stamp program of, 248
New York State Athletic Commission, 140, 142–45
New York Times, 154, 246–47, 272n18
New York University Law School, 82, 220
Niebuhr, Reinhold, 154
Nixon, Richard M., 124, 149, 150, 151, 213
No Child Left Behind Act (NCLB), 250–55
NORI (National Office for the Rights of the Indigent), 156-57, 158
North Carolina: capital defender project in, 221. See also Charlotte (N.C.); Greensboro (N.C.)
Northeastern Law School: changes in, 241; graduation requirements of, 239; hiring at, 135; public interest law and, 261; work-study program of, 131

Oberlin College (Ohio), 2, 89–90
Ocean Hill–Brownsville schools, 166
O'Dell, Hunter Pitts "Jack," 64
Office of Economic Opportunity: Legal Services Program of, 118, 148, 149
Ogletree, Charles, 134
Ohio: Kent State protests in, 124; murder case in, 234; school desegregation cases in, 105
Olive, Mark, 221
Orangeburg (S.C.): antiwar protests in, 124

Pace, Stephen, 68
Pacific Legal Foundation, 179
Parker, William Mack, 115